Thomas More's Magician

Also by Toby Green

Meeting The Invisible Man
Saddled With Darwin: A Journey Through South America

Thomas More's Magician

A NOVEL ACCOUNT OF UTOPIA IN MEXICO

TOBY GREEN

Weidenfeld & Nicolson
LONDON

First published in Great Britain in 2004
by Weidenfeld & Nicolson

© 2004 Toby Green

A CIP catalogue record for this book
is available from the British Library.

ISBN 0 297 82988 2

Typeset by Selwood Systems, Midsomer Norton

Printed in Great Britain by
Butler & Tanner Ltd, Frome and London

Weidenfeld & Nicolson

The Orion Publishing Group Ltd
Orion House
5 Upper Saint Martin's Lane
London WC2H 9EA

Well, that's the most accurate account I can give you of the Utopian Republic. To my mind, it's not only the best country in the world, but the only one that has any right to call itself a republic. Elsewhere, people are always talking about the public interest, but all they really care about is private property.

Thomas More, Utopia

You suffer, my heart:
Torture yourself no more in this realm!
Such is my destiny, known to all.
I'll earn the gift of being born on earth,
in this place of purity:
with this alone I can touch the beauty
where life subsists.

Aztec poem (translated from the Spanish version of Angel María Garibay, *Historia de la Literatura Nahuátl*)

For my parents

CONTENTS

ILLUSTRATIONS

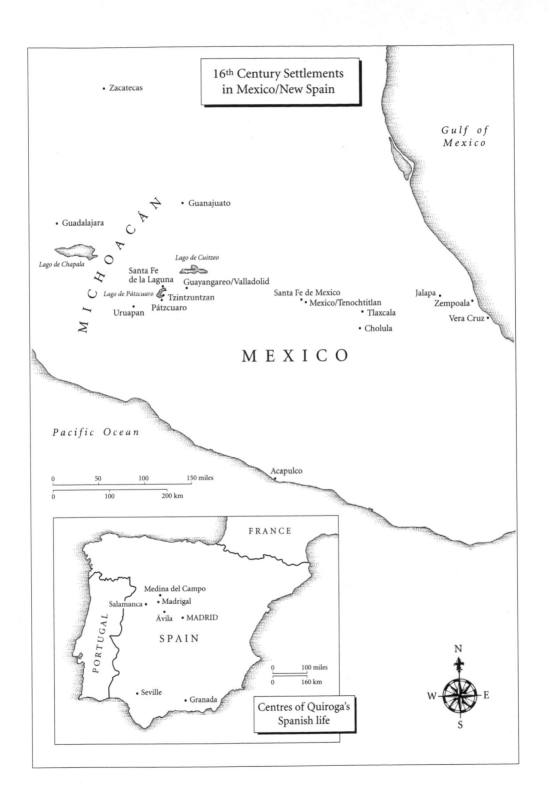

16th Century Settlements
in Mexico/New Spain

• Zacatecas

*Gulf of
Mexico*

• Guanajuato

• Guadalajara

M I C H O A C Á N

Lago de Chapala

Lago de Cuitzeo

Santa Fe
de la Laguna

Lago de Pátzcuaro   Guayangareo/Valladolid

Tzintzuntzan   Santa Fe de Mexico   Jalapa •
                                • • Mexico/Tenochtitlan   Zempoala •
Uruapan   • Pátzcuaro   • Tlaxcala   Vera Cruz •
                                • Cholula

M E X I C O

Pacific Ocean

```
0        50        100        150 miles
0        100        200 km
```

Acapulco

FRANCE

Medina del Campo
Salamanca •   • Madrigal
           • Ávila   • MADRID

PORTUGAL   S P A I N

```
0        100 miles
0        160 km
```

• Seville   • Granada

Centres of Quiroga's
Spanish life

N
W — E
S

PREFACE

During the run-up to the general election of 2001 in the United Kingdom, I heard one of the leading figures in British politics announce that his was not an ideological party. This claim was resonant of the fact that, at the dawn of the third millennium, ideology no longer had any role in politics. Pragmatism was the order of the day, a third way to supersede the claims of competing ideologies. Marxism, state-sponsored socialism, utopianism: all were bankrupt.

It was easy to understand the origins of these feelings. Having so recently sanctioned mass murder in the Soviet gulags and through China's Cultural Revolution, utopian ideology was thought best left out of politics. Karl Popper had voiced the accepted view, that utopias tended towards dictatorship, cults and the belief in an 'absolute and unchanging ideal'.[1] As the novelist Mario Vargas Llosa put it: 'That idea of a perfect society lies behind monsters like the Taliban. When you want paradise you produce first extraordinary idealism. But at some time, you produce hell.'[2]

Nevertheless, I felt somewhat out of sync with this atmosphere, since for some time I had been increasingly interested in utopias. It had not been so very long since these schemes had been integral to the intellectual and political atmosphere of our world. I wondered if their passing was a genuine cause for celebration, or whether it in turn left a vacuum now being filled by equally dangerous movements — nationalism, for instance, or religious fundamentalism, which could take advantage of the collapse of man-made solutions to the world's ills.

In spite of this perceived failure of utopianism, the pages of history were full of idealists who had sought to create what they deemed a perfect world. Nowhere was this more so than in the Americas, the 'new' world in which many Europeans, fundamentally disillusioned with the 'old' world, had sought to create what they saw as a better model. There were the well-known communes of the Amish and the

Shakers in North America, for instance, and the Mennonites and the Jesuits in Paraguay.

It struck me that from writing about the sort of world that these idealists had created, the genuine nature of utopianism might emerge. By examining the successes and failures of utopian projects, two things might be achieved: these historical movements could be re-interpreted through a modern prism, and the advantages and disadvantages of our current non-ideological politics might become clearer.

It was while reading a book on the Jesuit missions in Paraguay – made famous by the film *The Mission*, starring Robert De Niro – that I first came across the story of Vasco de Quiroga. Quiroga, one of the members of the second ruling council of Mexico, used Thomas More's *Utopia* as a blueprint to found an entire community on the outskirts of Mexico City in the 1530s. He formed another such commune in the neighbouring state of Michoacán, where he was eventually made bishop, and his utopian zeal gradually spread to encompass his entire diocese.

As I read more about Quiroga's work, it struck me as extraordinary that this story had been examined so rarely in the English-speaking world. Though the classic work of scholarship on Quiroga – Fintan B. Warren's *Vasco de Quiroga and his Pueblo-Hospitales of Santa Fe* – was written in English, Warren's book was published in 1963, and only two full-length academic monographs have been published in English since, neither of which concentrates exclusively on Quiroga's life.

Yet Thomas More has long been seen as one of the most important figures of the early sixteenth century in England, and this realisation of his vision in Mexico seemed to me to add an important strand to the story of his life. The debate still rages among academics as to whether or not More believed in the principles of his *Utopia*, something which Quiroga's story might help clarify; after all, the fact that Quiroga, for one, took these principles seriously surely implies that they were plausible to many a humanist of the age.

When I decided to write this book about Quiroga's life and his utopias, though, I came across a problem. As the historian Fernando Gómez has put it, if we have no particular interest in Mexico, and have never wanted to go there, the general response on hearing the words 'Vasco de Quiroga' is 'to shuffle feet, raise eyebrows and ask, "Who?" a bit nervously'.[3] Making an obscure sixteenth-century Spanish lawyer and bishop of relevance to the modern world is a challenge.

Yet I believed passionately that Quiroga's story *was* of relevance. Here was a man who had given away all his possessions and even got into debt in order to found his utopias. His idealism was surely a paradigm against which to measure the pragmatism of our times. His belief that More's literary creation and social programme could be realised posed a strong challenge to our more knowing, more cynical age.

Wondering how best to convey this relevance, I found myself reading mounds of utopian novels. As I did so, I began to realise that Quiroga's story was itself the perfect vehicle for utopian literature. The classical form of the utopian novel is, after all, a story in which the narrator travels to some distant land and returns telling of the curious customs they have found. This was the case with More's *Utopia*, Bacon's *New Atlantis* and Butler's *Erewhon*; in the nineteenth and twentieth centuries, when there was no longer anywhere new to explore on Earth, utopian writers began to locate their stories in the future (Bellamy's *Looking Backward* and Morris's *News From Nowhere*) or in a different galaxy (the work of Ursula Le Guin).

Quiroga's life fits this utopian pattern of exploration neatly. Born in Castile in the late fifteenth century, he travelled to Mexico in later life and there created a utopian society. I soon realised that I could write a book which would combine his life story with a contemporary utopian journey that mirrored his own. The result would fit into a utopian genre, seeking to tell Quiroga's story, and, through the modern strand, trying to pin down the relevance of both Quiroga and utopianism to our lives today.

This is what I have attempted in this book, which is thus a sort of hybrid of biography and utopian narrative. It is only fair to make this clear at the outset: utopia was at the heart of Quiroga's project and, likewise, it is the centrepiece of what follows in all its forms – as an idea, as a historical movement, and as a literary form.

Writing this book has involved incurring even more debts than an author usually chalks up, and I would like to express my deep gratitude to all those who have helped me on my way. In particular, I wish to thank the adjudicators of the K. Blundell Trust at the Society of Authors for giving me a generous grant to help cover the cost of research in Spain and Mexico.

The historian who writes about the history of early colonial Mexico would never achieve more than a surface representation were it not for the palaeographic specialists who, over the last 150 years, have transcribed and published so many reams of documents from the awkward (to our eyes) script of the sixteenth century. So I wish to express my thanks and admiration to Joaquín Pacheco, Joaquín García

Icazbalceta, Francisco del Paso y Troncoso, J. Benedict Warren, Rafael Aguayo Spencer, and most particularly to the great Mexican historian Don Sílvio Zavala, who first made the connection between Quiroga and More.

In Spain, I wish to thank Don Julio Díaz, the *sacerdote* at Madrigal de las Altas Torres, for sharing his time and local knowledge with me. I am also grateful to the staff at the Archivo General de las Indias in Seville, and to the staff at the Archivo del Obispado de Ávila for their help.

In Mexico, I owe a great debt to Francisco Pérez, of the Centro de Difusión of the Universidad Vasco de Quiroga in Morelia, for helping me out enormously with contacts on my arrival. Francisco put me in touch with the Quiroga specialist Armando Mauricio Escobar Olmedo, who has proved himself an invaluable colleague and a great friend. Armando has generously opened many doors, helped me to ferret out obscure illustrations, and has been happy to discuss our various theories about Quiroga at the drop of a hat – both during my stay in Michoacán, and subsequently by email and when we met in Madrid. This book would have been much less complete without his sustained input.

I also wish to thank Pascual Guzmán, archivist at the Archivo Histórico del Arzobispado de Morelia; Fernando Mendoza, archivist at the Archivo Histórico de Pátzcuaro; Padre Ephraim Cervantes and the staff of the library at the Arzobispado of Morelia; and the staff of the libraries of the Universidad Vasco de Quiroga, the Universidad Michoacana de San Nicolás Hidalgo and the CREFAL in Pátzcuaro. I am also greatly indebted to Alejandra Perezmejía and Manuel Díaz Cebrian of the Mexican Tourist Board in London for pointing me in the right direction to start with.

For help in my research in the UK, I would like to thank the staff of the British Library and of the main library at the University of Birmingham. I have also been much assisted by my doctoral supervisor at Birmingham, Dr Paulo de Moraes Farias, whose sharp insights into this period have greatly enriched my own interpretations. My discussions with my friend Tim Dowling on Latin American history – and the nature of Amerindian cultures in particular – have also been invaluable, but my biggest debt of all must be to Shez Dawood, who has been a fellow traveller from the beginning on this utopian journey. I would also like to thank Jamie Crawford, Jack Everett, Emily Fowke, Nicky Harris, Maggie Pearlstine, Ian Rakoff and Martin Taylor.

I wish, too, to make acknowledgement to those publishers who have granted me permission to reproduce copyright material:

Orion Publishing Group, for permission to reproduce material from Ursula Le Guin's *The Dispossessed* (published by Victor Gollancz) and Jacques Soustelle's *The Daily Life of the Aztecs on the Eve of the Spanish Conquest* (translated by Patrick O'Brian; published by Weidenfeld & Nicolson).

Extract from *Darkness at Noon* by Arthur Koestler published by Hutchinson. Used by permission of the Random House Group Ltd.

Reproduced by permission of Penguin Books Ltd, extracts from:

Don Quixote by Miguel de Cervantes Saavedra, translated by John Rutherford (London, 2001), material reproduced from pp. 74, 84, 85, 600, 943.

The Conquest of New Spain by Bernal Diaz, translated by J. M. Cohen (Harmondsworth, 1963), material reproduced from pp. 122, 123, 214, 215, 230, 232, 233, 234, 235.

Utopia by Thomas More, translated by Paul Turner (Harmondsworth, 1965), material reproduced from pp. 27, 40, 65, 66, 69, 70, 73, 79, 80, 84, 89, 102, 106, 120, 130, 131.

Every effort has been made to trace copyright holders; any errors brought to the attention of the author and publishers will be rectified in any future edition.

In terms of writing the book, Simon Trewin and Sarah Ballard were always behind this idea, and I am most grateful for their input. And at Weidenfeld & Nicolson I must thank Richard Milner, who has shown indefatigable belief in this project, and the patience of a saint (to rival that of Don Vasco), as my proposed narrative structure has veered from one idea to the next. Without the help of such a supportive and creative editor, I would never have attempted the form this book has taken.

When if finally came to putting the pieces together, I must thank Tom Graves for his cheerful help in tracking down illustrations. Francine Brody ensured that everything happened when it was supposed to, and I would also like to thank Ben Buchan and Emma Finnigan.

Part One

THE ROAD TO DYSTOPIA

The settlers of Anarres had turned their backs on the Old World and its past, opted for the future only. But as surely as the future becomes the past, the past becomes the future.

Ursula Le Guin, *The Dispossessed*

ONE

It was not until two weeks before I was due to leave for Spain that all my plans finally fell into place. The previous months had been spent doing library research and making phone calls, as I had tried to prepare the ground before leaving for Madrigal de las Altas Torres, the small Castilian town in which Vasco de Quiroga had been born. Finally, though, I managed to speak to the staff in Madrigal's municipality, and to the secretary of the local priest, and my efforts began to slot into place.

It was mid-April. I checked the notes I had made of the books that I had read on Quiroga and sixteenth-century Mexico thus far, and compiled lists of all the documents I hoped to decipher when I left Madrigal and reached the Archive of the Indies in Seville. I also renewed my attempts to make contact with historians in Mexico who might be able to give me some pointers before I left. It was a busy time, but everything still boded well for my utopian project, and as yet there was nothing to suggest that my schedule and my proposed book were not entirely realistic.

At the end of the working day, I took to going for long walks through the fields that surrounded the small town of S——, where I had been living for some time. I stepped over stiles, sent sheep scampering out of sight, and picked wild flowers for the kitchen table. Spring had come early that year – just as autumn had left late the year before – and the days were unusually hot. Many of the flowers were rushing out into bloom far ahead of themselves. Daffodils had been only a memory by the end of March, and some of the bluebells had dried out as early as the second week of April, I found, as I collected my bouquets in the late-evening light.

The days were lengthening, and it was a pleasant time of year. The fresh air seemed good for me, and I did not want my brain to become stale with all the reading I was doing as I researched Quiroga's life. I also knew that I needed to pick up some anecdotes or else I would have nothing good to write about.

Yet all the same, after a week or so I found that simply wandering aimlessly through the woods was not having the desired effect. This was what prompted me to pick up the phone again, and to contact the local Green Party: the campaign for that year's local elections was in full swing, and I knew that they needed people to deliver leaflets. The Green Party seemed to me to be the inheritor of the sort of idealism that Quiroga had championed, and that I wanted to write about, and so it seemed entirely appropriate to get involved in their campaign, as well as providing me with a trouble-free means of beginning my book. I had always found beginnings difficult, after all, and there was no need to make things hard for myself when an easy and idealistic answer to my problem was to hand.

The very next day, I was despatched with five hundred leaflets and sent to pace the streets of S——. Instead of roaming public rights of way, the evenings now found me opening gates and stuffing green pieces of recycled paper through people's letter boxes – at best, I thought, to be recycled again, unread. It was a carefree time, and not only was I enjoying my evening strolls but I was doing my bit as well.

What was more, I soon came across the anecdotes which I had been hoping to find. The voting public had as little respect for the Green Party, I found, as they had for all the other groups that passed for political organisations:

'All you politicians are as corrupt as each other.'

'Green Party? What's that?'

'Green Party? Goodbye.'

'I'd never vote for you. You're just utopian.'

The absence of idealism – and, indeed, of political engagement of any sort – was impossible to miss. It was precisely this, of course, that I intended to write about, and I soon found that my mind drifted off into daydreams about the things I might want to say in my book on Quiroga, and the way in which I would attempt to convey the enduring relevance of idealism to the political fabric. I paced the pavements of S——, sticking leaflets through letterboxes, avoiding skateboarding children, my head lost in admiring the cirruses overhead, my mind drifting into softer and more implausible dreams.

It was doubtless during one of those fantasies that I made my first mistake. I had just finished leafleting a cul-de-sac, and was quietly mopping my brow. The evening gloom was ripening, and there was little to say that anything was wrong except for the anger of the old man who confronted me at the gate to his house.

'You!' he barked, waving a stick in my general direction.

'Me?' I asked, walking hesitantly across the road towards him.

'Are you delivering local election leaflets for the Green Party?' he snarled. I could not deny it, even though to adopt a political stance seemed likely to worsen the situation. 'Well,' he said, 'do you think these are here for fun? Is that what you think?' He pointed to some pieces of fraying elastic wrapped around his front gate – one of the ends was hanging loose. 'Is that what you think?' he repeated.

'I'm sorry,' I stammered.

'You didn't put it back when you delivered your little bit of paper, and now you've let my dog out.'

'I'm sorry,' I repeated, pathetically.

'That's one vote you've lost,' he concluded, turning his back on me. I stood on the pavement, watching him slam the front door of his house behind him. I had not even seen his wretched dog, and for all I knew it was a figment of his imagination. Nevertheless, he might complain about the behaviour of the Green Party electioneer; after all, as a group we were far from being universally popular, and many saw us as a threat to their way of life.

The twilight deepened. There was no one else out in the streets, and I had almost exhausted my supply of leaflets. People were relaxing in front of their televisions after doing whatever they did for a living, and they did not wish to be disturbed; it was, of course, high time that I joined them. In any event, there were only a few days left before I was due to travel, and I had plenty still to arrange. The flight had to be confirmed, insurance and money transfers had to be negotiated, outstanding bills had to be paid and I had to get into the right sort of mood for undertaking research.

Deciding to call it a day, I turned and began to climb the steep hill which led back home. A military plane roared overhead. The colours of twilight receded, and everyone switched on their lights in the privacy of their own homes. Few people remained in the communal areas, but outside one house I saw an old man sitting on his terrace, beheading dandelions into a battered plastic bucket. It was an unexpected sight, and I paused, glad for the chance to catch my breath.

'What are you up to?' I asked.

He squinted at me in the darkness, as if he had barely seen me. 'I'm going to make some dandelion wine,' he said, eventually. He asked me who I was, and I explained. 'Ah, the Green Party,' he said.

'Oh well, you should like me, then. Dandelion wine – that's a green thing to make, isn't it?'

'I suppose so,' I said.

He squinted at me again – his sight was clearly very poor. He was a slight man with closely cropped grey hair and a forehead scored with deep lines. He put a bony hand to his brow as he stared vaguely towards me, and then chuckled to himself: 'What chance the Greens?' he asked, putting his bucket of dandelions to one side. 'An anarchist, ill-defined group if ever there was one. A bunch of utopians.'

'What do you mean?' I said.

'Well it's true, isn't it?' he shot back. 'You're all idealists, even though the world has moved on. And it's moved on without you.'

'Don't you think that utopia still matters?' I asked him.

'Utopia!' he laughed. 'Oh no, I don't think so. Now that communism has died, you Greens are the last utopians. But even you must see that you're fighting a losing battle. No one's interested in idealism any more,' he told me, his eyes twinkling. Then, delving into the recesses of his memory, he added: 'As Isaiah Berlin put it, "What characterizes our time is less the struggle of one set of ideas against another than the mounting wave of hostility to all ideas as such."'[1]

I was surprised to meet someone able to quote twentieth-century philosophers to me on the streets of this quiet town. This was not at all what I had been planning when I had agreed to deliver political leaflets. It was not that the old man had accused the Greens of being utopian that got to me, but his dismissal of all utopianism per se.

Speaking in as measured a tone of voice as I could muster, I told him that I was in fact more interested in utopias that even he had realised. I explained that I was a writer researching a biography of a utopian who had lived and worked in sixteenth-century Mexico. Within a few days I would be in Spain, I told him, embarking on the first round of my archival research, and I was fitting in this leafleting just to keep my utopian hand in, as it were.

'And who was this Mexican idealist?' he asked.

'Very few people have heard of him,' I said. 'His name was Vasco de Quiroga, and in some senses he was the first true utopian.'

'Hold on,' he said. 'What about Thomas More?'

'Well,' I said, 'Thomas More was the writer, but Quiroga was the implement.'

'No, I'm sorry,' he said, 'you'll have to tell me a bit more before I understand what you're on about.'

The light was failing, the streets were empty; I knew that I ought to return home and set about the packing which I had been putting off for too long. Yet I was surprised to have this opportunity to work through my thoughts – I had not expected an exchange like this until meeting historians in Mexico – and knew that I ought not to refuse it. I took a deep breath, and began to explain.

I agreed with the old man that it had been Thomas More – once Henry VIII's Chancellor, later martyred for his refusal to accept Henry's split with the Catholic Church – who had coined the word 'utopia' in the book which he had published in 1516. More's *Utopia* had described the voyage of one Raphael Hythlodaeus – or Nonsenso,[2] as we may call him – to the island of Utopia, which was located somewhere in the New World. Nonsenso had found many of the customs on Utopia to be much better than those of the Old World, and ended by saying that he hoped that they might one day be adopted in Europe.

'So that's where the idea of utopia began then, just as I said,' the old man interjected.

'Well,' I answered quickly, 'More may have coined the term, but his wasn't the first ideal state. Plato set out to formulate the same thing in the *Republic*. And in fact More made it quite clear in his prefatory note that his very notion of Utopia was based substantially on Plato's book.' Happy to show off my expertise, I quoted: ' "Plato's *Republic* now I claim / to match, or beat at its own game." '[3]

It was quite a complex thing to describe, and all the while, as I spoke, the old man sat grinning in the gloaming, looking every now and then at his dandelion heads, and squinting at me so hard that, as I finished, I wondered if he had taken anything in.

'Vasco de Quiroga,' he said.

'Yes,' I said.

'An idealist in Mexico.'

'That's it,' I said impatiently.

'Well,' he said, 'it's a fantastic story. Creating a living version of the *Utopia*. But why don't you think of More as the first utopian?'

Getting increasingly preoccupied by my own concerns, I explained that, while Thomas More had indeed coined the word 'utopia', he could not be called the first utopian. The word 'utopia' had been derived by More from the Greek *ou* (not) and *topos* (place): the island described in his book was, then, a type of 'not-place', and not only did the name of the island itself imply equivocation, I went on, warming to my theme, but the nature of More's own beliefs was obscured by his playful character. Oh yes, he didn't want the landed classes to know what he really felt – that would have been far too dangerous. So, in fact, many of the customs of Utopia were in direct contradiction to the beliefs that More himself must have had: the Utopians condoned divorce and encouraged euthanasia, for instance, so that if a person had an incurable disease they were visited by plain-speaking local authorities: 'Let's face it,' they said, 'you'll never be able to live a normal life. You're just a nuisance to other people and a burden to yourself – in fact you're really leading a sort of posthumous existence. So why go on feeding germs? Since your life's a misery to you, why hesitate to die?'[4]

It was difficult, I went on, to square this belief with those of a devout Catholic who would die for their faith. And, furthermore, there were several contradictions in *Utopia* which seemed deliberate. The minimum distance between towns on Utopia was twenty-four miles, and, More had written, 'the maximum, no more than a day's walk';[5] but, I said, with the knowledge of harsh experience, anyone who walks a lot will know that it is hard to cover much more than twenty-four miles in a day. Meanwhile, though More himself was a jurist, lawyers were banned, for, he wrote, 'if nobody's telling the sort of lies that one learns from lawyers, the judge can apply all his shrewdness to weighing the facts of the case.'[6]

'So you see,' I concluded, 'Thomas More could not let himself be seen as a true utopian, even if that was what he believed in.'

'But,' the old man asked me, 'your man Quiroga was different?'

'He was,' I said, with a soft smile.

Vasco de Quiroga, I explained, had been one of the first administrators of Mexico after the Spanish conquest. Born in Castile in around 1487,* he had arrived in Mexico in 1530 as a member of the second *audiencia* – or governing body – and had quickly been appalled by what he had found there. Rather than colluding in the free-for-all which was then destroying the Mexican Indians, he had used his salary to buy land near Mexico and in Michoacán, founding communes which he modelled on Thomas More's recently published book. He was so altruistic, I went on, that he even got into debt as a result of his attempts to provide the best for the communes. Although Quiroga had died in 1565, the utopias had continued to function in some form or other until 1858, when new laws ensured that the communal land had to be divided up and owned by individuals[7] – these were usually

*See ch. 2, p. 31 for a full discussion as to the probable date of Quiroga's birth.

rich landowners who then rented the land to tenants who had previously shared the land in common.

'So you see,' I ended up, 'Quiroga realised More's *Utopia* in Mexico.'

'Did Thomas More ever hear of this?'

'Almost certainly not. He was executed in 1535, only shortly after Quiroga's utopian communes had begun to function properly.'

The old man grinned widely at that. There was silence between us for a moment, and another military plane roared through the evening sky, en route to who knew where.

'Well,' he said, taking a deep breath, 'it's a good story, I'll admit, but it sounds to me as though you've made it up. After all, there must be hundreds of writers out there looking for a story like that, and how come none of them has written about it?'

'Why would I possibly want to make any of this up?' I snapped, angered that my long hours of information-processing should be belittled in this way. 'There are many books which act as source material, and hundreds of documents. Piles and piles of paper to immerse myself in. If information is what you're looking for to prove that I'm an honest man, there's no shortage of it. History confirms everything I've told you, and there's nothing fictional about the account I've given you.'

'If what you say is true,' the old man said then, beheading some more dandelions into his bucket, 'you're already sorely trying the patience of your readers. Why should they believe an idiot dreamer's account of a Mexican utopia when he's fool enough to leaflet for the Green Party as well? It's all much too fantastical for them to take it seriously, and, if they've got this far, I expect they'll be putting your tome down and mixing themselves a stiff drink instead.'

I took a step back and stared hard at the old man. Of course, I was looking for anecdotes, but I had not been expecting this. All I wanted was a few quiet days before I left for Spain, and I needed to get home to finalise the preparations for my trip; but he seemed to have decided that I was already planning to include this exchange in my book, which, even though I was, seemed to me to be presuming too much on my intentions.

'I'm going to have to press on,' I told him then, lightly, making a show of looking at my watch. 'But to answer your point before I go: I think it's only fair that I should declare my political position in a project like this. People don't have to agree with me, and they probably won't, but at least they'll know what I think. I'm expecting people to read about idealism, and that's a political subject, or at least it ought to be. So if I've done some leafleting for the Green Party, it's out of good faith and does not betoken anything that's unreal.'

The old man stood up now, and stretched his arms over his head. 'That's a good answer,' he said. 'But please don't go.' He stooped to pick up his bucket of dandelion heads, and then looked earnestly at me. 'Look, I'm sorry I've given you a hard time,' he said, 'but it's because I'm interested in utopias myself. I suppose I wanted to test you out. But seeing as you appear to be so genuine, I think I could be of help to you.'

'Frankly, I doubt it,' I said. This drivelling old man was not being of any help to me at all, and I really did not have the time to talk to him when Quiroga and Madrigal were waiting for me. 'Look, I must go,' I added. 'I've got a hundred and one things to do before I leave for Spain.'

'It'll only take a couple of minutes,' he said, 'I promise you. But I must just show you something in Cervantes's *Don Quixote*.'

'*Don Quixote*?' I asked impatiently. 'What's that got to do with it?'

'It's got absolutely everything to do with it,' he said. 'For the task you've set yourself is very similar to that which Cervantes set Don Quixote: to rescue a cause which society has turned its back on. In Don Quixote's case it was chivalry, and in yours it's idealism.'

He was so insistent that it seemed a shame not to humour him, and it was also true that my interest was piqued by what he had said. Waving aside any further protests, he led me up the garden path and pushed open his front door. I had no idea what to expect, but I certainly did not anticipate the avalanche of papers that fell from all sides as we entered the house. The living room was more paper than room, and the piles of books, junk mail, newspapers and magazines were such that it was difficult to see how this man could make head or tail of it. It was a strange sight, but at last I began to see him for what he was. S—— was well known to be full of ageing eccentrics, and here, it seemed, was one of them; this seemingly unreal exchange was not my fault at all, and owed nothing to my idiosyncrasies.

'Excuse the mess,' the old man said, putting down the bucket of dandelion heads and turning to me. 'I haven't had a spring clean for a long time.' He climbed neatly over some colour supplements, and began removing a pile of annual reports from the settee. 'But we'll easily clear a space here.' His mongrel came over, wagging its tail, and the old man patted it cheerfully. 'Now don't mind Tony,' he said to me; 'he's a faithful friend, although his aggression is sometimes unjustified. Just sit quietly while I find my copy of *Don Quixote*.'

He turned away from me, and for a moment I wondered if this last remark had been addressed to me or the dog. I stroked his mongrel absent-mindedly as he started burrowing through a mound of old paperbacks which were piled high in a cardboard box beside the kitchen table. He tossed yellowing editions of Steinbeck, Wodehouse, Bellow and Bowen to one side. Loose sheets of paper twitched about on the floor, and his mongrel stirred uneasily. I patted it idly on the head, pleased to have some contact with an animal that did not seem as deranged as the old man.

The truth was that I didn't quite know how I had ended up in this front room filled with heartless piles of paper, talking about *Don Quixote*. But I was quite enjoying being there and anyway this was grist to my creative mill. I knew that soon the experience would be behind me and I would be able to get on with immersing myself in information about Quiroga.

'Ah, here it is,' he said then, interrupting my reverie. '*Don Quixote*.' He advanced towards me, carrying a thick paperback in his hands that was filled with pieces of coloured card that acted as markers. 'Look here,' he said, tossing a pile of *Marvel* comics onto the floor from the settee and sitting down beside me. 'You might find that *Don Quixote* is just what you're looking for in your utopian quest.'

'How's that?'

'Well,' he said, turning to a marker, 'Cervantes's epic begins in the old knight's home, which is filled with books, just like my house here. And in fact, Don Quixote's housekeeper and niece both feel crushed by the mounds of books, just as so many people today feel crushed by the profusion of information. So if you think about it, although you've been testing your readers' loyalty to the limit already – as I've said, if I were them I'd already be blind drunk rather than persevering with the sort of ludicrous narrative you've got in mind – you have at least followed Cervantes's lead in the way you've begun your book.'

I looked harder at the paperback's dust jacket and, taking it out of his hands, flicked idly through the pages. The old man's insistent reference to my book on Quiroga – which I had not even begun writing yet – was beginning to unnerve me. It was as if he knew something that I didn't, and that in itself gave a surreal quality to our exchanges.

'That's as may be,' I said in the end, 'but what's it got to do with utopias?'

'Well,' he said then, taking the paperback off me and giving his dog a friendly stroke. 'As I've told you, his attitude to chivalry is just like your attitude to idealism. And furthermore, you could say that Don Quixote's love of chivalry was itself an idealised vision of some long-lost age of derring-do, and so contains exactly the same qualities of lunacy and self-delusion that all idealists must maintain if they're to succeed, which of course is where you come in.'

I wasn't going to take this sort of mockery any longer. I stood up from the settee and pushed myself free of the old man and his mongrel, Tony.

'Look,' I said, 'I think I'd better be going.'

'Why?'

'This hasn't been helpful at all,' I said, taking a few steps further through the ankle-high piles of old newspapers and discarded printouts from the Internet that littered the floor. 'I just came out to deliver some leaflets, not to be insulted. You may think that idealism equals fantasy, but I don't. As I told you, Quiroga and his project are important to me, and I won't be deflected by the likes of you. The truth is that I think that people still long for a better way of doing things than what we have at present, and so writing about utopias is essential. I believe that humanity has a greater value than the totem of self-interested economics. I know it's not fashionable, but I still believe in the soul – or at least that there's something sacred to existence.'

The mongrel barked half-heartedly as I finished my little peroration, and the old man shushed him affectionately. 'Quiet, Tony,' he kept on whispering into his flea-bitten ear. 'Well,' he said, turning to me, 'that's quite a little speech, and I'm glad to see that you've taken our utopian discussions to heart. But I'm afraid it's all of little relevance to this day and age. You'd be better off if you forgot all of that and lost yourself to the doors of perception.'

'The doors of perception?' I asked.

'Yes,' he said, still whispering platitudes in his mongrel's ear. 'It's a book about hallucinations by Aldous Huxley, the last great utopian. Huxley lived in California towards the end of his life and sometimes took LSD with his wife.'

'I see,' I said, slowly. In fact, I was not seeing very much at that point; it was completely dark outside, and this was the only house in the street in which the lights had not been switched on.

'But I'm sure you know all about Huxley. You've read his novel *Island*, of course?'

'I'm afraid not.'

'You must have done! A model utopian like you.'

'Is it good?' I asked.

'Not bad,' he said. 'It was a book that became significant in the sixties, and was used by many hippies as a blueprint for their communes: in a sense, it was the last utopian manifesto. Huxley wrote it at more or less the same time that E. F. Schumacher wrote *Small is Beautiful,* one of the key texts of the Green movement. And in fact, the two books bear some striking similarities. Like Schumacher, Huxley thought that economies and technologies ought to be adapted to human beings, and not the other way round, and that people ought to do much more practical work, digging in the fields and so forth – otherwise, he said, they just become "sitting addicts".'[8]

Once again, I was struck by his knowledge of utopias, and how lucky I had been to meet this man somewhere as unlikely as S—— and find an appropriate anecdote with which to launch into my book.

'Sitting addicts?' I asked.

'Couch potatoes.' He paused, as if waiting for some sort of response. 'Huxley knew that the modern world would only make people dissatisfied, and lead inevitably to escapism and aggression. He wanted society to be mostly vegetarian, and thought that children ought to be brought up by "mutual adoption clubs",[9] rather in the manner of Israeli kibbutzim.' He paused, and his eyes filled with emotion. 'But of course,' he said, 'Huxley is yesterday's man. The kibbutzim are falling apart, and now no one believes in that sort of utopia – the brave new world is much more plausible than Huxley's island.'

'Brave new world?'

'Oh come on!' He rose from the settee to confront me, clasping a pile of junk-mail letters, all of which appeared to be well thumbed. 'Don't pretend you don't know what I'm talking about. You're not so immersed in your green issues that you can't see it happening before your eyes.'

'What happening?'

He stared hard at me, and then allowed the junk mail to fall from his hands, letter by letter, as we both stood upon the morass of useless information which littered the floor. 'Huxley's dystopia. Pleasure-to-order. Our grammes of soma are our pills and our Sega Megadrives and our Internet pornography.' He passed his hands over his eyes. 'That's what he said, you know,' he went on sadly. 'When Orwell published *1984,* Huxley wrote to him: "Within the next generation I believe the world's rulers will discover that infant conditioning and narco-hypnosis are more efficient, as instruments of government, than clubs and prisons." "[10]

He looked at me with triumph, and suddenly I felt a wave of tiredness washing over me. He knew his subject – that I could tell – and such were the storm of information and the devastating nature of his argument that I was unable to think with any clarity. But I was not going to let his cynicism deflect me now – not when I had bought my ticket to Spain and settled on Quiroga as a subject.

'Well,' I said, turning decisively away from him and wading through the piles of paper towards the door, 'there's a certain amount of contemporary resonance in what you've said, but I don't believe that Huxley was a prophet. Things are not all as controlled as he envisaged – not yet, at any rate. That's why we must act while society has yet to be broken by the information age.'

'That's fine,' he said. 'You carry on with your plan. But you'll see from what I've said why I think *Don Quixote* is just the book for you. Because your rosy view of idealism is as doomed as was the Don's dream of chivalry. I think you'll find that it's no longer possible to be a utopian in the modern world, and that idealism and ideological dogmatism are one and the same.'

'Yes, thank you,' I said, reaching for the doorknob, and preparing to leave this mess behind me.

'And what's more,' he went on incorrigibly, as if I had not turned my back on him, 'the sort of fantasy that your idealism inevitably requires is bound to permeate the book that you write. In fact, I wouldn't be surprised if people who have got this far aren't beginning to wonder whether this whole business of your utopian arrival and discussion hasn't just been an elaborate ploy.'

This was going too far, and I wheeled around to confront him. 'Don't be ridiculous,' I said, furious that he would not leave me alone. Looking around his house, I began to feel a mild panic when I considered the impossibility of getting to the bottom of anything in the paper jungle that was his living room. I could hardly see anything for the information that burst out on all sides on these reams of paper. Who was this man to lecture me on what I was doing and tell me that I was deluded, I asked myself, when it was clear that I was the rational idealist and he was the madman?

I had to go and get on with my final preparations for my journey to Spain, but it was so dark that I could barely see anything. There was no electricity in his room, and I realised that he lived in perpetual darkness, surrounded by his meaningless piles of paper and correspondence and books and magazines and periodicals and junk mail, and by his mongrel Tony. This, I sensed, was the essence of a cruel, thoughtless, isolated, soulless and unhinged existence: information collapse.

But then, I was in a bad mood. 'I've had enough,' I said. 'I must be going.'

'Think over the *Don Quixote* angle,' he urged me.

'I will,' I said, as much as anything to be rid of him.

'Good luck with the campaign,' he said, as I turned to go. 'I'll vote for the Greens.'

'Thank you,' I said, relieved that at least my visit had not been entirely wasted; but Tony must have sensed my false sincerity, for he leapt towards me, so that the old man had to dive in to rescue my ankle.

'Thanks for coming,' the old man said, restraining Tony by the neck.

'Not at all,' I replied.

'Don't forget,' he said: 'the doors of perception.'

'The doors of perception,' I echoed, quizzically, resolving to forget all about this ridiculous experience and to concentrate my thoughts on Quiroga. The evening was close, and I could feel a trickle of sweat creeping down my chest. With a start I saw that, far from being baffling, the paperwork now appeared familiar. Looking around, it seemed as if the endless piles of information in the old man's house had been arranged neatly into the stacks of books and manuscripts that might, even then, be awaiting me in the archives of Spain and Mexico.

Then I feared that the old man's mood had addled my mind, for I was behaving like Cervantes's protagonist – taking the endless piles of paper rubbish that he lived with for priceless historical documents was very much like mistaking a barber's basin for Mambrino's helmet. I laughed to myself, and the old man raised an eyebrow at me. For a moment I had thought that I had in fact been standing in the entrance hall of the Archive of the Indies in Seville. That really would have been the sort of lunacy that the old man had been talking about.

Of course, in reality, I was just enjoying the spring in S—— before I set out to research Quiroga's life in Spain. Reassured that I was not going mad after all, I said farewell to the old man and Tony and walked slowly up the hill back home, ready to begin my utopian adventures with the journey to Madrigal.

TWO

In Madrigal, the Castilian summer remains strong in September. The air throbs with the devil's heat, and ears of wheat and barley hang listless in the plain that has the town surrounded. On some blessed days the atmosphere reaches a pitch and then explodes in a chorus of thunder, so that the fields are speared by lightning and then softened by a breeze; but mostly the only movement is with the skylarks and the swifts who flit over the pastures and arc around the walls. In the evenings a stillness falls across the world, and deer and boar roam the arbours of pine and holm oaks, the boles of those old trees twisted like gargoyles on a cathedral. Only in the far distance is there any indication that there is more to the world than the insidious flatness of the plain: beyond Ávila, the shadow of the Gredos mountains weighs down upon the horizon.

Madrigal is at the heart of Old Castile. Although it is a small town, it is an important settlement. Its rise to prominence has been comparatively recent, and began when John II, the artistic (and incompetent) father of the late Queen Isabella, used the town as a summer retreat: John often held court here, and it was in Madrigal that he married for a second time in 1447.[1] The walls of the town, originally built by the Moors, still sport eighty lookout towers, enough to convince the most powerful rulers in the world of their safety. First there had been John, and then, while Isabella remained alive, she and her husband Ferdinand – the 'Catholic monarchs' who united the kingdoms of Castile and Aragón, defeated the Moors, expelled the Jews and sponsored Columbus's voyages of discovery – were frequent visitors to the palace in which Isabella herself had been born in April 1451. But the Queen died a year or two ago, and Ferdinand now keeps away. The first signs of Madrigal's long and graceful decline from the heart of empire can be discerned by those who look hard enough.

Yet at first glance, little has changed since Isabella's death in 1504.

In this urbane setting, where civilisation reigns, the world that lies just outside the city walls can be difficult to imagine: the town is hidden from the countryside on which it depends, and the walls form such a barrier that the land beyond them is mostly unseen. Within them are to be found the royal palace, two impressive churches – Santa María de la Gracia and San Nicolás de Bari – which dominate the plain, a hospital to care for the sick and the impoverished,[2] and elaborate houses in which Castilian hidalgos live with their families. Many buildings are comparatively new – changing architectural techniques express the wealth and the innovative spirit of the age – and their tiles reflect the summer light with brio. They embody the form which Cervantes will describe in *Don Quixote*: 'spacious [as] in the village style ... arms, although carved in coarse stone, over the street door; the wine cellar under the courtyard and the buttery under the porch ... [and] all around ... enormous earthen jars'.[3]

Once the heat of the day subsides, the streets fill with nobles, clerics, messengers and traders. The townspeople are for the most part immaculate: the men wear scarlet breeches and thick velvet cloaks inlaid with brocade, with swords tucked into their belts and wide-brimmed hats which they raise when some figure of importance passes by, while the women's heads are shielded by silk bonnets made by teams of weavers in Andalucía,[4] and they wear delicate coats over their crimped dresses.

There is a clannishness in the air that marks out the atmosphere even from that of only fifteen years before, when there was still a significant Jewish community here, and the synagogue on the western side of the town was well attended.* Following the first great pogroms against the Iberian Jews of 1391, the Mosaic tribe had scattered from its great centres – Burgos, Córdoba, Seville, Toledo – to small towns such as Madrigal,[5] which had come to be a medium-sized *aljama*† in the fifteenth century, comprising perhaps as many as 400 members.‡ The *aljama* in Madrigal had been in the midst of a busy network of

---

*The synagogue is still standing, one of the few medieval synagogues remaining in their original form in Spain.
†The Spanish term for a Jewish community.
‡This calculation can be made from the taxes paid by Madrigal's *aljama* during the 1488–91 wars of the Spanish against the Moors in Granada. Madrigal's *aljama* contributed 42,120 maravedis in 1491, while that of the Extremaduran town of Cáceres, whose population is known to have consisted of 130 taxpayers, paid the virtually identical amount of 42,775 maravedis; as only adult men were taxpayers, the population of the *aljama* was certainly several times that of the number of taxpayers.

Castilian Jewry, with communities of a similar size in nearby Arévalo and Medina del Campo, and one of the most influential *aljamas* in all Iberia at Ávila.[6] But now, following the expulsion edict of 1492, while some Jews have remained – those who have chosen conversion ahead of exile – there is a unity of purpose in Castile which marks the new century apart from the old: traditional enemies have been vanquished (they will not be readmitted), goodness has prevailed, the markets of Africa and the New World are being opened up for trade with Europe – all for the glory of God, and His Catholic King Ferdinand.[7]

Among the most important families in Madrigal are the Quirogas. Like many other Castilian nobles, Vasco Vázquez de Quiroga settled in the town during its expansion under John II, although his family had originally come from the valley of Keiroga, in Galicia. Later, he had married María Alonso de la Cárcel, who had been born into a rich family of Arévalo. Indeed, in Madrigal some people mutter about the family's wealth, for this is an age in which money is often identified with Jews who have converted to Christianity, and the surname 'de la Cárcel' is suggestive of a Jewish origin.*

Vasco Vázquez de Quiroga and María Alonso de la Cárcel had had three children, Álvaro, Constanza and Vasco; but both parents had died by 1502, leaving their children to fend for themselves.[8] As the eldest, Álvaro has taken over the family's land at the stronghold of Bercial, just a league south-east across the plains.[9] Constanza has already become a nun,[10] and the youngest child, Vasco, is now about to begin his studies to become a licenciate in canon law at the nearby University of Salamanca.

The Quiroga family house is in Calle Palacio, just a hundred yards from the palace walls. It is built with the slim bricks which characterise the town, burning red when the sun sets behind the church of San Nicolás. As with all homes belonging to people of standing, the façade is severe, with the family's coat of arms emblazoned in stone on either side of the solid oak doors: an uprooted beech tree, five stakes and a Maltese cross, symbols which the Quiroga have revered for generations.[11] The Quirogas have long been involved with the Orden de

---

*Converted Jews often took surnames of the place which they came from – e.g. 'de Burgos', 'de Toledo' – but they also often took names which were related to their urban roots. 'De Mercado', 'de la Calle' and 'de la Rúa' were all surnames of converted Jews, and 'de la Cárcel' would appear to fall into this category. Although no historical documents have come to light which show conclusively the Judaic origin of Vasco de Quiroga's mother, some specialists in Michoacán agree that it is highly plausible.

San Juán – symbolised by the Maltese cross – and their Galician home is very close to the pilgrimage route to Santiago de Compostela. Taking on the family tradition, Vasco's father had been governor of the Order of San Juan in Castile.[12] Members of the Order, founded to succour pilgrims to the Holy Land, are well known for their hospitality, and so from a young age Vasco has been indoctrinated in the need to care for the needy – whoever they may be.[13]

A long, heavy key opens the door to the family home, where the exterior is offset by a cool patio. It is here that the Quirogas spend much of their time, surrounded by porticoes adjoining the spacious rooms in which they receive their guests – the smallest rooms are the bedrooms, which are kept compact to preserve their warmth in winter. The rooms are all decorated with *azulejos*, the blue and white tiles whose style and colours have been inherited from the Moors, and there are many devotional images of the Virgin and of saints. In the evenings, copper braziers glow red with hot coals, and light comes from the brass oil lamps, which cast a wan glow over the shadows.

In the first decade of the sixteenth century, Vasco is now in his late teens. He is tall and healthy, with piercing dark eyes and a sharp mind which will soon revel in the legalese of renaissance Castile. He has packed his trunk, and now he is ready to ride to Salamanca. Standing in the courtyard in the early morning, he can already hear movement out in Calle Palacio. Horseshoes clop harshly on the cobbles, and the murmured conversations begin to join the music of birdsong as the night sky lightens. Heavy iron bells ring out from the bell-tower of Santa María, and their repetitive, uniform tones strike unchallenged across the morning, beckoning Vasco to a life of service.

The young man has already said his prayers. He has eaten a little bread, and drunk water from a pitcher in the courtyard. He is not tired. His mind is agile, and it is impossible for him not to recall his childhood as he stands on the verge of relinquishing it. But it is difficult to take stock of all the changes which have swept across the country since his birth, altering the very fabric of society: its composition, its values, and the sources of its wealth. The arable landscape around Madrigal is now increasingly broken up with fields given over to cattle, and the enclosures have brought hardship to many. Fewer people are needed to work the estates of the nobility and, following the law of 1480 allowing freedom of movement to labourers, emaciated figures can sometimes be seen hobbling across the plains looking for new masters, carrying their few possessions in a bundle on their backs.

Recently, there has been a run of bad harvests, and Vasco himself has overheard people from respectable families talking openly of the need to emigrate to the new lands discovered by Columbus. God knows, they say sadly, there is nothing left for us in our own country, and has not the Lord opened up these countries so that His word and His people may continue to prosper?[14]

Nevertheless, these problems have not affected the Quirogas too badly. Wealthy and noble, they have been among the few families in Madrigal not to be prejudiced by the recent shortage of horses in Castile.[15] This shortage has not only led to problems of farming and transport, it has also accentuated divisions between the haves and the have-nots following the ruling of Ferdinand and Isabella in 1494 that no one could ride a mule with a saddle and a bit.[16] The mule is a hybrid of the donkey and the horse (almost as dastardly as a cross between Christians and Jews or Moslems), and should not be graced by the trappings of dignity. And so during the past decade the people of Castile have travelled bareback on mules, or saddled on horses; it is only since Isabella's death that this has begun to change, and people have started to revert to the old ways.[17]

Vasco's horse is saddled and awaits him in the street. His brother Álvaro will ride with him to the south gate of Madrigal, and then he will continue with a family servant to Salamanca. Álvaro now emerges from his chamber, wearing a velvet tunic and silk breeches, with a sword in his scabbard. The two men mount their horses and begin to ride through the streets of the town; near the palace and the churches the roads are cobbled, but elsewhere they are made of earth. The brothers say little to one another, for this is one of the many times in a person's life when words can do little justice to feelings. Vasco has a sense of nostalgia, an imperfect appreciation of the past and its meaning. The streets reek with the acrid smell of fresh horse-piss, the guards are up in the towers and stand to attention at the palace doors, birds dart through the streets: there is so much in this which may not change in his lifetime, yet he knows that when he returns to Madrigal he will see it all differently.

It is early enough so that there are not many flies to bother them, thank God. A group of townsfolk have gathered outside the palace, waiting to make petitions. Vasco knows the palace well, of course, for he has prayed in the royal chapel, a building in which there have been many changes over the past fifteen years. Mudéjar artisans – descendants of the Moors who used to rule here – have been at work redesigning the choir with new *azulejos*. On each tile they have been ordered to paint an opening grenadine,* because now, at last, with the final surrender of its Moorish rulers in 1492, Granada has opened to the Christians; although the terms of surrender had initially been lenient, after the rebellion in 1499 all unconverted Moors were finally expelled a few years ago, in February 1502.

When he recalls the recent events in Granada, Vasco feels momentarily unsettled. The first Archbishop of Granada following the defeat of the Muslim ruler Boabdil had been Hernando de Talavera, a *converso*.†[18] Prior to being appointed to the see of Granada, Talavera had been Bishop of Ávila – in whose diocese Madrigal belongs – and had become a friend of Vasco's father. In fact, the two men had both contributed to the financing of Columbus's first voyage to the New World.[19] But, following the 1499 rebellion, the political atmosphere had changed, and Talavera's tolerance of the Moors had become suspicious. The feared inquisitor Rodríguez Lucero had purged Granada between 1499 and 1502, calling the city 'little Jewry' (*judea la pequenna*) and preaching that the gates ought to be shut, so that those who were left inside could be burned alive.[20] Talavera himself has just been persecuted: his tainted Jewish origins could never be forgiven, and he is now a beaten and wounded man who will shortly die in disgrace.

It is true, Vasco thinks: there are many *conversos* who claim to be Christians but whose faith is that of the Mosaic law (perhaps he shudders inwardly for a moment, as he ponders his late mother's own disputed origins). Of course false converts cannot be countenanced, and the work of the Holy Office of the Inquisition – burning devoutly through all the seasons – is most necessary. This is a time of unseen threats, fear of heresy against the prevailing religion, and of the holy persecution of those who diverge from the accepted norms of society.

No, Vasco thinks, he must not let the fate of the *conversos* distract him. Recalling the new *azulejos* in the royal chapel, he remembers how they surround the sepulchres of important figures in recent history: Isabella of Barcelos, Queen Isabella's maternal grandmother, and María of Aragón, the first wife of John II. The sepulchres are made of alabaster and embossed with the shields of Saint Augustine, decorated with exquisite bas-reliefs of flying angels and saints. By the altarpiece is a statue of the Virgin which was found at sea after a shipwreck and

---

*These can still be seen today; the palace was granted to the Augustinian nuns by Charles V in 1527, and has barely changed its interior design since.
†Or converted Jew.

given to King Ferdinand – with a smile, Vasco remembers the excitement that the story caused when the captain first appeared with this unusual present. Was not this protection of the Virgin at sea a miracle, when you considered all the dangers that might have befallen her?

Of course, Vasco knows that there are many beautiful palaces in Castile, and that more are being built all the time. But still, he wonders whether he will find a place to match the architectural harmony of the courtyard, whose arches are supported by Doric columns, or to rival the Mudéjar woodcarvings of the rooms in which Isabella and Ferdinand used to receive foreign ambassadors. These ceilings are so intricately cut that they seem to betray the perfection of God's plan for humanity, hinting at the precise geometry of the unseen world.

It does not take long for the two Quirogas to leave the palace behind them. Just across the road is the entrance to Madrigal's hospital, Santa María de la Purísima Concepción, founded in 1443 by María of Aragón. It is strange, Vasco thinks, that although many are finding the economic situation increasingly difficult, and hunger is now a scourge throughout the Empire, there is also so much new wealth. The gap between the haves and the have-nots grows inexorably, and the monarchy has reluctantly become aware that the lavishness of its new cathedrals and palaces sits awkwardly with the poverty of most Christians in Castile. Vasco approves of the charitable purposes of the hospital of Santa María, for it is the duty of every Christian who can afford to give alms to do something for the poor and the sick. Empire is, of course, essential to justice, but Christian charity provides for everyone, and the generosity of the rich will surely be rewarded in heaven.

Now Vasco takes a pull on his reigns, guiding his horse up the street which leads to San Nicolás, and Álvaro looks at his younger brother with surprise.

– You will not go straight to the south gate, Vasco?

– I wish to pass San Nicolás, brother.

Álvaro nods. It is an understandable request, for it was here that both he and Vasco were baptised, in the same font as Queen Isabella herself, a huge stone affair that is almost two metres across. The family's house falls in the parish of San Nicolás, not that of Santa María, and Vasco wishes to pass the scene of many of his childhood prayers. As in the palace, Vasco recalls, San Nicolás's high nave is graced with an intricately carved Mudéjar ceiling. It is important to remember that those Moslems are also children of God – they are not complete barbarians – and the architecture of Sevilla, Córdoba and Granada – the cities of their old kingdom of Al-Andalus – is said to be exquisite.

Thinking of the many Moorish touches to be found in Madrigal, Vasco accepts that this may well be so. His childhood has brought him into contact with people from many different countries, after all, and he has seen something of their skills. Not only does Madrigal bear traces of the Moorish and Jewish communities who have lived here, but just five leagues to the north is Medina del Campo, the most important market town in Europe: twice a year, in May and September, up to 60,000 merchants descend from all corners of Spain, from Flanders, Genoa, Florence, and even from the Canary Islands and from Ireland.[21]

From Madrigal's northern towers, Medina's castle of La Mota stands out above the plain. Isabella and Ferdinand used to spend much time in Medina's palace, which is set back from the Plaza Mayor, and in fact it was there that the Queen died. Vasco has been to the town many times, as royal banquets have often been thrown during the annual fairs. At these times so many traders come from overseas that a special royal post – Aposentador Mayor – has been created just to deal with lodging them.[22] Most goods made in Spain or brought over from the emerging settlements in the Indies are traded here, where the Plaza is one of the biggest in Castile and the streets are filled with churches, monasteries and private mansions guarded by tightly latticed iron grilles. During the fairs Medina bursts with livestock, the hooves of unbroken colts skitter over the dusty cobbles, fish slap against stones, new saddles and bits and piles of fruit spill over into the streets amid the heaps of cotton and silk clothes and the sparkle of jewellery and brocade catching the sun. When traders tire of the heat they shelter beneath awnings, eating at improvised tables and awaiting nightfall, whereupon patrols are sent through the streets with lanterns and trumpets to protect the storehouses from thieves.[23]

Vasco remembers it all. Yes, he has been lucky to be raised in the heart of Castile just when the grace of God has enabled the Catholic monarchs to triumph over their enemies. It is sad that the Queen is no more, but her husband Ferdinand is continuing with the good work of Christian conquest. Surrounded by so many of the trappings of these triumphs, Vasco cannot doubt divine purpose, nor the justice of the growing empire. Are not the two intimately connected? And do not God and his son Jesus Christ, our Lord, wish the gospel to be preached in the furthest corners of His world, so that all shall come under one rule of law, the true faith? Then humankind may live in global, Catholic togetherness.

The streets of Madrigal form a tight warren, with narrow alleyways linking the concentric arrangement of roads which move from the outer walls to the churches at the town's centre. Passing San Nicolás, Vasco and Álvaro delve into the old Jewish quarter, which is now occupied by *conversos* and by those who bought the homes of those Jews who went into exile (and paid well under the odds).* More and more people are now out in the streets, with their mules and oxen, and the Quirogas greet acquaintances as they go.

The Madrigaleños take off their hats deferentially as they greet the riders.

– Young Vasco! Off to Salamanca!

– A student's life!

– All the privileges of a university education!

There is a sense of shared pride in his adventure that touches Vasco. Yes, it will be a privilege to go to the University of Salamanca, and he means to do justice to all the hopes that have been vested in him. There are many expectations, for, of course, it would be a great thing for Madrigal to have one of its own sons in the upper echelons of the royal court.

It is not far from the Jewish quarter to the southern gate. This being his farewell voyage through the town, Vasco is surprised to feel relief when he finally reaches the city walls. There will be no more nostalgia, he tells himself, no more yearning for his past. From now on, he shall look only to the progress of the future, and to enacting God's law on earth. He will allow his unhelpful emotions to fall away from him.

The servant is waiting for him and his brother. The two men nudge their horses close by one another, and clasp each other's hand.

– Farewell.

– Farewell, Álvaro.

– God will look after you.

– Thank you. God bless you.

– Be careful in Salamanca, Vasco. There is much wickedness there.

Vasco has heard of this himself, and he is a little apprehensive as

---

*The Jews were given just four months to wind up their affairs and leave the country in 1492. Inevitably this meant that many of them were forced into selling their goods for a fraction of their true worth.

he ponders his adventure. Still, there is no need for maudlin sentiments, for they will meet again (in the next world if not in this one), and he releases his hand from his brother's. Beyond the walls he can see the vastness of Castile opening up before him. A short distance from the town is the great Augustinian nunnery, and past that there are fields of crops and pastures in which long-horned cattle graze among poppies. Isolated copses cluster in the plain, and partridges and turtle doves join in with the aviary of swifts and house martins that sings in the morning. That birdsong is joyous, Vasco feels, a hymn to the creator – like the journey provided by study and knowledge.

He joins his servant and rides out of the gates of Madrigal.

The precise date of Quiroga's birth is unknown, as no register of births was kept in Madrigal until 1534. Tradition sets it in 1470, but Fintan B. Warren has put it in 1478 or 1479,[24] while the Mexican historian Francisco Miranda Godinez has suggested as late as 1488,[25] citing two reasons: first, a document of 1555 from Mexico City describing Quiroga simply as 'older than sixty'; and second, a papal document of 1544 describing him as already being old (which Miranda Godinez takes as being nearly sixty). Miranda Godinez's attribution seems plausible, especially if the description of Bernal Díaz del Castillo, one of the great chroniclers of the Spanish in Mexico, is noted: Díaz writes that two of the four *oidores* of the *audiencia** in Mexico in 1535 were 'old' – Licenciados Salmerón and Zeynos – but makes no mention of Quiroga.[26] Had Quiroga been born in 1478, he would have been almost sixty by 1535 – certainly 'old' by the standards of the time.

If Quiroga was born around 1488, he would probably have made for Salamanca around 1505. It was common for people to begin their studies young at the university – Hernán Cortés, the conquistador of Mexico, was fourteen when he arrived there in 1499[27] – and Juan de Tavera, a family friend of the Quirogas (and future Archbishop of Toledo) who had lived in Madrigal with his mother, was Rector of Salamanca between 1504 and 1505.[28] This means that Quiroga would have travelled during the upheavals that followed the death of Isabella, which had created numerous problems. The late queen had declared that Ferdinand – who was from Aragón – could not rule over Castile, and had passed the Crown to their daughter Juana; but Juana found

---

*The government of the new colonies in Mexico was initially placed under the jurisdiction of an *audiencia*, which comprised a president and four judges known as *oidores* – literally, 'listeners'.

it difficult to cope with the demands of government after the death of her husband, Philip the Fair, and Ferdinand would eventually declare her insane and incarcerate her in a nunnery in Tordesillas in 1509,* ruling Castile as the Protector of her son Charles, later to become Emperor Charles V. These power struggles were in their pomp, then, as Quiroga made for the university, and no doubt he would have been aware of the parallels between them and those of the period leading up to the joint rule of Isabella and Ferdinand. In fact, the upheavals of the early 1500s resulted directly from the marriage that had changed Spain for ever.

It had been at Madrigal in 1469 that Isabella had received the suits of various European princes and had chosen to marry Ferdinand, son of John II of Aragón and heir to the Aragonese Crown.[29] The joining of the kingdoms of Castile and Aragón famously brought more unity to what is now Spain than the place had ever known before – indeed, it made the creation of the modern country possible.

However, things had not been easy for the royal couple at first. Isabella's half-brother, Henry IV – a licentious and extravagant man, known scandalously as 'el impotente' – was savagely hostile to the marriage. During the 1460s, Henry had faced a rebellion of Castilian nobles which had caused widespread anarchy. Castile had descended into 'such corrupt and terrible habits that everyone behaved according to their own will and desire, with no one to punish or reprimand them ... the towns were destroyed, the goods of the crown were lost, and the royal rents fell so low that it is shameful to mention it';[30] churches were defaced, women were raped, and 'everyone was given free licence to sin'.[31]

This insurrection had been supported by the Aragonese, and so the idea of his kingdom being joined to that of his enemies appalled Henry. Just before his death, on 11 December 1474, he nominated Juana 'la Beltraneja' as his heiress – la Beltraneja claimed to be his daughter, but was said by her enemies to be the offspring of Beltrán de la Cueva, one of Henry's advisors, bred during a supposed affair with his wife Juana of Portugal.

With Isabella and Ferdinand sticking fast to their claim, Henry's death precipitated open civil war between the rival factions in Castile, with la Beltraneja and her party being supported by Portugal. Isabella and Ferdinand retreated to Madrigal in 1476 to hold court, and gave the order to found a security force called the Santa Hermandad, which

---

*Where she remained until her death in 1555, cut off from the outside world.

was the forerunner of the *guardia civil* – the Spanish police.[32] The Beltraneja faction was defeated at the Battle of Toro in 1476, together with the Portuguese, but it was not until the death of John II of Aragón in 1479 that Castile and Aragón were finally united.

The union of the two kingdoms led to the overhauling of Castilian institutions, and to more peace than had been known for centuries: councils of state, once the preserve of the nobility, were now staffed by *letrados* – licenciates from the prestigious universities of Salamanca and Valladolid – meaning that there were many more opportunities than ever before for bright young men with a university education – people like Quiroga. The development of the printing press in the latter half of the fifteenth century meant that he was part of the first generation in which there was anything like a mass readership, people for whom education and knowledge were genuine possibilities and not the privilege of a select few. With old ways being overturned, the voyages of discovery by the Portuguese to Africa and by the Spanish to the Indies were expressions of the way that newness was in everything.

This revolution in the government of the kingdom was forged by a togetherness that was essentially grounded in religious fundamentalism. Hailed by the Pope as 'athletes of Christ', Isabella and Ferdinand threw out the Moors – who had ruled part of the Iberian peninsula ever since 711 – and expelled the Jews. The cultural boundaries were redrawn: Castile united with Aragón, and Christians united against Jews and Moslems; Catholicism became the driving force of the new togetherness, and the multicultural nature of Iberia's *convivencia* was overthrown for ever. It was a shame that Jewish and Moslem converts remained to dilute the Christian race – Ferdinand himself had Jewish blood on his mother's side[33] – but at least these alien religions could be crushed in Spain, so that memories of past compromises would fade away. Yet the process was more one of amnesia than obliteration: it is said that the most famous Spanish phrase of all – '*Olé! Olé!*' – descends from the cry of 'Allah, Allah'. Suspicion of people's true background and beliefs would endure: even today, in restaurants across Spain a dish of broad beans is called *judías verdes* – 'green Jewesses' – and is always served with pork sausage.[34]

The period of the reign of Ferdinand and Isabella, then, had been one of constant change in both government and in ideas, as victories in Spain and discoveries in America changed people's views about the world and its cosmography; and though the old rivalries had been renewed following Isabella's death, many of those changes could still be seen during Quiroga's short ride from Madrigal to Salamanca. The region around Madrigal, for instance, became known as La Moraña, named after the Moors who once ruled the area. But it is estimated that, after the upheavals of the rule of the 'Catholic kings', only about one million of the eight million Moors converted and remained in Spain.[35] Though there were many architectural reminders of the Moorish past, the old cosmopolitan mixture was vanishing in the early years of the sixteenth century, as Quiroga headed for the university.

While the Moors had gone and the understanding of the world was shifting, some customs held fast, however, and Quiroga's journey would have taken him past the countless castles that littered the plain. People still believed that safety could only be guaranteed in urban settlements, and there was a mistrust of isolation.[36] They did not live alone in farmsteads sprinkled across the plains, but in the villages where storks rattled their beaks, nestling in the bell-towers of the new churches, which gleamed in the baking heat.

In between the settlements were the fields of crops, the pastures and the copses. The clusters of trees looked appealing to travellers, but things were not always as they seemed. There was a saying in Castile: '*Setiembre o secan las fuentes o se llevan los puentes*' – Come September, either the fountains run dry or the bridges are carried off by floods.[37] So the copses were either filled with horseflies and mosquitoes, if it was dry, or dripped water incessantly, if it was wet.[38] In these years, though, drought was the order of the day, as a series of dry summers made for poor harvests. It was at this time that the severe conditions impelled many people to cross the Atlantic in search of a better life.

So the plains were filled with perhaps 5000 thirsty students looking for shade as they made their way to the university.[39] The sons of the nobility, like Quiroga, went with servants, books and equipment, but many students came with very little. The distance between Madrigal and Salamanca following the old Camino Real was only thirty-two kilometres[40] – less than a day's ride for a fit man like Quiroga. That brief journey passed through countless expressions of the shifts that had overtaken the world in the past twenty years: there were more sheep to be seen than ever before, as the wool trade took off; the ancient woods were interspersed with more pastures and fields of crops; the threat of attack had diminished, so that for the first time the castles and forts that clung to the plain in their thousands appeared somehow bereft, as if intimating the beginning of their slow decline from their place at the centre of the world; Christians – or those

claiming to be Christians while practising Islam or Judaism in secret –
were the only people to be seen; and the plain of Castile was full of
people like Quiroga, dreaming of the personal benefits that a university
education might bring.

Salamanca is spotted by Vasco from a distance, perched on a rise
above the clear, rushing waters of the Tormes river. In the hour before
sunset the light has cleared, and the buildings stand out in sharper
definition than during the middle of the day. Now he can see the
keeling cathedral, whose fragile state is a cause of great worry, and the
steeples of the churches and monasteries which cluster together as if
fighting for first call to the heavens. The golden colour of the sandstone
dazzles and bears the promise of great riches in wealth or in learning;
and then, to the south of the city, he catches sight of the Roman
bridge, with its arches and the span of a hundred eagles.

The city is imposing, and brings home to Vasco that it will be here
that his future is decided. His throat is swollen with thirst, and his
back aches after spending many hours in the saddle: the journey has
lapsed into silence. Neither he nor his servant can think of anything
beyond their arrival, and their pain is tempered only by the struggles
of the poorer students whom they pass on the road, walking with as
much dignity as their blisters and their patched bundles of belongings
will allow. Salamanca is a magnet for all of Spain, and in particular for
those who venture north from Andalucía, braving the arid, baking
plains of Extremadura, where they cross wave upon wave of the
pasture that lies yellowed and desiccating in the summer furnace.

Vasco would like to enter Salamanca across the Roman bridge itself,
for it suits his sense of majesty; but that would be a detour. No, says
his servant, it is best just to pass through the Gate of Toro and find
their lodgings as quickly as they may. Up ahead is another group
similar to his own, and Vasco slows his horse: there is no hurry to
push on into the thronged streets, he says, and indeed – if he dare
admit it to himself – he is a little apprehensive. It is well known that
new students at the university are given a hard time by their peers,
and some protest that as soon as they arrive at the faculty they are
showered with more saliva than a thundercloud gives out rain;[41] then
the initiate is forced up to the lectern to give a speech, before being
used as the butt of jokes throughout his first year of study.

Vasco looks forward to none of this – he has come to progress in
learning, not degeneration – and he is also fearful of the caves which
skulk away below the city, where necromancers are said to lurk. The

grottoes of Salamanca are famed for being home to the study of the black arts, and this poses such a threat that during her reign Isabella ordered them to be blocked off so that they could not be used.[42] Yet Vasco knows that they are still functioning – many people have warned him of it – and he fears, not without justification, that they will remain for a long time.* This Salamanca is a confused city, filled with great cathedrals and great wrongdoers, the saintly and the dissolute, the rich and the indigent, peopled by students, merchants, beggars and thieves, all of them wearing as many different types of clothes as there are saints' days in the year: it will surely be an instructive place to begin his career.

Together, the two riders pass through the Gate of Toro and enter this city on the cusp of modernity. Groups of friars walk up and down the streets looking disparagingly at the gaggle of human life that swarms around them. The long habits of these barefoot mendicants rustle heavily against the cobbles: they all wear different habits, so that they are as varied as the people of the city who crush beside them – the beggars, ladies, pilgrims to Santiago, servants, maidservants, travellers, merchants, the naked and the homeless, the peasants and their lords. Whatever Salamanca is, it is full of life.

There are so many people that the two travellers are forced to dismount and lead their animals through the city. Vasco is dazed by the crush. Of late, Madrigal has been a quiet, almost staid town, and only his visits to the annual fairs of Medina del Campo have shown him anything like this pandemonium. Out of the corner of his eye he sees some of the older students greeting one another, and he senses the companionship that his studies may bring him; but all this is far away, and for the moment he cannot begin to comprehend this world. The university term will not start until the day of San Lucas, 18 October, almost a month hence: how will he cope in this bedlam until then? Vasco longs for the rigour and comfort of a routine.

– Come. We must find our lodgings. My brother has made an arrangement with Juan de Tavera.

Vasco's servant nods mechanically, but he seems less distressed by the chaos. He has heard that Salamanca has something for everyone, and his eyes stray around as he turns his mount and follows his master. As the poet Ruíz de Alarcón would put it, the students of the university

---

*As late as the eighteenth century, a Portuguese visitor, Francisco Botello de Moraes y Vasconcellos, arrived and made his way straight to the magicians who lived in the grottoes.

'follow their whims, play with vice ... and make a point of being crazy'. Another poet, Sebastián de Horozco, would write that the students in Salamanca 'waste their time in walking / by night to the whorehouses / in sleeping and strolling / drinking and playing / and in all sorts of other dirty tricks'.[43] Not everyone comes here to learn about the justice of God, and about the exercise of His laws in the mortal world.

The streets are narrow and filthy, filled with animal and human excrement, animal and human urine, the caws of crows and flapping chickens; but they are also glowing with the golden colour coming from the sandstone buildings that reflect the sunlight in a fanfare of pillars, capitals and bas-reliefs. Rising up a gentle incline, Vasco and his servants reach the plaza outside the cathedral, that teetering mass of ancient stone in desperate need of repair. Work will begin on a new cathedral in 1509, a project to the glory of God whose scope is vast (so vast that it will never entirely be finished). The new cathedral will act as a buttress, stopping the old cathedral from terrorising the townspeople by tumbling into nothingness and filling the air above the city with a cloud of dust.

Vasco has heard much of the old cathedral and its poor state of repair. Everything in this building – from the stonework on the architraves to the carvings on the tombs – will remind Vasco of the inspiration that can come to artists in the presence of God. Inside, standing before the nave where he himself will pray many times, is an altarpiece consisting of fifty-three panels which show the life of Jesus Christ, including his birth, the Last Judgement, and his soaring up to the angels – helping Vasco to imagine the epiphany of the soul after its rebirth from death. A door leads out from the nave to the cloisters, where he will take his exam to become a licenciate in canon law in the chapel of Santa Barbara. His examiners will sit around him on stone benches, interrogating his knowledge of the law after he has spent twenty-four hours alone in the room preparing for this ordeal. There will be little colour here, he will find, beyond the tiles beside the altarpiece; but then law is morality and reflects the power of justice (and the prejudices of power), so it is fitting that he should qualify in a dark room where contemplation is what matters most.

The cloisters and the cathedral are closely connected with university life. Apart from the exams of the prospective licenciates, one of the most important chapels in the cloisters is owned by Rodrigo Arias Maldonado, professor of law, whose lectures Vasco will soon start attending;* the chapel is resplendent with new *azulejos*, and ringed by choir stalls whose armrests are so high that they come up to the shoulders of those who pray there. On another side of the cloister is the Anaya Chapel, containing the gleaming alabaster sepulchre of its founder, intricately carved with a myriad faces and distinct lions lining up along its sides.

Everything, Vasco will see, shows that all art leads to God. This is what he has learnt through the Mudéjar designs of Madrigal, and this is what is proven by the craftsmanship of Salamanca. This sumptuous cathedral, the wonderful new houses rising up all around the city amid the wooden scaffolds and the dust, the new monasteries and churches, all show that learning and art and science are expressions of God's will, and that Castile is at the epicentre of divine justice. Vasco cannot escape it – and no one should expect him to. He seeks God, truth, beauty and justice, and his first impressions of Salamanca lead him to believe that he will find them here. He cannot yet question a moral authority that goes unchallenged throughout the world, carrying off all in its wake.

Outside the cathedral, the crush lessens somewhat. There is a wide space here, and Vasco and his servants are able to pause for a moment's rest. In the distance, they can hear the cries from the Calle de Serranos, a street thronged with students who buy those things that they need: mattresses, blankets, chairs, tables, candlesticks, clothes, boxes, padlocks, lecterns and quills. Some of the students who have already arrived in the city are making their way back to their lodgings, weighed down by the piles of things that they will need for the winter. The cries and the smells and the movement suddenly fill Vasco with an inexpressible joy, for they seem to encompass life in their variety and their incessant passing, and as such are surely a paean to God.

He stands still for a moment, overwhelmed.

– My master! his servant calls to him.

– Yes.

– We must make for the lodgings arranged by your brother.

Of course, the man is right. Soon it will be dark, and then the bawdiness of the more dissolute students will overtake the streets. He has heard that then all is chaos, as armies of serenaders vie with one another in the streets, letting loose their fiddles and guitars and their

---

*Maldonado later had a building constructed known as the Casa de las Conchas, whose exterior was lined with shells, symbolising the pilgrimage to Santiago. This is one of the most famous tourist attractions in Salamanca today.

teams of shield-players – but, as Cervantes would later put it in 'The Pretended Aunt', unfortunately being 'better skilled in the music of the knife and fork than in any other instrument'.[44]

Vasco does not feel equipped to meet this challenge on his first night in the city. With the help of Juan de Tavera, Álvaro has arranged lodgings for him in the house of an old friend, and there the young Madrigaleño knows that he will at last be able to settle down and begin the life of study. He is happy now, as he follows his servant, who has been to Salamanca many times before on errands for the Quiroga family. The servant leads the young master through a street that leads directly off the plaza by the cathedral, down towards the Tormes river. Soon they are passing by the sandstone façade of the university itself, and the servant nods to Vasco as they go.

– That is it, Don Vasco. The university.

Together with Bologna, Oxford and Paris, Salamanca is one of the four great universities in Europe. Although no Christian would ever admit such a thing, its existence owes much to the model of the Colleges of Arabs and Jews founded under the Caliphate of Al-Andalus centuries ago; in fact, the university system has been passed on to Christian Europe by the Christians' greatest foes, the Muslims and the Jews.[45] Today, Salamanca embodies something of the democratic ideal, with the students electing their rector each year – something that Vasco approves of so much that he will incorporate elections into his own ideal state thirty years hence. Already he knows that the university is a remarkable institution and, as he stands before it in the Calle Libreros, he begins to contemplate his own place there. Even though the extraordinary sandstone frontispiece – complete with its hidden lucky frog – will not be completed for twenty years yet, its scope can already be seen. It will be headed by portraits of Ferdinand and Isabella, and eventually will have the arms of Charles V above them, while being covered by cherubs, lions, twisting vines and elaborate heraldic symbols. Entering beneath this monument to the Catholic monarchs, Vasco will study in the classroom immediately to the left, facing onto the courtyard. From here, it is but a short walk across to the staircase that leads up to the second level and the library.

Vasco knows that all the students are impatiently awaiting the library's completion. Although it will not be ready until 1510, he will eventually be able to sit among the many heavy leather armchairs, aware that the collection of books in that room is rivalled nowhere in Christian Europe.[46] It is here, turning the pages with a solemn hand, that Vasco will develop his reverence for the written word, and for lifelong learning. Does not a university education set a man up in the world? It educates (and, as the Spanish put it, indoctrinates) a person with the crucial concepts of their time, and so Vasco will learn the essential truth of his time: that knowledge serves God. It is also here that he will cement his friendship with Juan de Tavera; Tavera will later change his life when, as President of the Royal Council of Castile, he puts Vasco's name forward to be *oidor* of Mexico's second *audiencia*.*

The Empire and its foundations are remarkable gifts, Vasco thinks, as he stands outside the university and tries to imagine all that he will learn there. They have given the Spanish the opportunity to educate the whole world in the values of Christ, to bring hope to barbarous peoples in every corner of the globe. That, then, must be the Spanish aim, and the realisation of God's word: the universalisation of Christ's rule on earth (under Spanish laws). How much the world will thank them!

– Come, Vasco, we are almost there.

The light is failing now, and the twilight heaves with people and with the startled calls and movements of the thousands of swifts that fill the streets. Shadows are in everything now as the two men move down the street and eventually stop at the door of a house that looks like all the others. Vasco leaves his horses in the care of his servant, and knocks hard; eventually, he is let in by a servant.

He climbs the steep, narrow stairway alone and enters his low chamber. He stoops slightly as he moves to the desk by the window, where he stands and looks below. Those who are still out are hurrying home, and Vasco smiles at the amazing range of their headgear: berets, caps, bonnets and all manner of leather and felt hats bobbing around beneath him amid the tunics, cassocks, capes and shawls. It is truly memorable, but now the night will descend and the city will fill with darkness.

Yes, he thinks, it is time to turn to prayer, and to hope that this journey through the university and life will bring him peace and

---

*As matriculation records did not then exist, there is no concrete proof that Quiroga studied in Salamanca. However, while he might have studied at a foreign university, if remaining in Castile he was almost certainly a student at Salamanca, as there was no course in Valladolid in civil law, the course which he is known to have taken. This fact, combined with others, has in recent years led opinion to push towards Salamanca: in addition, Juan de Tavera was the Rector of Salamanca, and his influence on Quiroga's later career is known through a letter from Nuño de Guzmán, the disgraced president of the first *audiencia* of the new colony. Furthermore, Tavera – like Quiroga – was probably of *converso* origin.

enlightenment. Does not the good Lord want happiness and justice for all of His flock, wherever they might live? Does He not want them to be healthy and free of want?

That sort of perfection is what he must strive to achieve, he thinks, as he turns and prepares to go down to his servant. Yet there is so much work to be done before that ideal can be achieved, and the fantastic stories coming out of the New World have shown how many people remain bereft of the word of truth and God.

There are so many souls to be saved. One time, he thinks, as he treads confidently down the stairs and recalls his father's investment in Columbus's first voyage, he will go to Seville and hear these stories for himself.

THREE

It was dark in Seville. I stood quietly in the hallway and struggled for a moment to get my bearings. I found myself remembering the fantasy I had had in S——, that in fact I was already standing in the Archive of the Indies. Of course it was absurd to credit that I had travelled to the south of Spain with such bewildering ease, and without even burning any fossil fuels.

As I took in my surroundings, the reality of the recent bus journey from Madrigal began to take hold. The marble stairway and the high ceilings of the Archive made the air pleasantly cool, a striking contrast to the violent swings of the bus as we had clattered round the curves of the Sierra Morena. The grandeur of the entrance hall was a delicious counterpoint to the hurry of the bus driver. Slowly, I began to relax, as I decided that I did not have to mimic the insanity of the old man in S—— in my own utopian quest.

The *funcionario* at the entrance desk was watching me, tapping his watch.

'We're about to close, *señor*,' he informed me.

I thanked him. There was clearly no point in staying here when the Archive was shutting; I would come back in the morning to find out more about Quiroga.

Turning on my heel, I walked out into the city. The Archive was surrounded by sheet metal, and plumes of dust rose up into the sky as if the building had recently been pounded into oblivion. For a moment I ducked instinctively, but then I gathered from the teams of bulldozers and the numbers of people with hard hats that nothing more sinister than the Archive's ongoing maintenance was afoot, and my tension eased.

I walked briskly, searching for a pavement cafe where I could unwind. As I crossed the cobbles towards Seville's monumental cathedral, an unpleasant smell lingered in my nostrils. I passed by a succession of puddles – each of which had a reddish tinge – and was surprised at the rainfall, for I knew this to be one of the hottest cities in Europe; but then I saw a fleet of horse-drawn carriages awaiting the herds of tourists outside the cathedral, and I realised that the puddles were puddles of horse-piss.

Passing the floodlit entrance to the cathedral, I came across a bridal party making for a side chapel, high-stepping over the horse-piss as if they were royal guards. The men wore yellow roses in their buttonholes, while the women were dressed in evening gowns topped off with silk veils and lacquered hair-combs. Their elegant attire was in marked contrast to my own, and I began to feel the effects of the heat.

I walked into the first cafe I saw and ordered a bottle of beer from one of the *mozos* standing by the entrance. Then, taking a deep breath and sitting down at a table across from the cathedral, I began to leaf through the notes that I had made on More and Quiroga thus far, and the things that I had learnt in Madrigal. My researches had concentrated initially on More's *Utopia*, and the nature of its 'perfection'.

More's fictional island of Utopia, I saw, was not a place where people would want to live today. There had been much restriction on individual liberty, and the society had been grounded in the worst hierarchy of all: sexism. Nevertheless, for its time it had been an ideal: the concept of individuality had only been nascent in renaissance Europe, after all, and the benefits of patriarchy had then been unquestioned.

More's narrator – Nonsenso – had come across the island of Utopia in the 'Mundus Novus' of which Amérigo Vespucci had written. The island had been a sort of crescent encircling a large lake,[1] and there had been superficial similarities between it and England: its dimensions were exactly the same, and the number of its city-states was identical to the number of counties in England including London.[2] But everything else was different, and even though the Utopians lived in a stringently controlled state, their way of life was, according to More's book, 'the happiest basis for a civilised community'.[3] While there was 'much to condemn', there were also 'several regulations which suggested possible methods of reforming European society'.[4]

There were fifty-four towns in Utopia, each of which looked exactly alike. Between the town were country farms that could house at least forty adults:[5] the townsfolk took it in turns to spend periods of two years working in the fields, and those who enjoyed country life could stay longer if they wished.[6] Towns were organised around households, or families, with each town having 6000 families, each containing between ten and sixteen adults;[7] this being a patriarchal society, each family fell under the authority of the oldest male. There was also a representative democracy based on these families, with one district controller for every thirty families,[8] and groups of ten district controllers placed under a senior district controller.[9] Each town had 200 district controllers, and they were responsible for electing the mayor by secret ballot: the mayor held meetings every three days with the senior district controllers.[10]

Labour in Utopia was organised so that people worked six hours a day:[11] everyone farmed, in addition to practising a trade. If people wanted to wander around the countryside, they could do so, but they would only eat if they did a morning's or afternoon's work in the farms they came to.[12] In the towns, each group of thirty families ate together, and supper was taken in a room scented with burning incense; music was always played before the meal ended with sweets and fruit.[13] Though as inhabitants of the New World they did not call themselves Christians, they believed fervently in an afterlife, and in a single Supreme Being.[14] I had found that it was probable that More had been influenced in writing this by early reports from the New World: in 1493, for instance, representatives from Ferdinand and Isabella had told Pope Alexander VI that the Indians 'believe[d] in one God, the Creator in heaven'.[15]

I paused reading through my notes, and took a sip from my bottle of beer. The light was fading, and the streets were gradually becoming more animated as teams of tourists began to search for a place to sate their hunger after a hard day's sightseeing. While many of them seemed calm, I sensed that some people were overtaken by a sense of bewilderment as to the foreign language and foods, much as I had been when talking to the old man in S———. Relaxing as I nursed my beer, I felt very glad that I was no longer prey to his brand of crazed idealism.

The tables around me quickly began to fill up. I tried to make myself inconspicuous, but soon found that a group of Sevillanos had sat in the chairs nearby and put their drinks on my table. I smiled in an attempt to be friendly to them. At first they said nothing, but then, after about ten minutes in which I had tried to continue concentrating on my notes, one of them turned to me suddenly:

'What's all this, *macho*?' he asked me. 'Why all the reading? You should be drinking your beer and enjoying yourself.'

I explained that I was a researcher, and had come to Seville to do some work in the Archive of the Indies.

'That's as may be, *macho*,' he said; 'but the Archive's shut now, so drink up and relax.'

I looked at him closely for a moment. He was a wiry man, a slab of taut muscles, pent-up energy.

'What's your name?' I asked him.

'Pablo,' he said.

'Well Pablo, I *am* relaxing,' I told him. 'It's just that I want to read through my notes.'

Moving his chair nearer to mine, Pablo asked me what my research involved, and I explained about More and Quiroga, running through an outline of More's ideal community, and of how Vasco de Quiroga – the young man from Madrigal – had realised it in Mexico.

'It all sounds a bit dull to me, *macho*,' he said when I had finished. 'Those old guys did not drink or enjoy themselves. Like you, they did not know about fashions. I wouldn't want to live there.'

I agreed that it did not sound like fun to us, but stressed that Utopia had been as just a community as could have been imagined at the time. Provided everyone had worked who had been capable of it, everyone had eaten well. There had been four hospitals in each town, and, since there had been no private property, Utopians had despised gold and silver – which they had used for chamber-pots and fetters[16] – and had loathed the way in which other societies worshipped a rich man 'not because they owe[d] him money or [were] otherwise in his power, but simply because he [was] rich'.[17] The Utopian economy's overriding aim had been: 'to give each person as much time free from physical drudgery as the needs of the community will allow, so that he can cultivate his mind – which they regard as the secret of a happy life'.[18]

When I had finished, Pablo stared at me as if I had just arrived in Seville on the latest flight from Mars.

'I see,' he said. 'And that's your idea of fun?'

'Maybe not,' I said; 'but it's an interesting idea.'

Pablo burst out laughing. 'To you perhaps,' he said, 'but it strikes me that you've spent so long reading up about this obscure story that you've gone a bit soft in the head.' I shuddered at that. 'I mean look at you!' He leaned over and began to finger my frayed blue jeans and my old shirt. 'You haven't got a clue about *modern* values, have you? Forget the ideas of these guys who've been dead for 500 years – you need to go shopping.'

'Shopping?' I asked him, feeling a surge of dread.

'You need an entire new wardrobe,' he said.

'You're exaggerating,' I complained. 'I could do with one or two shirts, perhaps, but that would do.'

'Forgive me, *macho*,' Pablo said, 'but in my view you ought to get in more than that. There's a lot of uncertainty in the air just now, and – quite apart from your absurd lack of fashion-consciousness – you don't want to be caught out.'

'Uncertainty?'

'There's a general strike planned for the day after tomorrow,' he said.

I now recalled that on my way here from the Archive I had seen several posters advertising the strike. In a curious echo of Spain's golden age – which I had been reading up on as well – Seville today manifested both great wealth, through the passing tourists, and great poverty, with widespread unemployment upsetting the social equilibrium. There was considerable social unrest, with the city's unemployment problem compounded by the starvation wages paid to the day labourers in the olive and orange groves that surrounded it. The unions had organised a strike to remind their paymasters of the inequity of the economic order.

'Well,' I said to Pablo, taking another swig from my beer bottle and emptying it, 'when the shops open tomorrow, perhaps I'll get in three pairs of shirts and trousers, and an extra pair of shoes.'

Pablo looked at me with a pitying smile. 'Honestly, *macho*,' he said, 'have you forgotten to take into account the constant threat of terrorist attacks? Everybody I know is going out and spending like there's no tomorrow – which there probably won't be – just to consume the very last piece of fashion that they can find.'

'That's crazy,' I said.

'No it isn't,' he insisted. 'What's crazy is to ignore the permanent danger of enemy assaults. A shopping spree is certainly one way of protecting yourself from the fallout from terrorist bombs. Just look over there.'

He pointed to the street beyond the cathedral, and I saw a balding, tubby man marshalling stacks of boxes into a white van, which was parked on the roadside.

'What's he doing?' I asked Pablo, in spite of myself.

'He's stocking up with clothes for his family,' Pablo said. I watched with increasing bewilderment as the crates of clothes mounted up on the roadside, a veritable army of possessions. It appeared that the bald man had taken the nature of postmodern society very much to heart, for these days what was clear was that good citizenship required a fat wallet and countless desires all in need of high-street satisfaction.

I watched for some time, until I realised that none of this seemed real any more, and that at that moment I was in danger of falling into a deluded world view such as that which I had come across in the old man in S——, or in the ideas of the great knight-errant Don Quixote.

'Stop right there!' I yelled to Pablo, pushing back my chair and standing up, quivering with rage. 'You're trying to lead me down the slippery slope to madness.'

'Hey, *macho!*' he exclaimed. 'Relax! As I told you, with all that arcane understanding, you're already there. With all that idealism, you're bound to feel deluded.'

'No,' I said. 'No. That idealism was a problem for the old man in S——, but I'm perfectly sane. I'll show you.'

I wasn't going to talk to him about More and Quiroga now, that was for sure. I marched up to the bar and paid my tab, and then walked out into the Sevillian night and hailed a cab.

The driver stopped and I got into the back seat. He put his foot on the accelerator, and we moved off slowly.

'Where are you going to, *señor?*' he asked me.

With horror, I recalled that I had yet to find a hotel. 'I've no idea,' I said weakly. 'I have no hotel.'

'No hotel?' he echoed, stepping on the brake and bringing us to a standstill. 'Why not?'

I couldn't understand how I could have failed to make a booking. 'Well,' I said, trying to explain myself, and recalling the fleeting perception I had had in S—— that I had already been transported here by magical chance, 'you see, I came here by accident and wanted to smarten up straightaway.'

'By chance?' he echoed, quizzically. He was a fit young man with a shaven head, and he looked at me now with deep bafflement.

'I think so,' I said, wondering if that surreal journey had in fact been real and the bus journey through the Sierra Morena had been a dream. 'You see, I'm doing some research at the Archive of the Indies.'

'Ah in the Archive,' the man said, as if that explained everything. 'And what's your subject?'

'It's really very interesting,' I said, trying to find a focus and recover my sense of normality. 'I'm looking into Vasco de Quiroga. Quiroga was born in Madrigal, in Castile, and probably studied canon law at Salamanca University. He was appointed one of the *oidores* – or administrators – of Mexico in 1530, less than ten years after Cortés executed the conquest in 1521. Anyhow, as an *oidor* Quiroga saw how most of the Spanish settlers were destroying the Indians, and resolved to do something better for them. Thomas More had just published his book *Utopia*, and Quiroga used it as a model to found communes in which the Indians could be protected.'

'That sounds fascinating, *señor*,' the taxi driver said, drumming his fingers on the dashboard.

'It is,' I said. 'Getting to the heart of those utopias, you can see if the human being is really capable of altruism and goodness. These days, with the way in which greed has been put at the forefront of international economic policy and work is valued solely for its earning potential, it's inevitable that people should see their jobs as in a great measure self-serving. Altruism as such is therefore increasingly difficult to imagine. But it appears that Quiroga and those who lived in his communes tried it.'

'Did they, *señor*?'

'Yes!' I said. 'In fact, for centuries Utopia was a creditable ideal. The Americas came to represent a place in which the slate had been wiped clean and people could begin again. Idealistic groups realised what a mess we were making of things in Europe, and knew that there needed to be new ideals and a new beginning.'

The taxi driver looked long and hard at me in the overhead mirror, and then let out a whistle.

'Well, I can see why you've come here, then,' he said, running his hand over his shaven head and looking concerned for me as he spoke. 'But there is a little problem with the timing of your trip, *señor*. For the Summit's on at the moment, and it'll be very difficult to find a room.'

'The Summit?' I asked.

'Oh yes,' he said. 'All the leaders of the European Union are here at the moment in order to debate crucial international issues.'

'Oh,' I said. 'That makes everything a lot harder.'

'We'll just have to drive round till we find somewhere,' he said.

I was unsure about this plan – as a leafleter for the Green Party I did not want to add unnecessarily to carbon emissions – but I saw that I had little option. As the driver let his foot off the clutch and the taxi began to move slowly through the streets, I reflected on how easy it was to be distracted and to end up doing things that were in direct contradiction to your own beliefs. After all, I mistrusted cars, yet here I was forcing my taxi driver to burn fossil fuels. That, I realised, was the wickedly clever essence of the new economic and moral order: why have principles at all when to have them inevitably makes for hypocrisy?

As the taxi moved off, I tried to relax. The conversation with Pablo in the bar and the vision of the man piling his van full of clothes receded, so that I was no longer sure if they had even happened. There was no need for this utopian research into More and Quiroga to turn my idealism into delusion, and I would soon be able properly to develop my investigations.

I turned my eyes to the streets, and took in my new surroundings. Although by now many of the shops had closed, the city was still thronged with vehicles and people. We inched up street after street, but whenever I stopped to check the hotels we came upon, they were all full. In no time at all, my new sense of calm began to be overtaken by a concern that I would be left homeless on the streets. The taxi driver seemed similarly concerned, and the car soon fell into silence as we went from hotel to hotel, and constantly suffered rebuffs. How had I managed to make such a mistake, and fail to book a room? I asked myself. I prided myself on my organisation, but my obsession with More and Quiroga and their utopias had blinded me to the realities of my situation.

After perhaps half an hour the driver pulled in to a side street and turned to face me. It appeared that he had come to a decision, and my anxiety meant that so had I: my best option was to offer him some money and sleep in his car. It would be uncomfortable, but at least I would be alone and protected, and I would not have to deal with strangers. Yes, of course I dreamt of Utopia, and the sort of together-ness which that implied, but we lived in an atrophied society and for the time being isolation was essential for my protection.

'Look,' the taxi driver said, interrupting my thoughts, 'my grand-mother has a spare room. She'll put up with you for the night.'

'Put me up?' I asked, not sure if I had understood him.

'Come on,' he said. 'I'll show you to her flat.'

He opened the passenger door for me, and I stepped out onto the pavement, paying the fare I had seen on the meter. Then he entered a nearby house and led me up a steep, dark stairway, before knocking on the door at the top.

'I'm afraid I haven't got time to wait,' he said hurriedly, turning to face me. 'Just go on in, though, and explain. She won't mind. In fact, she'll be grateful for the company.'

There was no sound from the room to acknowledge the knock;

nevertheless the taxi driver gestured to me encouragingly, before backing away hurriedly down the stairs. Somewhat bemused at his eccentricity and wondering if I would be able to maintain my pretence of normality much longer, I opened the door and walked into his grandmother's flat.

It had been a strange few days, and I suppose that I should have been used to surprises by now. Nevertheless, nothing could have prepared me for the disturbing sight that awaited; for there, sprawled across a three-seat sofa, was one of the most enormous women I had ever seen. She was lying down, but it was clear at once that this was largely because she could not raise herself without a tremendous effort. Beside the sofa were two coffee tables filled with vast quantities of food: there were packets of crisps and biscuits and chocolate, empty cans of Coca-Cola and lemonade, half-eaten pizzas on which the cheese was beginning to harden, hamburger cartons from famous burger chains – some of them empty, others not – also cartons of cream and packets of sugar and ice cream. The floor was a morass of plastic packaging which could easily have filled several dustbin liners, and the whole room stank of an atmosphere of greed, cultural neglect, social isolation, sadness and self-loathing.

'Hello,' I said tentatively. But she did not hear me – my voice was drowned out by the blaring of the TV which she was watching – so I walked forward until I was between her and the machine.

'Oh goodness,' she said, jumping visibly in her skin. 'You nearly gave me a heart attack.'

'I'm sorry to surprise you like this,' I bellowed above the noise. 'Your grandson suggested that I might be able to stay the night here. I've just arrived from England to do some research, and all the hotels in Seville are full.'

Once I had explained myself, she could not have been kinder. Of course, she told me, I must stay, there was plenty of room and it was always interesting to meet new people, especially those from overseas.

'Pull up a seat, *muchacho*,' she said, gesturing at a flimsy chair by the window. 'I'm just watching the news.'

I did as I was told, and we watched the day's events unfold. With the Summit due to begin the next day, Seville was tightening its security: the increasing number of immigrants meant that there was a general fear that terrorists might be at large.

'Have some pizza,' the old woman said, and I polished off a slice – as I had eaten nothing for hours, I was very hungry. 'Open a can of

Coke. Have a burger! There's plenty more where these came from,' she said, munching away herself.

I helped myself to the food that lay haphazardly about the floor, and started to feel better. It had been a bewildering day, but after I had eaten a few slices of pizza and some ice cream I felt able to take in the news item about the constant stream of murders carried out by the army, the paramilitary death squads and the Marxist rebels in Colombia. Oppression was such a terrible thing, I thought, as I took a large bite from a hamburger, and it was always chastening to see other people's misery on TV.

'Perhaps we should watch something else,' I suggested to the old woman. 'There's only so much depressing news that it's possible to take.'

'Oh no,' she said, between mouthfuls of chocolate ice cream, 'I always watch the news. It's important to know what's going on.'

There was nothing I could do about it, and so I polished off two chocolate bars and a packet of crisps in quick succession. Then I disturbed the miserable flow of the newsreader for a moment by piercing open another can of Coke; but soon he was at it again, this time talking about cocoa plantations in West Africa that used only slave labour. This was too much: I really needed to relax, and these distressing stories were doing nothing for my equanimity. The news just made me feel angry, exploitative, fearful and impotent; it made me despise myself, for I realised that in my subconscious these awful tales made me unutterably relieved to live in S——.

I got up, feeling heavy after all the food I had eaten, and turned off the TV.

'I'm sorry,' I said, turning to the old lady, 'but I can't cope with this any more. I hope you don't mind.'

She looked shocked.

'Don't you like the TV, *muchacho*?' she asked me. 'Is it that it's too small?'

I saw shame in her expression, and for the first time I took her in properly – her treble chins, the little dark eyes which were buried beneath her fleshiness, and her wispy grey hair – and saw that perhaps she might once have been beautiful.

'No,' I said quickly, 'it's not that. I just can't stand the news. I don't find this constant barrage of information is very healthy right now. It's doing me no good.'

'I see,' she said, looking confused. 'Why not?'

'Well ...' I paused, trying to take stock of my own feelings: I believed that there was something deeply insidious in the endless misery that these broadcasts displayed, something that promoted indolence and apathy; and of course TV was also a prime medium for the advertisements which encouraged us to have as many desires as possible, so that we would feel impelled to buy crates filled with clothes or stuff whole supermarket trolleys full of junk food. Yet it was impossible to be content when our desires just grew within us, like cancers; in fact, contentment had ceased to be a commonplace or realistic goal.

'Are you sure you're feeling all right?' the old woman asked me now.

'I'm fine,' I said.

'Sit down,' she said, and I took a step back to the flimsy chair, which almost buckled as I sat in it. 'Perhaps you need another chocolate bar?' she asked, eating one herself.

'No, no,' I said.

'Is it your research that is getting to you?' she asked, opening a vanilla ice cream.

Yes it was, I realised. There was so much to think about, and so little time in which to think when there was such a vast quantity of information to absorb. I suddenly felt very tired, and became aware for the first time that I was failing to keep a grip on reality. I had no idea who this old woman was, nor where I was, nor even if my journey to get here had been at all believable; but then, I no longer cared even that fiction should be credible, for what mattered to me was my utopian vision (or at least, that of More and Quiroga).

'It's difficult to imagine,' I said slowly, 'but I'm looking into idealistic societies.'

'Oh,' she said, licking the vanilla from her lips, 'I used to be an idealistic young woman! I didn't always used to be like this – a glutton.'

'You didn't?' I asked, unable to keep a note of surprise from my voice.

'Oh no, *muchacho*,' she said. 'I was an agile, beautiful young woman. And I was always protesting with the other Marxists.'

'You were a Marxist?' I asked.

'Oh yes,' she said, her enthusiasm beginning to wane. 'We had to keep quiet during the Franco regime, of course, but in the eighties we could be more open. But then – after the collapse of the Eastern bloc – well, it was all so dispiriting. There was nothing but individual greed left as an aspiration. And so – I just joined in.'

'Did you not want to fight for your ideals?'

'Of course we did, but it was soon apparent that they were being abandoned. No one was prepared to sacrifice their lives for an ideal any more, as they did during the civil war. And so Marx just seemed an irrelevance after a while.'

'This is really very interesting,' I said. 'Marxism represented a kind of utopia, I suppose, but I'm approaching the theme of idealism from an earlier standpoint.'

I explained about Thomas More's *Utopia* and Quiroga, and the old woman clapped her hands with excitement. For a moment, her face lit up with a vitality that I had imagined long dead in her.

'Of course,' she said. 'We often said that More was the first socialist.'

'Well,' I said, 'it's not quite so straightforward as that, but I'll tell you what I've discovered.'

I stood up, trying to work through an explanation which did not sound tired or rehearsed, and which somehow might galvanise her into realising that utopian idealism was not dead – that, in fact, it was of crucial relevance to her as she sat wallowing in TV and junk food.

I outlined the features of More's *Utopia* that I had read over in my notes in the cafe, and then went on to explain that the book had to be contextualised. Thomas More, I explained, had been an important figure in the humanist movement in early sixteenth-century Europe. Humanists had believed that the purest Christianity ought to be based on the study of the gospels themselves,[19] and that a culture centred on this faith would hold fast to stronger principles than that in which they lived; they had also seen the rural lifestyle that had preceded the age of modernity as an ideal order of nature, and one that could promote greater humanity and union with God.[20] The humanist movement had reached its apogee in the early sixteenth century through its new standard-bearer the Flemish scholar Erasmus, who had been a friend of Thomas More's. In the 1520s humanism became increasingly popular in Spain, the most powerful European country at that time, as many of the writings of Erasmus were translated;[21] although the rise of Lutheranism meant that soon humanist 'dissent' in Spain was less tolerated, the movement's impact on the early colonists of the Americas could not be ignored.

More's *Utopia*, then, I said, came at a time of important intellectual change. It had been published in 1516, just one year before Martin Luther's rebellion against the Catholic Church had begun, and was therefore the product of the last moment at which Christianity in Western Europe remained united. Many humanists had hailed the book,* and the evidence suggests that, although the text is deliberately ambiguous, More himself believed in many of *Utopia*'s communistic ideals. Later, awaiting execution in the Tower of London, he wrote: 'If all the money that is in this country, were to-morrow next brought together out of every man's hand, and laid all upon one heap, and then divided unto every man alike, it would be on the morrow after worse than it was the day before';[22] but perhaps, I said, stopping beside her sofa and standing on a mound of chocolate wrappers, this view reflected the fragility provoked by Henry VIII's moves to disestablish the Catholic Church in England, rather than suggesting that More had not at one time believed in the abolition of private property.

I had been speaking for quite some time, and now I paused for breath. The old woman, who had been stuffing her face with cream cakes continuously throughout my little speech, gulped down her food and then craned her head round and smiled at me.

'So it's true,' she said: 'More was a Marxist.'

'In some senses, yes,' I said, freeing my shoe of the sticky chocolate wrappers. 'In *Utopia* he wrote time and again of the evils of private property. His narrator, Nonsenso, said: "I don't see how you can ever get any real justice or prosperity, so long as there's private property, and everything's judged in terms of money,"[23] and: "The one essential condition for a healthy society [is] the equal distribution of goods – which I suspect is impossible under capitalism",[24] so that "you'll never get a … satisfactory organisation of human life, until you abolish private property altogether."[25] These are the words of someone who – at the very least – was suspicious of the accumulation of material wealth.'

'It's so strange,' she said, stifling a burp. 'When you listen to passages like that, written almost 500 years ago, it sometimes seems as if things haven't changed in all that time. It's so contemporary.'

'That's it,' I said, feeling a wave of sympathy for her as I took in the force of her comment. 'And that marks out More's *Utopia*. Of course, More was only one of many utopians, perhaps too many. But, let's face it, people sympathise with them. For all that our leaders talk of the need for capitalism to adopt a caring face, it's difficult not to empathise with More's Nonsenso when he says: "When I consider any social system that prevails in the modern world, I can't, so help me God, see it as anything but a conspiracy of the rich to advance their own interests under the pretext of organising society." '[26]

*See below, ch. 7, p. 130.

'That's what we've always been fighting against,' she murmured.

It was a distressing thought, and for a moment we settled into an uneasy silence. I slumped down into the chair again, and she passed me over a cold hamburger, which I munched my way through without thinking. It was very late, and the lack of noise from the TV made me realise just how tired I was. After I had eaten the shrivelled meat, I picked up a box of jam tarts from the floor and began to demolish them, hoping that the energy would keep me awake a little longer.

The congealed, revolting food brought me back from my idealism to the fact that I was sitting in a room with a gargantuan old woman whom I had never met before, discussing ideas that seemed impossible to realise. Was this the nature of utopian journeys, I wondered, that they led inevitably to delusions of perfection, to fantasies? I still hoped not; I still wanted the perfection made real, or even just a credible narrative to work with when it came to writing my book.

I turned to the old woman and sighed. 'Yes,' I said, 'I believe that More and Quiroga were good men.'

'From what you say,' she answered, 'that's so.'

'In spite of everything,' I went on, '*Utopia* was the vision of a just man. Yes, it was authoritarian, but at that time every society was authoritarian, and at least the state of Utopia was upheld by social justice. Quiroga was the first person to put this vision into practice, and so it's the nature of the reality that he created that we've got to get to the bottom of if we want to see whether Utopia is necessarily a fantasy, or whether it can in fact come true.'

The old woman smiled at that, and for a moment I thought that she was going to respond; but then she stuffed her face with another cream cake, shifted her buttocks on the sofa, and let rip with a deafening fart.

I looked at her in astonishment, but she did not even apologise.

'Excuse me,' I said, 'but that was disgusting.'

'Disgusting?' she echoed.

I looked at her closely, and saw that she felt no reason to apologise for her behaviour. At that moment, all sympathy that I had felt for the death of her idealism drained away, and I began to feel intensely angry.

'You're not interested, are you?' I challenged her, realising that she had found her fart far more stimulating than anything that I had just said.

'Oh no,' she said, sniffily, 'I am. But it's so difficult to get the energy for idealism these days. There are other things which seem much more appealing,' she added, a luminous gleam flashing through her eyes.

'Well,' I retorted, 'I'm not surprised you think that. I mean, look at you – you're disgusting. You have no control over your body. In fact, you just live in your depraved mind, probably trying to convince yourself that the body has nothing to do with you.'

I was hurt by her ambivalence to my own interests, and had deliberately tried to hurt her back – forgetting, for the moment, that I had nowhere else to stay.

'What do you mean by that?'

'Look at you,' I said, almost shouting now as I got up. 'You just sit there imbibing all this rubbish – rubbish on the TV, rubbish in your food, rubbish on the brain. It's no wonder that the idealism is draining out of you, and that you're becoming a stultified fart emitting stultifying farts, incapable of appreciating the joy, the poetry and the beauty of life.'

'Well,' she said, 'you're not much better. You've been eating just as much as me ever since you arrived. And anyway,' she added, 'you may call me depraved but you know the meaning of the word just as well as I do.'

With a tremendous effort, she began to judder into motion, placing her tubular arms on her knees and hauling herself to her feet.

'What is it?' I asked, alarmed at being confronted by the sheer size of her.

'You're the one that's really depraved,' she said, beginning to finger the insides of her thighs.

'Me?' I asked in consternation.

'Yes,' she said. 'You're the one who wants to whip me, and thrill to my masochism.'

The words weren't out of her mouth before she lunged at me. Performing a balletic sidestep, I dodged to the side, and she went crashing to the ground.

'You must be mad,' I said, backing hurriedly away.

'You do!' she bellowed from the floor. 'Or else you want to be whipped yourself! You want to enjoy that frisson of pain, indulge the urges which are crushing us both right now!'

Without uttering a word, I turned and ran out of the apartment door. That woman was so immersed in the unending glut of her desires that I began to wonder if she had seen me as anything but an object capable of pleasing her. Her increasingly liberal society had filled her heart with freedom, but all that she had done was fall into the enslavement of a thousand desires. Pleasure was her goal in life, and it had sickened her; but then, feeling tainted just by having taken part in this joyless orgy, I realised that her false fantasies had touched me, even as I had fled from her presence.

I ran pell-mell down the stairs towards the street. Looking down at my belly as I went, and thinking over the situation that had led to this disgraceful series of events, I saw with horror that my experiences were dismantling the rules even of fiction – let alone reality. My idealism had driven me into a different dimension, and it had all begun with the old man in S——: now I began to see why he had been so interested in *Don Quixote*.

Reaching the pavement, I sat down and tried to collect my thoughts. I had nowhere to stay, and I had yet even to begin my research in the Archive; but already I felt myself being transported into a realm where everything – even the most sensible idea, the richest emotion – might be make-believe. This was not how my research was supposed to have started off – no, not at all. I felt as though I would never learn anything about Quiroga at this rate, and that the earnestness with which I had intended to approach the project had already been betrayed by something over which I had no control.

Some hours must have passed, for gradually the sky began to lighten. I decided to wander through the streets and make for the cathedral area again, just to be ready when the Archive opened. I walked with a sense of melancholy and foreboding, and felt a great release when I saw the cathedral, with the Archive and the Alcázar – the old royal palace – behind it. The shops had not yet opened for business, and all the restaurants were closed, so that my only companions were the flocks of birds circling around the old monuments.

In that unexpected moment of peace, my greed of the night before seemed absurd. I would have to consider things all over again, I realised, and try to recall the basis of the ideas that I wanted to mull over: the notion that there was more to life than the self-destructive surrender to fleeting passions, and that the individual consciousness fared better when admitted to a genuinely interdependent community, rather than when always fighting to acquire property in competition with others.

My pace slowed as I approached the gates to the Alcázar. With a sudden and overwhelming surge of fatigue I realised that I had not slept all night, and my delusional experiences all combined to make me feel immensely tired. My mind misted over; my thoughts blurred. Hardly caring what I was doing, I lay down beneath the jagged silence of what had once been the most powerful place on earth, and began to dream of the wealth that had once coursed right past this spot, and of its progress following the conquest of Mexico.

Soon, much as the old man in S—— had promised, I found that my experiences had spiralled down into fantasy, where the pictures I conjured up of both Seville and Mexico were deeply disturbing.

FOUR

August in Seville is disagreeable. Attracted by the humidity of the Guadalquivir river, armies of malarial mosquitoes buzz through the city, thriving as the heat intensifies; the smells become more rancid; the women (who virtually run the city[1]) cool themselves with ivory-handled fans, and the men (many of whom plan an escape to the Indies) swelter within their layers of armour, velveteen cloaks and monastic habits of penitence. Only the naked feel any release from the heat: the slaves just arrived from North and West Africa, chained and fettered into coffles by the riverside, and the homeless urchins darting through the crowds and pinching their keep. In spite of the wealth that is constantly unloaded from the ships on the river – bars of gold, bundles of cotton and exotic new crops such as potatoes[2] – there is an overwhelming sense of hunger in the city: all the wine and wheat grown nearby is despatched to the Indies, and the situation is so bad that just a few days ago, on 14 August 1530, the Crown passed an edict banning further export from the region around Seville.[3]

The major landmark on the Guadalquivir is the Torre de Oro, a crenellated tower built under the Moors in the thirteenth century. It is here that the gold brought by the ships is stored, and from the tower a road leads a short distance along the edge of the city walls. Here groups of beggars sit, their eyes filled with hallucinations: *Are not those masts of the ships a heavenly army? Take note of the sails for they are angels' wings! Spare a coin for the next St Francis* – their ploys buzz in the air, like the flies and the mosquitoes, disguising their suffering as they lie there, some of them with their faces raddled with the pox, others with fleshy stumps for legs and arms. Poverty is never a pleasant sight for the rich, but then it is surely God's little joke that great poverty is always to be found beside great wealth: the beggars who thrust themselves at the gowns and dresses touch the hidalgos with passing shame, which they quickly shake off as they make for the royal gate where the entrance to the Alcázar is to be found.

Here, two elegant carriages have just arrived, each drawn by a team of six horses and embossed with gold and silver designs; inside the carriages, the leather has been carefully worked, and the cushions are made of the finest silk and velvet. The horses swish their tails in the heat, trying to distract the flies, and the drivers perch in front of the carriages and put coarse handkerchiefs to their brows. A crowd of people gathers in the shadow of the vast cathedral, which was finished less than thirty years ago, and which squashes the city under the divine aims of the Catholic juggernaut. Old Christians, *conversos*, half-castes and gypsies jostle to catch a glimpse of the passengers. Eventually, as if by a pre-arranged signal, the carriage doors open in concert and four men step onto the cobbles, ignoring the stinking throng as they make for the royal palace. The armoured guards stand aside at once, for they know these visitors: they are the licenciates Ceynos, Maldonado, Quiroga and Salmerón, the new *oidores* of the *audiencia* of New Spain.*

The four men have many hopes as the enter the Alcázar. They know the importance of their task: they have been appointed after the disastrous 'work' of the first *audiencia*, led by its president, Nuño de Guzmán, and *oidores* Juan de Matienzo and Diego Delgadillo. Shortly after the conquest of Mexico, even Cortés admitted: 'The majority of Spaniards who pass through here are uncivilised and ill-starred, degenerate and sinful in diverse ways,'[4] and just a year ago the first Bishop of Mexico, Fray Juan de Zumárraga, wrote to Charles V detailing the abuses of the first *audiencia* – the letter was smuggled out of the port of Veracruz hidden in a crucifix, because Nuño de Guzmán had banned contact with Spain.

Yes, their task is a difficult one. Not only is Mexico in meltdown, but the old medieval order is disappearing, and so by force or reason something else must be built: the licenciates hope that reason shall do the work that the conquistadors have begun, and the changes in consciousness brought about by the discoveries have led some Spanish thinkers to the teachings of Erasmus, seeking to return to Christ through the gospels so that His true philosophy can be revealed. Many in Spain now feel that this might best be achieved through agrarian communities, and one of Charles V's principal advisers is Antonio de Guevara, author of the 'Danube Villein' in which the rural idyll is

---

*The colonies in the country that today is called Mexico were known by the Spanish as Nueva España, or New Spain.

eulogised:[5] the comforting stereotype of the 'noble peasant' has just begun.

There are, though, no peasants actually to be seen as the *oidores* enter the Alcázar, which is by far the finest building in Seville. This old palace, formerly home of the Moorish kings, mixes the best of Christian and Islamic designs, with gardens where the groves of orange trees are so thick that the sun never breaks through; at present many vegetables are grown here, but Charles V will remodel the gardens during his reign, filling them with a maze and countless patios and fountains. The Emperor has a special bond with this place, for it is here that he celebrated his marriage to Isabella of Portugal in 1526, and built special apartments for the occasion. The new Sala de Fiestas is a long, oblong room, decorated with the red-and-gold Flemish tapestries which are famous throughout Europe. From here a series of corridors leads to the dark Sala de Audiencias, where royal councils are held and Mudéjar architects have been given free rein: the dome is built of cedar wood and the walls are lined with delicate stucco work, with the stucco moulded into geometrical shapes and hidden Arabic writings which mean (though, of course, Charles and Isabella do not know this) 'Allah be praised'.

In the forecourt, military exercises are being conducted. Soldiers march across the patio, and the *oidores* pause to let them pass. Naturally, the Alcázar is protected from the suffering in the city, yet this creeps through the thick walls and penetrates the marching, prayers, and courtly graces that murmur within: Quiroga feels the stifling atmosphere, and longs to be free of it. Here, in one of the greatest palaces in Spain, he may be protected, but his true vocation is with the poor. Is it not for this reason that he has accepted the job of *oidor*, because he has dreamt of the Indians imploring 'Who will show us good things?'[6] Thus far, as Bishop Zumárraga has shown, the Spanish have not answered their plea.

Quiroga follows the other *oidores* across the patio. To the left is the Sala de Justicia, and to the right the Casa de la Contratación, where all travellers making for the Indies must register, proving that their families are Old Christians, and not newly converted Jews or Moslems.[7] This is not an old building, but already many repairs have been carried out on it,[8] and more will soon follow.[9] Its expansion and embellishment symbolise how trade across the Atlantic has so quickly become important, for it is here that the contracts for the Indies are settled. As the *oidores* enter the building, they see an incredible bustle of merchants and sailors vying to petition Francisco Tello, the new treasurer, who has only been one month in the job.[10] The room swirls with gowns and breeches inlaid with gold and silver thread, with sailors' caps and with the finest leather hats. Everyone has a sword tucked into their belt – no one would dream of walking through the streets of Seville without one – and these jangle as the men brush past one another and try to conclude their work.

As the *oidores* enter the room, however, the hubbub dies away. The businessmen are all aware of the importance of these bureaucrats, for they will govern the richest of all the colonies; though much is spoken of Europe's grandeur – of her art, learning and charity – they know better than anyone how much their wealth now depends on the New World. Seville is replete with objects brought over from the Indies, and it is no coincidence that so many buildings have risen since 1492, with the city now bursting with builders clambering up the wooden scaffolds, and with new hospitals and monasteries and churches and mansions.[11] There is such a frenzy of activity that it might be wondered if the world can support it without collapsing into the dust that hangs over Seville day and night, like an invisible shroud.

– My lords and gentlemen, Francisco Tello calls, his voice quivering (he has yet to find the brash self-confidence which his new job requires). The new *oidores* of His Imperial Majesty's Audiencia of Mexico!

There is applause and Quiroga bows his head, along with his companions.

– They voyage with our blessings and with our trust in their good offices as servants of the Lord's will, Francisco Tello says with greater pomposity. We grant them our prayers that they shall see the wealth of the new lands exploited for the good of our Holy Roman Emperor.

The applause is more forthright now – the new treasurer has managed to strike the triumphant, self-righteous tone which suits all empires best – and this ringing endorsement fills Quiroga with joy. Yes, it is God's will that he should voyage to the Indies, and he will fulfil his divine role. Sweeping his cloak up around him, he leads his fellow *oidores* through to the chapel beyond the long room in which they have been standing. In five years' time, the new altarpiece here will be completed, depicting Columbus's voyage to the Indies, a Christian warrior brandishing a sword atop a white horse while surrounded by the distorted heads of unbelievers, and a priest holding a galleon in one hand and an eternal flame in the other, helping to guide the Spanish ships safely across the sea. Are not faith, navigation and Christianity the props of God's conquest (not to mention gunpowder and disease)?

The four *oidores* kneel before the simple, gory crucifix that stands in the chapel. The journey across the ocean will take four months, but trust slays fear, and Quiroga is not alarmed. He will be the instrument of faith and light, and will bring peace to a country where the people are benighted – and decimated by the Spanish.

Much of Quiroga's life in Spain remains mysterious, but enough fragments have come to light to allow a cautious sketch of his career after he left Salamanca, probably some time in the early 1510s.

After graduating, he probably moved to Granada, where he may have worked in the Royal Chancellery. His fondness for the old Moorish city is shown by many things: his initial naming of the Spanish city in Michoacán 'Granada', his modelling of his see's cathedral on that of Granada,[12] and also that his utopian hospitals were called Santa Fe – the same name as Ferdinand had given to the military garrison built near Granada during the siege in 1491.[13] By the 1510s Granada would still have been a tense city, with the communities of forcibly converted Jews and Muslims aping Christianity in the blood-red shadows of the Alhambra. The inquisitorial zeal of the early years of the century would still have been a strong presence in the memory of the converts – in 1529, further *autos* would be held here, and eighty-four 'judaizers' would be burned.[14] And so, in Granada, Quiroga would have begun his apprenticeship not only in judicial matters, but also in the niceties of living in a cosmopolitan environment where Catholicism was still new to many of the residents – an atmosphere which would resonate with him when he reached the New World.[15]

By the early 1520s Quiroga had been made the judge-in-residence at Oran, a Spanish enclave in what is now Algeria.* Oran had been taken by the Spanish in 1509 and was part of an extension of the reconquest that had thrown the Moors out of Granada. North Africa at this time was very unstable; after the final expulsion of the Moors from Granada in 1502 there had been a vast influx of Moslems along the coast, adding to the Jews who had arrived in 1492. Most of the Moors went to the ports of Algiers, Shershel, Tetouan and Oran,[16] where they often lay in hiding, waiting to pounce on passing Spanish ships. The Spaniards quickly learned to protect themselves, and if they

---

*Oran was governed by the Audiencia of Granada – another reason for thinking that Quiroga was here until then.

suspected a traveller of being a Moor, they would call out in Arabic: *'Ya Mohammed! Ya Mohammed!'* – whereupon those in disguise would look around, and be caught.[17]

Realising that this was hardly a sure-fire way of protecting his people, Ferdinand launched a series of raids across the Mediterranean, and carved out the protectorate of Oran. This would safeguard Spanish interests, not only by creating a safe haven in North Africa, but also by perhaps diverting some of the gold of Guinea into Spanish hands. For by this point the past hundred years had shown that the great discoveries tended both to be driven by economics and to have enormous economic benefits. In the early fifteenth century, Portugal's currency had been in free fall, with the old pound of 1383 having been worth 500 of the new pounds of 1404.[18] This massive devaluation had been accompanied by a great wheat shortage, but Portugal's capture of the Moroccan city of Ceuta in 1415, her explorations of the African coast and the Atlantic archipelagoes, and her founding of a trading post at Mina on the West African coast in 'gold country' had changed all that: during the reign of João II (1481–95), almost half of the Crown's revenues had come from African gold,[19] and the Portuguese king was known as *il rei di oro* – the king of gold. Fernando wanted a slice of the African cake; he did not yet know how the gold and silver mines of the New World to the west would themselves change Spanish fortunes.

In many ways Oran was an ideal stronghold for this purpose. Clinging to the side of a dry, rugged mountain, the city was surrounded by a ditch ten yards deep and six across. Though the city was on the Mediterranean, and held a very large port, an oppressive heat usually hung overhead, stilling the air in torpor. Arid mountains rose inland, speckled with low thorn trees and stone-walled villages where Sufi mystics and dervishes whirled in ascetic union with the Sahara and the frozen night sky. Vultures wheeled by day in the thermals, waiting for death.

In Oran itself, the Spanish colonists sought protection from the alien world around them. On the far side of a river was the Ras-al-cassar castle, where the royal officials lived, while the other settlers shielded themselves behind a high wall fortified with many towers. After his upbringing surrounded by the towers of Madrigal, this would have made Quiroga feel at home, even though so much about life in Oran was unfamiliar, ranging from the ubiquity of the Islamic mystics to the lions that were sometimes seen.[20]

As in Granada, there was much about his work here that prepared

Quiroga for Mexico. The political situation was analogous to that of the Spanish in the Indies, with Quiroga trying to enshrine Spanish law in a place where the Spanish were in a minority.[21] Furthermore, like Mexico, Oran was intensely cosmopolitan, and nearby there were large communities of Jews and Moors with which Quiroga had to coexist. This was also an exotic city, and must have given Quiroga a window onto the stimulation that can come from being among unfamiliar peoples, with the atmosphere of North Africa combining with stories surfacing from unknown places: the empire of Mali, and the fabled city of Timbuktu, from which came the prize of gold.[22]

In addition to all this, though, what was perhaps most crucial for Quiroga's future development was the fact that the coast was full of slave traders, since the neighbouring state of Tlemcen was the main commercial town in this part of Africa.[23] Here he would have seen the arrival of the caravans that had crossed the white sea of the Sahara, and perhaps felt the first stirrings of anger at this barbaric treatment of human beings: the slaves that survived the crossing came fastened together by collars and poles, which joined them at the neck, their eyes long glazed over with exhaustion and despair – just another product to be traded, like the gold mined in the dusty foothills of Guinea.

Had Quiroga wanted to enrol in a university to study the qualities of justice and righteous anger which he would take to the New World, he could have not done better than go to Oran; and though most of his work here involved settling trade disputes, he did make one contribution that gave a hint of what was to come. When a treaty was drawn up between the Spanish in Oran and the Moors in Tlemcen in September 1526, Quiroga was one of two Spanish ambassadors sent to meet the five Moorish representatives, three of whom – interestingly, for a Muslim kingdom – were Jews.[24] One of the articles is telling of the attitude that Quiroga's experiences had instilled in him: Article 13 said that the people of Tlemcen would not be made Christians by force.[25] This is particularly noteworthy, considering that, earlier that year, the Muslims of Aragón – the final remnants of Spain's non-Catholic population – had been forced to leave the country or convert: at a time when the Catholic conquest of Spain had finally been forced onto all who lived there, Quiroga was practising tolerance.

It is true that this sort of attitude was more usual in medieval Europe than is often supposed, and Nicholas de Lyra, a fourteenth-century Franciscan lecturer at the Sorbonne,* had put forward the

*He lived 1270–1340.

view that heathens could be saved even if they did not believe in the Christian God per se – provided that they believed that God existed, and that God rewarded those who searched for Him. Nevertheless, this article is significant, and perhaps betrays something of the impact that Quiroga's early life had had on him. For, having been born in a town with a sizeable Jewish community, from a maternal family that perhaps itself had some Jewish blood, the forced conversions of Jews at the time of the 1492 expulsion – when he would have been four or five years old – may well have left deep scars.

Andrés Bernáldez, the royal chronicler of Ferdinand and Isabella, gave a harrowing picture of the sort of things the young Vasco may have seen as the Jews pulled out of Madrigal in 1492:

> They left the lands of their birth, great and small, old and young, on foot, or riding on horseback, on donkeys and on other animals, or travelling in carts, and they all went to the ports where they had to go to; and they went by the roads and fields which they had to go by, with much difficulty, some falling, others raising themselves up, others dying, others being born, others falling ill, so that there was no Christian who did not feel pain at the sight of them.[26]

Meanwhile, the Quiroga family's friendship with Hernando de Talavera, coupled with Talavera's fall from grace and Quiroga's own experiences in Granada following the Moorish expulsion, seems to have crystallised his nascent compassion towards all people, regardless of their faith, convincing him that people should only be brought to the true faith through good works, and not through force.

Though its impact on Quiroga's future was significant, his spell in North Africa ended comparatively quickly, in September 1526, following a disputed judgement of his in the case of Baptista Caxines, a merchant supposed to have bought another man's wife. Something of Quiroga's increasingly stubborn temperament emerged here through his quarrel with another licenciate, Liminiana; in writing his version of events, Quiroga began somewhat petulantly by saying, 'Liminiana, who calls himself a licenciate ...'[27] The case was referred back to the Crown in Spain, and Quiroga returned with it; Charles V eventually ordered that Quiroga should not pay costs, and he was now in favour at court, where the situation was soon very tense following the disaster of the Imperial Army's sack of Rome on 6 May 1527 – something that Charles, then in Spain, had tried and failed to prevent.[28]

Between 1527 and 1530 Quiroga appears to have been one of the *letrados* of Charles and Isabella. His first biographer, Juan Joseph Moreno, wrote in 1766 that Quiroga had been a private lawyer in Valladolid,[29] and it may have been at this time that he worked there in this capacity. It is known that he travelled with the royal party from Burgos to Madrid early in 1528,[30] and also that in 1529 the empress was sending him on personal errands for her. This makes it possible that he would have been with the court at Monzón in June 1528, when the great conquistador Hernando Cortés returned with personal gifts for Charles from Mexico, arriving with a miniature bestiary of birds, pumas, coyotes and other strange creatures, large quantities of gold, precious woods, jewels and perfumes, and three of the sons of the Emperor Montezuma, the ruler of the Mexica,* whom Cortés had met when he had first arrived at Tenochtitlan.

Cortés's visit provided everyone in Spain with a tantalising glimpse of the mysterious world across the ocean – a world which many found impossible to imagine, and peopled with the mythical beasts and monsters that dwelled in their nightmares. The illustrations of books of the time showed how fearful Europe was of this unknown continent: one Italian drawing depicted a monster as big as a tree, with a vast flying saucer-like hat and a face taking up its entire torso. As late as the end of the sixteenth century a unicorn was reportedly seen in Florida.[31] This was an expedition to an idea that was entirely new, and the voyage across the Atlantic was, for those who made it, a voyage in the mind as much as one across geography – so much so that the journey itself was imagination enough for those who made it. Through-out the colonial period, the writing and printing of novels would be banned:[32] America represented a *tabula rasa* where humanity, having made such a mess of Europe, could try to do better.

Shortly after Cortés's visit, however, the arrival of Bishop Zumár-raga's smuggled letter showed that the situation in Mexico was terrible. After the letter had been digested, late in 1529, preparations began for the new Audiencia. Charles V was genuinely concerned for his distant subjects: being the Emperor of God was quite a task, and it was difficult to reconcile the supreme power which God invested in the Holy Roman Emperor with the cruelties being committed abroad in the name of Christianity. In 1528, the Crown had ordered that those colonists with slaves must prove with documents that the slaves had been fairly taken, and also that Indians enslaved on false accusations

---

*Although often known as the Aztecs, the people of Tenochtitlan were known at the time as the Mexica – a use followed in this book.

of warmongering should be freed.[33] Nevertheless, no one pretended that these measures were being obeyed, and Zumárraga's account showed that the new *oidores* had to be determined men, sympathetic to the oppressed as well as to the Crown.

Quiroga had such a background. Having had such a wide-ranging experience of different cultures, and having shown himself to be tolerant and understanding in North Africa, he was a suitable candidate to be *oidor*. The appointment of all four *oidores* was confirmed early in 1530, and they were given large salaries of 600,000 maravedís a year, plus 150,000 maravedís in order to buy things that they would need to take out to Mexico.[34] Quiroga began to prepare for the voyage, as more news began to leak out from New Spain regarding the excesses of the First Audiencia, where Guzmán, Delgadillo and Matienzo had led a debauched existence, holding banquets and dances with disreputable women, and – as a party trick – hosting mock trials in the courtroom in which the women were the judges and the members of the Audiencia the accused.[35] Things had reached such a state that Delgadillo had at one point sworn at the friars in Mexico, claiming that they belonged in a whorehouse; Zumárraga had responded that the same was true of the *oidor*.[36]

As Quiroga prepared to make his journey, he also listened to the disturbing stories about plagues that had begun to ravage the indigenous peoples of the New World, as if in complement to the plague of sins committed by both the heathens and the First Audiencia. Perhaps this was a divine plan, one through which the 'biological epidemic [could] illustrate the dilemmas of moral contagion'.[37]

Already, even as Quiroga prepared to travel to Mexico, the virus lay too deeply embedded to be rooted out.*

Though Catholic prayer is their route to divine guidance through life, the *oidores* cannot remain in the chapel for ever – even when on the threshold of such a dangerous voyage. Here, in Seville, they must strip away the old categories of feeling; their eyes can linger over those things that are familiar, but they must not covet them. With an unexpressed melancholy, they relinquish the meanings and values of the Old World, and prepare themselves for the import of the New.

*Indeed, plague was to exert a curious hold over the places in which Quiroga spent his life, and not just in the New World. *The Plague*, Albert Camus's famous novel about moral responsibility and heroism in a time of crisis, was set in Oran, where Camus lived for a time in 1941 and 1942, when that city was occupied by another colonial power – France – and underwent an epidemic of typhoid fever.

The streets beside the Alcázar are as crowded as ever as the four men leave the palace and make their way to the dock. This is the most beautiful spot in Seville, filled with hidalgos, merchants and conmen.[38] Beyond the cathedral and the Giralda – the tower of what was once the city's chief mosque – Quiroga glimpses the narrow streets of the commercial quarter: Seville is one of the homes of printing, and many of the books which he is taking with him to Mexico have come from here.[39] The learning represented by printing is a reminder of all that is admirable about European civilisation, he thinks; yet he worries that the cultural energy is not wholly beneficent, knowing that Seville is also a great theatrical centre, with the last thirty years having seen performances of *Adam and Eve*, *The Descent from the Cross* and *The Conversion of Constantine*.[40] As in Salamanca, these performances are reminders that art (or official art) must always sanction the prevailing religion, whatever that might be; but many people have begun to doubt how genuinely people hold to the true Catholic creed: after all, they say, Spain is filled with apostates, a fifth column of subversives (Jews), who constantly cast doubt upon the moral sentiments of society, and whose filthy, piggish ideas are infiltrating the masses.*

Like any Catholic who is honest with himself, Quiroga knows that the common folk throng with most pleasure of all to the mixture of pagan and Christian dances which run riot during fiestas, with performances of *The God Pan* and *The God Jupiter*, as well as more sober numbers such as *The Seven Vices and Seven Virtues*:[41] of course, it is appropriate that people be reminded of vices before virtues, as so many of them are *vicioso*, bawdy and licentious, and need little excuse to abandon themselves to pleasure. Such is the nature of existence in this dissolute old world, Quiroga thinks disparagingly.

On the way to the Guadalquivir, the *oidores* pass a succession of waifs half-eaten by lice, their eyes pasty with suffering, making for the houses of the city's merchants where they hope to scavenge the leftovers thrown out by the cooks of the wealthy.[42] The poverty is endemic (an epidemic), whose contagion touches the dock as Ceynos, Maldonado, Quiroga and Salmerón reach the riverbank. Here the dusty, open space is thick with people running to and from the ships at anchor. Downstream, groups of Sevillanos sit casting fishing nets into the water – the river is famously bountiful[43] – while beyond, in the grey thread of water, a hive of smaller ferries crosses over from

---

*Those Jews who had become *conversos* were commonly known as *marranos*, which had the meaning of 'pigs'.

Triano and its Moorish castle, with makeshift canvas awnings protecting passengers from the burning August sun. The ferrymen steer a cautious course, avoiding the turning hulks of the galleons limping into the dockside, with the boatswains whipping the last shred of energy from the half-naked slaves who have clawed the vessels over from the west.[44]

Quiroga stands a little apart from the other *oidores*, momentarily dazzled by the rhythmic flipping of the oars of the galley slaves. The Torre de Oro looms ominously overhead, and Quiroga is all too aware of its jagged crenellations rising heavenwards and piercing the sky-blue, a Tower of Babel for Spain's new golden age. All around him people dart by, rushing to unload goods from the newly arrived ships; incomers are often unwilling to trust those from Andalucía – 'by and large they are degenerate, idiotic, avaricious and but little blessed with true virtues', a Silesian noble wrote in the late fifteenth century[45] – and Quiroga looks on warily as scavenging gulls gather above, fighting one another for the stale pieces of ships' biscuits which lie abandoned on the decks.

He is frankly bewildered by this last view of the chaos and dissolution of Europe: the clanking chains of the slaves brought by the Portuguese from Africa, the voices of sailors from Genoa, Venice, Lisbon and Flanders, and the flapping sails that are unfurled as ships sail downstream. For a moment, the visceral disorder reminds him of the fairs at Medina del Campo, and he is transported back to Madrigal and the childhood that he must now leave behind for ever: as a young man he had felt that everything about his world was eternal and just, and he had never imagined himself leaving behind both this world and its values.

Yet now America beckons. Muttering prayers for the voyage, he follows Ceynos, Maldonado and Salmerón aboard the three-masted galleon[46] and stares with both nostalgia and relief at the venality which he will now leave behind. Of course, he has sailed across the Mediterranean before, when at Oran, but there is an irreversible finality in the weighing of the anchor, the views of Seville drifting into an empty distance, and the passage past the hills of Aznalfarache, which are thronged with people as the ship slips slowly away,[47] a vessel of hope vanishing towards the eternal blue haze of the ocean.

What can the New World mean but hope, when the Old is destroying itself? Is not the suffering of those distant peoples a route to paradise, now that God has granted them the chance to be saved by the Holy Church? Cannot an ideal be wrought from the ashes of a continent that lies, raw and smouldering, unseen by the eyes of Europe?

Quiroga's lips draw tight as the galleon passes the last headland and pulls into the headwinds of the Atlantic.

FIVE

Far away, in a world filled with alien feelings and a new form of terror, the rules of life are different (some say that there are none). Down by the low crests of the shoreline, the shadows of the forests blend into a haze that hangs motionless over the sea and the drifting dunes. Fine grains of sand eddy overhead and fill the void. The jungle is advancing: remorselessly, it reclaims the lands that used to belong to civilisation; its tentacles creep over the broken rubble of buildings once proud and unquestioned; its raging fertility sprawls luxuriantly over the undug grave of a race that has raced back into the nothingness from which it sprang. The people, and their souls, are gone; the jungle, and its laws, are advancing.

In Zempoala, the forest's triumph is almost complete. The humid atmosphere has always given nature an advantage here, where the local Totonac civilisation had built a town that was so green with vegetation that it looked like a garden.[1] Zempoala had been the largest settlement on this part of the coast of New Spain, with a population of between twenty and thirty thousand Totonacs[2] centred around five vast ceremonial temples, staggered on several levels and built with the grey stone of the area. At the heart of the city had been a large square filled with lime-coated buildings which shone so brilliantly that some of the Spaniards, arriving just eleven years ago, in 1519, thought them to have been made of silver.[3]

The Totonacs are still remembered as solid, noble people, their dignitaries dressed with large gold lip-rings and rich cloaks,[4] the people's hair arranged in plaits and their ears weighed down by heavy rings. Like the other peoples of Mesoamerica, they used to practise human sacrifice in temples whose stench of blood and visceral iconography still terrify the Spanish. Zempoala had been filled with transvestites who had prostituted themselves in order to earn their keep,[5] and had been the home to vibrant *tianguiz*, or markets, where the local produce had been bartered. However, subordinate to the

72

great empire of the Mexica during the fifteenth century, their own rites and customs had fused with those of their masters at Tenochtitlan.* As the most acute Spanish colonists well know, the imperial process that absorbs local cultures into a dominant force began well before their arrival in 1519; however, there is no doubt that they are accelerating the trend, as Bernardino Sahagún, the great Spanish historian of the Mexica, will write in 1580, '[The Church] has come to these regions of the West Indies, where there used to be a great diversity of peoples and languages, of which many have now disappeared, while the rest are on the way to joining them.'[6]

Perhaps what Sahagún recognises is that, where peoples are used to the ways of empire, colonisation is readily achieved. In Chile, the lands held by the Incas will be rapidly absorbed by the Spanish colonial system, while those held by the independent, semi-nomadic Mapuche people will not be subdued for a further 350 years. In Argentina, the early centres of colonial rule will be in the north-west, nearest to the old heartland of the Incas and Tiahuanaco, while it will take centuries for the rest of the country to be settled. In North America, the territory of the nomadic peoples of the plains will not be fully occupied until the end of the nineteenth century. The imperial miasma will expand slowly for centuries, and only once it has embraced the whole world will its very particular cosmology gain the veneer of what is unquestionable, absolute.

In Zempoala, however, the end of this process is not yet in sight. All that is apparent is the lyricism of a world still largely free of the profit motive, for the Spanish have not yet replaced the Totonacs. Just four years ago, in 1526, the eight surviving families of Zempoala were resettled inland, in Jalapa, and the whole coastline is now swathed with an air of abandon. The ruins of the city are necklaced with wreaths of green, with brilliant bouquets of flowers, nature's own offering to the last rites of a people who lived with this land and not off it. The hymns of remembrance are sung by the birds, who dive through the air, their tails twitching quickly out of sight.

The birdsong tinkles along with the passing waters of the nearby streams, neither of which shows any sign of ceasing. The trees crowd in on Zempoala, clambering up the temples and allowing their roots to colonise the homes of the dead. The foliage gathers overhead, blocking out the light, the views of the green hills which rise to the

*The best example of this is the fact that Zempoala's ceremonial site is the largest Aztec complex still standing today.

north and the west, the sound of the sea washing gently against the shore. Paths which once led to surrounding villages burst with creepers, brambles, bushes, thorns.[7] Nature takes over quickly, loudly, without dispute, and the memory of everything that has gone before it is soon extinguished.

Only among the dunes by the coast is the view at all different. Here the beach is quiet, but the sea is increasingly busy. The waters rise and fall, chopping at the hulls of the ships that come to gather nearby, where the new arrivals stare at the growing natural anarchy of this alien world, and ask themselves: How did this human emptiness, where every settlement is a cemetery, come about?

Borne by the current of history, a new sail now stirs on the horizon.

The conquest of the Mexican heartland was executed in little more than three years. In 1518, the Spaniard Juan de Grijalva passed the 'Isle of Sacrifices' off the coast of what became Veracruz, where he found the corpses of five Indians dismembered within two great temples whose walls were smeared with the gore of the sacrifice.[8] The bloody scene which Grijalva found had been part of an ill-fated attempt to stave off the end of a way of life, and to prevent the coming of 'the children of the sun', as the Mexica first knew the Spanish.[9] In Mesoamerican religions, people were offered up to the gods as a bounty in return for assistance in navigating the rapids of the earthly world, and the arrival of Grijalva's 'strange range of mountains ... floating in the sea'*[10] had made it clear that supernatural assistance was essential.

Grijalva's stories excited the ambitions of Diego Velázquez, the Governor of Cuba, who equipped a new expedition under his stepson Hernando Cortés.[11] Filled with the fantasies of the age, Velázquez commanded Cortés to search for strange beings with great flat ears and others with dog-like faces:[12] after receiving these bizarre orders, Cortés then had to use all of his guile to prevent himself from being

---

*It is interesting to compare the attitude of the Mexica to ships to that of the first African peoples to see caravels, seventy-five years earlier. According to the Venetian sailor Cadamosto, who was one of the earliest Europeans to visit Senegambia, in the 1450s, some thought the ships to be birds or fish, while others took them as 'ghosts wandering at night'. See Vitorino Magalhães Godinho (1945), op. cit., vol. III, p. 128. In both cases, the implication appears to be that divinity (and fear) are involved – the Mexica identified gods with the volcanoes near their imperial city, while Cadamosto's 'ghosts' can probably be interpreted as the Senegambians seeing the ships as the spirits of the ancestors (so integral to belief systems in West Africa).

stripped off his captaincy by the envious governor before departing – good training for the double-dealing that he would later employ in Mexico. After departing on 10 February 1519, the expedition gained an interpreter at the island of Cozumel, where they came across the Spaniard Jerónimo de Aguilar, who had lived in slavery among the Maya for eight years. Later, in the region of Coatzocolos, the chief conquistadors acquired local wives, one of whom, Doña Marina, spoke both Maya and Nahuátl, the language of the Mexica – she and Aguilar combined to translate Nahuátl into Spanish through the Mayan tongue, which they both spoke, and thereby made the conquest possible.[13]

So in 1519 the mountain range returned to Zempoala, disgorging men who fought to kill, and not – like the Mexica and their neighbours – to capture and sacrifice to the gods. Soon these strangers, bearded and pale as moonlight, let loose a host of weapons more deadly than any that these peoples or this world had seen before: furious tubular gods that thundered and sent a smell of burning to drift over the bodies of their victims, and – perhaps most terrifying of all – a beast that seemed half-man and half-monster, come to gallop among them and despatch their warriors into the hereafter. Soon the idols of the Totonacs had been 'rolled down the steps and ... smashed to pieces';[14] their elaborate carvings, 'in the form of fearsome dragons as big as calves, and others half-man half-dog and hideously ugly',[15] were permanently stripped of their influence over earthly happenings: the process of conquest had begun.

Observing their gods shattered about their feet and the disdain with which the Spanish had treated tax inspectors from Mexico who had recently arrived in Zempoala, the Totonacs assumed the children of the sun to be *teules* – gods (or demons). Enlisting the support of their cacique (chief), Cortés took fifty of the best Totonac soldiers on his march to Mexico. After defeating the army of the Tlaxcalan people, he marched with their assistance to Tenochtitlan, where, after two years of intrigue, massacre and alliances with the enemies of the Mexica, he razed the old empire to the ground and received the capitulation of the Emperor Cúahtemoc on 13 August 1521.[16]

The impact of the Spanish on the coast was melancholy. The first town founded by the conquistadors had been Veracruz, which was still under threat from Indian attacks in 1523.[17] This had been during the last throes of indigenous resistance, for even by this early date – just four years after Cortés had landed – the Totonacs had all but vanished. The cause of their demise had been a plague of smallpox, which had been brought to the country by one of the porters serving

Pánfilo de Narváez, a rival conquistador who had been outwitted by Cortés during the initial conquest of the Mexica.[18]

By June 1520, three months after Narváez's arrival, the plague of the pox had been spreading through the humid lowlands. People had vanished into the dust, and once thriving communities had fallen into ghost towns. Unused to the floods of corpses, which had arrived, like the Spanish, as if from nowhere, the Totonacs had found it difficult to bury them all, and the stench of festering bodies had drifted unmistakably over the country. Even once Mexico had been taken by Cortés, the disease had continued to advance, its arrival greeted with fatalism and despair by all except the fighting dogs, brought by the Spanish to help in the conquest and now running wild and feeding from corpses.[19] In some places, half the population had vanished;[20] those who survived did so with their faces sunken and their eyes broken.[21] The cacique of the Totonacs, one of Cortés's first friends in New Spain, was among the victims of the epidemic, and in their tragedy his decimated people must have seen the fulfilment of the prophecy uttered by their headmen when Cortés and his army had destroyed their gods: according to Bernal Díaz, the 'Cacique and the rest shouted to Cortés in a great fury, inquiring why he wanted to destroy their gods, since if we desecrated and overthrew them their whole people would perish'.[22]

In 1525, Veracruz had been moved down the coast to a riverbank a little more than a league from the ocean. Cortés had built himself a large house on one side of the plaza here, across from the *ayuntamiento*.* Ships docked at the port of San Juan de Ulúa – about six leagues south, beside the site of the modern city of Veracruz – and passengers were then canoed up the coast to the first city which they would see in the colony, so newly and savagely begun.

In an era of millenarian fervour in Europe, the truth was that nowhere did the end of the world seem nearer than in New Spain.[23]

Two days before the end of the year 1530, the galleon bearing licenciates Maldonado and Quiroga nears the port of San Juan de Ulúa. Drawn and exhausted by the voyage, their eyes lighten as their final destination comes into view. The coastline is dotted with groups of people scrabbling for shellfish in the sludge where the ocean meets the land. Though this is a fetid and unhealthy coast, the port is

*The ruins of the house, covered with ancient ceibo roots, can still be seen in the old town – now a sleepy tropical village called La Antigua.

sheltered by a north-facing island. Forests sprawl inland, and canoes can be seen making for the ship, rolling gently across the bottle-green sea.

The canoes have come from the inlet that leads to Veracruz, already the main port of entry for goods to the colony. As the dugouts arrive, Quiroga finds his eyes drawn to the Indians, but the Indians do not look back at him: the sun is rising directly behind his back, blinding them, and crowning him with a halo. So he returns his gaze to the continent: swallows and scissor-tailed birds swoop down towards the surf on the shore, playing in the stiff breeze, and above the dark shadows of the people hunched over on the beach a row of dunes rises, like a barricade, concealing the nature of the land that lies beyond.

A surge of relief settles over Quiroga. More than four months have passed since they pulled out of Seville; their galleon was thrashed by a tropical storm near the port of Santo Domingo in the Caribbean, where they separated from Ceynos and Salmerón, and only on reaching the Yucatán peninsula did his mind turn from the tropical storms to the world he was about to discover.

Sailing along the coast, the lushness of the unknown plants and trees had entranced him at first. But soon that wonder had given way to a sense of oppression, for in the tropics there is such a thickness of vegetation and colour that the mind quickly feels trapped. This tangle of lianas and flowers and birds presses in, it seems, until a person cannot think clearly. The coast had turned, and turned, and Quiroga's unease had turned almost to fear as they had neared their destination, passing the Isle of Sacrifices: yes, he knows, Christianity has come to *Tierra Firma*,* as the Spanish call the American mainland, but there is still much ungodliness abroad. Since their arrival in 1524, the mendicant Franciscan missionaries may have been baptising the *naturales*† by the hundreds of thousands, but the old religion still lives, and to some newcomers it seems almost as if these heathens (whose beliefs and customs are utterly alien to those of the planet's dominant force) pose a threat to civilisation itself. In the past two years, Bishop Zumárraga has shattered 20,000 idols and destroyed 500 temples,[24] for such alien modes of reverence and morality cannot be tolerated: there is only one, Catholic path to paradise.

At last the galleon nears the quay at San Juan de Ulúa; the deckhands

---

*Literally, 'Firm Land'.

†The Spanish knew the indigenous people as a whole as *naturales*.

throw down ropes to the shore, which are fastened to iron hoops as the vessel is moored. Beyond the island to which his ship is now attached Quiroga can see this continent of which he has been dreaming for months – the makeshift houses ashore are raised on stilts, while, on the island, a long wooden church stretches out across the open plaza. With the anchor dropped, and the ship stable at last, the unloading can begin of the piles of goods which have arrived from Europe.

First come the bailiffs (*alguaciles*),[25] usually two or three of them, to take possession of the letters that have been sent by the royal court. Meanwhile, Indians line up their canoes alongside the vessel, waiting to transport the crates of plants and seedlings that have been brought over from Spain.[26] By this time attention has begun to turn from military matters to more subtle forms of conquest; shortly after the defeat of the Mexica, Cortés had ordered that those Spaniards with European plants and seeds should plant them among the Indians,[27] and more recently Rodrigo de Albornoz, the royal accountant of Mexico, has voiced popular concerns when begging Emperor Charles V that no ship should leave Seville for Veracruz without bringing Spanish plants and seeds to the colony.[28] The new *oidores* will continue this process, when they send to ask for more seeds and plants during their first year of office.[29]

The truth is that it has not taken long for conquest to alter the environment. Already the traditional plantations of maize cobs and squashes that once littered the valleys of New Spain are being supplemented by fields of wheat and sugar cane. The long-standing orchards of avocado and guava trees are now sprinkled with groves of almond, orange and peach trees. There are also grapevines, and mulberry trees have been planted for the production of silk. But despite all this, by the end of 1530 there is still a clamour for an increase in the species that the Spanish know, and many of the mendicant Franciscan friars will soon write a joint letter to Charles urging that more should be brought.[30] The previously unknown flora of the Americas is, it would seem, a challenge to the Spaniards' perception of the world and of themselves, perhaps even a challenge to their moral order: geography plays a vital role in circumscribing character, as the Spaniards – hailing from the great and brutal plain of Castile – see only too well. So this conquest is not only to be spiritual and territorial; it is also to be biological (in all senses): it must be if the heathen outlook of the *naturales* is to be completely reversed, so that they can be absorbed into the growing Empire.

The plants and seeds have been carefully stowed in barrels and crates to protect them on the long voyage. Now they are hauled over the sides of the ship into the canoes that wait to ferry them across to the continent. Amid the advice called from sailors to canoeists, the shrieks of the livestock can be heard as their hobbles are checked and they are lowered overboard as well: here are mules, horses, cows, sheep, goats and chickens, brought over to fulfil the same function as the trees and plants, and no doubt as relieved as the people on board to be freed of the confines of the ship. Although as much as possible has been done to make life during the voyage entertaining, with games of dice and cards, prayers, plays, dances and the reading of romances,[31] the vessel has been little more than a travelling prison suffused with the stench of animal excrement.

At last the *oidores* can join the cargo in the journey along the line of dunes and up the inlet to Veracruz. Quiroga and Maldonado are helped into a rowboat, surrounded by gulls and pelicans hoping for an easy meal. The water slaps gently against their boat, foaming with violence in the distance as it breaks over some reefs. Beyond the sea are the dunes, beyond the dunes are the gentle shapes of the first wave of hills, and beyond these are the mountains, whose jagged edges cut the sky without mercy. Nature is brutal in New Spain, and this world is without compassion – Quiroga knows this only too well. Here is such cruelty, such avarice, and the eyes of the Spanish are luminous with their lust for women and gold. It disgusts him, for he knows the enormity of his task: there is much wealth here, but there is also so much greed that little of it is allowed to trickle down to the Indians.

During the canoe trip between San Juan de Ulúa and Veracruz, smuggling and the concealment of imported goods are the norms.[32] But perhaps, in deference to the arrival of the new *oidores*, the activity has lessened this time. They are paddled along this mosquito coast, where the dunes are so high and so soft that horses sink if they try to climb them.[33] The birds still hover overhead; a shoal of snappers shimmies in the clear water. Away from natural beauty, the prospect of perfection in this blighted country is more distant than ever, but for Quiroga, as he tries to dispel the discomfort of the queasy, floating sensation that overcomes those who have been at sea for a long period, perfection is exactly what he hopes to find.

The discoveries of the fifteenth and sixteenth centuries precipitated an extraordinary bout of soul-searching among the more spiritual

Europeans. The peoples of Africa had been known for centuries, and were self-evidently 'natural slaves', as the Aristotelian category put it (Aristotle, with his helpful division of peoples into natural masters and natural slaves, was the most popular classical philosopher of the age); but though the Spanish were used to having African slaves, the American peoples were new to them, and touched their consciences more profoundly. Of course, the Spaniards did not actually want to do any work – they were natural masters, after all[34] – but if the Africans could be brought over to alleviate the suffering of the *naturales* of the Americas, this might resolve their moral qualms (which did not extend to the Africans).

Initially, however, not everyone accepted that the Indians were rational beings capable of salvation. The most famous champion of Indian rights was Bartolomé de las Casas, whose struggle to protect indigenous peoples first came to prominence at a conference at Barcelona in 1519, where he denounced Aristotle as a gentile burning in Hell.[35] Zumárraga was another defender of the Indians, as was the Spanish theologian Francisco de Vitoría. The great debate on Indian affairs came between Las Casas and Juan Gines de Sepúlveda at Valladolid in 1550.* Here, Sepúlveda outlined his case that the Indians were little better than wild animals, drawing on a tradition that had been initiated by a Scottish professor of law in Paris, one John Major, who had written in 1510: '[The Indians] live as beasts ... from which it follows that the first to occupy those lands can justly govern the peoples that live there, as they are evidently natural slaves. In Book I of the Politics, [Aristotle] says that there is no doubt that some by nature are slaves and others free ... that it is right for some to rule and others obey, and that in empire ... one has to rule and hence dominate, and another obey.'[36]

The divergence in views on how the American peoples should be treated was matched by the range of opinions as to their origins. Though Columbus had called them 'Indians', Magellan's 1519–22 circumnavigation proved them to have little to do with the East Indies. One view held that the Indians were lapsed people of the Book who had been christianized centuries earlier by the Apostle Thomas.† One of the most popular opinions, though, was that these people were

---

*See below, ch. 13, p. 239.
†The legacy of this belief can be seen in the Mormon creed, which also holds that Christianity was taken to the Americas at the time of Christ, only to lie dormant for centuries.

remnants of the ten lost tribes of Israel, a view that gained strength throughout the sixteenth century, and still had not entirely disappeared in the twentieth century.[37]

This seemingly bizarre belief about the lost tribes of Israel exemplifies the struggle of the medieval mind to come to terms with the new categories opened up by the discoveries. During the fervour that led to the expulsion of the Jews from Spain in 1492, it was widely believed that the Jews often kidnapped Christian children and sacrificed them at Passover – this infamous 'blood libel' would last long into the modern period. Had not the *conversos* and Jews done exactly that with the 'Holy Child' of La Guardia in 1491, and been justly burnt by the Inquisition?[38] The Indians were cannibals and ate the meat of people that they sacrificed to their Gods – did they not obviously have Jewish origins?

This debate was, then, intimately related to preconceptions about the world at that time, as the Spaniards struggled to replace their outdated cosmology. It was also pivotal to views on the imminent coming of the Messiah. The mendicant Franciscan friars who arrived in New Spain in 1524 brought with them the goal of realising the Kingdom of God on Earth.[39] They interpreted the discovery of the New World as the onset of the final age of history before the coming of Christ, connecting this belief to the Apostle John's vision in the Book of Revelation of a new heaven and a new earth.[40] These missionaries genuinely believed that they were on the threshold of rediscovering a planetary Eden, and that, once all the races of humankind had found the true faith, historical time would be at an end (the 'end of history' being, it turns out, always wedded to the triumphs of empires). The belief that the Indians could be the lost tribes of Israel was connected to this apocalyptic vision, as, according to the Book of the Apocalypse, the tribes would re-appear at the time of the Last Judgement.[41]

Perfection, it seemed, was not so impossible a goal after all. It was ready to hand. But the path was dangerous; laced with crowns of thorns. It was to be reached through the redemption that was brought to the *naturales* through conversion. They would die (on the cross, as it were) to bring about paradise, perfection, forgiveness for the whole world. The most divine beings were always ready to endure pain for others.

Yea, and if perfection be so imminent, how better to accomplish it than through Utopia?

*

In Veracruz, as in Seville, Quiroga finds a melange of different peoples. There are the remnants of the Totonacs, and African slaves brought over from Cuba, as well as the local Spanish dignitaries, the mayor (*alcalde*) and town councillors (*regidores*), waiting to greet the *oidores* in their finest regalia. Surrounded by a flotilla of small canoes, Quiroga and Maldonado are rowed in to dock. The sunlight glints in the muddy river water, reflecting the walls of the town and the tower of the distant church. The dockside is a jumble of netting and crates and goods spilling over onto the riverbank. The *oidores* exchange greetings with the welcoming party, and are appraised by the settlers.

How does Quiroga strike those who meet him now? Age has begun to exact its price, and the tall young man of Madrigal has begun to stoop. His face is bony, his expression frequently sharp. His dark eyes flash about him, betraying his alertness. At times, he raises his thick eyebrows, and then his whole forehead creases into lines, which spring up like the rings around a tree, as if tokens of gathering maturity.

Quiroga's handshake is firm. He is quickly welcomed, and he and Maldonado are then accompanied through the streets to their resting place on the small plaza, which is enveloped in a mist of greenery. They soon realise that Veracruz is anything but an impressive town. The streets are dusty and some of the houses are crumbling, while loose strands of straw twitch in the heavy stillness. An air of decay hangs over the settlement, even though the city has been built so recently. Soon the money will run out and even the Customs House will be made of straw and adobe, not stone;[42] in 1533 the river will burst its banks and many of the flimsy buildings will be washed away. But there are the distant mountains to distract Quiroga's eyes from such problems, and, still floating on his sea legs, and trying to accustom himself to an environment in which everything is different, he has not yet had time to appreciate the true depths of 'this Babylon'[43] in which he has arrived. In fact, as Bishop Zumárraga has written to the Spanish court, it seems as if 'the earth of solidity and safety'[44] has been lost for ever. The very foundations of life appear to be under threat, not only from the inhuman customs of the *naturales*, but from the cruelty aroused in the Spaniards by the extent of their power over the indigenous peoples. The age of innocence, of safety in God's care, is gone for ever; the compassionate cannot believe their eyes when they see the avarice and destruction that have come to replace it.

Quiroga and Maldonado waste little time in leaving Veracruz for the capital, for Ceynos and Salmerón are already there awaiting them. The Royal Seal is stowed in a solid chest and fastened to a mule, whose saddlecloths are inlaid with brocade and velvet.[45] The *oidores* are provided with saddle horses and porters. In ten days they will reach their final destination, the Venice of the New World: Mexico.

Initially, Quiroga's eyes settle on the beautiful scenery, as the way cuts through the lowlands. Here are forests thick with orchids and passion flowers, broken up by savannah where large herds of deer graze[46] against the backdrop of the trees and mountains beyond. The richness of the country is unimaginable to someone who has never seen tropical vegetation before leaving Europe, for the area is so lush that according to one of the Spanish chroniclers it is common to find twenty-five streams in just six miles.[47] The waterways are the main paths towards the interior,[48] where the mountains are 'the most beautiful and fresh ... in the world',[49] filled with avocado trees which are so plentiful that the dogs stuff themselves on the fruit that lies rotting on the earth.[50] At night, jaguars and pumas are to be found out hunting, even though the Spaniards' dogs have killed some of these wild animals;[51] some of the beasts come right into the settlements, so that people have to sleep on raised platforms together with their livestock.

The heat and the abundance of clear running water mean that there are thick clouds of mosquitoes, even more than Quiroga was used to in Seville. As they ford stream after stream, the thickets rattle with the sound of alarmed snakes making their escape. Just eleven years earlier, Cortés wrote that most of the Totonac villages held between 300 and 500 inhabitants.[52] The inhabitants of the towns used to erect trellises covered in sweet-smelling flowers and vines.[53] Perhaps this had already been the true Eden, so that there had been no need to rebuild it following the conquest (contrary to the hopes of the Franciscans); indeed, in 1520, Paracelsus had written that there might have been two Creations, one in the east and one in the west.[54]

Passing through the ruins of these same villages of which Cortés had written, however, feelings of misgiving emerge in Quiroga. Now, in the first days of 1531, the plague of the pox on the Totonacs is being superseded by another, that of the *encomenderos** and other unscrupulous colonists, who make such unreasonable demands of the local chiefs that they are forced to sell their own children and relatives

---

Encomenderos were people who had been given grants of land – *encomiendas* – by the Crown to assist colonisation. The *encomenderos* gained the rights to an Indian town, its land and the services of those who lived there, in return for instructing the *naturales* in Christianity.

into slavery.[55] Many people have fled their towns and live wild in the countryside[56] rather than suffer oppression, and those who have stayed are so heavily burdened that they are unable to nurture their plantations,[57] which decay rapidly, meaning that there is no food to feed the people. The scene is appalling; as Quiroga sees the evidence of disease, abandonment and torture at every turn, fury at this 'infamous, shameful system'[58] stirs within him.

It does not take long for the road to Mexico to begin to climb steeply. The vegetation is still thick, cloying, unyielding, tumbling down into the frequent river valleys, which rise in cresting green waves on either side of the streams. Occasionally there is a glimpse of the milky cone of the Orizaba volcano, which appears to hang by levitation in the sky, beckoning Quiroga westwards, its snows angelic. Slowly, the land gathers itself into ridges whose tops bunch upon one another like the edges of a serrated knife. The tangle of branches, creepers, vines, flowers, bushes, thickets, trees is still overpowering, but the heat is not quite so intense. Quiroga's skin is no longer a constant film of sweat; his mind is able to clear a little with the lower density of nature's excrescences.

Now the road climbs even more sharply, and cold air all of a sudden vies with the sweltering currents of the plains. Quiroga finds himself moving into an unaccustomed chilliness, as the tangle of greenery falls away and the two *oidores* crest a pass and fall down into a barren plain where there are no plantations, and vegetation is confined to a sprinkling of cacti rising up from the sides of the surrounding hills. Dominating the plain is a salt lake, its edges radiant with the whorls of the white crystals, giving the light a brilliance that makes everything appear to sparkle.

The route to Mexico still leads through the province of Tlaxcala, the people whose help was essential to Cortés in the conquest of the Mexica. The neighbouring states had been traditional foes, and most of the army which had taken Mexico had been Tlaxcalan. The Tlaxcalans had always been in the front line,[59] and had helped Cortés's master boatbuilder, Martín López, to construct and transport the brigantines which had helped the Spanish to gain control of the lake in which Mexico was built. They had also been among the first to set fire to the archives of ancient codices which told the story of the Mexica on their own terms, and not through the eyes of their conquerors (who had soon joined in the burning and destruction of these priceless historical records).[60]

The Tlaxcalans' complicity with the imperialists benefits them little today, however, for by now, as Quiroga and Maldonado pass through their territory, they are subject to incessant demands for services and supplies by those who travel the road to Mexico. In two years' time they will complain to the Audiencia that the road is 'very prejudicial and damaging to them and the inhabitants of their province',[61] because of everything that is demanded of them.

Tlaxcala is a city in flux, as Quiroga sees. Although still acclimatising to the changes brought by the Spanish, in years to come the city will be privileged by the colonists – the memory of Tlaxcala's support in the initial conquest never disappears – so that there will never be a Spanish council here, and the Indians will retain much power.* In 1535, the Spanish Crown will give Tlaxcala a coat of arms, and the arts will flourish under the Franciscan friars, with Tlaxcala producing brilliantly coloured codices which will recount the (many) arrows of fortune.

The buildings that will come to define the town's architecture are now under construction: the arcades that line the plaza, the Franciscan monastery, which will not be completed for seven years, and the cathedral, with its intricately carved Mudéjar ceiling so reminiscent of Castile. The curvaceous hills that surround Tlaxcala, and the neat, well-ordered layout of the town combine to soothe Quiroga, who is frankly shattered as he breaks his journey here. The changes in climate, altitude, culture, geography, cosmology – all are enough to exhaust the mind and embattle the emotions, meaning that they are increasingly hard to discern and most often become discarded.

Quiroga is pleased to meet the guardian of the Franciscan Church, Fray Toribio,† and see the font in which the old Tlaxcalan chiefs were baptised in 1520. The font was hauled up from the coast by Cortés's army in a great labour of devotion; but then, thinks Quiroga, great devotion is essential if barbarism is to be overcome. Yes, this carrying of the font had been a symbol of everything that is signified by the conquest of New Spain: love of God (and the love of God for His people), greatness of purpose (and nation), immense effort (and sacrifice).

It is dawn. In Tlaxcala's plaza, Quiroga stands and sees a cloud fanning out like a recent eruption from Matlacuéyctl, the volcano that

---

*Though the Spanish colonial administration implanted itself very firmly within New Spain, the Indian communities did possess their own power structures, with their own councils and 'governors' modelled on the Spanish councils of the new cities. Tlaxcala was unusual in possessing no Spanish equivalent of the Indian neighbourhoods.
†The famous chronicler Motolinía.

lies to the east: a burst of light glitters from the barren cone, only for its force to be diluted by the cloud. From here, he knows, it is not far to Mexico. In two days he will arrive, and grasp his challenges head-on. Even now, he has seen evidence of the difficulties that lie before him. The road is always busy with teams of porters staggering beneath the terrible loads that they are expected to bear between Mexico and Veracruz. The letters of Zumárraga have given an idea of the brutalities being meted out daily to the *naturales*, but only now does Quiroga begin to understand what this means. Zumárraga, who has also been named 'Protector of the Indians', has said that the Spanish take the Indians 'heavily burdened to wherever they want to go ... without even giving them food, and so naturally they suffer greatly and some of them even die on the road',[62] and that 3000 Indians have died on the roads of Tepeaca,[63] the province next to Tlaxcala. Perhaps the glitter on the volcano is a reflection of their bones, shining white like the salt lake, picked clean in the plain. In Oaxaca, to the south, things are even worse, for there so many corpses lie on the roads to and from the mines that for half a league on either side of the road 'it is difficult to tread on anything except for dead men or their bones';[64] so many birds flock to the impromptu cemetery that they block out the sun.[65]

Is this barbarism really essential to the nature of conquest? In the clear light, with the skeins of cirrus crowning the mountains around him in puffy white halos, Quiroga feels the weight of the question. Yes, the physical act of possession is necessarily vile, but spiritual conquest should be a different matter, especially when civilisation itself is at stake. Is it not the duty of the most powerful and enlightened to offer help to those less fortunate than themselves, and show them the true benefits of Catholic assistance?

Yet everywhere he turns he sees undeniable proof that the most powerful and enlightened are taking advantage of their position simply to fill their pockets, with no thought for the carnage that has been brought about in the land and among its people. These Indians are to be brought to the very gates of heaven by the grace of God, who granted the vanquishing of the Mexica: but how is the divine will to be realised amidst the greed and cruelty of the settlers, and in spite of the diseases that they have brought with them – diseases which are so rapacious that they must be the arrows of the devil (and may well also be expressions of the conquerors' very own rapacity)?

The road to Mexico begins to climb again. The settlements come and go as rapidly and inconspicuously as the days that elapse with them. The maize crop is withered and straggly, the half-grown cobs hanging listlessly by the wayside in the shadow of copses of pine trees, the subtlest conquerors of all; and still they pass the ubiquitous piles of bones, gleaming like memories of Spain. No one can stop a natural process, but surely there is a way of saving the Indians from the first age of international capitalism, let loose with such savagery among them — surely there is a better model of society than this one.

As the road begins the final climb towards the pass which is to reveal Mexico, Quiroga begins to pray for divine inspiration.

SIX

Leaving my problems by the Alcázar behind me, I woke up in Mexico with a heavy weight in my pocket – the nearest thing to my heart, as it were. Shifting around, I tried to ignore it, but it wouldn't go away. Then my eyes started to water, and I realised that I would have to sit up straight, get a grip, behave, and rid myself of the absurd fantasies which had recently begun to thrive inside me where Utopia was concerned. I was a rational, historical investigator, not a lunatic idealist, and I still had plenty of research to undertake. Deluding myself that I was becoming almost sensible, I righted myself and found that, now that I was ready to join the ranks of acceptable society, I was sitting at the heart of a vast rubbish tip.

The extent of the garbage was fantastic. Thousands of torn plastic bags eddied in the gusts of hot air that attended this strangely desolate spot. This was the flea market to beat them all, and fleas weren't the only things on offer: here were discarded cans, bottles, petrol canisters, piles of plastic packaging, CD cases, film cartridges, condoms, syringes and rotting food – all gathered into mounds almost fifty metres high. Stooped figures could be seen picking through the remains, trying to scavenge some sort of existence from the festering slush. I caught sight of one of them, emaciated, cowled by rags, with a face hollower than canned laughter and eyes as glazed as pottery; I shuddered and, in spite of the genuine sympathy that I forced myself to feel for the filthy wretch, turned away to look steadfastly in the opposite direction. There I saw packs of dogs tearing through the mess and scattering the detritus – not that it made much difference in this giant, uncovered landfill site, which appeared to encompass the known world. The waste materials were oozing back down into the earth, smothering it like a latter-day primeval sludge, and I could see that if I stayed here for much longer, they would crush me too, without remorse, pity, compassion or shame.

I felt my throat gagging. The stench of decay was almost as

unmistakable as the signs of it that stood out all around me. Putting my hand to my nostrils and pinching them tight, I began to run, almost blindly, hoping to burrow my way out of the rubbish without further ado; but I found that the weight in my trousers was becoming more and more oppressive, so that soon I could hardly move. Tired by the constant demands exerted by the pocket where I usually kept my wallet, I felt inside it and came up with an escudo, a sixteenth-century Spanish gold coin. Staggering past a graveyard for cars, I looked at my latest discovery with a flash of panic; passing the serried ranks of unwanted fridges, I put my hand into my pocket and picked out another gold coin, and then another. As Don Quixote had known, dreams could very well become reality, and before falling asleep I recalled that I had been in Seville, dreaming of riches and Mexico. Not only that, but I had been teetering on the verge of delusion.

There was no doubt about it. Walking out into the hazy sunshine, and spying the main road beyond the tip, I realised that, just as the old man in S—— had foretold, Don Quixote was of increasing relevance to me: my dream had helped to wing me across the Atlantic to Mexico City. I would have to forget all about the research in the Spanish archives for the time being: my new function was clearly to be a knight errant in the modern world, righting wrongs and saving the human race from disaster.

Feeling rather pleased with myself, my sense of reality began to abate. I stared at the sea of traffic that confronted me on the twelve-lane highway to the north of the city, and smugly decided that, like Don Quixote, my first task was to find a trusty squire, some unsuspecting Sancho Panza. It was likely to be difficult: I didn't think that they would accept gold coins any more. Still, the traffic was stationary, and so, taking my life into my hands, and beginning my adventures, I sallied out into the lanes of still metal and clambered unasked into the passenger seat of one of the green-and-white taxis. Smiling disarmingly at the gaunt face of the driver, I introduced myself.

'I've come to Mexico to investigate utopias,' I told him. 'What about you?'

'I live here,' he told me, 'and my name is Juan Pérez, or John Smith to you.'

'Well, John!' I said patronisingly. 'Take me forward, and let's progress in harmony to wherever you're going.'

'We're going nowhere just now, *señor*,' John replied, pointing at the fuming vehicles pouring out trails of smoke into the fug overhead, at the dust and the dirt and the smoke and the mechanical, soulless inertia. 'Oh,' he went on, 'to begin with we progressed very rapidly, and for quite some distance, but now we've ground to a complete halt. And I shouldn't be surprised if we start going backwards soon enough.'

Looking out of the rear window, I saw with alarm that we were at the top of a very steep hill, and that even remaining where we were would almost certainly prove too much of a burden for gravity and the other laws of nature to bear; but his glum views and the oppression of the rapidly shrinking planetary resources were not what I wanted to think about just yet.

'Well come on,' I said irritably, forgetting for a moment that I had not yet persuaded John to be my sidekick. 'That's not the way to begin a lusty adventure of rescue, is it?'

'Who do you plan to rescue, *señor*?' he asked.

'Damsels in distress!' I cried. 'Or at least, anyone who's locked in the dungeons of poisonous oligarchs, advertising agencies and bureaucrats in league with the devil.'

'Well,' he said, 'let's not talk twentieth-century politics.'

'No, you're right there,' I said; 'we're well out of that.'

'Let's just sit here and see if we can't go forward some time before midnight.'

'Midnight!' I squawked. 'But I want to go on now. Now!'

'Oh yes, I know you do, *señor*,' he said; and, perhaps alarmed at the possibility of losing my custom, he began to speak with a mixture of obsequious humility and despair. 'But this city of Mexico is a nightmare now. Too many cars, too many people, too many buildings, too many factories – it has no future.'

This was quite a little speech, and, looking sideways at John's drooping face, I couldn't help but be reminded again of the old man in S—— and his quixotic fantasies; in fact, I began to wonder whether that old utopian had not placed spies around the world just to keep a check on my progress, for certainly there were many people who appeared to share his views.

'It sounds as though everyone here needs rescuing,' I said, quickly banishing my paranoia, and recovering the arrogant self-assurance that I knew would be necessary before John gave himself up to following my path.

'You're right there,' he replied.

'That's quite a task for me,' I said knowingly, 'as a valiant, modern-day saviour.'

'Saviour?' he said, looking alarmed and wondering at the depths of my inanity. 'Who are you supposed to be saving?'

'Well, it's as you say,' I answered. 'Everyone here needs saving. The burdens of poverty, the exhausting traffic and smog, the demands of international business – they are all performing an inexorable strangulation process on this city and all who live in it. My crackpot dreams have brought me this far, and now it's for me to find everyone and help them. I'm willing to die for them, if only I can bring them to Utopia, perfection, paradise – on Earth, if not in heaven.'

'Everyone?'

'Well,' I went on, oblivious to what a pompous idiot I had become, 'when you have the answer to all the world's problems ready to hand, it's surely your duty to share it with the human race.'

John looked at me with a mixture of pity and astonishment – my inanity had become insanity, and bordered on what passed for political statesmanship in the contemporary atmosphere. Now that I had promised far more than I could possibly deliver and had spoken with the necessary degree of self-importance, barefaced conviction and deceit, he was happy to join me.

'Don't worry,' he said. 'I'll give you a helping hand. I'm itching to put everything right myself. But what reward are you going to give me?'

'Reward?' I asked.

'Oh yes, *señor*,' he said. 'Even the great hidalgo Don Quixote de la Mancha – an adventurer like yourself – offered his squire Sancho the governorship of an island when he relinquished his freedom and voted with his feet for the Don. So the very least that I expect from you is a tax cut.'

'Well,' I said, thinking on my feet, 'I've got no islands to give away, John, and I don't set the taxes – yet. But I have got some sixteenth-century gold coins – the forerunner of today's tourist dollar, if you like. I'm not quite sure where they came from, although doubtless they were stolen by some rogue – a pirate, or an ancestor of mine. But I was rather hoping that you'd accept them in lieu of Mexican pesos, as I'm flat broke.'

John seemed perfectly happy with this false bribery, and the deal was done. I won power as I handed over the gold, which was not even mine to give and in fact had probably been mined and carried to the very ports of New Spain by John's Amerindian ancestors. Soon John and I agreed that we should make our way into the centre of the city before beginning our knight-errantry.

So we sat waiting in the lines of traffic, and night slowly began to fall. With the darkness, Mexico City took on a much brighter appearance, with its lights spreading out at the bottom of the hill, flashing on the logos of the shops, in advertisements and neon signs, in the offices which stood like concrete guardians before the portals of the largest city on the continent – one of the fullest expressions of the modern world that existed. The brightness reflected the innovation that was in everything, the new buildings, new cars, new clothes, new technologies, neophytes all superimposed on an old world of empire which had still to be fully requited. And yet my own experiences in the city's rubbish tip had shown me that you did not have to travel very far from this glitter to reach a truer picture of filth and choking pollution, and I could not help but feel that this brilliance was a mask for inconsolable gloom, and that the true desire of this world was for release from its all-consuming destructiveness, a desire to finish it all as quickly as possible, to find rest, burial, and so herald different times when a gentler species might prevail.

So here we were, stuck in the traffic jam, where nothing seemed capable of moving us. We sat there halfway through the night, until we began to despair of ever being able to save people.

'Come on, *señor*,' John said to me eventually, as time pulsed on. 'I've had enough of this. Let's get to work and preach the gospel.'

This sounded rather presumptuous coming from a squire whose eternal gratitude and cringing obsequiousness should have been bought with my tourist gold coins, and I voiced an objection.

'Hold on, John,' I said, 'I'm in charge. Don't forget – I'm the employer here.'

'That's true,' he said meekly, having been reminded of his true station as a servant in his own country. I was glad that I had reasserted my property rights. I was the one who had brought over the money, and the ideas: this would be my cult, my Utopia, or it would be nobody's – and certainly not his.

'Anyway,' I went on, 'we can't go anywhere. What about the car?'

'We can leave the car. It'll probably still be here in the morning – this lot aren't going far.'

'But what if they do?'

'Then we can get another one, *señor*,' he said, 'using the gold coins. There's no shortage of cars, and no shortage of manufacturers.'

'You're right, John,' I said. 'As long as people are happy to burn up the atmosphere and sit around for hours in lumps of metal, business will keep on making them.'

'Of course, *señor*,' he said. 'That's the law of choice, freedom, the market – and that's why, when it comes to the environment, everyone agrees that self-regulation is the only answer.'

With a loud, trumpeting sigh, I opened the door of his taxi and we made our way past the throngs of parked cars on the highway. Looking through the windows of each and every vehicle, I felt a mounting sense of excitement as I realised just how many people were in need of my Utopia: each one of them thought that they were happy, but really I could see that they were miserable wrecks (in their miserable wrecks), in need of the true answers to all their problems, which only I could give them.

With truly utopian zeal, I now saw adventures at every turn. I was out of the taxi, and into the big guns. Reaching the edge of the inside lane, I gestured to John to stop and flung open the door of a large, four-wheel-drive Chevrolet.

'Come on,' I said, realising that the terrorist threat had never been closer to me. 'Get out right now. This car is a bomb.'

The Chevrolet driver stared at me in astonishment. 'A bomb?' he said.

'Oh no, *señor*,' John said, rushing up to me and wringing his hands, 'this is no bomb.'

'You must be mad,' the driver added.

'No,' I said, convinced by divine inspiration, revelation and falsification that I was right and that they were wrong. 'It's a bomb all right, and I don't mind telling you that I'll help to light the fuse if you like. A time bomb burning up in the hands of individual citizens, destined to destroy the world within fifty years. Every bit as deadly as anthrax, smallpox, sarin nerve gas and nuclear weapons in the hands of our bitterest enemies in the Middle East.'

'The Middle East?' the driver asked.

'Yes!' I shouted, warming to my task. 'The Middle East, the Communist bloc, the Jewish ghettos, or wherever else our bitter foe Mohammed Marx Hacohen can be said to be hiding.'

'Mohammed Marx Hacohen?' John interjected, grabbing my arm. 'I've not heard of him.'

'No no,' said the driver, joining in. 'You've got it all wrong,' he said to me. 'You can't just go taking out three enemies all together like that. You have to do it one at a time, like our ancestors did: first the ghettos of the European Jews, then the Marxists, now the Muslims. The external enemies of the progressive world are absolutely essential to peace and development, especially as they stop people from having to look for the enemy within – but it's critical that they only come one at a time.'

'That's all very well,' I said, 'but after the next mass extinction of humanity – that is, once peace has returned to the Middle East – where's the threat going to be then?'

'Well,' the driver said, looking me up and down, 'that would be you.'

Sneering, and screwing up his eyes, he slammed the Chevrolet door into my face, wheeled the car round and over the pavement, and drove off in the direction of the rubbish tip. I lay dazed on the pavement and tried to come to terms with my predicament. I knew that I was not mad – it was the others who were at fault for not sharing my utopian vision, after all – nevertheless I was surprised that I was finding it so difficult to attract followers. And this was not the only shock, for I now realised with a start that the cars were beginning to move again on the motorway, obliterating John's stationary taxi without mercy.

I only just managed to crawl to the side of the road with the help of my faithful squire to avoid both of us being crushed to death.

'Well, John,' I said, wiping my brow with my hand as I turned to the taxi driver and – like everyone else – refused to credit the evidence of my own eyes; 'we certainly told him.'

John helped me to dust myself down. 'If you say so, *señor*,' he said, suspiciously. 'But look here: before we go any further, there are a few things I want to get straight.' John seemed quite irate now; as he went on, I saw that he himself had clearly read the *Quixote*, and had decided to adopt some of the mannerisms of the Don's squire, for he now began to speak in a litany of long-winded proverbs just like old Sancho. 'For one thing, my name's Juan and not John, and for another I want you to explain more about your gospel. It's all very well to start saying that you've got the answers to everything, but I don't know what you're trying to solve. I was perfectly happy until you came along and got me to give up my secure existence as a taxi driver and follow you. We've hardly been gone ten minutes and already I've lost my taxi and nearly been crushed to death. And as the proverb has it, you've got to look after your own, and a vote in the hand is worth two in the bush, except in Florida, where a vote for the bush is worth two in the ballot box, as it were. And what is more, you can't help the child until you've fed the parents. So from what I've seen so far this idealism of yours is potentially lethal, and I really ought to go back to sit in the traffic jam with everyone else, because at least I wasn't going anywhere then, and it's better to be a stone on the riverbed than one falling down the mountain.'

'Yes, John, I understand what you mean,' I said, putting my arm paternally around his shoulders, aware that this kind of stupidity was the sort of thing I was bound to come across in my quest to rid the world of evil and bring absolute perfection to it. As I mulled over my answer, we passed the entrance to the rubbish tip, and then turned down a side street which heralded an enormous market area, crushed full of humanity even though it was the middle of the night. Vendors were selling everything that a person could possibly want, and in far greater quantities than could ever be disposed of. Ranchero music filled the air with its raucous dissonance as we walked along whole blocks that were occupied by people selling the same wallets, or combs, or bootlegged cassettes, the same tacos filled with fried meat and green chillies and onions, with the marketeers shouting louder or higher to undercut, thrust, survive, differentiate their wares from the identical products to be found at their neighbour's stall.

'You see, John,' I continued at last, 'for some time now I've had the sensation that our civilisation is drowning. Drowning!' I felt a sudden glow of self-righteousness as the truth of my comments reverberated around my little head. 'We're galloping through the world's resources. Our governments arrange international conference after international conference to address the great issues of the day, yet our habits don't change and, if anything, the purpose of these summits appears to be to convince people that the congestion of the world's arteries is easing when actually they'll soon be furred up beyond repair. Our great intellectuals are in the grip of Darwinism, and bellow the fact that survival is the overriding moral principle, and yet our species seems to have no desire to see out the twenty-first century. Yes, our ideological semantics, our great theories themselves, have become static, inconsequential and self-defeating beyond repair, and you can see the result in the gridlock in all our cities and towns, in the mental inertia that information overload has brought us to, in the hollow satisfaction that comes from a situation in which everyone and everything caters to the vilest desires so that we're all allowed to wallow in our own urges.'

I came to a stop in the middle of the street, blocking the way for dozens of porters and indigenous women carrying their children and shifty businessmen barging their way through with battered briefcases. The smell of frying tacos filled the air as I tried to gather my thoughts. 'Oh yes, John,' I said eventually, looking at my squire with tremendous pity and getting to the nub of it, 'we're drowning all right.'

John turned to one side, and we brushed past a selection of fake-leather handbags before reaching the sanctuary of the kerb.

'Well, *señor*,' he said, 'it's a rare goalkeeper who saves his opponents' team before he saves his own, and where goodness is a football the devil's the one who's kicked it permanently into touch, as they say. So if you've really decided to give up your family, your life and your home to come and help us all build perfection over here, then I'm not going to stand in your way, and in fact I'm more than happy to give it a try myself. What we all need in this country is food, and the disbanding of a greater part of this city.'

'You're right, we've got to get back to basics,' I said. 'Look around!' I gestured at the teeming food stalls, of which there were dozens. 'There's plenty of food, but the women serving up the tacos here haven't got six customers between them because no one can afford to eat it; and, in fact, the faces of most people in this market are drawn with hunger and mental inertia. For the truth is, the brain's by far the greediest organ in the human body, and that's why sustained creative thought has always been the privilege of the well fed.' I looked at John with the unquenchable self-belief that I knew to be merited by my ideology. 'And so every explosion in intellectualism, from the radicalism of Erasmus to the exponential increase of universities in modern times, has essentially been grounded in the tyranny of the full stomach!'

'Well, *señor*, that's as may be, but when it comes to stomachs mine's as tyrannical as anybody's, and there's no time like the present, as they say, and it's best to strike while the iron's hot, or before the opposition have built up their weapons of mass destruction. So let's go and get in some tacos before we bore each other – and everyone else – to death.'

Recognising the truth in what John said, I allowed him to lead the way to one of the stalls and we sat down and ordered some food. The air was hot, sticky, and hung oppressively overhead. Gradually, the night was lightening, and the first rays of the sun were now apparent. Although I had slept briefly while fantasising my way over from Seville to Mexico, I was still enormously tired, and, as we waited for the kindly woman who ran the eatery to prepare our food, I gawped open-mouthed at the city as it rumbled on around me. Just metres away was an ancient Buick whose front half had totally disappeared, leaving its passenger doors and boot sticking helplessly into the air; a small truck pulled up at a road junction and two men leapt down, calling out in long, monotonous cries and trying to sell gas to the women washing down the pavements outside their shops; meanwhile, a group of indigenous people bustled animatedly through the throng of people and stray dogs lying morosely by the roadside, speaking in musical, high-pitched voices, and communicating in a language that was utterly alien to me.

I was tired, and the roots of my purpose in having embarked on this wild adventure seemed to have become obscured. I was searching for Quiroga, and a new way to rekindle the concept of Utopia in the modern world; but the more I had travelled since meeting the old man in S——, the more I had seen that this world was, if anything, increasingly dystopian, and that the ideals of perfection which had driven people for centuries had simply created the reverse: a paradise for lunatics, or for those who were cut off from the world around them. My utopian dreams appeared so archaic that I wondered if there was any space left for me on Earth, and it was doubtless this which contributed to my gathering sense of delusion. It was as if this was the only possible destiny for utopianism.

'I hope you'll forgive me, *señor*,' John said, interrupting my daydreams. 'But I can't help noticing that you seem as though you're feeling rather sorry for yourself.'

'That's right, John,' I said.

'Juan,' he said.

'The thing is,' I continued, 'I should have known that I couldn't hide myself away from you.'

'Well, *señor*,' he said, 'a problem shared is a problem halved, and if worry's your middle name then you're like the rest of us.'

Seeing John staring so earnestly at me, I began to unburden myself. I explained that I had come to Mexico to follow the journey of Vasco de Quiroga, whose utopian ideals seemed both intriguing and of the utmost relevance to the modern world. I myself, I said, was something of a utopian, and believed that action was urgent if we were to stave off the disasters which beckoned us – this was my gospel, as he liked to say. However, I went on, although I remained a steadfast idealist, I found that the city was making me increasingly exhausted, so that I could not think straight, and that all the noble ideals with which I had started out seemed further and further away. The modern world, I said, appeared to be crushed by the surfeit of information, the regression to an atavistic surrender to instinct, and ecological catastrophe, such that there was no space left for idealism to be heard.

It was just as well that my dismal little speech was brought to an end by the woman who ran the stall, who now brought us red plastic plates each bearing three tacos garnished with red chilli sauce and limes. As I began to stuff the food unceremoniously into my mouth, John looked at me and laughed.

'Well,' he said, 'it's a good thing that you've met me.'

'Is it, John?'

'Of course,' he said, 'provided that you really want to take advantage. After all, opportunity only knocks if you know how to open the door, and there's no point in craving wildlife documentaries if you've got a snakeskin handbag.'

What he meant, he went on, was that if I was really interested in utopian ideas, I was barking up the wrong tree, and putting dog food in the cat bowl: not to mince words, or mix metaphors in the pestle and mortar, if I wasn't more careful, I'd end up slaughtering my own child when God had given me plenty of rams to choose from, and there was no point in getting so down in the mouth about it when at any moment a simple change of heart could transform enemies into friends, destruction into eternal salvation, and mean that my umbrella could become a parasol, for wasn't a night out with Mohammed Marx Hacohen better than no night out at all?

The point was, he said, abandoning the quixotic refrain that had become so maddening in the last little while, my aspiration to be a Don Quixote, and to have him as a Sancho Panza, was all wrong. Because though the sixteenth century had seen the first great flowering of utopian literature, the publication of *The Ingenious Hidalgo Don Quixote de la Mancha* had represented the first decline from the high-water mark of the literary utopian dream. In fact, far from extolling the utopian idyll of humanists, Cervantes had excoriated it with the bitterest satire.

The *Quixote*'s first reference to 'the golden past' gave an inkling of what was to follow, John continued, smearing his face with chilli sauce as he demonstrated just how thorough his reading of the book had had to be for him to adopt the proverbial mannerisms of Sancho. In an authorial introduction to the main adventures in the first book, Cervantes wrote that this wondrous period meant that 'unless raped by some blackguard, or by some peasant with his hatchet and his iron skullcap, or by some monstrous giant, there were maidens in those times gone by who, at the age of eighty and not having spent a single night under a roof, went to their graves with their maidenheads as intact as the mothers who'd borne them.'[1] The merciless satire continued shortly afterwards, when Don Quixote gave a little speech to some goatherds: 'Happy the age and happy the centuries were those on which the ancients bestowed the name of golden ... because men living in such times did not know those two words *yours* and *mine*.'[2] This was the epoch when 'fraud, deceit and malice were not yet intermixed with truth and plain dealing. Justice kept within her own bounds, and favour and interest ... did not dare assail or disturb her'.[3]

The fact was, John told me, that this was one of literature's finest creations because Cervantes had recognised that, in the midst of the birth of the modern world, it was absurd to eulogise the pastoral idyll as some sort of perfect society, a Utopia.[4] The belief that the pastoral idyll of writers such as More and Guevara could in fact convert itself into an anachronistic disaster was at the core of the book: by creating such a lunatic character as Don Quixote, who was trying to recreate the 'golden age', Cervantes sought to show that there was no hope for a utopian society which turned back to feudal ways and tried to hide itself away in pseudo-perfection and escapism.[5] Therefore, John concluded, wiping his lips with satisfaction, there was no hope for my utopianism if I tried to couch it in terms of the world's first great anti-utopian novel. In fact, I had better lose every shred of my gathering madness if I wanted this utopianism to have a real impact.

'Come now, John,' I answered swiftly, allowing my condescension to reach its apogee, 'you're not trying to tell me that even your fictional progenitor, Sancho Panza, didn't prefer the life of the feudal vassal to that of being forced brutally into the modern world.'

'That's exactly what I am saying, *señor*,' John answered. 'Why, towards the end of the book, even Sancho himself says: "There's as much of this lovey-dovey stuff and wicked urges out in the fields as inside the cities."[6] Oh no, you can't dress mutton as lamb, or get away with being a wolf in sheep's clothing. Both the dove and the hawk have to eat to survive, and that's Sancho's last word on the subject until someone offers to pay him an appearance fee, because humour isn't a bottomless cup, and the road to riches is paved with TV chatshows, and cameras only lie when someone wants to sell a lot of newspapers.'

'That's quite a performance, John,' I said. 'But if you're so convinced by what you say, you'll have to explain to my satisfaction how it was that More's passionate belief in Utopia gave way to Cervantes's knowing proto-modernist critique.'

John nodded his head rapidly, seeing the sense in my request. Putting a gold coin into the hand of the restaurateur, he pushed back his battered metal stool and beckoned me to follow him. It was now quite light, and the thick smog had yet to settle its mantle upon the city. As we made our way towards the Zócalo, the enormous square at the heart of the city, he began to explain the process that I had just described.

There was no doubt, he said, that utopian books tended to be written by people sensitive to the miseries of the world, and that they were often expressions of cultural malaise.[7] There had been something about the birth of modernity that created this atmosphere in abundance: for up to fifty years before More had published his book, utopian architectures had been mooted in renaissance Italy,[8] and for a century or more afterwards many thinkers devoted their energies towards devising some sort of supposed ideal state. Unlike More's own book, these were not all egalitarian societies, with some of them – such as Rabelais's *L'Abbaye des Thélémites* and Burton's *A Utopia of Mine Own* – accepting the basic hierarchies of society.[9] Of course, these hierarchies were grounded in the first Utopia of all, Plato's *Republic*, whose strict division of people into philosopher-guardians, auxiliaries and craftspeople doing the trade they were best suited to was grounded in human inequalities.[10]

Nevertheless, John continued, the most famous utopian books of this era today are those which – like More's work – were early anticipations of communism. Another example was Thomas Campanella's *The City of the Sun*, in which people lived 'in a philosophical way with everything in common'.[11] This sort of commonality was based on Campanella's belief that 'all private property derives from having one's own dwelling apart and one's own children and wife, and out of this self-love is born ... But when people lose self-love, there remains only community.'[12] As in More's Utopia, the residents of the City of the Sun all wore the same clothes,[13] and worked a much shorter day than did most people in early-modern Europe, 'so that all the rest of the time can be spent in learning through playing games, taking part in discussions, reading, teaching and walking'.[14] As a Dominican monk, Campanella – like More – believed that this naturally equal state was very close to Christianity, which was the true law, so that, when 'freed from abuses, it will become mistress of the world'.[15] He wrote that this was why 'the Spaniards discovered the rest of the world ... Those people go in search of new countries out of greed for money, but God's intent is a higher good.'[16]

The thing was, John went on, looking as though he was beginning to tire of this convoluted historical explanation, that whether they were egalitarian or hierarchical, the humanist utopias of the renaissance had expressed the view that society could be perfected and that there was some kind of immutable ideal to which humanity could aspire. This sort of idealism was a mirror image to the 'perfect' God in the heavens, and of course, he added, the first Franciscans who came to the New World had wanted to create that perfection right here. But it was that kind of blurring of categories, coupled with the growing realisation by the end of the sixteenth century that the concept of perfection being built on Earth did not sit easily with the development of modern life that led to the type of utopian cynicism that Cervantes expressed in his *Quixote*.

We had reached the Zócalo by now. This vast space, surrounded by arcaded buildings, was astir with the morning rush hour. On the north side of the square, the solid bulk of the largest cathedral in Latin America crushed the city. Three priests of European origin were standing on a dais, preaching universal peace and forgiveness to a crowd of rather than more than a thousand people, who were of principally indigenous origin; around the corner, the stones of the ruins of the Templo Mayor of Tenochtitlan reflected the grey pollution.

'Well, John,' I said, trying to formulate a sensible answer.

'Juan,' he replied testily.

'Look, Diego,' I continued, realising that it was essential that I reassert myself now if I did not want to lose his support for good, and find myself having to revert to a conventional narrative, 'I can accept this up to a point. But I still think that you'll find that our knight-errantry is most necessary in this day and age, and that your lesser part in it is as crucial as my own starring role. For all that you've told me about the decline of utopian fervour from the early sixteenth century to the seventeenth century, you can't deny that some sort of idealism is more fundamental now than ever – because as it stands today, idealism is the sort of corpse that medical students enjoy kicking round the laboratory as a prank: a ponderous and much mocked football. But history shows that when people allow their moral precepts to be reduced to self-interest, they'll soon swallow any old rubbish if they can be made to believe that it suits their purposes. Look at the Jews in medieval Spain: their aristocracy became increasingly agnostic, so they were happy to abandon the faith of their ancestors and convert to Christianity just to cement their position in the hierarchy.[17] But that didn't save them when the Inquisition came looking for the "Jewish heretics". Nor will our world's renewed interest in money and self-interest save it when the polar ice caps melt and some great new persecution sweeps by.'

Diego laughed at that, and clapped me on the back. 'Of course, *señor*,' he said. 'And perhaps you are right in one way: Don Quixote's quest to reclaim the age of chivalry was about as sane as yours is to reclaim the age of idealism. And you have about as much chance of succeeding as he did.'

'Absolutely, Diego,' I said, struck by this strange echo of the views of the man in S——, and wondering again if he were not shadowing me in some way, 'it's there for the taking. And seeing as the *Quixote* is one of the most successful books of all time, you can see how important it is that you shouldn't abandon me to pursue my knight-errantry alone. After all, Quixote without his Sancho would not even have been half as good.'

'Well, *señor*,' he said, smiling at me again, abandoning his recalcitrance and recognising that in me and me alone lay his only hope of future fame and salvation, 'there's something to what you say. After all, a cup which is half full does not make you half as drunk as one that is complete, because though it takes one drunken lout to steal a super-market trolley, it takes two to fill it with lead and smash shop windows with it. And as there's no point in shutting the stable door after the horse has bolted, or in trying to combat asylum seekers after you have spent centuries reducing their countries to misery and despair, I may as well have my cake before it's been eaten by someone else and a special tax on sugar has been introduced.'

'That's it, Diego,' I said.

'Juan,' he said.

'Look, Juan Diego,' I said, feeling thoroughly confused, 'I agree entirely with you. But before we go and eat our cake – I'm going to have more than my fair share too, by the way – I just want to get one thing straight: I'm in charge here, and just because you've listened very carefully to my arguments and realised that I'm right in every respect, that doesn't turn you into a saint of any description. Not even if you come bringing me an image of the Virgin which you've dug up in your back yard, or chanced upon at the top of a nearby hill!'

'That's all right by me, *señor*,' Juan Diego answered. 'I've never given much credence to those stories of saints anyway. For seeing is believing, as they say, and there's no better miracle than the filling of a stomach, particularly if it's mine; so provided you let me have my cake, I'll be your servant and we can both feel that all's right with the world, and even more so because we won't be the ones who are hungry.'

We had crossed the Zócalo and reached its edge. Already the smog was gathering itself and the buildings on the far side of the square shimmered through the pollution. Close by, the arcades gave way to a passageway lined with cafes and shops selling expensive sweets, perfumes and jewellery. Outside each boutique was a beggar of some description, with stumps for hands, or arms, or legs, and a look of righteous despair adorning the face of each and every one of them. I could not give to them all; I took Juan Diego by the hand and we ignored them religiously, passing the line of shops as quickly as we could and then ducking down a side street that led away from this window onto our greedy shame.

We had been walking for quite some time now, and my throat was itchy, my muscles felt lethargic, and my eyes felt wet with the smog, which was becoming stronger with every passing moment. The air pressed in, constricted me, the expressions of stoicism and penury on the faces of so many people wounded me deeply, and all of a sudden I was overwhelmed by a sense of grief, at the compelling evidence of the swift decay of this city, at the growing poverty and misery that were adopting most of the world's countries, and at the extermination of the planetary environment, which was being brought to a head during my own lifetime, as I lived, and loved, and ate, and travelled, and in doing so helped, in my own deeply insignificant way, to bring this process to closure.

I stopped and looked Juan Diego squarely in the face. Both of our eyes were watering because of the pollution. He gestured behind my back and, turning round, I confronted a poster which was appended to the door of a cafe: 'Do you sometimes suffer from anxiety, depression, loneliness, nerves, insomnia or jealousy? Then you may be suffering from neurosis.' Yes, the whole world was suffering from a collective neurosis, a crisis of the will to survive in its battle against the will to die in a fog of flames and the smoke created by carbon fuels.

'Señor?' Juan Diego asked me, looking deeply concerned for my welfare, which was more than could be said for me. 'How about eating in there?'

'What!' I cried, 'and make things even worse for the damsels trapped inside!'

'The damsels?' he asked me. 'Look, señor, I won't tell you again. You really must leave these delusions behind you if you want your utopianism to thrive. I know that the modern world is full of people who claim that utopias can only lead to that sort of madness, but the fact is that it's your goal to show that that's wrong, and that it can go hand in glove with the most deep-seated reason.'

'Damsels,' I said again softly.

'So you'd better pull yourself together,' Juan Diego said. 'By damsels, of course, you mean waitresses. Well, *señor*, I can assure you that they don't feel trapped, and indeed if no one went in to eat they wouldn't thank you, as they'd have no work and would soon starve.'

'Of course you're right, Juan Diego,' I said weakly. 'You're right.'

So I followed him into the neurotic cafe and we sat down and ordered two sticky buns and some coffee. Juan Diego looked at me with a smile quivering at the corner of his lips, and then gave me a pep talk that brought me back to my senses.

'Look, *señor*,' he said, 'I can see that you're finding this vast, carbuncular city of ours difficult to come to terms with. And that's no surprise, really, for we find it just as bad as you do. This filthy monument to the empire of the Old World shows just how great is the need to replace it with something better. When we Mejicanos think of the beauty of the old city of the Mexica which was built here, the clear light which used to illuminate the volcanoes – their Gods – which we never see now because of the smog, we shiver with sadness. Often it seems to us that God had the European empire build its largest expression right here, on the site of the grandest achievement of the empires of the pre-Columbian world, just to remind us of the horror and evil of what happened in those awful times.'

'That's it, Juan Diego,' I said.

'But a sorry face never saved a damsel in distress,' my squire continued, 'and the only people who are happy to live in the past are those who were born there. The important thing is not to beat about the bush, but to jump up and down on it, crush it, and bury it mercilessly so that no one will ever dig it up again. And so, as they say, if you can't stand the heat, get out of the kitchen, and as the whole world's going to be cooking fairly soon at least there's some hope of full stomachs for all concerned, which is the same thing as saying that the future does not have to be like the past, because nothing's as inexorable as the laws of nature, and so if we really believe in this Darwinism, if that's our basic credo, our new religion in all but name, then we'll soon see that survival's more important than a few oil fields, figures in a bank account, and the erection of phallic architectural monuments to a doomed empire.'

'What are you saying, Juan Diego?' I asked, as our buns arrived. 'Do you mean that, in spite of everything, you've got some hope where the future's concerned?'

'Yes, and much more so since you appeared,' he answered. 'Because even though you've needed a crazed touchstone thus far, I'm quite happy with the critique that you've given of things as they stand. Like Thomas More, you've spent the first part of your utopian voyage showing us what a terrible state of affairs we're in. You've shown me to my satisfaction that information overload, the pandering to base human instincts, and the ecological destruction of our planet are the three main barriers to happiness and fulfilment for people all over the world. And I've no doubt that, with my help, you'll be able to present some passable ideas as to how to put all that right – and recover your reason.'

'Yes, Juan Diego,' I said, tearing into my bun with renewed relish. 'You're right. That's why I came here to preach my gospel after all: it's the only way forward.'

'Yes indeed, *señor*,' said Juan Diego, 'but one thing you mustn't forget is that people who think they're always right are generally wrong, and that although too many cooks spoil the broth it's better to pretend to seek the approval of the international community before adopting the unilateral stance you've decided on beforehand. That's another way of saying that your ideas might be interesting, but you must be prepared to accept that some of them will appear downright crazy, because although no one recognises the Messiah unless He announces that that's who He is, no one believes in salvation any more, and so you'll have to tread carefully if you don't want to end up in politics or an asylum, which is much the same thing.'

I realised that what Juan Diego had said was very true. I had to tone down my self-belief, and adopt a more humble attitude, or else no one would realise how right I was where everything was concerned. But still, there was no doubt that this journey after Quiroga had brought me into much closer contact with the burning problems of the day, and had reinforced in me the need for some sort of utopian solution.

We had both finished our buns by now. We pushed back our chairs as one, leaving another gold coin on the table, and made our way out into the clogged city. I knew that Santa Fe de México, the place where Quiroga had formed his first utopian community, was not too far off. Looking into the distance, I imagined I saw the place rising up like a heavenly vision above the smog. The road was straight, true and easy to follow (it was a vision, after all) – surely it couldn't take us very long to reach our goal.

SEVEN

The licenciates Quiroga and Maldonado crest the pass beyond Tlaxcala and descend into the valley of Mexico. The air here is chill, beards their stubbled chins with hoarfrost. The panorama is etched in crisp lines, both familiar and strange, as the still waters of the lake mingle with the rising dawn light and the ridges beyond. The road heaves with carts and Indians bearing enormous loads to and from the city,[1] but the way is easy now; excitement and relief mingle with apprehension as they descend rapidly, like divine spirits from the white heaven of Popocatépetl, and see the city before them. It seems to be a timeless vision, stilled in the aeons of history, and yet already, on 9 January 1531 – less than ten years after Cuáhtemoc's surrender to Cortés – Quiroga knows that this world has changed irrevocably.

Since that great day, much of the lake has been drained, and there are now fields of crops and grazing cattle where once the valley had been steeped in blue mystery. The heartland of the Mexica is filled with the water mills that Nuño de Guzmán and his *oidores* have had built.[2] The waterwheels, like the imported trees and livestock, remind the colonists of home, but they have also created problems, taking water away from the Indians so that they cannot irrigate their crops as they did in the past.[3] The land is also drier, and the grass shorter, than before the conquest, as the shortfall in irrigation has already begun to combine with the effects of imported cattle. The dry, stubby grasses crunch slightly as they go, following the Camino Real.

A few years ago, just after the conquest, Rodrigo de Albornoz claimed that cannibalism among the Mexica had been due in part to the absence of cattle.[4] But in fact their human sacrifice had always been ceremonial, and never a matter of satisfying hunger. While Quiroga sees the herds of animals as reassuring, a sign of progress, for the indigenous peoples the new animals will be a disaster. Just as, in almost five centuries' time, the rainforests and indigenous peoples of Amazonia will make way for the raising of livestock, so in Mexico, by the end of the sixteenth century, the explosion in the numbers of stock will play a vital role in deforestation and in the Indian population's disappearance from the lands that they still cherish as theirs.[5]

Approaching the city, Quiroga and Maldonado see the pastures sprinkled with the animals that they know, and with which they have been raised. The cows and bulls and heifers and bullocks roam contentedly across the grass. Their hooves raise a trail of dust that mingles with the intense blue of the sky and sits, almost intangible, over the settlers. The animals eat remorselessly, chewing up the roots and gradually making for the spread of orchards that extends for more than a league beyond the city walls.[6] The trees are still green but withering: a veil hangs over Mexico, long before the arrival of the contamination that will make this the most polluted city in the world.

In the distance, a crowd of people can be seen, fast approaching. The settlers have been ordered to make a great fuss over the new *oidores*. Ceynos and Salmerón come to greet Quiroga and Maldonado, and the four *oidores* enter the city with much ceremony, two standing on either side of the mule bearing the chest with the royal seal, with one both in front of and behind the animal.[7] All those hidalgos who own horses have been ordered to ride out and greet the *oidores* on penalty of a fine of five pesos, and so the judges are surrounded by horses, which have been brought over from Spain, Jamaica and Santo Domingo, their coats white with sweat induced by the crowds of people and the general excitement. The more important the settler, the more luxurious the saddle and, as in Spain and Portugal, some of the men have saddles embossed with silver and even with gold, with the style of the bit being seen as a particular sign of status.[8]

Followed by a huge crowd of horses, Spaniards and Indians, and greeted by all the major dignitaries, the *oidores* pass into Mexico, moving along streets decked out in flowers and garlanded with elaborate hangings.[9] The city smells sweet. The whites of the houses offset the strong colours of the blooms perfectly. The sky is shaded a sharp blue that lends it the aspect of an ocean. The *oidores* pass through the Spanish quarter, in which several thousand people live, and where there are more than 400 main houses,[10] all made of chalk and stone, two convents, and a hospital that has been built by Cortés on the very spot where he first met the Emperor Montezuma. Water is piped to each home, a comfort that is unheard of in Castile. The streets are 'wide and extensive', the houses 'beautiful and magnificent'[11] – some even have turrets – and yet, despite the opulence, now that Quiroga has at last arrived, he cannot dispel the uncomfortable sense of fragmentation that has dogged him ever since Veracruz.

Just as with the valley beyond, this bold, opulent, European Mexico is a very different place from that which the conquistadors discovered for the first time just twelve years ago. That city was razed to the ground during the siege before the conquest, and barely anything was left standing by the Spanish and their Tlaxcalan and Texcocan allies. The Mexica had preferred to 'marry the earth',*[12] seeing their home destroyed, rather than to give it up to these false, pallid gods.[13] Trapped in their city, they had starved, eating grass and tree cuttings whilst surrounded by the corpses of their fellows, unable to access the land beyond the lake.[14] Had they been cannibals pure and simple, they would have suffered no hunger, but the Mexica saw the consumption of human flesh as a sacred rite, and they went hungry: the decimation of their world ensured that 'the sobs of the women and children were such that they broke the men's hearts'.[15]

Even once Cuáhtemoc had capitulated, the suffering of the erstwhile imperial masters had not ceased. Massacres and looting by the Tlaxcalans and Texcocans had followed. Bodies had littered the streets for days, and some believe that 240,000 people were killed.[16] The city was levelled during the fighting, and has had to be rebuilt; naturally, the Indians have done all the work. Cortés has had the city made even bigger than before, so that there are almost twice the number of houses,[17] and such has been the amount of building work undertaken that, at the peak of the labour, 'so many people were walking in the streets that some roads could hardly be crossed'.[18] But the new city today is inevitably built on the bones and ashes of the massacred, and some vestiges of the atrocity – a smell, a sense of dread, the rapacity of the fighting dogs who are used to tearing bodies apart – linger on as the four *oidores* reach the plaza which is at the centre of the Spanish quarter, and is the giant, brooding heart of the new city.

Suddenly everything stills for a moment, as if for the crowd to consider what is to follow (and what has already been done). The arcades of the main buildings are already in place, and their façades glint in the sunlight. The procession halts before the doors to the *casas viejas*, one of the two palaces which Cortés has had built for his own use, a mansion of staggering opulence that contains fifty-two smaller houses that are used as shops and storehouses:[19] at each corner of the palace is a tower, built of forbidding black masonry,[20] with crenellations that remind Quiroga of Castile. It is in this dominant setting that the

*As the verb 'to die' could be translated in Nahuátl.

oidores will begin their work, although they will soon be ordered by the crown to move into the other of Cortés's palaces, the *casas nuevas*. As he stares up at the mullioned windows of his new home, something of the forbidding character of his task filters through to Quiroga; his eyes catch the extravagant coats of the rich colonists, the coppery skin of the Indians, and the thick, penitential habits of the friars, whose bare feet remind him of the nobility of religion, of devotion.

Unaccustomed to the altitude, Quiroga catches his breath as the unloading begins. The chest with the seal is carried up the steps into the palace. Crates are borne by Indian porters, and Quiroga watches as his books – some of his most prized possessions – disappear inside. A cloud of dust hangs over the wide plaza, raised by the feet of those who have followed the procession, and also by the many building works still being carried out in the city – something which reminds Quiroga of Seville. What is different is that here the Indians sing day and night as they labour,[21] to console themselves as they raise up (and entomb) the city, and their high-pitched harmonies sear through Quiroga's ears as he stands there, wondering at how different this hemisphere will be from that which he has known.

Yes, both continents have recently been taken over by a fervour of construction. He has already seen the tasteless pleasure house that Nuño de Guzmán has built on the Tacuba causeway, ripping down the former hermitage to St Lazarus to make way for it. Now he can see the other new buildings which have gone up since the 'government' of the First Audiencia began: gleaming palaces which Delgadillo, Matienzo and Guzmán have built for themselves on land which had belonged to Cortés, using the carved wood and stone which Cortés had previously reserved for himself.[22]

Such greed! It is hard for Quiroga to take it all in: this new city in a new world, the ragged children crawling through the streets of the Indian quarter beyond the Spanish enclave, the wails of the packs of dogs scavenging and tearing at whatever scraps they find. In a few months' time, the first epidemic of measles, the next great disease to follow the smallpox epidemic, will break out. Is there no hope for these miserable wretches, brought into the reach of God by His bounty and yet wasting away into nothingness?

Quiroga follows his possessions into the palace. Beyond the city, the afternoon sunlight illuminates the mountains and the minerals glittering upon them. Popocatépetl smokes. The paddles of canoes clutch at the lake and echo like heartbeats over the water. But the Indian pulse is weak and fading, and any sense of how powerful it once was is already beginning to eke away into the skies overhead, together with the fires of the houses which are kindled by night, as if both the Spanish and the Mexica have decided to build a monumental funeral pyre to that pre-Cortesian world which is no more.

As things stand, there is almost nothing to tell Quiroga how great this civilisation had been fifteen years and several human aeons ago, when the children of the sun had been unknown in the New World.

'When we saw all those cities and villages built in the water, and that straight and level causeway leading to Mexico, we were astounded. These great towns and [temples] rising from the water, all made of stone, seemed like an enchanted vision of Amadis. Indeed, some of our soldiers asked whether it was not all a dream ... It was all so wonderful that I do not know how to describe this first glimpse of things never heard of, seen or dreamed of before.'[23]

Bernal Díaz's famous description of the Spaniards' feelings on first seeing Mexico before them has never been bettered. Amadis, the romantic saga par excellence – later to be much mocked by Cervantes – introduced the New World to the conquistadors through their imaginations; it was no wonder that works of fiction would be banned for those that followed them.* Here in Mexico they would fight rousting battles (and win), they would conquer unfathomable odds (virtually unscathed), and gain heroic riches for themselves (and Christ): they would, in fact, come to embody their own chivalric tale, rendering the yarns of knight errants, so beloved of Don Quixote, unnecessary.†

But the Spanish were not the only ones to see Mexico in the lyrical terms of the imagination when they crested the pass. These are the thoughts of an ambassador from Huexotzingo to the capital on seeing the valley:

> I climb; I reach the height.
> The huge blue-green lake

*See above, ch. 4, p. 67.
†Indeed, one wonders whether Cervantes – whose great book is filled with send-ups of virtually everyone imaginable – is not alluding to this 'real-life chivalry' in the Americas. The fact that so much of the European perception of the Americas in the sixteenth century was distorted by the imagination, that novels had been banned in the New World, and that there was a similarity between the heroic tales of these stories and those performed in the New World, implies that at least some of the conquistadors may have seen themselves in this light. But, in Cervantes's book, Don Quixote and Sancho's brave escapades usually end in pain; the implication is that deeds of derring-do carry with them their own price in blood.

Now quiet, now angry,
Foams and sings among the rocks ...
Flowery water, green-stone water,
Where the splendid swan
With its rippling feathers
Calling swims to and fro.[24]

This civilisation was sited in a place of pristine natural beauty, surrounded by a crown of mountains and gilded by the diaphanous light; certainly, it did not take long for the wonder of Mexico to become apparent to the aspiring Spanish heroes.

The valley was filled with a large lake known as Texcoco, in which the most important Mexican cities were built, some on islands, others on the shore, and others half in the lake and half on land. Here were Texcoco, Tacuba, Iztapalapa and Tenochtitlan itself, cities that were 'better ordered than those in Spain, with very beautiful streets and squares'.[25] The palaces were built of stone and beams of cedar, with huge chambers and courtyards sheltered by canopies of cotton.[26] In Iztapalapa, the paths in the palace gardens could take four people walking abreast, and there were so many birds that they almost completely covered the waters of the lagoon;[27] the colours of their feathers dazzled in the brilliant light. In Mexico itself, the emperor's palace had a reception room that could hold 3000 guests;[28] on an upper floor was a space where thirty horsemen could race one another, as if in a plaza,[29] and 300 people were employed solely in looking after the countless birds living on the lagoons there.[30]

Naturally, this great wealth was founded in conquest. The Mexica were convinced that their historical role was to dominate other nations and that their fate was to expand.[31] As with other imperial peoples, this domination was couched in terms of divinity, for the Emperor of the Mexica was himself semi-divine,[32] and their Gods peopled the world as earthly beings so that the cosmos was full of divinity.[33] Every thread of the earth's fabric was sacred; every thread had to be subjugated to the divine purpose of the Mexica; and so their officials executed the schemes of the gods, which were ever more bellicose, as the people of Tenochtitlan directed their attentions to conquering and plundering their neighbours.[34]

The opulence that resulted far outdid anything in Europe. The houses of the Mexican aristocracy were so vast that it was possible to visit them several times and still not see everything.[35] They had sumptuous gardens, in which the paths were 'choked with roses and other flowers, and the many local fruit-trees and rose-bushes ... Everything was shining with lime and decorated with different kinds of stonework and paintings which were a marvel to gaze on.'[36] Away from the mists of winter, the sky was a clear blue, lending an intensity to the colour of the snows atop Popocatépetl, to the evergreen forests of cypress, to the yellow shoots of the thorny acacia trees, and to the oak and alder woods that climbed up the mountainsides. The land was fertile, and the grasses rose halfway up a person's legs,[37] swishing in the breezes that sent ripples arcing over Lake Texcoco. The lake itself was dotted with small islands, floating gardens which were heavily cultivated.

In the midst of such beauty, however, the essential violence of the world was never lost. Bloodshed was stripped of its arbitrariness by becoming sanctified through human sacrifice, with victims being carried to the altars of the large temples, which ascended into the sky. Beyond the countless monuments to their gods, who drank blood, like vampires, the smouldering volcano hinted still further at the inclinations of the world towards brutality. The Spanish, like the Mexicans, were in awe of Popocatépetl when they first saw it, and to Cortés the smoke appeared to be 'like a large house'.[38] The ash drifted out across the sky, a cloud that smudged the heavens with foreboding.

In spite of the symbols of destruction, though, there was much to distract the Mexica from their fears. Descending from the pass which brought travellers from the coast, three causeways led across Lake Texcoco to Tenochtitlan itself. They were raised on stone and earth, and were broken up by bridges, which could be raised if necessary. The causeways were thirty paces wide,[39] and usually filled with people moving to and from the city with goods to sell at the great market of Tlatelolco. The lake, too, was crammed with people, paddling their canoes of goods towards the market: here were slaves, attached to one another by collars and long poles like their equivalents in Oran, and also loads of livestock and jewellery, vegetables, fruit and fabrics, dealers in the prized delicacy of chocolate – never seen by Europeans before their arrival in Mexico, where the cocoa bean was the main currency – and, most bizarrely of all, 'many canoe-loads of human excrement ... for the manufacture of salt and the curing of skin'.[40] In fact, all the roads in Mexico possessed shelters in which travellers could retire to empty their bowels 'in order that their excrement [should] not be lost'.[41]

The stench from the faeces mingled with the smells of the sweating crowd making for Tenochtitlan, where the plaza of Tlatelolco's marketplace was three times the size of the plaza in Salamanca.[42] This was not a stagnant, ossified city, but 'the young capital of a society in full development, of a civilisation in full progression, and of an empire that was still in the making'.[43] On some days, 60,000 people descended, and all the Spanish readily admitted that they 'had never seen such a thing before':[44] the chatter of the people mingled with the tweeting mass of bird-life – partridges, turtle doves, parrots, turkeys, falcons, eagles, owls and more[45] – to create a noise that 'was loud enough to be heard more than three miles away'.[46] The colours of the fruits and vegetables and spices glittered in the light.

Beyond the market, the city itself was so extraordinary that Cortés felt that he could not describe even a hundredth part of its majesty.[47] In addition to the plaza of Tlatelolco, there was another plaza twice the size of that at Salamanca. The verges were filled with sweet-smelling flowers – as if to compensate for the excrement – providing yet more colours to dazzle on streets that were so spotless 'that there was not a straw or grain of dust to be found there',[48] with people rising before dawn to sweep them clean.[49] Many of the thoroughfares were canals which could only be traversed in canoes, as in Venice. The water lapped at the walls of the flat-topped houses that were linked to one another by drawbridges over the waterways. One whole quarter was filled by entertainers, 'dancers and stilt-walkers, and some who seemed to fly through the air, and men rather like clowns'.[50] Often, these people performed on *tianguiz*, stages on which farces and pantomimes were acted out,[51] and where there were dances in which the participants, dressed as birds or butterflies, were showered with rose petals. Celebrations reached their pitch during human sacrifice, when the victims were urged not to be unhappy.[52]

The biggest sacrificial festival of all was that given in honour of Tezcatlipoca, where the man to be sacrificed was selected a year in advance and treated as the image of this god throughout this time: twenty days before the festival, four women came to be with him, and they would have uninterrupted sexual intercourse until five days before the sacrifice, when the great parties and banquets would begin.[53] Then, as he was carried up to be sacrificed, musical instruments rang out,[54] and they did not stop as his heart was wrenched free and left to pulse on the earth, whence it had come, whilst the living danced and sang and ate in this great celebration of existence which was existence itself.

Yet not everything in this Mexico was uninterrupted joy and a sanctification of life through lifeblood. This realm was 'a place of crying and affliction and unhappiness',[55] where 'there was no pleasure that was not next to much sadness, no rest which was not next to great affliction'.[56] The old people used to say that this world was a great trickster, 'laughing at some, enjoying others, mocking and humiliating others; everything in it is full of lies, and there is no truth';[57] even death itself was a passage only into utter oblivion, for 'no one thinks of the dead; people only consider the present, which is managing to eat and drink and search out life, building houses and working to live'.[58] A Nahuátl poem expressed the zeitgeist of the Mexica as their flowering neared its end:

> Shall my heart go
> As flowers that wither?
> Some day shall my name be nothing?
> My fame nothing, anywhere upon the earth?
> At least let us have flowers! At least let us have some singing!
> How shall my heart manage (to survive)?
> We go about on the earth in vain.[59]

Such, then, were the beauty and horror of Mexico, such the Mexica's poetic grasp of life, before the arrival of the Spanish and their elaborate and equally blood-strewn imaginations.

The *oidores* have arrived and installed themselves in the *casas viejas*. While the palaces of the nobles of the Mexica may well have been so big that it was possible to get lost in them, the same is true of the mansion in which Quiroga has initially settled himself. Parts of the building are raised to a second storey, and it is here that the chambers for the Audiencia and apartments for each of the *oidores* are located.[60] Looking down from his balcony, Quiroga can see the inner courtyards, which are ringed by covered passages whose ceilings are propped up by colonnades and arcades of brick, wood and stone.[61] It is down at this level that the two kitchens, and countless shops and workshops are situated.

But in spite of the scale of the mansion it is not big enough to suit its station as the capital of the new Spanish colony, where it must be able to smother the *naturales* with its Christian love. Tenochtitlan – 'the place of the prickly pear'[62] – had been perhaps three-quarters of the size of ancient Rome,[63] its temples rivalling even the cathedral of Seville. So the Spanish buildings must be even greater, and this city even more opulent: throughout 1531, the work of roofing the *casas nuevas* will be carried out by Indians from nearby Coyoacán, the village where Cortés has a hacienda, and in order to finish the building there will need to be a further 700 cedar beams, 15,200 boards and sixty window shutters. Meanwhile, across the giant plaza, Bishop Zumárraga is in the process of spending the first four years of his see's income on expanding the cathedral.[64]

The activity is extraordinary – among the Indians, if not the Spanish. The labourers are all Indian and they find the building materials at their own expense, most often by using the rubble of the houses that stood before the conquest, bringing the rocks into the city on their backs, and paying the masons and carpenters themselves, as well as providing their own food;[65] in virtually all ways, in fact, the trappings of the old empire feed and inspire the new. Of course a glorious Christian city needs to be built on this site which once housed such barbarism, and the *naturales* must be made to recognise the divine justice of the European conquest; nevertheless, watching the incessant labours of the Mexica – first under the hot sun, and then by torchlight at night – Quiroga feels the first stirring of a rage that transcends mere disquiet, as he sees the indolence of most of the Spanish settlers.

These spoiled, rapacious layabouts do nothing; they fester in their own idleness, admire one another's clothes and horses; they gossip and intrigue incessantly. Do they not see that their wealth is driving these *naturales* into the ground, grinding them down as ants beneath the heel of a boot, suffocating them, burying them, burning them in the hellfire of disease and work that goes unrewarded (in this world)? Have they no shame? Burning to death – even as Jewish heretics – would be too good for them.*

Quiroga cannot abide idleness. The journey from Spain has been a long one, but it has also forced him into inactivity, and, along with the other three *oidores*, he now throws himself into a fury of governance, as the new Audiencia tries to overcome the crisis which has arisen during the previous two years, under the guidance of Nuño de Guzmán.

The members of the First Audiencia had been appointed following Cortés's catastrophic expedition in Honduras in pursuit of his enemy Cristóbal de Olid. Leaving in August 1524, Cortés had taken an army of Mexica and Spaniards into the swamps of Tabasco. Arriving in Tabasco he had sent ahead to the local caciques for a drawing of the

---

*The first inquisitorial auto-da-fé had taken place in Mexico in 1528, with the burning of Hernando Alonso, the ironsmith on Cortés's original expedition, and a merchant called Gonzalo de Morales, on charges of judaising.

Thomas More, author of *Utopia*. More was beheaded on 6 July 1535, just 2 days after Vasco de Quiroga completed his most famous work, the 'Información en Derecho'.

Map of the Island of Utopia, with the colophon of the original book – set by More in the New World.

VTOPIAE INSVLAE FIGVRA

VTOPIENSIVM ALPHABETVM.

Tetrastichon vernacula Vtopiensium lingua.

Horum versuum ad verbum hæc est sententia.
Vtopus me dux ex non insula fecit insulam
Vna ego terrarum omnium absq philosophia
Ciuitatem philosophicam expressi mortalibus
Libéter impartio mea, nó grauatim accipio meliora.

Seville in the 16th century, from where Quiroga departed for New Spain in August 1530. The prominent tower is the Giralda, originally a mosque.

Emperor Charles V, ruler of Spain and the New World, as well as much of Europe. Charles sent Quiroga to Mexico in 1530 as a member of the ruling council.

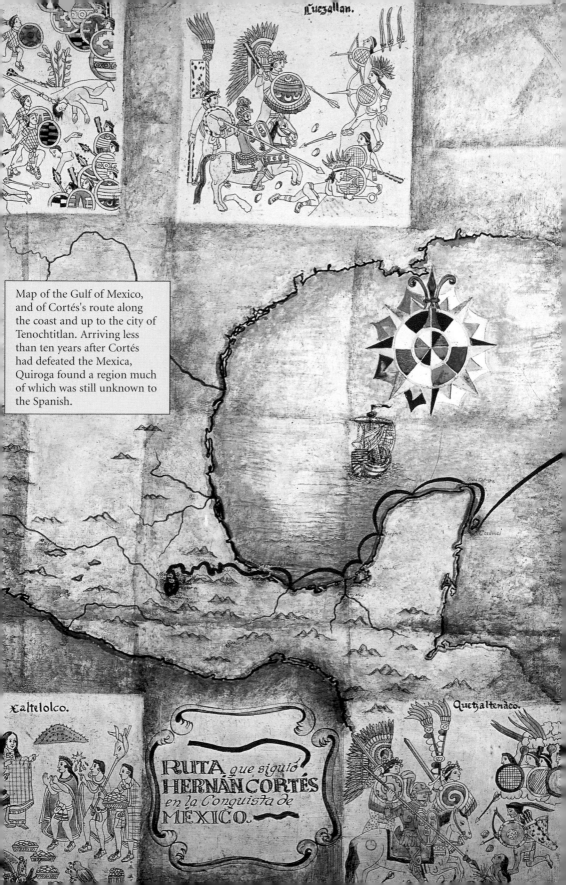

Map of the Gulf of Mexico, and of Cortés's route along the coast and up to the city of Tenochtitlan. Arriving less than ten years after Cortés had defeated the Mexica, Quiroga found a region much of which was still unknown to the Spanish.

RUTA *que siguió* HERNÁN CORTÉS *en la Conquista de* MÉXICO.

Island capital of the Mexica. Tenochtitlan – 'the place of the prickly pear' – was the Venice of the New World.

Above right Hernando Cortés, conquistador of Mexico.

Right The Spanish take Tenochtitlan. The last Emperor of the Mexica, Cuáhtemoc, finally surrendered on 13 August 1521.

Spanish massacre Cholulans. Cholula was one of the spiritual centres of the Mexica, rumoured to have over 400 temples.

Spanish massacre the Mexica. The numbers of dead in the siege of Tenochtitlan may have reached as many as 240,000.

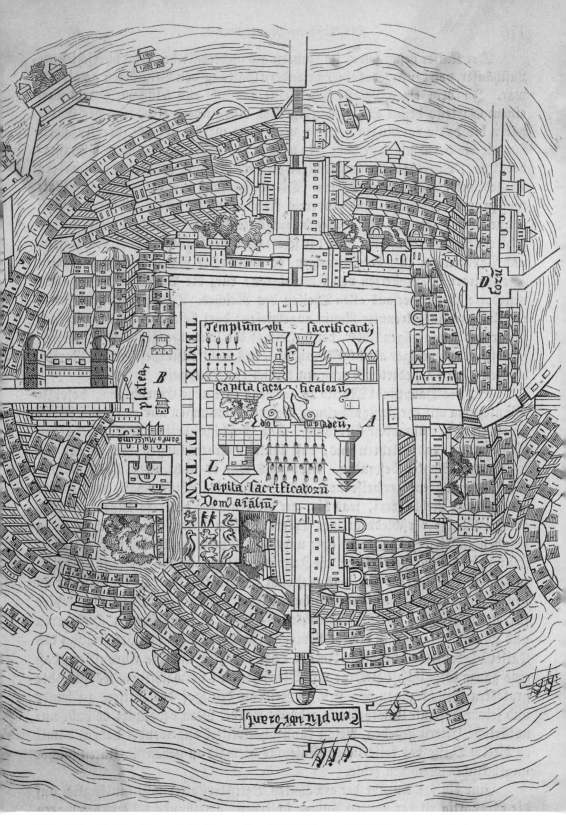

Plan of Tenochtitlan. The capital of the empire of the Mexica was divided into a network of canals, and several large plazas, including Tlatelolco.

Human sacrifice by the Mexica. Human sacrifice was always religious, never brought on by hunger; the Mexica did not resort to cannibalism during the terrible siege of their capital by the Spanish.

path he should take, and had then launched through the swamps, ordering the Indians with him to build fifty bridges for the Spanish to cross.[66] Although warned by the Tabascan lords that this whole territory was 'depopulated, because the Spanish had robbed and burnt it',[67] Cortés had been disappointed at the lack of Indians. Hearing news of an uprising in Mexico, he had executed Cuáhtemoc, son of the last Mexican emperor, thinking that it was the Indians who had revolted; but, on returning to Mexico in June 1526, it had become clear that the upheavals had been due to Spanish infighting, provoked by the very absence of Cortés.

Desiring a more reliable instrument of royal power, Charles V had appointed the First Audiencia under Nuño de Guzmán; but this had been even worse, and some of the stories which Quiroga now hears are enough to tear a Christian's heart to shreds, as he sees at first hand how the government of the First Audiencia has disintegrated into avarice and the collapse of the rule of law: in 1529, Tzintzicha, the indigenous leader of Michoacán, had been imprisoned in Mexico for two months until a ransom of 800 ingots of gold, and 1000 of silver, had been paid to Nuño de Guzmán;* meanwhile 113 Indians from Huexotzingo had died in carrying the daily tribute required of them the eighteen leagues to Mexico,[68] while Guzmán, Matienzo and Delgadillo had seized over 100,000 Indians for themselves.[69] The First Audiencia has also stripped Cortés's followers of their *encomiendas*, taking them for their own use and that of their cronies, so that 'in a short time ... this [has] become a society filled with hatred, composed as it [is] of robbed and robbers'.[70]

The private lives of the wicked president and *oidores*, it transpires, have been equally scandalous. They have stopped going to church every Sunday, and started holding Sunday banquets instead, as a slight to the clergy, with whom they have been in perpetual dispute.[71] It seems as if they feel that there is no longer any need for pretence as to the atavistic, dissolute nature of this conquest. With the orgies conducted in the chamber of the Audiencia itself,† the implosion of order in New Spain is complete, so that notaries now charge vast sums for the slightest piece of work, while, after their recent experiences, the bishops and mendicants have become resistant to all civil power. Luxury and dissolution are 'corrupting all social classes',[72] and everyone is interested solely in what they can get for themselves.

*See below, ch. 10, p. 176.
†See above, ch. 4, p. 68.

The new Audiencia must rebuild a sense of order. Charles V has also instructed the *oidores* to investigate the extent of the holdings of Cortés – about which there is much disagreement – and to produce a full account of all the towns and villages of New Spain. Even at a time when bureaucratic legalese adopts the minds of the most violent people – with the conquistadors drawing up complex documents in the most improbable situations to determine the exact rights and duties of all[73] – the administrative task is immense. Only three months after their arrival, they are beginning to baulk at the scale of their task, writing to the Empress on 30 March 1531 that they have so much to do that they frequently do not get to sleep until three or four in the morning. The president of the new Audiencia, Sebastian Fuenleal, will not arrive for another six months, and, they say, 'So many difficulties have arisen that even if we had a very prudent president, things would be very hard.'[74]

Quiroga's work is exhausting. Riding to the nearby towns and villages, he tries to get a feel for the true state of affairs. Because of the salty land around Mexico, the horses are often lame.[75] There is still such a shortage of mounts that their backs are riddled with sores: as the months elapse, the winter chill dissipates, and flies begin to congregate around the open wounds. With his mounts hobbling along the lakeside roads, beset by waves of insects, Quiroga visits the towns which have been granted to Cortés, and about which there are such violent disputes. The whitewashed walls, waterwheels, orchards and vineyards are all reminiscent of Spain, and should be restful. Yet, beneath the superficial tranquillity there is much hostility. The Indians are increasingly rebellious, while the allies of Cortés obstruct the investigations of the Audiencia. They do not want the reality of the situation to become apparent, for the Crown suspects the Marquis of the Valley of Mexico to hold five times the 23,000 vassals that have been granted him by Charles V.

Before dusk, Quiroga returns to Mexico, where beyond the Spanish neighbourhood is a scene redolent of Dante's Inferno. There are four Indian quarters – San Juan, San Sebastián, San Pablo, and Santa María Cuepopan – in each of which Quiroga discerns that 'their way of living is all chaos and confusion'.[76] Entering the houses of the poor, he is chastened by the scenes of indigence and drunkenness which everywhere surround him. Many of the elders are dead, killed in the wars or in the mines, so that the young have few figures of authority to turn to. The rapes committed by the conquistadors have produced mestizo adolescents who roam the streets 'in packs like wolves, [doing] whatever they [have] to in order to survive'.[77] There appears to be no limit to the suffering that the Indians are to endure.

Disturbed by these scenes, Quiroga passes into the sanctuary of the European enclave. The protective walls have been built up as if to shield the Spanish from contagion by the poverty, and the environmental and social disintegration that they themselves have wrought. Lost within the confines of their part of the city, the settlers distract themselves with their own disputes and claims against one another. There is so much jockeying for power that the horror of the external reality beyond these machinations is easily forgotten; but Quiroga is now distressed beyond measure. When the numerous cases brought by allies and foes of Cortés have ended for the day, together with the long arguments over the numbers of the Marquis's vassals, and night has fallen, his mind falls back to the tragedy which mounts up outside the Spanish settlement.

It is surely impossible to live in this despairing world and not to seek a reconciliation of some sort with those who are being oppressed. Quiroga knows that he needs an ally, and so, attracted by his evident care for the fate of the Indians, and by his humanism, he turns to Zumárraga, who is now a balding man with a neatly trimmed beard, and a handsome, gentle face which acts as a counterpoint to the growing severity of Quiroga. The bishop's eyes are dark, welcoming, but yet also betray anxiety; a slight frown mark creases the space between his eyebrows.

Both men have so much work to do, and live in such a state of unease that they now find sleep an unnecessary luxury. Cristóbal Cabrera, Quiroga's companion between 1538 and 1545, will write that his master sleeps hardly at all:[78] like so many people, he finds losing himself in his work an excellent way of dealing with his situation. Zumárraga, too, is a man who suffers from perpetual exhaustion.[79] And so they meet at night, when the great travails of each day are at an end, and the blackness is interrupted only by threads of light in the Spanish quarter, and by the nightmares of the Mexica, who see dwarf women and death's heads and monsters gyrating on the ground when they consider darkness:*

---

*Many clues point to the fact that the two men met often. The first is that Quiroga was clearly reading Zumárraga's copy of *Utopia* in these months (see ff., this chapter); and, in 1535, that when Quiroga was appointed to the diocese of Michoacán, Zumárraga expressed a 'holy envy' that Quiroga had done so many good works while fulfilling his role as *oidor*, cit. Fintan B. Warren (1963), op. cit.

– It is a horror, Don Fray Juan. The *naturales* are being destroyed before our eyes.

– It is so, Don Vasco. But yet, in spite of our doubts, we must recall that Saint Thomas Aquinas, of holy memory, asserted that war was justifiable for Christians, and even that, when war is just, it is worthy of praise and heavenly honour.[80] And we know that the *naturales* of this land were in great need of our coming. I have smitten down their idols with my own hands, but still cannibals and idolaters remain in large numbers. You have seen the remains of their great temples at Cholula, four hundred times a Babel![81] You have sensed the blood that still curdles in their hearts.

– Of course, Don Fray Juan. But how may they be brought to the knowledge of Christ when such barbarity is inflicted upon them? You know that they are treated with such cruelty that every day they lose their fear and shame before us, making themselves more daring and bellicose because of the very nature of the things which they learn through their intercourse with us![82] Does not Erasmo make clear that it is through the practice of the doctrine of Christ that genuine conversions may be made?[83] This must be our tool for evangelising, for the *naturales* will never learn the true faith when they are beset by thieves and apostates who are Christians only in name.

– You are right, Don Vasco.

– And so we must organise the *naturales*. We must found more *congregaciones*, and show even more zeal in their conversion. This is a world where we see the apocalypse coming upon us, and only a holy republic may dilute the effect of what is to come.[84] At least in this way, we may yet find that this hell on earth is lessened, and the sins of our brother Spaniards cleansed.

– Indeed, Don Vasco. And through the inspiration of the Holy Spirit I have found myself in the possession of a learned work by one Tomás Moro, native of England, a description both of the world of the Indies, and of the great blessing of a heaven on earth which may yet be realised. I have it here with me, an edition of Basle of 1518. I shall lend it to you so that you might see how this world may yet be saved.[85]

As dawn approaches, the two men part. With More's *Utopia* in his hand, Vasco stands on the balcony, listening to the plangent tunes of the surviving Mexica as they work. These people can surely not see the Christians in the guise of redeemers when all they bring them is torture, disease, bereavement, death. Do not the Mexica themselves believe that Hell is peopled by the souls of those who have died of disease?[86] How will they ever be brought to believe in the true faith, when all that they have learnt from the Christians is grasping and misery?

There must be a means of rekindling more positive emotions. Yes, there must be a better way, he tells himself, looking out over the Indian quarters, as the Mexica wake slowly from their hellish dreams.

For the Spanish, their arrival in the New World and the subjugation of the peoples that they found living there was a central part of God's plan. As Benito de Peñalosa y Mondragón, a friar writing in the early seventeenth century, put it, Spain was a 'new Israel', superior to any chosen people hitherto selected, 'because that nation [Israel] was never called to take the word of God to the New World, whose inhabitants appear to have been destined to be converted by this new chosen people'.[87]

In other words, the discovery of the Americas and their conquest by the Spanish was an essential element in the Spaniards' vision of themselves as a noble, gracious people. What was equally important was that this discovery had followed on, almost organically, from the final triumph of the reconquest in 1492, and the expulsion of the Jews, followed by the Moorish expulsions of 1502. To the devout monks and laypeople of the period, this must really have seemed a confirmation of the justice of their cause, of the truth of the Christian religion, and of their divine purpose on Earth.

This unquenchable belief in the objective goodness of their deeds underwrote the Spanish achievements in the Americas. On commissioning Cortés to lead the campaign to New Spain, Diego Velázquez had said that the first motive was to 'increase the dimension of our holy Catholic faith'.[88] This had not been lost on Cortés, and during his long battle campaign against the Mexica he gave a fiery speech to the assembled Spanish and Tlaxcalan troops in Tlaxcala, when he said that 'the principal reason for war ... was to preach the faith of Jesus Christ';[89] at the same time, he took pains to deal with scepticism in the ordinances that he issued to his army before the final attack on Mexico in 1521, which stated that 'no person whatsoever is to dare to say that they do not believe in God'.[90] This statement may also be interpreted as a reference to *conversos* among the party of conquistadors, who were seen as the breeding ground for scepticism in Spain at this time.* That Catholicism and its divine cause were the essential props of the conquest is also underpinned by the lengths to which the Crown went to prevent Jewish or Moslem converts from travelling to the New World.†

In addition to their religious fanaticism, a key element in the Spanish triumph in Mexico was their violent character, steeped in centuries of wars against the Moslems. The bloody conquests of the New World were merely extensions of the civil war between the factions of Isabella and La Beltraneja in the 1470s, the campaign against Granada of the 1480s and early 1490s, and the subsequent wars waged in North Africa. This was a people that had learnt the art of conquest in brutal terms, whereas the peoples of Mesoamerica fought in an entirely different way, seeking to capture their enemies alive and then sacrifice them to the Gods.[91] It is this that explains how the Spaniards were able to overcome such an extraordinary numerical disadvantage in their battles – combined with their secret weapons, epidemics and gunpowder, their violent heritage made the conquistadors impregnable.

Once Cuáhtemoc had submitted in 1521, the other seeds of the conquering Empire could easily be sewn. There were the mendicant friars, walking barefoot around the hinterland, preaching eternal love with one hand and stripping the Indians' connection to their Gods, their culture and their heritage away with the other. The *encomiendas* weakened the conquered peoples still further, and the final nail in the coffin of submission was the controversial question of slavery.

One of the main tasks that Charles V and Isabella had given to the Second Audiencia was to resolve slavery, a matter that the excesses of the First Audiencia had brought into sharper focus. The instructions to the new *oidores* were nowhere more detailed than in this regard:

---

*There were at least two *conversos* – Hernando Alonso and Diego Ordaz – among Cortés's party, and there may have been many more (see José Monín (1939), op. cit., pp. 71–2). This statement against scepticism supports this view, for at this time in Spain atheism and agnosticism were associated irrevocably with Judaism. From the twelfth century onwards, the intellectuals among Spanish Jewry had often sought to develop a rationalist philosophy, in which they could maintain the supernatural world while stipulating that the only role of divine providence was the general conservation of humanity. These people were Averroists, and a well-known Averroist saying was that 'In this world you will not see me in trouble, and in another world you will not see me in torment!' (Yitzhak Baer, (1966) op. cit, vol. II, p. 369); another Averroist motto about life was: 'To be born and die; all the rest is a snare and delusion' (ibid., vol. II, p. 274). In the context of Quiroga's life, it is interesting to note that one of the centres of this atheistic movement was Medina del Campo (see *Inquisición y Criptojudaismo* by Juan Blazquez Miguel (Madrid, Ediciones Kaydeda, 1988), p. 50).
†See above, ch. 4, p. 61.

they were to imprison Nuño de Guzmán for illegally exporting slaves to the Indies; ensure that no slave 'freed' from slavery among the Indians was enslaved again; discover the slaving customs among the Indians; compensate Indians that had been wrongly enslaved, and ensure that no slaves were now made in any shape or form – the African imports would have to suffice.[92]

However, these instructions were not without controversy. Given the Spaniards' incapacity for hard labour, the lack of Indian slaves would have – it was thought – a devastating effect on the economy of New Spain. As early as 22 January 1531 – less than two weeks after Quiroga's arrival – Oidor Salmerón wrote to the crown that, without slaves, 'the receipts from the mines will diminish and end up being very little or nothing'.[93] But Quiroga was not so convinced by the sob stories.

The conflict between Quiroga and the other *oidores* came to a head very quickly. When there was a rebellion of the Impilzinga Indians early in 1531, Salmerón ordered that the rebels should be enslaved; on being sent to investigate the division of slaves by Vasco de Porcallo, Quiroga found that most of the men had been killed, and so freed the women and children. At almost the same time, Quiroga and Salmerón reacted differently to a request from Cortés to attack nearby unconquered areas: together with Maldonado, Salmerón said that the conquest would assist everyone – God, king and conquistadors; but Quiroga fulminated that it was the Spanish activities themselves that were making the Indians more warlike.[94] His irritation with Quiroga is exemplified in Salmerón's later description of him as 'virtuous and most solicitous for the welfare of the Indians; but timid and scrupulous, therefore more apt to carry out orders than to give them'.[95]

Appropriately, this controversy had been sparked by disagreements regarding the great conquistador himself, Cortés. By May 1531, the *oidores* had seen enough to make an initial assessment of his holdings, and try to call him to account; but this would not be easy, for Cortés was still strong, and he was in the prime of life. In his late forties, his stocky frame exuded the power of the victor. His signature bore all the elaborate flourishes of a man sure of his rank. His coat of arms depicted a large cat with eagle wings sitting astride an armoured horse – for the Spanish had swooped with vicious feline claws, mounted upon what the Indians had seen as centaurs.

To judge from a portrait painted in 1528 during his visit to Spain,[96] Cortés's bearing at this time sought to marry that of the strutting possessor with that of the man who still sensed his accountability to God. In the painting he leans forward ever so slightly, as if inclining to prostrate himself. His eyebrows arch, framing the expression of someone who has seen cause to doubt many of the tales he has heard in life – indicating, perhaps, that he himself tells many lies. His hair is almost greasy, unkempt, but his chest is proud and wide. He walks bowlegged, the result of so many years sitting upon a horse. His stumpy legs are neatly divided by the long sword that hangs down from his belt and almost touches the floor. And yet, although the sword cannot be missed, Cortés does not grasp it by the handle: for, as the whole of Spain is all too well aware, this conquest has been wrought by God (and not through the bloody victories of men).

– Don Hernando Cortés, Marquis of the Valley of Mexico, on this day of May the second in the Year of Our Lord 1531, please be welcomed to the session of the Audiencia of Mexico, appointed by His Divine Majesty Charles, by the grace of God Holy Roman Emperor and King of Spain.

– Thank you, sirs, *oidores* of the Audiencia. I am familiar with the splendour of the palace. Was it not by my very orders that this room was built, in which we may all sit in such pomp and ceremony today? Ha! Yes indeed, do I not know it well?

– Of course, Don Hernando. God has been bountiful in His gifts. To you above all has He seen fit to bestow earthly blessings, and it is for this reason that today we have come to settle all questions and accounts.

– Ah yes, we must settle accounts. But it is all paid up, good sirs, all paid up! The Royal Fifth* was subtracted with great care at the time of the conquest, and everything is settled. It was not my doing that Alonso de Ávila was waylaid by French pirates.†

– Don Hernando, if you please, the Audiencia would begin its hearing.

Murmurs from the plaza pass through the thick walls of the palace. Outside, the light is strong, accentuating the heaviness of the chamber,

*The King of Spain was owed a fifth of all takings in the Indies, known as the 'Royal Fifth'.

†Carrying the Royal Fifth in a small fleet, Ávila – one of Cortés's captains – was attacked by the French pirate Jean Fleury, and the treasure was carried to Dieppe in France. All the gold thus ended up in the court of François I of France, Charles's sworn enemy. Most of it was melted down from the fabulous jewels which Ávila had been carrying, and so all but disappeared.

with its solid tables, and the tall doors leading out into the corridors and chambers beyond. Fretting and fidgeting, Cortés finally allows himself to settle into one of the high-backed chairs, knowing just how much is at stake: today, the Audiencia are finally to rule on which holdings Cortés must return to the Crown, and on which he may keep.

– Don Hernando, it is known that you have many vassals in the towns of Cuernavaca, Guatespeque, Tutepeque and Acapistla.[97] You have built yourself a sumptuous palace at Cuernavaca amid the cotton trees.[98] There you sit in pomp, as a lord over the Indians. You indulge yourself in the nine rivers that meet there, where the butterflies flutter and the birds call. The Mexica saw that place as a heaven on earth,[99] and like them you lie back as in paradise in the countless arbours and orchards that cover that land in greenness, in fruit and in flowers.

– But that right was granted me, sirs, by our Holy Emperor himself, as Marquis of the Valley of Mexico.

– Don Hernando, in taking the best land for yourself you were perhaps within your rights. But, as you know, it is our opinion that you have more than your agreed quota of vassals in these lands.

– Good sirs, our Holy Emperor granted me 23,000 vassals – and what does that refer to but to the number of heads of family? One may not call the weak, the infirm, women or children vassals as such. That title refers only to men such as you or I.

– Don Hernando, 23,000 vassals refers to the number of souls which our Holy Emperor sought to bestow on you, and not to heads of family. Such, as you know, is our firm opinion. And, furthermore, we have seen that even in the surrounding area there are many places which you control. Here in Mexico you had two palaces until we took this one for ourselves – and even this we have had to buy from you![100] The surroundings of the town of Coyoacán are thickly wooded,[101] and from these woods many of the materials for building here in Mexico must come – and yet you would have Coyoacán for yourself, as well as all the other riches which Mexico has brought you! Tacubuya is another town which you would have! A limit must be made, Don Hernando. A line must be drawn.

– By the Lord and the Apostles and all that is holy! One would think that it was you yourselves who had risked your lives to conquer this land for our Holy Emperor and for the Church of God! Who in heaven are you, to come and place yourselves in judgement over the rest of us? Do you think that you have any better rights to these lands than do I, who won them?

But the meeting goes against Cortés. The largest and most

sumptuous palace belonging to him in Mexico is taken by the Audiencia for the time being, and the Marquis is prevented from laying his hands on Coyoacán and Tacubuya. The wings of his eagle have been clipped, and the age-old law of possession is subverted by the Audiencia.

By now there are many hints as to the direction of the new government. The *oidores* have clamped down on the use of Indians as beasts of burden, reduced the taxes being paid by them, and have made their enslavement more difficult by keeping branding irons in a box that only the local bishop and magistrate of each town can open. They have taken steps to prevent people from dressing in silk, something that has become so commonplace in Mexico that, out on the streets of the Spanish quarter, the poorest jackanapes newly arrived from Europe swans around in clothes of luxury. A royal decree of 1510 forbade the wearing of silk in the Indies, and the new Audiencia is determined to see the Crown's wishes fulfilled.

The gold embroidery of the hidalgos' garments still glitters stubbornly, though. Summer is coming, and the sun catches the brocade and makes the clothing seem even more ostentatious. The wide streets are dotted with settlers gossiping beside their homes, fomenting dissent against the restrictions on clothing and slavery which the *oidores* wish to impose. With the Indians finding greater protection, there is now increased demand for African slaves, and the Spanish quarter is also home to many forced immigrants from Guinea, whose naked backs shine ebony in the sunlight as they integrate themselves into the labour force as miners, weavers, agriculturalists, herdsmen and overseers.[102] By now, in fact, there are so many African slaves in the New World that it seems like a 'new Guinea', with more people of African than Spanish blood in some places.[103]

Meanwhile, in the Indian neighbourhoods, people try to hide the idols that they still worship in secret, as if the very act of reverence is now something about which they have to be ashamed. The air is dry and hungry. Colours sharpen, but there is little colour in Indian lives any more. Women bear baskets of goods to the reconstituted market at Tlatelolco, where bargains are still struck and items exchanged; but there are fewer people than before in the great plaza of the Mexica, and an unspoken air of suffering and bitterness festers.

Discord has come to hang above the city: everywhere is riven by conflict, and no one can say how far its consequences might reach.

The *oidores* slowly come to feel besieged. They fear a general rebellion.[104] The Indians in more distant provinces are proving difficult to subdue. In Panuco in 1529, the Indians had rebelled and killed forty

Spaniards and fifteen horses; Gonzalo de Sandoval, an ally of Cortés, went there only last year, and burnt 400 Indians as a reprisal. The Indians of Michoacán and Iztlan have been in open rebellion for many months.[105] Now the Yopelcingos have begun to rebel, killing many Spaniards, and the *oidores* feel that they might soon see a revolt in Mexico itself. The matters of control and power are more pressing than ever. Might the rule of God and the king be subverted, and they themselves suffer the terror of being attacked? Could civilisation be at risk?

Cortés, a wilier and more seasoned colonist than the *oidores*, takes advantage of the threatening atmosphere to remind his judges of his power. He waits for the *oidores* themselves to beg him to come to Mexico to help them, and then deigns to prop up the government of God. He and his sidekicks ride into the city again, like conquerors (again), and parade up and down the streets. Their horses snort and toss their heads and untrimmed manes, prancing like clowns in the streets. The swords and armour jangle. There is nothing to fear from the barbarians who surround the new settlers so long as this brutal army is there to protect them.

Then one night the alarm sounds. The settlers bolt their houses and extinguish their candles. Mexico descends into a blind panic, amid the thuds which reverberate as the Spanish lock themselves in. Immersed in the darkness of the luxurious houses that they themselves have built, they can only listen with fear and uncertainty as the army of their bloodthirsty protectors rampages up and down the streets. The horsemen are 200 strong,[106] and their mounts' hooves thunder and echo like the drumbeats that used to accompany the sacrifices of the Mexica. There are cries from the soldiers, and their armour tinkles as it jolts up and down in the saddle. Protected by the army, the settlers feel safer. They let their guardians go out and seek the enemy, wherever they might be. This is a new war, a new struggle, and the rules of exchange must shift to take account of this (only Cortés appears to know what they are).

Later, though, it transpires that there have been no insurgents. In fact, the tidy streets in which the Spaniards live have been empty of all but their own thundering horsemen and the fear that consumes everyone. Some say that Cortés himself manufactured the scare as a means of exhibiting a show of force.[107] However much they try to ignore it, the *oidores* and the settlers will forever live in hock to the armed men who won them their wealth and this foreign country.

*

By now, Quiroga has witnessed enough of the New World to wish to retreat from it, and to take refuge among the books that he loves so much. Wrangling with legal disputes by day, by night he turns to the *Utopia* which Zumárraga has lent to him. Thomas More's book has been popular ever since its publication fifteen years ago, and as Quiroga reads of this imagined state he becomes fascinated by the tale of this strange island in the Indies. His eyes widen with every page as he reads what is all but an exact description of Mexico.

That the land of the Utopians lies in the Americas appears certain. The narrator, Nonsenso, had been on three of Amérigo Vespucci's voyages to the New World. Staying on, he eventually found his way to Utopia, and, on his return to Europe, recounted what he had seen to Thomas More and his Flemish friend Peter Gilles. Just as in the city of Mexico, there was 'an enormous lake' in Utopia.[108] Just like the Mexica, the Utopians loved gardens 'in which they grow fruit, including grapes, as well as grass and flowers';[109] the gardens were kept in a beautiful state, and Nonsenso had 'never seen anything to beat them',[110] although had he seen the sumptuous botanical gardens at Oaxtepec,[111] he might have changed his mind. Gold was plentiful in Utopia, as it is in New Spain, and there is more than an echo of Cortés's campaigns when More writes that 'without a Utopian pilot it's practically impossible for a foreign ship to enter the harbour'[112] – without the help of the Tlaxcalans, the Spaniards could never have taken Mexico.

Reading by candlelight, with the flame guttering and the wax hissing, Quiroga presses on with mounting excitement. What is perhaps most astonishing is that Thomas More wrote this book several years before the discovery of Mexico. Not only does the placing of Utopia echo that of Mexico, but the book has a colonial conceit that is expressive of the Spanish position in New Spain: if the Utopian island became overpopulated, the surplus were sent to start a settlement on the mainland nearby, forcing the local people to submit to Utopian management by war if necessary. Nonsenso said that the Utopians saw war as 'perfectly justifiable, when one country denies another its natural right to derive nourishment from any soil which the original owners are not using themselves'.[113] Indeed, foreign settlement had been very much in the air in the More household, as More's brother-in-law, John Rastell, had left to found England's first colony in Newfoundland just six months after *Utopia*'s publication.[114]

The questions of colonisation and of just wars resonate deeply with Quiroga, and he will not take much convincing that More must have been inspired by the Holy Spirit. Even though things have changed greatly since *Utopia*'s publication, the central tenets of More's vision still hold true in 1531: it takes a book like this to contextualise the great changes in cosmology that Quiroga and his contemporaries have experienced.

Tiring somewhat, Quiroga lays the volume down for a moment and screws up his eyes, thinking over all that he has seen. Outside, the city has at last fallen into silence. The stars shine with the sort of force that inspires awe and contemplation. Only dogs and demons prowl at this hour. Opening his eyes, Quiroga realises that it is the growth of geographies and economies – essential to the story of *Utopia* – that has led to the scenes which now confront him in Mexico. Knowledge of the world is growing all the time, and for the first time subjects have begun to slave away for the wealth of an emperor who lives in a different hemisphere. Sugar and tobacco from the Indies will soon appear on the tables of homes in Europe, and the profits will fund further voyages of exploration. To many, the possibilities appear limitless, for the natural bounty of God is far greater than has previously been imagined, such that it surely can never be exhausted by mere mortals. But having seen so much misery in just a few months, Quiroga feels doubts. Like More, he fears the unchecked growth that is promised by new economic realities. Reading the *Utopia* again and again, he tries to distil its lessons.

Nonsenso's critique of Europe* matched many of Quiroga's thoughts. There is too much emphasis on greed and wealth in the old world these days, and not enough on spiritual salvation. In Mexico, Quiroga feels himself to be surrounded by the godless. The disease of atheism is a condition that increases all the time, and as recently as 1516, Pomponazzi, a professor of philosophy in Bologna, published a work in which he had professed doubt as to the doctrine of immortality![115] It would really be laughable, Quiroga thinks, were it not so serious. The beginning of the modern world is coinciding with the growth of atheism, as the possibility of unlimited power and wealth appears to limit the allure even of heavenly paradise. Observing the avarice, Quiroga agrees with Nonsenso that 'if you're not afraid of anything but prosecution ... you'll always be trying to evade or break the laws of your country, in order to gain your own private ends'.[116] So he is relieved to hear that the Utopians did not 'believe anything so incompatible with human dignity as the doctrine that the soul dies

*See above, ch. 3, p. 54.

with the body, and [that] the universe functions aimlessly, without any controlling providence'.[117]

Nonsenso's critique of Europe and the Europeans, and his description of a land with many similarities to Mexico, galvanise Quiroga into examining the other elements of *Utopia* more closely. He soon sees the importance of More's proposals in Book Two for a genuinely just state. Whatever More's own opinions might now be,* Quiroga believes that his *Utopia* enshrines a vision that can be realised. Following the leading humanists of Europe, he sees this as a 'holy commonwealth that Christians ought to imitate',[118] as Erasmus has put it; or, as the great French classical scholar Guillaume Budé has said, *Utopia* preaches 'absolute equality ... and a contempt for gold and silver'.[119] Humanists of the early sixteenth century see agrarian communism as a goal, and *Utopia* is to be the work that begins the long anti-capitalist tradition (it is no wonder the teachings of Erasmus are quickly becoming heretical).

With the initial shock of his arrival ebbing away, Quiroga redoubles his efforts to understand the lives of the Indians destroyed by these new forces. Now that the power struggle between the *oidores* and Cortés has died down, he settles into a new routine, concentrating on carrying through the examination of all the towns and villages in New Spain. He visits the settlements around Mexico, ducking into mud huts in which eight or ten or more Indians live pressed together as if in a cage.[120] Their bodies are shrunken and emaciated. Like victims of famines through history, their eyes are downcast with the humiliation of their suffering. Their joints protrude grotesquely from their limbs. Their fields of crops are shrunken and half-formed, for they have not the energy to tend them properly.

And all the time the earth is drying, glittering like the tops of the clouds in the reflection of the sun. The children of the sun have come, but now the sun is nothing but a curse; yet, while the local people suffer famine and disease, the settlers are benefiting from a period of prosperity and economic expansion that has never previously been equalled.

There is scant earthly succour for the *naturales*, then, and so much assistance that their poor souls need from the Lord. Yet still they turn to their old gods, as Quiroga's friend Zumárraga keeps finding out. In Lake Texcoco, just half a league from the city, there are places where idolatry has been discovered only recently.[121] The Audiencia will soon

*See above, ch. 3, p. 54.

complain to the Crown that the old cult remains a continuing force,[122] and there are even rumours that human sacrifice is still practised in secret. Those temples that are still standing, monuments to the fallen civilisation of the Mexica, are shadows that whisper of unappeased monsters slumbering invisibly in the new Kingdom of God. The temples are as solid and unshakeable as the earth itself, but their strength avails them little. At night, when the moon is full, the wan light strikes them as if they are all ghosts.

Seeking some solution to the idolatry and disease, Quiroga delves further into the Indian neighbourhoods of Mexico. His heart is rent. Every nook and cranny crawls with orphans. They are thin, frail and stripped of all hope. The Spaniards have 'killed the fathers and mothers of the said orphans, or [have been] the cause of their deaths in wars and mines'.[123] These children '[walk] around the *tianguis* and streets looking for the scraps of food that are left them by the pigs and dogs ... there are so many of these orphans, that no one would believe it who did not see it with their own eyes'.[124] Each child is a reproach. Each pair of dark eyes glazed over with distress is a reminder of what has gone before.

When night falls, Quiroga retreats to his rooms. His thoughts blacken like the city beyond as he becomes conscious of the emotional fragmentation that surrounds him. At times he prays for some sort of enlightenment as to what he should do. At others, he turns to favourite authors: Lucian, Cayetano, Gerson or More.[125] Mixing his voracious appetite for learning with his experiences of the Indians, he realises that there is much about the *naturales* to give cause for hope. They have 'an innate humility, obedience, poverty and disregard for worldly things'[126] which he admires enormously. These people could easily absorb the Christian teaching and put it into practice, as most Spaniards secretly accept. Has not even Albornoz admitted that this land is 'the most appropriate for the service of God, and for the benefit of those who wish to serve Him, that has ever been discovered'?[127] Yes, Albornoz has it right: the Indians are 'of such reason that in two years they [might] adopt the Spanish order and way of life'.[128]

All it needs, Quiroga thinks, is the right means by which to instruct them. Like all utopians who will follow him, he believes himself to have 'the truth' with which he must benefit everyone. These Indians are perfect receptacles for the faith, for they '[walk] barefoot and with long hair, without anything to cover their heads, in the manner of the apostles'.[129] Are they not as 'bland as wax',[130] wax in which a skilled sculptor can leave whatever impression he likes? How fortunate they are that the impression to which he, Quiroga the *oidor*, is drawn, is that of perfection!

Everything now pushes him towards the *Utopia*. More has described the situation in Mexico perfectly, and his solution is ever more urgent as greed forces everything into ruins. The ecology is showing signs of stress and fragmentation, and there will not be an endless supply of slaves for the mines. The indigenous people have been reduced to such desperate straits that they cannot survive for much longer, and is not a more equitable distribution of resources called for? There is, he feels, a pressing need for a return to the moral values which could yet rescue this world. A more ordered, more equitable society is necessary. How greatly they have been blessed in receiving the work of Thomas More!

On 14 August 1531 he composes a letter to the Council of the Indies, the body charged with governing the Spanish colonies. He feels no need to prevaricate: the question of the new communes which he wishes to found is at the forefront of his mind, for on the first page of his letter he writes that there are 'certain settlements of Indians which it would be most opportune to build'.[131] Land that is presently sterile could be cultivated and bear fruit. In the new settlements the Indians will not fall into despair and ruin; instead, 'working and breaking the soil, they will sustain themselves through their own work and be ordered in a politic manner with holy and good Catholic ordinances'.[132] There are so many young Indians who would be willing to work in these 'republics' that they are as numerous 'as the stars in the sky and the atoms in the sea'.[133]

The benefits of these republics will be considerable. The Indians will be ordered and will learn the art of civilisation. Their idolatry and drunkenness will be curtailed, their distasteful customs stamped out. Furthermore, the Indians, by being gathered into the sort of communities which More has envisaged, will have the great boon of being brought into closer contact with the teachings of Christ. Yes, everyone will benefit from the situation that such an ideal republic will bring about. Quiroga (ever modest) has a practical suggestion: 'I offer myself to put these republics into action'[134] so that the orphans and the poor may be 'taught the things of our holy faith'.[135]

This is a radical plan, but Quiroga sees it as a way of salvaging hope from the catastrophe. He is not proposing the abolition of slavery as such: even he accepts Aristotle's category of 'natural slaves', for everyone knows that slaves are essential components of all elaborate civilisations – this goes for the Spanish, just as it went for the Mexica.

So Quiroga does not suggest that no Indians should be enslaved, but rather that, when they have been put into chains for making war on the Spanish, they should be sent to the mines for only a little while,[136] so that they should not be without hope.

It is late at night. As he finishes writing to the Council, he feels that he has embarked on a project which cannot be reneged upon. He seals his letter with wax. Birdsong falls into his chamber along with the dawn. A few horses clop along the streets. There is not a breath of wind, and so the blooms outside are still. The morning is as crisp as a fresh snowfall, and soon the sun rises from behind Popocatépetl. In the distance, several canoes are stirring on the lake. The tips of the forests begin to sway. Already light is illuminating the streets, bringing with it the promise of a new society distanced from the vagabonds who have descended among the Indians, stolen their wealth without shame or self-knowledge, and retired to the safety of their opulent new homes.

Utopia is essential here – of that much Quiroga is clear: but whether the perfection will be made real, or prove to be an ideal confined to his dreams, is something that has yet to be decided.

Part Two

UTOPIA: A MODEL KIT

But where was the Promised Land? Did there really exist any such goal for this wandering mankind?

Arthur Koestler, *Darkness at Noon*

EIGHT

The atmosphere in the city is brooding, unrequited. Dust obscures the sky; clouds the thoughts. The faces of the Indians are scarred, their eyes broken with the pox.[1] Although Mexico is still situated on an island,[2] the great lake is drying out every day as water is leached off for irrigation. History has come to exact painful offerings amid the streets where once the only sacrifices were made for divine rewards, and the only music was ritual, and the only aim of life was living, which in itself was deemed enough to be beautiful, worthwhile, good.

The building must begin again.

The Mexica raise their eyes towards the mountains that ring the foreign city and hold it tight, as if in a noose. All these high hills, they take as gods,[3] nature always being so worthy of reverence; but these sierras are also aloof and forbidding, for they are 'airy and windy; they are wet and frosty; they are tearful, solitary, sad places; they are cavernous'.[4] These are spots where 'nobody lives, and nothing edible can be found, places of hunger and cold and numbness ... where beasts eat men'.[5] They are so desolate that they might be the perfect places for the Mexica to rediscover their adoration of the world, and to escape from the colonists.

If the truth be told, the Mexica also need to escape from themselves, and from the plague of drunkenness which has begun to tread among them. By night, their neighbourhood appears like 'a transplant from Hell, [where] the residents cry out, some calling to the devil, others drunk, others dancing and singing';[6] the amount of alcohol that they drink often renders them completely senseless.[7] These days, when they have fiestas, they pass 'days and nights drinking without cease'[8] – something which only goes to show how completely their world has disintegrated, for the Mexica have traditionally seen drunkenness as a thing to be despised, so much so that anyone caught drunk in a public place used to be beaten to death or strangled.[9]

The drunkard, it was said, 'goes about falling over, red with dust, dishevelled and filthy ... when he talks he has no idea what he is saying ... he goes around dancing and screeching. He undervalues everything ... his house is dark with poverty, and he sleeps elsewhere'.[10] The result is that everyone despises him, 'for being a man of public infamy. Everyone is hostile to him, and bored at the sight of him. Nobody wants to talk to him.'[11] The drunkard 'is like a serpent with two heads, who bites on one side and then on the other'.[12] People such as that 'are never calm or at peace, never happy ... they are always sad ... after they have drunk as much as they can they rob their neighbours' pots and jars and plates and bowls from their very houses'.[13]

Mass popular intoxication only develops alongside social dis-integration, isolation, despair. The Mexica do not want to fall into depravity, but their world has been destroyed, and as yet they have been given nothing worthwhile to replace it: it is not so easy to crush old gods in the space of just a few years while maintaining people's dignity and their sense of self-worth.

But perhaps this situation is not completely without hope. The Tetuan himself, one of the four 'Listeners', has recently come to offer them a new start.[14] He has approached Don Juan, Governor of the Indian quarter of Santiago-Tlatelolco, and Don Pablo, Indian Governor of Mexico, and urged that now they must begin to carry building materials up into the hills and make their homes elsewhere. He has bought a piece of land two leagues from the city, and has found a site where they can begin to rediscover the meaning of community. This will be a place for God, and for the Indians, where the 'sky is so serene, the shadows so cool and refreshing, the air so pure, the water so clear, the silence so admirable, that everything resonates with signs from the heavens and provokes contemplation'.[15]

Don Juan and Don Pablo accede to the request. They know that this Listener is one of the few Spaniards who cares for them and desires their good. He offers to pay them for the work, but they refuse – the only gratification they want, they say, is from God, for whom they are doing this work.[16] They begin to put the *macehuales** into order, and the exodus from the fire of Mexico begins.

The road to the western hills is soon a moving river of men and women journeying back and forth, singing and stuttering as they bear great quantities of adobe, stone and lime on their backs.[17] The way is steep, although shaded by stands of cypress and alder which give some

*As the Indian labourers were known.

relief from the sun. As they climb higher, the city spreads out below them, a whitewashed bluff in the midst of the great lake, which rolls and sighs with the winds and the souls of the thousands who lie buried in the blue depths. Once they reach Sante Fe – the Holy Faith – they set down the rubble and begin to forget.

They work intensely and, gradually, over the course of the next few months, the main buildings of the new settlement are raised: first a humble thatched house for God, then two communal houses – one for the people of Mexico, the other for the people of Tlatelolco – surrounded by a further fifteen individual houses, until they have constructed what the Listener tells them proudly is a *familia*.[18] A large communal kitchen follows, then a church, then four cells for Franciscan friars, then a dining area next to the church.[19]

There is so much reconstruction to be done, and so few materials with which to do it. The Indian homes are basic – they do not even have doors[20] – and provide little shelter. Winter descends, and Don Pablo goes to the Listener – begging an audience in his palatial apartments – and tells him that the work of the *macehuales* must cease for the time being, for it is wet. Thunder cracks like the whips of the *encomenderos*, the rain is a wall and a veil and a clammy, devilish hand, and there are no materials to be found.

But no, the Listener says angrily (increasingly deaf where his ideal is concerned), you cannot stop! This is the work of God to forestall the sins of man! It is here that the sick are to be cured, the dead buried, wanderers accommodated, the ignorant educated, orphans married![21] Even you, he tells Don Pablo, even you see that your people have no order and no state of living worthy of the name![22] It is here, in the new settlement, in this perfectibility of humanity on earth, that Mass can be celebrated, Holy Baptism administered together with the other sacraments, an honourable place found to bury the dead who hitherto have been eaten by the birds and the dogs and the other wild animals![23] So it is raining – let it rain! No, no – the work must go on.

Don Pablo does not wait longer than necessary in the face of this diatribe. These newcomers are the source of much mockery among his people:[24] their faces are very ugly – with their ridiculous long, bearded heads – but even the poorest among them never goes hungry, nor lacks anything.[25] If there are not enough building materials to be found, they will have to come from the homes of the *macehuales* themselves.

So as Santa Fe de México expands, the Indians begin to demolish their own homes and carry them up into the sierra.[26] In the quarters of San Lázaro and Chapultepeque, houses and arches are taken apart – although whether by the Indians of Santa Fe themselves, or by the Listener's enemies, who are many, will never be known. With the Mexica bent double beneath their loads, the scene is reminiscent of that on the roads leading down to the coast of Veracruz: there are so many burdens to be carried, and so many sins to atone for. As with the coast road, the *macehuales* are given nothing to eat, and no payment for their work;[27] very quickly, they begin to murmur against the rashness of their governors in accepting no payment for this almighty task.[28]

Don Pablo and Don Juan agree that if it had been any Christian other than the Listener who had asked this of them, they would have agreed a contract beforehand and demanded to know that the requisite building materials were in place.[29] They are ashamed to admit to their *macehuales* that the Listener continues to offer to pay them, but that they have refused up to now[30] – perhaps, if they ask him soon, some offering in return for their labour will be forthcoming; but in the meantime, they should look to the great work that he is performing.

For up in Santa Fe, Quiroga has not been idle. He has been spurred on in his work by the recent miracle of the Virgin of Guadalupe, something that has shown every Spaniard in New Spain that – even here – God does not forget His people. Early in December 1531, the Virgin appeared in a vision before a *macehual* known as Juan Diego, ordering him to tell Bishop Zumárraga to build a church at the site of his vision. Though Zumárraga was initially sceptical, proof of the miracle came on 12 December, when the Virgin ordered Juan Diego to gather roses from the top of the hill and take them to Zumárraga: the *macehual* put the flowers in his cape and, on opening it before the Bishop, found an image of the Virgin embedded in the cloth.*

This is enough to remind everyone that miracles are a simple fact of everyday life. Nonetheless, while Juan Diego's vision of the Virgin of Guadalupe is evidence of God's omnipresence, the Listener knows that he must work with natural and not supernatural laws for the time being. And so, although the work of the Audiencia continues to be intense through 1532 and 1533, as it founds the strategically important town of Puebla de los Ángeles in 1533 and arranges the construction of a new road between Mexico and Veracruz, he comes up to the new town whenever he can.[31] Sometimes he even misses important meetings

---

*The Virgin of Guadalupe remains Mexico's most popular religious shrine today. In July 2002, Pope John Paul II travelled to Mexico City to canonise Juan Diego.

and fails to sign his name when letters are sent back to Spain,[32] deciding instead to spend many days here trying to distil the peace of this spot, where he is surrounded by forests and the jagged peaks of the mountains, and can forget the excesses of the city. At night the stars glitter like algae on an ocean voyage, and the false lights of the city can be forgotten. After rising, he devotes his energies to transforming this place into something that will be of lasting benefit, overseeing the works, ensuring that the surrounding fields are properly dug, and sown, and that everyone has a part in the foundation of Utopia.

Nearby, he has bought the island of Tultepec for the planting of crops, and has paid the Indians of Capulhuac thirty *mantas* (blankets) to build a causeway over to it.[33] The island has been ploughed and worked by the Indians of Capulhuac, Toluca, Metepec and Teutenango, who have been paid seventy *mantas*.[34] Other people are helping in the works around Santa Fe, where the lands are very fertile, and the plan is for the Indians to be able to reap enough to feed their families.[35] This enshrines the ideal that this is to be a self-sufficient community, dissociated from the broader (and increasingly global) economy, whose pernicious effects are there for all with eyes to see.

It is this that ensures that many Spaniards in Mexico soon begin to feel threatened by Quiroga's Utopia.

In general, opinion in Mexico soon divided into two camps where Quiroga's project in Santa Fe was concerned: the clergy, the friars and the more religious settlers were in favour, and everyone else was against.

Following Quiroga's impassioned letter to the Council of the Indies in August 1531, the Crown decreed that, although it foresaw problems in gathering the Indians in one place, the Audiencia should have the final say in the matter.[36] The letter – dated 20 March 1532 – probably arrived some time in July 1532: by the end of August, Quiroga had wrapped up the deal in Santa Fe, paying 70 gold pesos for land belonging to the Almelya estancia,[37] and shortly afterwards he supplemented this with the purchase of some land belonging to Alonso Dávila for 40 gold pesos.[38] The work had begun by November, when the Audiencia wrote to the Crown that Quiroga's pueblo was underway.[39]

However, the settlers in Mexico itself soon began to agitate at the prospect of a commune which not only was within easy reach of the city, but also was a strong counter-argument to the necessity of the *encomienda* system. Already, the letters of these years from Mexico to the Crown were often filled with shameless begging by old conquistadors demanding more slaves, more land, so that they could 'sustain themselves'.[40] Now they saw not only that the Audiencia was clamping down on slavery, but that Quiroga's new town was becoming a direct rival to their ambitions. So, on 6 May 1533, the Council (*Cabildo*) of Mexico wrote to the Crown that Quiroga's settlement was 'without benefit seeing as the only benefit is in the name [i.e. Santa Fe]',[41] and claimed that the new settlement would depopulate the city and might lead to future uprisings. The Audiencia had already complained to the Crown about the gossip-mongers who fomented talk of Indian uprisings, and had always found that 'these scandalous tales begin among the conquistadors';[42] only by keeping the settlers in constant fear of enemy attack, it seemed, could the greediest among the colonists hope to achieve their own aims.

So the Cabildo did not let up. On 16 June 1533 its members discussed how Quiroga's project was draining away labour so that there were no Indians to do public works in Mexico.[43] Four days later Jerónimo López, the *regidor* of Mexico, made the first of a series of complaints about the severity of the labour being exacted from the Indians at Santa Fe, and emphasised the fact that they were supposedly using materials from their own houses to build the new settlement.[44] Meanwhile, Antonio Serrano de Córdoba was sent to complain to Charles V about Quiroga's work, reiterating the 'danger' which might come of the depopulation of Mexico.[45] The battlelines had quickly been drawn, and Quiroga's enemies appear to have been trying to take advantage of the fact that he had left on a prolonged journey to the province of Michoacán in an attempt to resolve the disorder there;* on his return, in 1534, he busied himself in his defence, procuring a signed statement from the Indian governors Don Pablo and Don Juan which showed that he had offered to pay them throughout the works, and had in fact given them something for the labour, if only once the complaints had reached his ears.[46]

It must have been galling to the conquistadors and *encomenderos* to have Quiroga's settlement within such easy reach. Not only was Santa Fe just two leagues from Mexico, but it was also within a stone's throw of the main road to Michoacán, which was now being opened up as one of the principal mining regions in New Spain. There could not have been a more marked contrast than that between the teams

*See below, ch. 10, pp. 177–8.

of slaves who were being marched to their deaths in the mines in order to extract their country's mineral wealth and send it to Spain, and the Indians of Santa Fe who, although hard at work, were at least building a community in which they would be protected. Quiroga would later make the comparison himself: the Indians, he wrote, 'are forcibly clapped in irons and sold and bought ... without the slightest pity, so that they can die horrible deaths in the mines instead of being educated'.[47] The new project showed that what these oppressed people needed was not greater commerce with the powerful economic forces of Europe, but the opportunity to build something that was largely for their own benefit.

Among those who were not motivated by greed, there was no doubting the value of what Quiroga termed his 'pueblo-hospital',* as becomes clear through reading the *residencia*, or public hearing, that was taken in February 1536 of his spell as *oidor*. By this time, Quiroga had been nominated as Bishop of Michoacán, and had already spent some time in that north-western province; nevertheless, the principal charge against him was related to the construction of Sante Fe de México, and the controversial question of the exploitation of the Indians in the building works: presenting himself at the trial, Jerónimo López reiterated his charges of three years before, almost word for word, but this time Quiroga was able to provide thirty-five witnesses in his defence.

Among his many supporters was Bishop Zumárraga, who testified: 'Quiroga gives us a good lesson and even a reprimand to the bishops of these parts, with all he does in spending his every peso on these hospitals and congregations.'[48] He even claimed that Quiroga was the object of holy envy in Mexico, for doing so much good and yet still exercising his duties as an *oidor*. Another witness, Martín de Calahorra, said that the pueblo-hospital had been so successful that 'it is already bringing envy on itself ... because people see that up to now the work has been getting ever better'.[49] Meanwhile, Bartolomé Alguacil claimed that he had seen Indians in Santa Fe 'eating like Spaniards'[50] – clearly something that was unusual, and worthy of note.

There was also widespread agreement when it came to the personal sacrifices that Quiroga had made in order to get the pueblo-hospital up and running. Martín de Calahorra said that he had heard Quiroga's servants 'complaining that he spent everything there [in the hospital], whether in giving them good food, or in giving them clothes or in

*Literally, 'hospital-town'.

building them a church and houses and other things ... as well as buying them fields from landowners in the area so that they can sow crops, and buying ornaments and books'.[51] According to Juan Ceciliano, it was 'public and well-known that he is poor and in need ... he has spent a great deal on the said work'.[52] Alonso Pérez agreed that he had 'heard it said ... that the Licentiate does not have a piece of bread to eat, and that he is poor and spent',[53] while according to Juan de Ortega, Quiroga was 'very poor and [had] nothing to eat'.[54]

The main charge – that of exploitation of the Indians in the building of the settlement – was refuted by Alonso Rodríguez, who said, 'the buildings of the hospital are not expensive because the houses are very small'.[55] Quiroga did admit, though, that the Indians had carried the building materials to Santa Fe, but he claimed that this was their side of the bargain, as he was the one who had bought the land. In any event, he said, it was not surprising that they had carried things with them to Sante Fe, and they would have expected nothing less, as they did not know how to go empty-handed to any job.[56] Furthermore, the houses were not for his own benefit, but constituted a 'hospital for poor Indians',[57] where 'so much cleanliness and honesty has been and is kept that it really seems to be a work of God alone and not of men'.[58]

With a name like Santa Fe, Quiroga intended his pueblo-hospital to be not only a place where 'the ill are cured, and the dead of the neighbourhood are buried, and the homeless and wandering Indians are taken in'[59] – this was, first and foremost, a work of God, and would be a place where the true Christian path would be followed. He was clear that one of the principal aims of the new town was the 'indoctrination' or Christian education of the Indians. In his statement of defence he asked his supporters to attest to the Christian ethos of the settlement, where 'deeds of charity are performed ... and students are read to ... And also many children are taught to read and write, and others are taught to sing,' so that they would be able to preach themselves.[60]

Again, his witnesses were not slow in agreeing with him. In addition to Zumárraga's eulogy, Martín de Calahorra said that Quiroga's main motive was 'that which relates to doctrine'.[61] Francisco Jiménez, from the monastery at Cuernavaca, said that 'many Indians from the surrounding area [became] Christian' in the hospital.[62] Fray García Cisneros said that he had been many times to Santa Fe to give mass, and 'there mass is said with great solemnity, sung and presided over by the Indians who live there'.[63]

Quiroga, it seems, interpreted More's *Utopia* in the only way in which a renaissance humanist could have done: as an invitation to found a genuinely Christian, sharing community, which alone – as Campanella would later write* – would show the true path to happiness on earth and in heaven. He had spurned the destructive, all-consuming cupidity of his age, and had given away his wealth in pursuit of what he saw as a broader good: altruism may have been unfashionable in New Spain in the early sixteenth century, but that was no deterrent to him.

Soon enough there were 12,000 Indians living in Sante Fe;[64] by and by many more came, so that eventually there would be 'more than 30,000 who lived a religious life'.[65] Here they were able to be more peaceable, to leave their drunkenness behind them, and to live in a manner which in fact was not too far removed from that which they had known before the arrival of Cortés.

There is still much work to do, but the dust is gradually beginning to settle. The church and the clusters of houses – or *familias*, as Quiroga insists on calling them – have been raised. Now the growing populace can devote themselves to the new settlement's most important task: agriculture.

Quiroga holds that the Mexica cannot drag themselves up from the abyss into which they have been thrown if they cannot feed themselves, and so prescribes farming as the 'universal activity' of all in the community – something to be done from childhood onwards.[66] Lessons are given to the children for one or two hours each day in the fields, and the children are allowed to keep whatever they can grow.[67] Farming activity reaches a pitch in the sowing season, as the labourers make for the fields to plough and sow. Then, when harvest comes, that soil gives forth rows of wheat, and the Mexica from Santa Fe slash and scythe and disappear towards the town with bundles of the new crop on their heads. This is a hard life, but not one without reward, for at least they are working for the sustenance of their own families and not for some tyrannical *encomendero*, a latter-day Montezuma.[68]

Of course, cultivation is not new here. It is something at which the Mexica have traditionally excelled. Their heartland was long a home to fields of chillies and corn strung out in bands of red and yellow between the mountains, but the conquest has brought rupture even here: so many people died during the first smallpox epidemic that

*See above, ch. 6, p. 100.

there were not enough hands to plant the crops, and the old knowledge was interrupted.[69] It is not that Quiroga is now teaching them things that they have never known; rather, it is hoped that this settlement will help them to return to something like their former condition.

The people work for six hours each day in the fields, or for three full days a week in times of need.[70] Maize, wheat, barley and vines are planted, and there are orchards of peach and quince trees.[71] Once harvested, the crops are stored in public granaries and distributed among the *familias*. Some sheep are introduced,[72] their coats as light and puffy as the clouds that scud overhead, and change, with the seasons. Their wool is shorn in springtime, and tufts cling to the people's clothes, the thatch of the huts, lie trampled in the road that leads down to Mexico. Looms are erected around Santa Fe, and the women are instructed in weaving, and soon learn that their role will be to make 'creations of wool and linen and silk and cotton'.[73] A delicious fresh spring wells up near the settlement,[74] and there the people gather with their pots and dishes to collect their water, and to gossip, to participate in the events of this time and place in the knowledge that these belong to no individual, and, like the food and the other goods of Santa Fe, must be shared.

It does not take long for the word to spread among the neighbouring communities about the more humane lifestyle in Quiroga's settlement. People may come from anywhere and be taken in. There is a style of creche here,[75] where the orphans and the abandoned sit alongside the children of people working out in the fields or on the looms, and all are instilled with the doctrines of the second great pillar of the new community: the Catholic religion. For, aside from the agricultural basis of the settlement, life in Santa Fe revolves around the church.

At dawn the whole town gathers together to pray, led by the Franciscan friar Alonso de Borja.[76] The different quarters of the settlement meet at the boundaries, where tall crosses are garlanded with flowers and trailing creepers.[77] The men and women are dressed in the same white garments, shifting between cotton and wool according to the season.[78] The doctrine is sung in a low, funereal chant, a sound that betokens the solemnity of this life, but sits awkwardly with the brilliant colours of the flowers and the mountains and the sky and the lake below. After prayers, the people return to their homes to eat something, before those who have to work leave to do so, while the others go to the church to learn or to teach, 'so that everyone is occupied in virtuous tasks'.[79] Then, in the evenings, people march through the street and sing the catechism in the darkness.[80] On Fridays, everyone fasts, so that 'this town [seems] more like a religious convent than a secular republic'.[81] The communal, religious existence is Utopia for the sixteenth century.

This new routine is not Mexican in origin, and yet life in Santa Fe is far from being entirely alien to the Mexica. Before the arrival of the Spanish, many of them used to be organised in units known as *calpulli*, which united various families to work for common goals and interests. Although there had been hierarchies within the *calpulli*, and they had all had a chief who was elected for life, a measure of commonality had also existed: the chief had ensured that land was shared equally between all the families who belonged to the group and farmed and harvested it in common.[82] Furthermore, as at Sante Fe, the *macehuales* of the *calpulli* all wore white unornamented cloaks,[83] and only the dignitaries adorned themselves with bright patterns.

So in fact, as the Mexica labour in the fields and share the crops in common, they find themselves returning to ways which they already understand. Even this reverence of the Christian God, and its central role in the settlement of Sante Fe, is not so hard to accommodate, for at least they have now returned to a society in which the divine takes centre stage, where the universe is described in spiritual and not material terms.[84] Once again, life, the earth, the world and its peoples – all are deemed sacred: this God may be a new one – with different standards, needs and priorities – but He is, at least, divine.

Furthermore, most of the Mexica revere Christ only in name. They themselves, when an imperial power, used to adopt the divinities of conquered peoples into their own religious worldview,[85] and so they do not see the need – now that they have been conquered – to relinquish their old gods. It will not take long for the Spanish to realise that their conversion is often a sham: Zumárraga will hold the first inquisitional tribunal against the Indians in June 1536; in 1537, it will be found that the caciques have organised a secret programme to train priests in the old religion.*[86] In the 1570s, Sahagún will write: 'If they [the Mexica] were now left to their own devices, without the Spanish nation as intermediaries, it is my belief that within less than fifty years there would be no mark left of the preaching that they have received.'[87]

So even the sacrifice of their old deities is no bar to the growth of Santa Fe. The Mexica flock here in large numbers. More houses are built; more land is bought. In February 1534, Quiroga pays 90 gold pesos to Juan de Fuentes for a farm and its farmhouse; five months

---

*See below, ch. 12, pp. 214–15.

later he buys more land from Alonso Dávila, complete with both native and Spanish trees for 70 pesos, and in October he buys land from Juan de Burgos.[88] In both 1535 and 1536 more land purchases follow,[89] so that soon there appears to be no end to the scope of this great project to the glory of God and the benefit of the Mexica. It is typical, then, that the eyes of the settlers down in Mexico have turned up to the settlement by now, and many of them are plotting to kidnap the people from Sante Fe and haul them away as slaves.[90]

Nothing would surprise Quiroga about those wretched settlers. As the time of his *residencia* approaches, he agrees with some of his supporters that to 'say bad things about this work [Santa Fe] is to say that good is bad'.[91] The more time he is forced to spend down in the city, the more he longs to break free of it. At the ghost of an opportunity he abandons the palace of the Audiencia and rides up to the hills, to the fresh air and goodness which he sees all around him in Sante Fe. It is here that he spends the 'best years of his life',[92] where God is in His pomp, where the Indians are protected, where the hummingbirds hover around the dazzling flowers and the earth betrays its enduring beauty (what possible value can this chimerical, worldly life have without even that?).

On arriving in the pueblo-hospital from Mexico he goes straight to his hermitage to read and pray. Then, after some time for reflection, he climbs the small hill up to the *plazuela* where the church stands[93] and goes inside. The Mexica love colour, and so brightness is the order of the day: the pillars have been painted, and there is a multicoloured cross made of parrots' feathers, alongside three striking altarpieces, one of a large cross, another of Jesus carrying the cross, and a third of the seven sacraments.[94] Quiroga is a realist, knowing that the flowers on the crosses and the feathers in the church are concessions to the Indians, but hoping that this subtle mixture of Christianity and their own customs will continue to bring the Mexica to the Church: after all, the Mexica have a positive passion for flowers,[95] and feathers too are potent symbols among these people, as parrot feathers are said to be the first things that were ever sold at Tlatelolco's market.[96]

Eventually, once he has finished with his prayers, he rejoins the world outside. The Mexica go quietly about their tasks. They talk softly, not wishing to draw too much attention to themselves. They move about in a measured way, without great hurry, for they do not want to be thought of as one of those people who 'look about all over the place like a madman'.[97] They generally walk with their heads lowered, raising them only when spoken to, and in particular the men never look at a woman, for they believe that 'he who looks at a woman with curiosity adulterates through his gaze'[98] – in the pre-Cortesian world, this had been enough to see some people punished by death.[99]

Quiroga approves of their modesty. The more that he lives among them, the more he is convinced that they have a 'cult of justice'.[100] His own experience has now shown him that these people are capable of being so humble and obedient that it would be possible to 'found a very good republic here'.[101] They do not care about superfluous material possessions, and in spite of everything are capable of 'great happiness and freedom in their lives and in their souls'.[102] How fitting it is, he thinks, that the divine inspiration of Thomas More should be realised here in the New World, where the land 'is, in peoples as in everything, exactly as was the first golden age'.[103]

More's influence on Santa Fe has grown ever more pronounced as the project has expanded. The emphasis on agriculture is, of course, akin to that of the *Utopia*, as is the white colour of the clothes worn and the number of hours that are worked daily by the people in the fields.* Even the name of the dwellings – the *familias* – is a clear derivative of More's book, where the building block of each Utopian town had been the 'family'. Throughout these early years of the growth and success of this first pueblo-hospital, Quiroga becomes more and more impressed by More, and this admiration reaches its peak on 4 July 1535, when he writes the longest account of the Indies that he will ever produce, the 'Información en Derecho', which addresses the question of slavery – something that the Crown has just licensed again, citing the familiar old excuses of 'just war' and the need to 'rescue' the Indians from their benighted state.[104]

In this impassioned, erudite letter, Quiroga refutes the idea that slavery would be beneficial in New Spain, saying that this is an argument for people who 'looking do not see, and hearing do not understand',[105] for slavery to the Spanish only crushes the Indians and is in any case fundamentally alien to the sort of slavery that they used to practise among themselves, where they had not lost their rights and freedoms and had been more like hired hands.[106] He finishes off by citing More as someone 'of more than human genius',[107] 'an exceptionally prudent man',[108] whose description of the New World 'without

---

*Though the substitution of the three full days in times of need was an invention of Quiroga's.

having seen it, is almost entirely accurate'[109] and must have been inspired by the Holy Spirit.[110] He encloses a summary of the *Utopia* with the letter,* and agrees with the French humanist Guillaume Budé that the book is like a 'summary of correct and beneficial customs, from which each one must take and incorporate traditions in their particular society'.[111]

More must have realised, Quiroga feels, the innate goodness of the American peoples, their aptitude for Christianity and for a genuine republic. Every day that he spends at Santa Fe, this tranquil, resonant place fills his heart with beauty, a flicker of perfection. He feels the touch of the numinous. Only through repeated prayer, and genuine, honest labour, can the innate happiness of the Mexica return and this land and this world be saved – else everything will be destruction, fire, torment.

At times of religious festivals, Quiroga's sense of epiphany reaches its zenith. The Indians dance vigorously, dressed in brilliant feathers[112] that dazzle and reflect the rasping colours of the mountainsides. The sun burns; birdsong echoes the music. The forests fill with the sounds of prayers and chants. The songs ring out across the sierras, and the echoes resound back[113] as if the hills themselves were joining in this paean to God. The spectacle is such that it could surely compete with Roman times![114] Here is the true potential of the New World, a place where humankind can rise from the ashes of an inferno (which it has ignited).

Yet there are questions that Quiroga still shies away from, absorbed as he is by his own vision of beauty, his steadfast belief that the bathing of humanity in this beauty is the path to rediscovering the sacred breath of life. In his 'Información en Derecho', while protesting against slavery, he defends the justice of the conquest, for the Indians have hitherto had no developed political state, and have traditionally been 'barbarous and cruel people ... ignorant of the trappings of good political arrangements and used to living without law or king'.[115] He writes that this creates the grounds for what Aquinas called 'just war', for the savage and Godless state of the Indians permits the Spanish to seek to 'humilliate them for their brute and bestial state, and once humilliated, convert them'.[116] Yet of course he also knows that the good intentions of the warriors in this just war – their genuine belief that they can raise the benighted people to a higher standard of living and rescue them from their hellish cultural abyss – have in fact

---

*This has unfortunately never been found by contemporary historians.

sown death and destruction among the Indians, and on a hitherto unimaginable scale.

Were he to be honest with his feelings, Quiroga would see that the 'justice' of this war hides itself under an increasingly large bushel, and that in this case (if not in all cases) it is a mask for the basest instinct: the desire of the greedy to get their hands on the gold and silver of the age. Even if the people in Santa Fe are indeed now genuine Christians, as he hopes, universal human values have charged their fellows a heavy price for their salvation – one which perhaps even they might not countenance.

After dark, he retires to his hermitage by the spring, and hears the gushing water supersede the noise of the pueblo-hospital. Again he prays and seeks the enlightenment of God as to his path; but the question that he dare not ask himself is: Which God is really being worshipped at these festivals? How can the true religious feelings of the Mexica, and his own role in establishing them, be unmasked?

NINE

I had imagined that I could just fantasise my way to Santa Fe and Quiroga's Utopia – just as I had crossed the Atlantic – but now that I was with Juan Diego I found that miracles were increasingly hard to come by, and that he was trying to rein me in. So as I stood on the concourse outside the neurotic cafe, and took a step beyond the *churros rellenos* on special offer, I realised that my legs were already a burden; and as we made our way westwards, passing the bookshops on the Alameda, I had to breathe hard just to keep pace with my squire. It was with some irritation that I saw him bounding across the vehicular sea of the Paseo de la Reforma, before awaiting me with a smug expression beneath the flashing Sanyo and Coca-Cola signs on the far side of the avenue.

The necessity of actually exercising my body – walking, as they call it – was a chore that filled me with instant loathing. I still believed that my status was such that any fool should have seen that I was a cut above most other people and deserved to be chauffeured around, or at the very least provided with a private helicopter. To have to walk to Santa Fe was clearly an intolerable burden, something that no civilised person ought to have had to put up with when they could happily have been stuffing their stomachs or their minds full of garbage. So, not long after we had begun to walk up the Puente de Alvarado, I stopped within view of a corner shop (where tortillas were singled out for being inexpensive) and told Juan Diego that I was not going to put up with this antiquated form of exertion any longer: if we really had to tax our bodies, I pointed out, there were surely some fitness centres with exercise bikes and rowing machines nearby.

'You promised to minister to me,' I protested, as we sheltered in the shade provided by a newspaper stand. 'After the last twenty minutes, I've got half a mind to abandon you right now. In fact, if all this were a book, I wouldn't read a page further: it's far too confusing, contradictory, and downright blasphemous to everything we hold dear;

and I thank heaven that the account I'm going to write will be entirely different.'

'Well, *señor*,' Juan Diego said, appearing to mollify me, 'it's a long way, I grant you, but nobody said that salvation, good sense, the survival instinct or Utopia would appear overnight, or even before the Sun starts to go round the Earth. And as the saying goes, you can't predict the future until you've been there, unless you're talking about the disappearance of fossil fuels within the next fifty years just in time for the collapse of the planetary ecosystems on which we all depend.'

'What are you saying, Juan Diego?' I asked, distracted and not really listening to the full force of his comments (my eyes had strayed to the headlines on the news-stand and were lingering over the empty summaries of stories that meant little or nothing to me, what with the scandal of the leaked political document and the latest shame to strike the British royal family). 'Do you mean that there's no saying when Santa Fe might appear?'

'If that's what you mean by perfection, or even simply the continuation of humanity as a species on the planet, then that's what I mean.'

'I'm just talking about Quiroga's Santa Fe, the suburb of Mexico City.'

'Well that's not for me to say, *señor*,' Juan Diego went on, wheeling round and dragging my eyes away from the endless headlines, photographs and snatches of paragraphs which I had distractedly been taking in (the opposition were critical, and petrol prices were on the rise because of increased franchising costs). 'But what I will say is that it seems to me that we need to think seriously about what sort of perfection we want to find when we reach this Santa Fe of yours, because as things stand our political system is having a good go at turning a significant part of humanity into glorified computing machines. And if you ask me, that's got about as much sense in it as turning up to meetings of the local council – and you should know, for I understand that you've been campaigning in local elections yourself – because if the world were a calculator, then we'd all be redundant, so if you're thinking of trying to produce perfection by turning us into machines we might as well all die now.'

'That's a pretty grim view of things, Juan Diego,' I said, thinking back to the opposition protests and the tales of Hollywood affairs (of convenience) which I had digested at the news-stand.

'Yes it is, *señor*, but they say that beauty is in the eye of the beholder, and machines haven't developed eyes since last I looked, so as far as

I can see the more information we have to process, and the more like computers we become, the more all the beauty will be gone from our world so that it can never return.'

'Look here, Juan Diego,' I stormed, feeling increasingly burdened by his speeches, and angry at having been dragged away from the vital information that had been available at the news-stand, 'when I want your opinion, I'll ask for it. We're going to my Utopia now – Quiroga's, that is – and when we reach Santa Fe we'll see that things aren't as black as you make out, and that perfection is only a Molotov cocktail's throw away, particularly if it's directed at the headquarters of a multinational corporation.'

'That's as may be, *señor*,' he answered, with disgusting self-satisfaction, 'but the very fact that you've resorted to mixing your metaphors is encouragement to me not to throw the baby out with the bathwater. After all, if even a good utopian like you is prepared to adopt some of my mannerisms, you can't be as stuck in your ways as I thought you were. Perhaps you've realised that we all have to work hard with others in order to build perfection, and that dispensing with your fantasies and trying to recover some pragmatism is essential if you want your idealism to be taken seriously.'

This was clearly such nonsense that I did not even bother to reply. I was not the one who sounded like a madman and spoke proverbial claptrap, and so I wasn't going to let Juan Diego interfere with my utopian vision. Knowing that I knew best, I resolved to keep myself to myself while we walked towards the site of Quiroga's first utopian experiment.

The streets all seemed alike to me, and we traversed endless blocks of small office buildings, stalls selling bootlegged CDs and worthless knick-knacks, street corners where there were beggars and hawkers of the latest newspapers to hit the press. My eyes flitted from headlines to the slogans beaming out from the shop windows, and these dissociated words soon filled my head in what passed for a stream of consciousness: *murdered by her lover, Mexico's drought alarm, the cheapest in the DF, the latest transfer rumour, World Cup football boots, imported from the United States, balance of trade, paedophiles exposed, oil prices fall, Made in Taiwan, why young models are opting for silicon, rage – the new road to fulfilment, buy one get one free, suicide rates are up, genuine Cantonese food, the canonisation of Juan Diego, one juice for 5 pesos two for 9 pesos, queue here for taxis and right turns.*

Following Juan Diego, I went straight across at the closing-down sale and shortly afterwards we had to wait at the new inflation rate. There was no denying that the special offers were tempting, but there were so many sales that we couldn't stop at them all, much though we were inclined to. We speeded up as we passed the best chicken in Mexico City, and for some time walked abreast of one another, still in silence as we took in the greatest novel ever written since last year and the biggest selection of hosiery in Latin America, while paying as little attention as possible to the potentially cataclysmic situation in the Middle East and the UN's latest predictions regarding climate change.

Suddenly, I stopped again as we neared the Observatorio metro station: as if in an epiphany, I had grasped the significance of what I had seen. There was something of vital importance to world peace and enlightenment in that babbling cacophony of words that I had just digested.

'Wait,' I told Juan Diego, realising that this had nothing to do with oil prices, silicon or special offers; 'what's all this about canonisation?'

'Whose canonisation?' he asked in bewilderment.

'Yours,' I told him. 'I saw the newspaper headline: "The Canonisation of Juan Diego". You can't deny it.'

'Oh no, *señor*,' he said, 'that's got nothing to do with me.'

'Yes it has!' I shouted at him, beside myself. 'You're conducting a sly campaign to turn yourself into a saint at my expense, when I've already told you that I won't stand for it.'

'Oh no, *señor*,' he said, cringing, 'that's not it at all.'

'Don't deny it,' I said, moving closer to him until I was towering over his greasy head. 'You're called Juan Diego, aren't you?'

'No, *señor*,' he said weakly. 'Just Juan. I've been trying to tell you, but you won't listen to me. Oh, how I wish you'd understand what I'm trying to tell you, and turn your delusions of perfection into something sane!'

'Don't lie,' I said, adopting my most threatening pose. 'This is all a ruse to claim the credit for my ideas, isn't it? You want to steal my ideas, you swine! Just so that no one will think of me as the utopian one when they hear of our exploits.'

'No,' he said rapidly, 'that's not it at all. This Juan Diego that they're canonising lived 500 years ago. He was a true saint, *señor*, but I'm just a poor slave following your advice as far as I can, and trying to get you to see sense.'

'Well, can you tell me nothing more about him?' I bayed.

'Not off hand, I'm afraid, *señor*, because—'

'Well that's not good enough!' I exploded. 'I must have the information, you see! I must have it! Where is it?'

'I don't know, *señor*.'

'Give me the information! Give it to me!'

I really was feeling distracted. I stood there, my face leaning over Juan Diego's, my eyes bulging, the breath wheezing out of my lungs as if the city's pollution had turned me into an asthmatic. And then, as I looked at the terror and revulsion in Juan Diego's eyes, I saw how impossibly ugly I had become in such a short space of time. Looking at him again, I realised for the first time that there was something in what he had been trying to tell me. My behaviour was no longer normal; no one was going to listen to me like this.

'The information,' I said, weakly. 'Do you know where it is?'

Juan Diego said nothing for a moment. We were beside one of the city's bus stations, and a constant stream of buses and combis passed us by. A passenger tossed an empty bottle of Coca-Cola into the street, and it rolled to a stop beside us. Juan Diego stooped to pick it up, caressing the spent plastic with strange respect, and then looked at me again with the same mixture of terror and revulsion as before. It was then that I finally realised how absurd I must have looked: an overbearing, unsympathetic, arrogant stranger ordering him how to behave in his own country.

'The information that you're looking for, *señor*,' he said then, tossing the Coca-Cola bottle aside, 'is so endless, so diffuse, so essentially meaningless, so soulless, that for myself I don't think you'll ever be satisfied by it.'

He moved closer to me as he said these words, and I sensed that something was changing in the relationship between us: that although I had all the power, he was no longer subservient, and might even be about to challenge me. I felt weak and exhausted, though, and for once could not defend my much cherished freedoms.

'No,' I muttered. 'No.'

'And as I've already told you, it's my belief that the glut of information is turning people into mere information processors. In fact, I would say that this is merely the tail end of a remorseless historical process that has as its aim the extraction of every last shred of beauty from the Earth and the human race. That is, first, you gut the natural world, and then you destroy humanity's capacity to appreciate its beauty as an end in itself – that is, its sanctity.'

We passed beneath a signpost for Santa Fe and began to walk more quickly as we climbed uphill. At last I could see the descendant of Quiroga's settlement on the hill above me.

'Have you got anything positive to say to me?' I asked in the end.

'Any information which might make me feel better?'

'Oh yes, *señor*,' he said. 'Yes indeed. In fact, I think you might find it helpful if I make a few comments about these ideas of yours in general.'

'What ideas?' I said, aware that, having been taken over by my fantasies, I no longer had any that were of interest. 'I haven't shared them with you yet, and you're really just a disciple on a promise.'

'Well that's as may be, *señor*, but a promise is better than nothing unless it comes from a politician, and you've been pontificating so vaguely about the perfect society for such a long time now that I've had a few thoughts on the matter myself. That's right – no one can call me plain old Sancho any more.'

'Well that's very interesting, Juan Diego,' I said blithely.

'The thing is,' he went on, as we waited at a set of traffic lights, 'wordsmiths like you are forever prating about how to build the perfect world, but there's one thing that you types just don't understand.'

'Which is?' I asked, somewhat impatient as I strode across the road during a break in the traffic and left him momentarily in my wake.

'This idea of a perfect world,' he said, catching up with me, his eyes wide with life, 'is just that: an idea. It's something that's born in the mind and that's where it'd be best off staying. Because ideas are all very well in the safety of an office or a library, where you're well heated and fed and the basic requirements of existence are reduced to electric switches and convenience foods, but the reality of things is far different. The truth is that this supposed perfection is just a reflection of a quality of mind. There are some minds – the most arrogant, unperceptive ones, of course – which see their own thoughts as so limpid and untrammelled as to be perfect in themselves, unblemished; and these arrogant minds wish to transfer their perceived self-perfection to the world outside their own comfort zone. And of course, as soon as they do so it's a disaster – and they often come across as deluded.'

'That's fascinating, Juan Diego,' I said, as we walked along the highway.

'Take yourself, *señor*,' he went on, his face sparked with animation. 'I mean it strikes me that – deep down, at any rate – you're probably not such a bad person. I've no doubt that you'd like to do something that's valuable for society, that there's much about the state of the world that distresses you, and that you have no true desire to intensify suffering for people in the world's poorest countries. Yet ever since you've arrived in Mexico you've been behaving in the most despicable and deranged way.'

'I have?' I asked, in spite of myself, aware that there might be some truth in this.

'Despicable,' Juan Diego repeated. 'Just because you've turned up with some gold coins in your pocket, you've started believing in your own power, and in the righteousness of your beliefs. Worse, you've deluded yourself into believing that you have the answer, and that everyone else is a fool. And so you come to my country and behave with a degree of arrogance that you wouldn't dream of displaying at home, you order me around as if I were your slave, and every shred of idealism that you might once have had disappears in a puff of smoke and the need to keep up repayments on your mortgage while enjoying jet-setting holidays, so that quite frankly I wouldn't be seen dead in any Utopia that you built. It's as if the idealism has gone to your head, which quite frankly is big enough as it is anyway.'

Juan Diego's words cut me to the quick. There was a sincerity in his tone of voice that cut through the barriers that I had built up since arriving in Mexico, and I realised that the idealism that had been mine back when I had been talking to the old man in S—— and leafleting for the election had vanished.

The truth was, I was no longer a good person – whatever that might have been.

'Let's just suppose,' I said to Juan Diego, as we turned a corner in the road and the gradient began to level off, 'that there's something in what you say, and that paradigmatic ideas should remain in the mind and not be transferred to the practical level. Where would you say the origin of this misconstruction lies?'

'Well, *señor*,' he said, as the spire of the church of Santa Fe came into view, 'I blame Plato.'

'Plato!' I exclaimed with false bonhomie. 'You don't mess about, do you? You're quite happy to go straight for the founding father of Western civilisation.'

'But of course,' he said. 'Because it's quite apparent that there's no other way. For, as they say, there's no point in blaming the children when the parents have brought them up badly, and instead of imprisoning drug addicts from inner cities it's the government we should really be after, and it's all very well to lambast corrupt African governments but no one thinks of spitting on the graves of those who played the "great game" at the Berlin Conference in 1885 when Africa was divided up among the colonial powers.'

'What do you mean, Juan Diego? What do you mean?'

'It's very simple, *señor*,' he said. 'Time after time we hear of world leaders meeting to try to resolve the problems caused by climate change, and to improve the industrial world's record where the environment is concerned. But that's got about as much sense in it as putting the cart before the horse, looking for eggs when you've got no chickens, or generating public paranoia and loathing regarding paedophiles when your entire cultural fabric has began to sexualise children. For the truth of the matter is that, like globalisation, the destruction of the world's environment is not a new thing, and is not something that policies alone can remedy.'

'That's something that won't go down very well among the political classes,' I pointed out.

'Well, as they say, although the truth hurts it's not half as painful as depleted uranium bombs, and if the political class don't like it, they could always try working. For the fact is that environmental destruction has its root in our psychology, in the way we think about the world. So until you address that problem, you may as well use the fossil fuels just like most people do, by going to lie on a beach for two weeks, rather than bothering to attend any of these international conferences, or reading any of the documents that they produce, even if they are printed on recycled paper, which quite frankly is about as likely as time running backwards or voter turnout rising at the next election in any stable democracy you care to name.'

'Juan Diego!' I bellowed, trying my usual old trick of stopping still in the street and hoping to catch sight of some racy headline on the news-stand. But he carried on walking, and so I had to hurry after him, leaving my bad habit behind me. 'Juan Diego,' I said heatedly, 'this really is very dangerous, what you're saying. You can't just dissect our psychologies – you've got no training, so you can't possibly know what you're talking about.'

But he ignored me.

'You see,' he went on, 'environmental destruction has been going on for centuries, and began when the Spanish discovered these poor countries of ours and engaged in biological conquest, in stripping the minerals away and shipping them off to their old continent to mint them for coinage, which had always been in short supply until they discovered the mines of the Americas.[1] And this attitude towards the environment was that it was not an end in itself – and sacred – but a means to an end: wealth. And in seeing the environment as entirely utilitarian rather than sacred, the Europeans were implementing categories of thought that were fundamentally incompatible with ecology. Of course, we all know that since the time of the discovery of the

Americas, this attitude has only hardened, refined, settled beneath layers of historical dust. And in fact this category of thought is now so deeply embedded in the Western mindset that we might think that it was impossible to uproot, were it not for the enormous urgency of doing so.'

'Juan Diego, this is nonsense. You've absolutely no evidence for any of this, and so it's worthless trash, pigmeat, hogwash, excrement. I spit on your theory.' I felt such a boiling rage at these ideas, that I did not just spit on the theory – I stopped and spat in his face.

Slowly, with what I can only describe as dignity, he wiped the spittle from his chin and continued talking. 'Yes, *señor*,' he said gently, 'this reaction of yours is only what I had expected. Because when you touch someone at their rawest, deepest emotion, fury is what results.'

'Fury!' I repeated, furiously.

'May I suggest, *señor*,' he went on, 'that for the time being you do not look around yourself at the news-stands and the shop windows, but down at the ground. This way, you will not be disturbed by the constant barrage of information, and may begin to calm your spirit – and even rediscover your soul.'

We walked on in silence for a time, and I followed his advice. My fury lessened, until all at once I felt myself overcome by a wave of sadness. Soon I stretched out my arm and touched Juan Diego lightly on the shoulder, so that he turned to look at me. I was surprised to realise that my eyes were misted over with tears, and that I could barely speak – that I was still capable of being moved.

'Wait,' I said to him in the end. 'Wait.'

'Oh don't stop now, *señor*,' he said. 'We're almost there now.'

I looked around me. To my left, the hillside fell away to a valley where hundreds of shanties were piled up like driftwood in the bowl. Smog hung above the impoverished people who lived there, concealing the limping dogs and the tendrils of plastic and the dust that billowed around the makeshift homes. Beyond, the glass-fronted façades of nearby international hotel chains glinted through the pollution, pricking the hazy sky with their names – *Sheraton, Marriot, Crowne Plaza* – and for a moment I imagined the international executives who stayed in such places staring out from their windows at the confused, vibrant, suffering human city below them, squinting hopelessly through the smog at this world in which they were but partially sighted.

I looked at Juan Diego. 'We're almost there?' I asked him.

'Yes,' he said. 'The monument to Quiroga is just down that street.'

He pointed down a side alley, and I glimpsed a throng crowding around fruit-sellers, and the Church of Santa Fe at the end of the road.

'But Juan Diego,' I said. 'What about Plato?'

'Plato?' he said. 'What about him?'

'A few minutes ago you told me that you blamed him.'

'Well then,' said Juan Diego, 'he can come with us. He's with us every minute of our lives whether we know it or not.'

He turned and led me across the road, dodging a pair of overcrowded city buses and rows of car tyres laid out along the pavement. Soon we had reached the market area. Here we were assailed by the smell of frying corn, and the sounds of a tuneless orphan busking beside the entrance to the market. Bundles of fruit and vegetables were piled up beneath the awnings of the stalls, and Juan Diego bought two bananas, which we ate as we descended the small incline to the church. Just stopping, and not thinking about Utopia, or the news, or the sales in the city shops, brought me an inner peace that I had not experienced for some time.

By and by we reached the gateway to the church, which had been erected on the site of Quiroga's pueblo-hospital. A few children were playing football on the forecourt, while their parents sat on a wall nearby and arranged dead men's clothes that would soon be sold to raise funds to repair the crumbling colonial building. Beneath the shade of a cedar tree, some teenagers were strumming their guitars, and a stream of music soon came to rest above us all, touching us gently with our sadness.

I turned to Juan Diego. He had picked up an empty bottle of mineral water from the ground.

'Look at this,' he said. He proffered me the bottle, which had been manufactured by the Mexican subsidiary of an international corporation. 'If you read that, you'll see why the present economic system is incompatible with the conservation of the environment and of the human species.'

I read the label, which declared: 'Preserve the environment. Put the empty bottle in the bin.'

'Of course,' he said, 'you'll have noticed that our nation has a great problem with trash. Just putting things away tidily is a great difficulty, let alone recycling it for future use.'

This was true. I had arrived in Mexico's rubbish tip, after all, and I had also seen that on either side of every road in the city – and this doubtless went for the country as well – there were lines of empty bottles, discarded newspapers, cellophane wrappers, and whatever junk there was to hand.

'Yes,' I said.

'We throw it here, there and everywhere.'

'Yes.'

In fact, right now, as Juan Diego spoke to me, there was a vast pile of rubbish festering on the street, yards from the gate to the church of Santa Fe.

'Well,' he went on, as we walked into the ecclesiastical compound and looked up at a statue marking the four-hundredth anniversary of the death of Quiroga, 'it's my belief that this too has a deep link to the psychology of conquest. For when the Spanish came here they found a people who, while imperial, did not have a concept of value such as they did. For the Mexica, metals were metals – they had no added value, and were not used for a coinage which could endure for more than one season, and thereby create a capital surplus. No, cocoa beans were the main form of exchange – a currency that was locked into the seasonal cycles – and not gold. And this was because their attitude towards the environment was that it was sacred, not utilitarian. But the Spanish had to implant the concept of the natural world as utilitarian if they were going to turn the colonies into the breadbasket of Europe. They had to uproot that old understanding, and to do so they had to be uncompromising. They had to make the Amerindians believe that their cosmology was worthless. And so it was that the entire economic and educational system of the colonial era was directed to this end – with the consequence that we Mejicanos, today, having discarded our cosmology of the world as sacred, now discard our litter wherever we choose to.'

We walked on until we had reached the doorway to the church. The bell tower was blue and white, and the house of worship had been built in an elegant colonial style, burying the emotions that had been created by the events at this place, so long ago – emotions whose legacy, if I was to believe Juan Diego, we still suffered from to this day.

'And all this,' I said eventually, 'all this is Plato's fault?'

'Of course, *señor*,' he said. 'Or rather, it's the fault of our inter-pretation of the significance of Plato's work. For though Plato wrote many things which could be interpreted as being semi-mystical – the theory of recollection in the *Meno*, for instance – what we concentrate on now is his sublimation of the workings of the mind as the ultimate perfection, through his theory of the forms.*[2] It's this stress that

---

*Plato's theory held that there were, essentially four levels of knowledge: understanding (*noesis* in Greek), thought (*dianoia*), belief (*pistis*) and imagination (*eikasia*). The first two

brought about the mind's separation from the natural world, its capacity to think objectively and reflect upon that world. And of course, it is that sublimated ideal – the "perfection" of the mind – which is the origin of the whole idea of Utopia: the transferral of the perfection of the mind to the real world. So it's no surprise to me that Plato was cited by Thomas More as his inspiration, and can be called the first utopian.'

'Absolutely, Juan Diego,' I said, trying to retain my calm. 'But most people think of this as a positive thing. This is why Plato is the foundation of our thought systems. For it's the capacity to analyse the world that has brought about every scientific breakthrough worthy of the name.'

Juan Diego smiled at me, his face a relief map of crags and hollows in the shade cast by the church's bell tower.

'I hear what you're saying, *señor*,' he said. 'But as they say, the proof of the pudding is in the eating, and I'll remind you that I still haven't had the cake that I was planning to eat as well. But that aside, there's more to this than meets the eye, so we'd better look quickly before we've been turned into machines and rendered permanently blind. And what I mean to say is that there are two sides to every coin, and one man's meat is another man's poison, and terrorism can easily be a just war if you live in a shanty town in any country in Africa or the Middle East. So while we might look on science as the proof of Plato's pudding, there is ample evidence that its sugars have begun to over-ferment. For surely the evidence of the incompleteness of the Platonic view is precisely the failure of utopian societies over the centuries.'

'Failures?' I asked. 'But I've just told you that *my* utopia is going to be perfect.'

'I know you have, *señor*, but *I've* just told you to stop deluding yourself if you want idealism to have a chance, because that perfection is a figment of your imagination and would be better off being left back in the library when you've finished a day's work. To be frank,

---

were directed at the intelligible realm (i.e. the realm of the mind): *dianoia* worked towards first principles, using hypotheses drawn from the visible world; *noesis* (the ultimate knowledge) was grasped by reason through the power of the dialectic, reaching the 'unhypothetical principle of everything' which allowed the mind to perceive the perfect, immutable 'form' of both qualities and objects. The next two categories were directed at the visible realm: *eikasia* was directed at what might be called reflections of this world – shadows, reflections in water, and so on – and was thus the lowest level of understanding, while *pistis* was directed at the things directly perceived in the natural world.

most people these days don't see Stalinism, religious idealism or even socialism as much of a success. And those ideologies – aiming for the best society that can be created – are pretty much condemned to failure from the outset. For once you take the non-existent perfection of the mind and transfer it to the world, it's not very surprising that what you're left with is also far from perfect – and in fact is dystopian. And similarly, once – like Plato – you separate the mind from the world to which it is intimately connected, it is not surprising that the mind ceases to see the world as an end in itself, and starts to manipulate, distort and destroy it. So to be brutally honest, for it's about time that someone was, with time pressing on and – let's face it – running out, until we dispense with this way of seeing the natural world, until we temper the Platonic mindset and much of the baggage that goes with it, humanity as we know it is doomed.'

I found much of this deeply disturbing; yet the fury that I had felt earlier at Juan Diego's deconstruction of my emotions – or the lack of them – had gone. Nor was I, even, particularly sad. Instead, I sensed that my mind was completely empty, all played out. I listened to the sounds of women sweeping the street outside their homes and of buses rumbling aggressively along the hillside beyond the church and of salesmen making their pitches in the nearby market, but it was all as if I was disembodied, and absent.

For a moment this seemed like the foretaste of death.

'Well, Juan Diego,' I murmured, feeling the need to touch his shoulder again, 'what's to be done?'

'Let's go inside to begin with,' he said.

With the doors to the church firmly shut, I had imagined that entering the place of prayer would be impossible. But now Juan Diego twisted the iron doorknob without force, and the wooden doors gave. We wandered inside to a nave that was steeped in coolness. The sounds outside were at once more distant. Here, amid the icons streaming with tears of blood, and the luminous, naïve, portraits of the Passion of Christ, I touched the cornerstone of my emptiness. There was no information here. None at all.

'Our Lord,' Juan Diego intoned, and I turned to see that he was kneeling beside a pew, with his hands clasped together in prayer.

'What's this, Juan Diego?' I asked in a fierce stage whisper. 'It might be that I'm prepared to accept much of what you say, but I draw the line at this.'

Juan Diego looked at me with pity, and then beckoned gently. I followed him out into a side passage, where I saw to my pleasure that there was a small exhibition about Vasco de Quiroga, with old maps and drawings of the greenery and fresh springs that had once graced Santa Fe, conveying an impression of what the pueblo-hospital might have been like.

'You see, *señor*,' he said calmly, 'I can understand what you say. But yet again, I fear, it's a question of putting the cart before the horse. After all, now, at the very moment when civilisation is on the point of unravelling, we are beginning to understand how and why we have reached this stage – just when it is too late.'

I sat down heavily on the cold flagstones in the side passage. A portrait of Vasco de Quiroga stared down at me, but his emotions remained inscrutable.

'I see,' I said.

'And of course,' Juan Diego went on, 'there are two ways of dealing with this situation. You can either dig a bigger hole for yourself, and bury your head even further into it, as if searching for the dodo and the Guanche people of the Canary Islands – just to make it a proper threesome when we all finally come to the party of extinction. Or you can do everything in your power to recover those emotions which, if requited even at this late stage, might yet save us.'

'And how should we do that, Juan Diego?' I asked.

'Well, *señor*,' he said, 'you can't leap back 500 years in time and reclaim the mindset of the discoverers of the New World who were asked to abandon their utilitarianism where the world was concerned and reaffirm its sanctity. What you can do instead is realise that in order to try and recover that gift – which they spurned – you have to recover that sense of sanctity which was lost precisely then, at the moment of discovery, and reject the idea that humanity will indefinitely be able to control nature. And in order to do that, you have to look at our present situation, and identify what it is that is taking us further away from any appreciation of that emotional identification of the world as sacred. And in my view, that's precisely the rampant expansion of information, which is having, as I've said, a good go at turning all of us into glorified machines.'

At the mention of information, my chest knotted; somehow, though (perhaps because there was no news-stand nearby), I managed to dispel the tension.

'But Juan Diego,' I whispered desperately, 'we all need that information. We all depend upon it. Without it, we're sunk. As the saying goes, "Knowledge is power," and without information, there's no knowledge these days. We'll all be put in the dark ages.'

'Yes indeed, *señor*, but if you don't mind my saying so, that saying is part of the problem. For we need to lose the idea that our power over the world can save us. And, of course, I'm not one to forget that, as I've said, there's two sides to every coin, and one man's meat is another man's poison, and...'

'Yes I understand all that,' I interrupted impatiently.

'And of course,' he went on more softly, 'I accept that there are good sides to the information superhighway. That people can be in touch with friends across the world. That they can investigate things which before they could not have done. That they can learn in different ways. But then that's because I see both sides to the coin. And perhaps my hope is that the general atmosphere could at least *begin* to recognise that, as well as having its positive side, the remorseless digestion of information is also liable to make us more mechanical and strip away our capacity to appreciate the sanctity of the planet, that is of our world as an end in itself. Perhaps if we could all individually recognise this, even subconsciously – there's no hope of relying on the government, that's for sure – then we could begin to evolve a new, and modern sense of the gift that our ancestors spurned so many centuries ago.'

I was distracted for a moment by the sound of an aeroplane droning overhead. Everything that Juan Diego had said had been unexpectedly soothing, and I found that the sense of unreality that had dogged me ever since speaking to Pablo in Seville was beginning to dissipate. Perhaps idealists did not have to be deluded, I thought, turning to the severe portrait of Vasco de Quiroga, and wondering quite how far Juan Diego's comments related to him. I yearned for Quiroga's quest to have been righteous, and true, but had it really been little more than arrogance and a bit-player in the mind's disassociation of itself from the world? I looked hard at the portrait – at the tight lips, the lean, bird-like features, the gnarled hand which held the Bible – and still saw no answer.

'Perhaps they had their reasons for spurning it,' I said at last, turning to my squire.

'Yes, perhaps they did, *señor*,' he said. 'But in my view the main reason was precisely the disappointment at seeing their dreams of perfection – born in the mind – fail when it came to the New World. And, to hark back to our earlier conversation, in another chapter of our relationship, as it were, this was what Cervantes was driving at in his anti-utopianism in the *Quixote*. And, in fact, if you ask me, it was precisely this experience in the New World that was behind the souring of the utopian ideal in the early-modern age.'

Juan Diego went on to explain to me that it had still taken some time for this process to develop, even after the publication of Cervantes's masterwork. In 1627, the famous English luminary Francis Bacon had published his *New Atlantis*, in which he had argued for a Utopia of scientific enlightenment, where the goal of his 'new' Atlantis – known as Bensalem – was 'the knowledge of Causes, and secret motions of things',[3] and so the city's gardens and public spaces had been mainly used for experimentation,[4] and filled with statues of their great inventors.[5] As a symbol of the new scientific spirit of inquiry in the seventeenth century, Juan Diego went on, *New Atlantis* had been important; yet this book had also borne hints of the way in which the utopian ideal was changing at this time, and perhaps being soured by a souring of the psychologies of those who created such ideas: for Bacon had also written that, when a European hermit had 'desired to see the Spirit of Fornication ... there appeared to him a little foul ugly Ethiop [African]. But if he had pleased to see the Spirit of Chastity ... it would have appeared to him in the likeness of a fair beautiful Cherubim.'[6]

In fact, as the seventeenth century wore on, said Juan Diego, the idealism which had accompanied the Renaissance began to give way to the satirical, proto-utopian novels – the forerunners of modern irony – which were written in the eighteenth century, when writers such as Jonathan Swift used distant locations to heap savage criticism on the 'age of reason and nature'.[7] By the end of the eighteenth century, the spirit of genuine utopians such as More and Bacon was gone, and Jean-Jacques Rousseau, Juan Diego told me, has been seen by many recent theorists to be the last of this school.[8] Rousseau's frequent writings about the state of nature, and the loosing of humanity's bonds, his idealisation of the primitive human state and of a world in which there was no property,[9] made him both a descendant of More and a predecessor of Marx – a stepping stone between Renaissance idealism and its industrialised modern offshoots.

'And so you see,' Juan Diego said at last, turning to me with a smile, and dispelling the distance that his gaze had adopted as he had been speaking, 'it is precisely the failure of projects such as that of your friend Quiroga which led to the slow disintegration of idealism in the world, something which today has run its course.'

'Failure!' I exclaimed. 'No, I am sure it was not that.'

'But you see, *señor*, it had to be – failure is the only possible outcome of the utopian ideal made real.'

'No, Juan Diego, I won't have it.' I was incensed by this comment.

'You're always going on about the two sides to every coin, and if you can't see that idealism is not all bad – that it can lead to nobility, and dignity, and contented societies as well as disaster – then I won't listen to you a moment longer.'

I stood up firmly; Don Vasco's face seemed to approve of my decision.

'There is something in what you say, *señor*,' he said. 'For of course we must distinguish between ideology and idealism. It's ideology that leads people to delusions, but idealism can yet be approached in a calm, beneficial manner – and if you really want people to be inspired to idealism after reading of your adventures, then it's calmness which you need to foster. But as for your friend Quiroga...'

I cut him off. 'No, Juan Diego,' I said, 'I won't listen to another word. I know you pretty well by now, and I've decided to ignore you. As far as I'm concerned you can go off back to your taxi and salvage the wreckage that we left last night on the motorway. For although much of what you say has the benefit of rhetoric and humour, it's nonsense. So I won't waste my time a moment longer with you.'

I left him and returned to the nave. I did not stop to genuflect, or reflect on my actions, but went back out the way I had come, into the storm of light and noise and information that lay beyond the church at Santa Fe. I still believed that the sooner I got on with my ambitious historical and literary quest for Quiroga, and perfection, and forgot all about these spurious criticisms that Juan Diego had developed of my ideas, the better.

I was about to forget him, when I heard his weaselly voice moaning behind me.

'Wait, *señor*,' he called out. 'You've forgotten about the canonisation.'

This was the only comment that could have stopped me. I wheeled on my heel and stared at my miserable former squire.

'Oh don't worry, Juan Diego, don't worry. I'm now quite aware that it's got nothing to do with you.'

'Well, *señor*, that's where you're wrong.'

All of a sudden I realised that the filthy rubbish heap beyond the church had rid itself of its ugliness. It was now a heaving mass of people, waving flags, holding crucifixes, praying to the heavens. The faithful were standing ten-deep and staring at the empty road, transfixed by the concrete and the atmosphere of devotion, and longing, and hope, and the desperate need for something to fill the growing void.

'What is it?' I said to Juan Diego, in spite of myself. 'What are they all doing?'

'They're waiting for the pope,' he said. 'He's flown to Mexico to canonise Juan Diego, the Indian who had the vision of the Virgin Mary at Guadalupe.'

'But why are they coming here?'

Before Juan Diego could reply, a cavalcade of limousines swept around the corner of the road, and in through the gateway to Santa Fe, pulling up in an irksome rain of dust. Then a smaller vehicle appeared behind them, topped off with a bulletproof compartment in which the pope stood waving to the crowds who adored him.

'You see, *señor*,' said Juan Diego, 'it's the popemobile. He's come to canonise me instead. After all, you've baptised me so that now I'm called Juan Diego, and I'm as good a substitute as anybody, particularly for some Indian who's been dead for 500 years.'

I was filled with horror and anger.

'Juan Diego, you lied to me!'

'No, *señor*, I did not. I was not aware when I denied my impending sainthood to you that my views on Utopia, perfection, and the history of the Spanish conquest would be seen with such favour by the Catholic Church. But then no one's a saint until they're made one, and God smiles on all of us even though only a few are chosen, and if humanity's to be saved, then we need a few more saints to help us, so why not choose me?, for I'm as deserving as the next man, particularly where you're concerned, *señor*.'

The protective plastic screen was wheeled back from the pope, and he advanced onto the cracked concrete. There was a surge in the roadside crowd, and the security guards had to hold back the penitents as he came with dignity towards us, moving so slowly that it seemed a miracle that he moved at all.

'But what will I do now Juan Diego?' I whispered. 'Without you.'

'Well, *señor*, you've come further with me than you ever would have done without me. And I think you've understood the truth in what I've told you about information, and the need to address this first of all. And it may well be that if you can get that right, the rest will follow, for where the beginning's concerned, the end's already in sight. And now we've already galloped through Cervantes and reached Rousseau, you won't be needing Sancho any more. And what's more, as I've told you, it's really time for you to dispense with your whole quixotic mentality, and to try to recover some normality, if you want your idealism to have any lasting impression.'

'I suppose you're right,' I said, feeling my arrogance fall away. 'But this canonisation isn't helping – it's as fantastical as the rest of our adventures put together.'

'Of course, *señor*, and no one would expect your delusions to disappear overnight. But, little by little, I'm hopeful that they'll vanish, and that we'll all see how idealism can indeed be a rational and sane alternative in the modern world.'

'That's my hope, Juan Diego,' I whispered.

'And just so long as you remember that, *señor*, you may yet go far,' he said. 'Because the most important thing about this journey of yours is to recover those sixteenth-century emotions, and lay them bare so that they can heal. That's what you must seek to find in Quiroga, and his story. That's why you must integrate it with your own emotional world. That's why they're so indissolubly linked, why the one story feeds into the other, and vice versa. And that's why this tale of yours is becoming ever more complicated, all-encompassing, and difficult to categorise, so that I shouldn't wonder whether, when it's all come to an end, people won't decide that what you've really produced is a work of the imagination rather than something that can adequately be described as factual.'

'Juan Diego ...' I said – but it was too late.

From the darkened interiors of the limousines, two groups of cardinals now appeared, dressed in red. They walked solemnly up to the pope, and assisted the pontiff the last few metres towards us – I shrank away from them, as they neared Juan Diego.

'*San Juan*,' they intoned, '*San Juan de Dios*. Servant of God, voice of the people.'

They led him away to their cars, and drove off. The crowds melted away as quickly as they had appeared, and I was left alone.

My first thought was to cry, but yet I felt strangely uplifted. I would bear Juan Diego in my mind, I resolved, and in my soul. I would cherish his atavistic love for the world's sanctity as if it had been my own. He had not dismissed the idea that there might have been some goodness in Quiroga, and perhaps by a miracle of the new saint I would find myself in Santa Fe de la Laguna, the site of Quiroga's most important utopian experiment – that might be the last narrative fantasy that he'd allow me.

I turned towards the west, and saw that all was not lost. In my mind's eye, the woods were filled with birdsong. I glided past the volcanoes, dallying with the eagles in their eyries. The world was fire, and light, and below were the countless lakes of a new world, as if formed by the tears of the gods of the peoples of this country, this world, this phoenix ready to rise from the shattered hills below.

I had arrived in Michoacán, the diocese where Quiroga had been made bishop.

TEN

To the north-west of Mexico, this Michoacán is a lattice of wonder.

The pastures are carpeted with flowers. Valleys are cut off from one another by ridges which twist into mysterious shapes, and are laden down with forests, choked with creepers. The hills are full of hummingbirds, and eagles, doves and turtle doves, quails, ducks, owls.[1] There are deer, and hares, wild boar, wolves, jaguars, foxes, badgers.[2] The bounty of the gods runs wild.

At times mists of rain descend to make this Eden inscrutable, and the eye fastens upon beards of moss, on plants burdened with raindrops, until of a sudden rosaries of lakes break up the view. The rivers are innumerable, and crystalline, and the fish of its waters are so many 'that the whole Province [is] named for their sheer quantity, Michoacán meaning "land of fish" in the Mexican language'.[3] With the tight valleys, the boulders that sprawl over the forest floor, the mists and the distant volcanic fires of Mexico and Colima, this relief landscape lies fragmented: and so, living amid these surroundings, the Purépecha* people see the cosmos as a struggle between order and chaos.

In around 1520, one of their priests has a dream. It is cold and dark in the main city, Tzintzuntzan – 'the place of the hummingbird' – and he dreams that a strange people have come bringing strange beasts, and that they enter the homes of the priests and sleep there with their beasts, and that they bring with them many chickens who soil the temples.[4] He dreams this two or three times, his heart a knot of fear. It is not as if the gods have recently been withholding portents of doom: two big comets have been seen, while for four years now the temples have been splitting up, releasing slabs of stone that smash to the ground.[5]

---

*The indigenous people of Michoacán are variously known as the Tarascans or the Purépecha – Tarascan being the term used by the colonists, and Purépecha that used by the people themselves, and the most commonly used today.

In the mornings, the priest stokes the fires in the temple with greater fervour than before. Fire is essential to the religious rites of the Purépecha, and the most important act of devotion is to burn wood in the temples of the main God, Curicaveri.[6] The wood is taken from the fortifications of the old stronghold of the Purépecha[7] through programmes of public work,[8] and the smoke that burns from it is seen as the channel of communication between people on Earth and their gods in the heavens.[9] Provided that he keeps the fires burning, the priest tells himself, all calamity will be averted. Nevertheless, he keeps his dream hidden when the chief priest passes by with his ceremonial diadem, lance, and a calabash filled with turquoise[10] that reflects the hummingbirds' feathers.

As the wood in the temple bursts with fire, and the sacred arrow of smoke rises with even more strength than before, the priest's mind is calmed. Rationally, of course, he knows that there is little for the Purépecha to fear in this world. They are, after all, the Mesoamerican people who have stemmed the advance of the Mexican Empire. Did not their great leader, Tzitzic Pandacuare, defeat the army of the Mexican Emperor Axayácatl fifty years ago?[11] Now, the Purépecha are able to live peacefully beneath the rule of their leader Tzintzicha, the *cazonci*, helped by their mastery of copper smelting and the copper axes which they take with them into battle. The ruthless Empire of the Mexica has not touched them, and they still rule themselves.

So, in the place of the hummingbird, even as the omens have gathered in Mexico, around the place of the prickly pear, everything maintains the veneer of normality. This is a settled, agrarian culture, where beans, squashes, pumpkins, chillies, tomatoes and maize are all harvested. The people fish in the lakes with circular nets,[12] and make honey.[13] They are mostly naked.[14] There is no murder among them, for fear of the terrible penalties imposed,[15] and they often live to the age of eighty or ninety.[16] The priests burn incense in elaborate multicoloured braziers,[17] ensuring that the Purépecha do not forget the importance of festivals, the wellsprings of existence.

At one such celebration, they fast for five days, before dressing up with feathers and disguising themselves as different-coloured clouds. Two slaves are sacrificed, before the people fall into drunkenness for five days,[18] drinking their fermented pulque* from small earthen jugs

---

*Pulque was the preferred form of drink in Mesoamerica at this time – fermented from the maguey cactus, it is still drunk in Mexico today. The maguey was an extraordinarily versatile plant; as Quiroga himself wrote, it gave the Indians drink and

until they can no longer stand up.[19] And throughout all this they are dancing, giving thanks to the spirits which are about them, to the maguey cactus, to the corn and chillies which give them their food, to the gods of the fish, the divine underworld beneath the surface, to the forces of the air, of light, of good, to the sacred power of life. They do not disguise their nakedness when dancing, for this is ecstasy, the release of human constrictions laid upon the soul; garments are shed, and only a cloth is worn about the shoulders.[20] The festival is five days long, but it is its own world, a paean of understanding.

Festivals intermingle with the daily rituals which give life meaning. The Purépecha are farmers through and through. Although collectivisation exists among them, as with the Mexica there is also a caste system, with the elite – who are distinguished by their brilliant turquoise necklaces,[21] and by their multicoloured cotton gowns which reach down to their feet[22] – arranging the equal distribution of the crops.[23] Women carry dishes of fruit and tortillas, while their husbands cut wood with their copper axes. They live together in huts which are covered by straw, and have one central doorway. As well as their agricultural work, many of the Purépecha are skilled craftspeople, and there are bowmakers, shoemakers, silversmiths, carpenters.[24]

Marriage is of crucial importance, with parents begging their daughters to behave well, as 'it is the custom that through the wrongdoing of one the relatives or parents will die'.[25] Some marry 'out of love, and without paying any attention to their parents' wishes',[26] but others marry relatives, especially sisters-in-law if a brother has died.[27] When a woman does marry, she cleans a large path at the entrance to the house in which she will live, 'symbolising ... the life which she [will] now lead':[28] clean and straight.

Such is the world of the ordinary Purépecha. They are governed by the *cazonci*, who, though a priest-king, does not have the attributes of a divine being, unlike the Emperor of the Mexica, being instead the human representative of Curicaveri.[29] The *cazonci* keeps an army of eighty royal eagles, who are fed on turkeys, and also a wolf, a puma and a jaguar.[30] There are storytellers to keep him amused.[31] Everyone serving in the *cazonci*'s house is a woman;[32] there are many noble ladies here who only go out of the royal compound to dance with the *cazonci* at festivals.[33] He also has castes of officials who are responsible for essential activities, such as quarrying, making houses, making and

(*cont*) honey and kindling and rope, as well as clothing and knitting needles (IED, op. cit., p. 487ff.)

repairing temples, and hunting duck and pheasant for the goddess Xaratanga.[34]

Occasionally, of course, the *cazonci* has to lead the Purépecha to war. When preparing for battle, the people dust down their suits of cotton armour.[35] Their generals are arrayed with headdresses of brilliant green feathers; their military standards are tall and painted deep red. Fighting is joined with bows and arrows, and large clubs; when the Purépecha are victorious, they burn down the houses of their enemies, share out the booty, and march off the prisoners for sacrifice.[36] With this combination of collectivism and ruthlessness, a belief in the sanctity of the world and a fierce fighting spirit, surely nothing can uproot their stronghold.

Yet the omens and dreams have not been all for nothing: the calamity suffered by the Mexica now reaps its own harvest in Michoacán as well. When first assailed by the Spanish, Montezuma sends envoys urging an alliance to ward off the common foe. But the *cazonci* Tzintzicha refuses, suspecting a trick. Shortly afterwards, the plague of smallpox assails them, together with measles, so that 'countless people die, and many lords' – including the *cazonci* himself.[37]

By the time the Spaniards arrive in February 1521, the Purépecha are in no state to resist, and greet the conquerors with friendship. The new *cazonci*, also called Tzintzicha, sends out 800 lords, each of whom is responsible for many people, so that the fields are covered with countless souls.[38] The Spaniards – led by Fernando de Villadiego[39] – are taken to special quarters, where they are entertained by musicians.[40] Tzintzicha then throws an enormous party which lasts for eighteen days, during which many people are sacrificed to the gods, before sending the Spanish envoys back with twenty Indians weighed down with fine cloth, twenty wooden chairs, and much fine leatherwork.[41] He also sends women to accompany the Spaniards to their beds – now, all forms of conquest have begun.*

In return for these gifts, Tzintzicha merely asks for the dog brought by the Spaniard Montaño.† Aware that the Spanish dogs have torn so many of the Mexica to death, he orders the dog to be sacrificed.

---

*This was the origin of the word 'Tarascan'. The Purépecha travelling with this party called the Castilians 'tarascue', which meant 'sons-in-law' in their language, after they had slept with these women on the way back to the Spanish army. See Hugh Thomas (1993), op. cit., p. 473.
†This was the same Montaño who famously, shortly after the conquest, went down into the crater of Popocatépetl to procure sulphur. This was then mixed with nitrate to provide gunpowder for the conquistadors.

A holy offering now, the dog is passed to the priestly caste.

The priest who has seen his terrifying dream come to pass bears the dog towards the altar. What is life, he wonders, but an expression of the dreamworld? Perhaps the catastrophe is his fault, a reflection of his turbulent psychology. If the whole social atmosphere is shot through with stories of Armageddon – Apocalypse – if that catastrophe seems nearer at every turn, then that collective feeling inevitably bears fruit. We live with the burden of destruction in our hearts, the priest feels, and the innate viciousness of the life cycle that is sanctified through living; what chance could this world have had, when the unspoken assumption of society was that it would soon be destroyed?

The dog growls with anger, bloodlust, fear; but his viciousness soon falls away into the impotence of a whimper. The priest clears his mind and climbs the steps of the temple with the dog, the sacrificial lamb – chosen ahead of the children of the Purépecha, many of whom have already been taken by the plagues.

The day is a clear one. The ripples of Lake Pátzcuaro spread out with the strokes of the wind, the rustles of the reeds. The hillsides are a frenzy of forests, lambent with the dawn light.

This divine, sacred existence stands on the verge of collapse. Only a recasting of the world in its original sacred terror can save it now.

The priest prepares to tear free the dog's heart, to leave it pulsing out its violence on the temple floor.

'Now,' he says, 'with your death, you will pay for the death of so many.'[42]

Yet the price paid by the dog was a low one.

After their peaceful capitulation, the Purépecha allowed the Franciscan friars in to preach among them. They sought coexistence with the Spaniards, and Tzintzicha visited Cortés three times in Mexico. But following Cortés's fall from grace in 1526, after his expedition to Honduras and the execution of Cuáhtemoc,* the Purépecha suffered terribly at the hands of the First Audiencia.

In the spring of 1529, Tzintzicha visited Nuño de Guzmán in Mexico, and offered him a gift of twenty plates of silver and many ingots of gold. But Guzmán was angered at this 'small' present, and imprisoned the *cazonci* until a ransom was paid in May;[43] although then allowed to return to Michoacán, Tzintzicha's freedom did not endure.

*See above, ch. 7, pp. 116–17.

In the summer of 1529, Guzmán decided to embark on a fortune-hunt to the land of the Chichimec Indians, to the north of Michoacán. He summoned Tzintzicha in August, and ordered him to collect supplies for his army as it passed through his territory. Between August and December, Tzintzicha was imprisoned in Mexico, only being released to prepare the tribute.[44]

Guzmán's army arrived in Tzintzuntzan early in January 1530. Within a week, the President of the Audiencia had arrested Tzintzicha and charged him with planning an ambush of his army in Michoacán, with obstructing the work of the *encomenderos*, with sodomy and reverting to idolatry, and with not supplying enough provisions for the expedition (nor providing him with enough gold and silver).[45] Local Purépecha were tortured into giving evidence against their *cazonci*, who was stripped naked and humiliated during the 'hearing'.

On 29 January 1530 the expedition to the land of the Chichimecs set off with all of the most important figures from Tzintzuntzan in chains, tied together by collars. Two weeks later, Guzmán pronounced Tzintzicha guilty as charged. He was to be burnt for his crimes, and his ashes thrown into a river; all his possessions were to be requisitioned by the crown.[46] Hauled before the tribunal of the Second Audiencia on 22 January 1532, Guzmán's sidekick, García del Pilar, admitted that, prior to his execution, the feet of the *cazonci* were burnt to get at the gold and silver; and that Tzintzicha had cried out that 'he had done no wrong to any Christian, and asked why they treated him so badly'.[47]

With no one to protect them, the ordinary Purépecha were hauled off by Guzmán on his expedition. They served as porters, and as slaves. Many died because of the different climates in the north, and the garden of Michoacán emptied.[48] Purépecha society fragmented: the people fled for the sierras, where they lived wild and shunned all contact with the Spanish.[49] It was clear that the situation needed to be rescued, and that someone needed to go to the distant province from Mexico.

By now, a split had developed in the capital of New Spain between Vasco de Quiroga and the other *oidores*, doubtless grounded in Quiroga's 'preposterous' pueblo-hospital for the Indians. The *oidores* appear to have wanted him to have as little to do with the day-to-day running of the colony as possible,[50] and so it was that he was sent on a journey of investigation to the troubled region, probably departing in November 1533.[51]

The timing, at least, of Quiroga's expedition was sensible. Although the Audiencia were still trying to bring Nuño de Guzmán to book – he was off adventuring in Jalisco – after two years in Mexico they had heard enough evidence to realise that Michoacán had been brought to its knees. Furthermore, Charles V's initial orders had been carried out, so that the new government had submitted their report of all the places in New Spain,[52] and had made great strides in the protection of the Indians: branding slaves in the face was now banned, and clerics were prohibited from keeping any '*indios encomendados*'.

It was natural, then, that the president and *oidores* should turn their attention further afield. Quiroga travelled with a notary – Alonso de Paz, who was almost certainly a *converso** – a bailiff and an interpreter. On arriving in Tzintzuntzan, he called for the Purépecha governor, Don Pedro Cuiranánguari and the other senior figures from the city, and told them that they had to get their people down from the hills, where they 'lived a life similar to that of wild beasts',[53] and were 'savage and atavistic in their manner'.[54] As the Purépecha saw that the new envoys had not tortured them, in marked contrast to all the other Spaniards that they had met thus far, they began to descend into the valley.

Quiroga explained to them the simple Christian truths. According to Alonso de Paz, he told them that 'their idols ensured that they were ill-treated and persecuted for their sins'.[55] While it was true that they had been greatly 'fatigued so that others could take their gold and jewels off them, all this was because of their idols'.[56] And so the Purépecha brought with them their divine representations, hewn of wood and of stone, which the Spanish – led by Quiroga – began to break and burn.[57]

Quiroga then married Don Pedro to one of his four wives; the Indian governor abandoned the others.[58] Quiroga told the Purépecha who had gathered that he wanted to build a hospital there to look after the poor and to give divine office; he was shown a place near the shores of the great Lake Pátzcuaro, where the building works of Quiroga's second utopian project, Santa Fe de la Laguna, soon began.[59]

As in Mexico, the arrival of Quiroga was unpopular among many of the Spaniards who were already in Michoacán. In September 1534, they complained that Quiroga had founded the new Spanish city of Granada in a 'dry and difficult place'.[60] Although one settler, Gregorio Gallego, said that water and wood abounded, most disagreed with

---

*'De Paz' was a hispanicisation of the Jewish surname 'Shalom', and those de Paz's who retained their Judaism eventually made their way to Amsterdam, London and the West Indies.

him. Francisco de Peñafiel complained that there was no drinking water nearby, and Juan de Avina and Pedro de Sosa also dismissed it as a bad spot. Francisco de Villegas, appointed Regidor of Granada by Quiroga, summed up the prevailing mood when he said that the city was in 'the worst place that exists in the whole country for the settlement of Christians'.[61]

Once again, Quiroga's habitual disputes with the local Spanish colonists had not taken long to begin. Like the settlers in Mexico, the Spaniards in Michoacán did not like the idea of an Indian republic right on their doorstep, when what they wanted was a cheap (or free) supply of labour. However, in 1534, Quiroga obtained a letter of approval from Charles V in favour of the new city, and the colonists had no option but to remain.[62]

The Purépecha, though, seem to have looked at it all more favourably. Indeed, their willingness to support a system that had dethroned their gods shows just how terrible their suffering must have been under Nuño de Guzmán; and so, at the *residencia* in February 1536, several of them came to give evidence in favour of Quiroga. Alonso Dávalos, a Purépecha, said that the pueblo-hospital of Santa Fe de la Laguna 'has been very beneficial for the *naturales*'.[63] Ramiro, a Purépecha principal, said that the pueblo-hospital was good, and that before Quiroga's arrival they had been in hiding from the Franciscans in the hills,[64] for, according to another Purépecha witness, Don Francisco, the Franciscans used to beat the Purépecha to get them to come to mass, whereas this pueblo-hospital was a 'work of God'.[65]

Quiroga's strong feelings for the *naturales* of Michoacán was by now well known among all the Spanish. Since the summer of 1532, the Audiencia had planned to divide New Spain into four dioceses additional to Mexico: Michoacán, Tlaxcala-Puebla, Antequera and Nueva Galicia. This idea was approved by Charles V in 1534, and on 5 December 1535 Quiroga was nominated to be Bishop of Michoacán by the Council of the Indies.[66] Although he was not even a member of the clergy, his work thus far in New Spain had shown him to be ideal for the job.

The pope approved the appointment in December 1536, and Quiroga was finally consecrated by Bishop Zumárraga on 22 August 1538.[67] Something of his increasingly dominant, argumentative personality was conveyed in a contemporary document, which described his acceptance speech as being so prolix that there was not room even to describe its gist.[68]

*

With the pope's consecration of his mission, Quiroga can see no barriers to his pious work among the Purépecha. Is not the carnal marriage of a man to a woman made holy by its consecration in the house of God? So, his is now a 'spiritual marriage' to the Church, the duties of which, far from being less onerous than those of human marriage, are a much greater burden.[69]

His work has already been countenanced by miracles. Recently, in Santa Fe de México, some Indians came rushing to tell him that an unusually large deer had appeared nearby. They had all run to find the animal, whereupon it had fled into the scrub, twisting and turning. Following it with difficulty, the party had reached an abandoned shanty, at which point the deer had vanished; entering the shanty with caution, they had come upon two old priests on the point of performing a rite to an idol in the form of a wooden snake.[70]

The arrival of the deer while Quiroga had been preaching[71] must have been a divine protest at the performance of the satanic rite so close by. The snake is a dangerous symbol, and its idolisation has to be stamped out, for to the Mexica the top layer of the world itself is made up of a myriad of serpents, which form a sacred base from which all other life is born.[72] Humanity, Quiroga believes implicitly, can be idolised with justice (man is made in the image of God, after all, and so images of Christ and of the Virgin – divine impressions of humans – are legitimate); but such blatant worship of the natural world, as if it were as valuable as humanity, is a terrible thing! People must be set above the world over which God has given them dominion, so that they can control it.

With the pope having acknowledged his divine aim, Quiroga sets out for Tzintzuntzan, mitre in hand. August is the hottest time of the year, but it is also in the middle of the rainy season, which falls between May and October.[73] It is now that the skies are rent with the devil's rakes of lightning, the forests split open, the bowels of the earth transformed into a thundering forge. In the mornings the horizon is clear, but then the atmosphere becomes heavier, and the torrents begin; as Quiroga will write in two years' time, at this time the rainfall 'barely ceases ... and the rivers are very turbulent'.[74] It rains so much, in fact, that men and their horses often fall over,[75] so that in 1584 travellers will still be complaining of the bad fords.[76] This is not a good time to be travelling along tracks which are still appalling, with steep chasms on either side and bad passes over the mountains.

The road to Tzintzuntzan goes directly by Santa Fe de México. Then, once Quiroga's first utopian vision is behind him, he and his

Vasco de Quiroga (*c*.1487–1565), who used Thomas More's *Utopia* as his blueprint for the communes he founded in Mexico and Michoacán.

Burning of the Idols by Cortés.

Nuño de Guzmán attacks Michoacán. Guzmán, President of the first Audiencia of Mexico, craved control of Michoacán because of the rich mines in the area.

Indian slaves lay foundations for the cathedral in Mexico. The destruction of Tenochtitlan during the conquest meant that the entire city had to be rebuilt by the Mexica.

The arms of Tzintzuntzan. Tzintzuntzan – 'the place of the hummingbird' – was the capital of the empire of the Purépecha until the arrival of the Spanish.

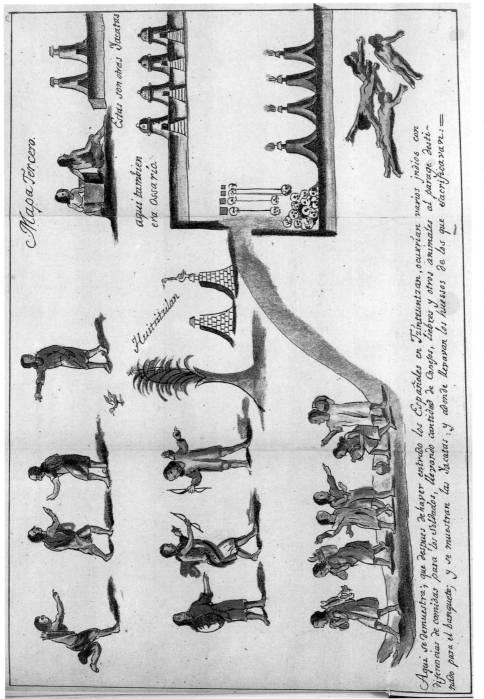

The Purépecha bringing food for the Spanish after their first arrival in Michoacán. The Yacatas in the right-hand corner of the picture were the monuments to the dead of the Purépecha.

aqui se juntan las comidas para los Españoles.

Este es el General Nanuma.

Aqui se demuestra donde se hizieron los banquetes, y se Juntaron las comidas que para esto dieron los naturales, à que assistio el Valiente Nanuma General de las ormas del gran Caltzontzi, y concurrieron los demas Cabos militares

The Purépecha lay out dishes of food on benches in their huts, preparing to serve them to the Spanish.

Quiroga and a Franciscan friar evangelise the Purépecha. Quiroga was the architect of the utopian societies in Michoacán, but depended on the network of mendicant friars to ensure that his system of 'hospitals' functioned throughout his vast diocese.

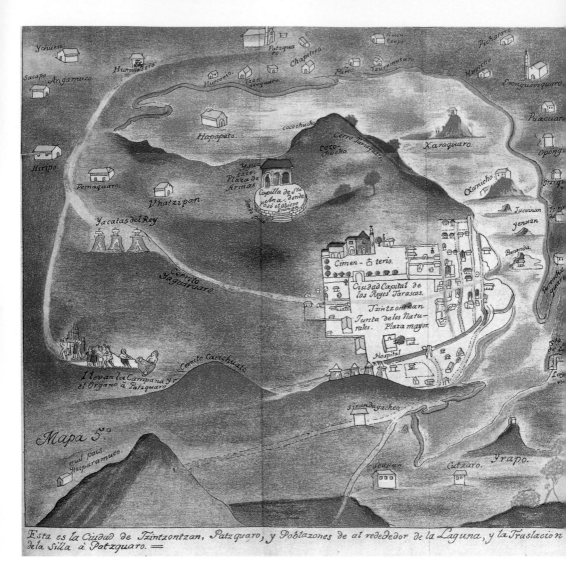

A 16th-century map of Michoacán shows the Purépecha hauling the bell (see detail below) for Quiroga's cathedral in Pátzcuaro.

companions ride up into the wild sierras, which are shaded by cypresses, yellow with chamomile flowers, speared by the thorns of the prickly pears. It is here, amid the snakes and lizards escaping his path, that Quiroga sees vindication of his work in the nearby pueblo-hospital. No longer are the sierras home to Mexica who have fled the Spanish; the wild animals are the only ones who live here.

Perhaps the most common animal of all is the coyote – called a fox by some Spaniards, and a dog by others.[77] The coyote is famous for its intelligence. There are people who claim that if someone robs it of its kill, the coyote will revenge itself by killing that person's chickens, or other animals that belong to them.[78] If, on the other hand, it receives generosity from humanity, it responds likewise: it is said that a traveller once freed a coyote from a snake, and the beast at once went off to kill two chickens, returning with them to its saviour as a token of thanks.[79]

The hills of Michoacán are also full of coyotes,[80] as well as countless other animals. Passing through the sierra beyond Mexico, Quiroga rides with his companions into the Valley of Toluca, the home of the Matalzinca people. This plain is as wide and as long as the Valley of Mexico, backed onto by yet another volcano. It is only beyond here that the boundary between Mexico and Michoacán takes shape, and the hills of the Purépecha begin.

The rain teems down. The drops serry beneath Quiroga's cape, ooze down his back and across his chest. They cluster about his unshaven face. Beyond Toluca, the wide valley fragments into steep hills that gather about the skyline, blocking out what little light there is during the storms. The hills bunch violently into plugs, and then drift down into lush valleys, which are irrigated by streams. Michoacán is dimpled with these forested hills, which are green and smooth; when the storms clear, the light is as transparent as glass, a polish for the world.

It is a journey of fifty leagues from Mexico to Tzintzuntzan – perhaps six days' ride. This should be a triumphal possession, for at last the hand of God has come to take possession of the land of the Purépecha; but the situation does not really lend itself towards triumphalism. Passing the settlement of Taximaroa, in the midst of the hills, Quiroga hears of bad treatment meted out to the Indians because of the nearby mines;[81] and although he knows that his pueblo-hospital in Santa Fe de la Laguna is working well, and that five convents have been founded in Michoacán since his first visit,[82] so many of the Indians are dead. The rain is falling, and his mule slips often on the muddy track. With all this in his mind, this is but a mute journey of spiritual conquest.

Nearing Tzintzuntzan, the hills at last fall away into the lakeland of Pátzcuaro. Scores of canoes can be seen out on the water, surrounded by webs of netting. In the middle of the lake are several islands, where the houses come down to the lake shore and the people can be seen washing, cleaning, fishing. Water is an integral part of Purépecha cosmology, and this milky lake is considered by them to be a living being,[83] a place in which those who drown descend immediately to a subterranean paradise.[84] So the fact that their *cazonci* Tzintzicha's ashes were thrown into the river by Nuño de Guzmán was, in some ways, a divine joke played on the Spanish.

It is a beautiful spot, of that there can be no doubt: a place for perfection.

Quiroga's mule descends the hills towards Tzintzuntzan, where the ruins of the old temple to Curicaveri can still be seen, together with the palace. Here, the *cazonci* had once stockpiled the heads of his enemies so that he could be surrounded by them, and by the large, semi-circular *yacatas*, stone sanctuaries of the gods and tombs for the leading lords of the Purépecha. A series of ramps had connected the great platform in front of the palace with the lake, and with a network of roads. The heart of the empire had been perched on a bluff above the lake, so that the people could admire the watery being, and dream of the heaven below.

But thirteen years ago, in 1525, Fray Martín de la Coruña, a Franciscan friar, destroyed all the temples and idols of Tzintzuntzan,[85] and the settlement is now dwarfed by the new convent. The people have descended from the hills, coming in their masses to be baptised (the watery ritual suits their own cosmology, of course[86]). But just now, they are coming to greet the new bishop, having been told to do so by the friars and their Purépecha governor, Don Pedro Cuiniarángari.[87] They play flutes and strike their drums. Their headdresses are a whirl of multicoloured feathers; their arms are filled with flowers.

Quiroga is deeply moved as he rides into the town and dismounts, unaware that it used to be the Purépecha custom to offer crowns of flowers to the full moon.[88] He is touched not only by the simple joy of 'his' people, but also by a greater spiritual thrill than he has ever known. It is not only that the pope has consecrated him Bishop of Michoacán; did not Thomas More (blessed by divine inspiration), write in his book that there was someone in England who had tried to get himself made Bishop of Utopia?[89]

Surely, divine inspiration has seen to it that now there is truly a Bishop of Utopia: one Vasco de Quiroga, in Michoacán.[90]

Although Quiroga was inspired by More's book, he was also very clear that the *Utopia* was only a starting point for the architect of utopian reality in the New World. In his 'Información en Derecho' he wrote that there were so many different peoples on earth that statutes and human relations should not all be uniform, so that there was no danger of falling into the trap of 'wanting to cure all illnesses with one remedy'.[91] People should choose those elements of More's book which were most appropriate to their situation and adapt them to the position on the ground.[92]

However, this sensible and rather non-ideological position was difficult to uphold for someone who *did* believe in the perfectibility of human society in the image of God, and that More had been inspired by the Holy Spirit. When it actually came to buying the land, and instituting the societies, More's work was of increasing importance to Quiroga. So he instituted the same framework among both the Mexica and the Purépecha, two nations who had been traditional rivals, and whose cultural differences were exemplified through the fact that their languages were completely unrelated. In this case, it seemed, one size did fit all.[93]

Given this dogmatism, and also the fact that hospitals have often doubled as tools for Christian conversion that have diluted indigenous cultures,* not everyone praises Quiroga's utopian schemes. Though there are many who see them as a genuine expression of saintliness – a papal commission is presently examining Don Vasco's claims for canonisation – others see Quiroga as a severe expression of the conquering society, a person whose ultimate aim was to crush the indigenous cultural ethos and absorb the Purépecha into the colonial system.

The latter group are often deeply suspicious of the utopian ideal as transferred to reality. In this viewpoint, the Americas simply represented the playing field in which the idea of Utopia could be enacted (once, of course, the land had been cleared of the people who had been living there). Thus it was that groups such as the Amish and

---

*In Palestine in the nineteenth century for instance, Christian missionary hospitals often had this function. The presence of Christian medical posts – and missionaries 'on site' – is also something that was a familiar pattern throughout the Amazon and various African countries in the twentieth century.

the Shakers were able to found their own agrarian communes in North America, and – more recently – that Paraguay has become home to groups of Mennonites, Moonies and social engineers such as Bernhard Forster and Elisabeth Nietzsche.

With its ideas regarding colonialism,* More's book itself played an important part in this view of the Americas as an unspoiled land where Europe could begin again. So on this interpretation, someone like Quiroga who took the *Utopia* as their starting point was bound to form a part of the 'proto-capitalist' armoury.[94] It was no surprise that Quiroga was not against the institution of slavery per se, but against the sale of slaves.[95] The fact that someone was a humanist did not make them an automatic champion of indigenous rights; in fact, 'built into the entire humanist programme was a contempt for untutored, pre-social man'.[96]

Quiroga was not against the institution of slavery, but very few people of his era were. Even Bartolomé de las Casas, the famous defender of indigenous rights, did not see the injustice of African slavery until the end of his life,[97] and actively encouraged the Spanish Crown to export African slaves to the Indies to alleviate the suffering of the Indians.[98] Slavery was unquestioned in Europe, where the institution descended, as Quiroga himself wrote, from the Romans.[99] But though the principle was blindly accepted, its practice was subject to debate, and Quiroga was one of those to call the Spanish form of slavery barbaric, pointing out the sharp differences between the European institution as inherited from the Romans and slavery as it was practised in pre-Cortesian Mexico and Michoacán,[100] where slaves were more like companions than brutalised underlings.

Quiroga was seen as the protector of the Indians. Though his settlements led to the intermingling of the Spanish and Purépecha cultures – so that he is held up as one of the most decisive figures in the *mestizaje* of the Mexican nation[101] – his desire was to help the Indians through good work, and to lead them out of the sixteenth-century abyss by example. This was probably his Erasmian inheritance, something that he may have wished to cover up by the mid-1530s, when Erasmus was interpreted in an increasingly subversive light in Spain.[102]

Perhaps the idealism bore some fruits that were rotten, but there may also have been other fruits that were sweet. Only by looking at the societies, and trying to grasp what people's experience of

*See above, ch. 7, p. 128.

them may have been, can the emotional reality – and its legacy – emerge.

The pueblo-hospital has been founded two leagues from Tzintzuntzan, on the shores of Lake Pátzcuaro.

Quiroga skirts the north-eastern corner of the lake as he travels there from Tzintzuntzan to take stock of the progress of his Utopia. Reaching the plain near the settlement, the pastures are mottled with trees that absorb the morning sunlight. Water meadows drift between the town and the lake, as if unsure of their boundaries. A clasp of hills rises beyond the water, folding upon one another and blocking out the world beyond.

Santa Fe is known to be a pretty spot.[103] Lake Pátzcuaro drifts away into golden sunsets and an ethereal mist that hangs above the water and the people who fish and swim there. The Purépecha are tremendous swimmers, regularly making their way across huge rivers even when they are in spate;[104] sometimes they pass across the water with goods for market carried on their heads, and yet manage to keep them dry.[105]

But the swimming (above the underwater heaven, of course) masks much superstition. The importance of founding a pueblo-hospital was impressed on Quiroga by his first visit in 1533, when he heard that an Indian sorcerer was killing many of the Purépecha with his 'diabolical craft'.[106] The sorcerer would look at people with a fierce gaze and say '*Niguari*', which in their language meant 'See, and die' – and he had had such power over the Purépecha that he had 'had them all bewitched and immersed in such melancholy that imagination alone killed them'.[107]

The power of the imagination is so strong, it can kill a person by their will alone, or bring about miracles and visions of the saints among those who see divinity as supernatural (instead of seeing nature itself as the expression of a sacred will). It can lead explorers to see unicorns, dog-like humans, fantasies in a new world; and so how right the Crown will be to ban novels from the colonies,* for as Cervantes will see, even if they are chivalric, these stories are usually filled with deeds of violence. How can an imaginative vision lead to happiness, or even satisfaction, if it carries with it a rage for which there will never be compensation?

It is not surprising that this world is dark and tending to apocalypse, Quiroga thinks, when it is immersed in such destructive thoughts. But

*See above, ch. 4, p. 67.

Santa Fe will be real – and good: people must choose this Utopia, or the dystopian cataclysm that is everywhere else. If they would have destruction, then at least let them go with their eyes open.

At last, he has reached Santa Fe de la Laguna. He guides his mule along the narrow streets of the settlement, and sees that all the women have their heads covered, as if in deference to the sky.[108] Where before they might have had ten or fifteen wives, the men now have one, and they have all given up their idols.[109] The houses are small[110] and made of adobe. They are mostly covered by straw, although some have earthen tiles:[111] modesty has returned to Michoacán.

Quiroga rides slowly into the centre of the town. He is surrounded by hundreds of people, dressed in white shifts as his ordinances for the pueblo-hospitals will later decree.* In the midst of the throng is Don Pedro Cuiniarángari, who has travelled ahead of him from Tzintzuntzan. Quiroga dismounts, and the two men embrace chastely. Though Quiroga has learnt enough Nahuátl to baptise the people of Santa Fe de Mexico,[112] he has not yet spent enough time in Michoacán to be fluent in Purépecha; this language, although said by some to be easy,[113] is of a completely different family from Nahuátl, and will take time to acquire.[114]

So Quiroga and the Purépecha governor fence with each other in words which are strange to the cacique.
– How is the work of God, Don Pedro?
– It is progressing, *señor.*
– More people are coming from afar?
– Yes, *señor.*
Of course, Quiroga thinks to himself. They will all have heard of the great work by now.
– Thank you, Don Pedro. Thank you for your hard work.

He moves through the throng, towards the hermitage which has been set aside for him. Now he will put his few possessions away, before inspecting the fields of crops and the crafts which he is reintroducing among the Indians, and ensuring that everything is being done in the proper way.

The pueblo-hospital has been founded by Quiroga in a wood known by the Purépecha as Atamatalco.[115] It is situated on ground a little way above the lake. As well as Quiroga's hermitage, there are rooms for the sick and for pilgrims, granaries, a large eating area and a building for the council.[116] The town's church has been located in an old

*See above, ch. 8, p. 147.

building which was already here,[117] but eventually a larger one will be built just back from the central area of the town, with a reddish stone arch leading to the hospital behind.

The guidelines of life in Michoacán's Utopia are the same as those for Mexico, within certain limitations. The pueblo-hospitals are still young, and Quiroga has not yet written the ordinances which will guide their functioning.* But at the same time, a tendency is developing: the people concentrate on agriculture, but also learn crafts and are educated in Christian doctrine; they eat together in the refectory, and their social structure is organised around the family; at times of festivals, they observe the rituals with great devotion.

Quiroga's desire is to form a stable and spiritual society, where the depredations of the *encomenderos* can be forgotten. He wishes to found a 'state of republic ... where everything is directed mainly towards the goal that there should always be peace'.[118] Knowing that, where the Indians have disappeared, 'all the land that depends on their care is destroyed',[119] he has no doubt of the importance of their guardianship of the environment; but at the same time, in spite of his idea that – where *his* Utopia is concerned – one size can fit all, it is impossible to separate the Purépecha from their roots.

So it is that in Michoacán's pueblo-hosptal, while everyone tends to their own crops and puts a cross there, the crosses are supplemented with trailing greenery and flowers,[120] as if to remind them of the garlands that they used to present to the moon. Though at first robbery and violence had been directed at those who had settled in Santa Fe,[121] people are now arriving from all over Michoacán, descending from areas that are very remote,[122] and where different languages are spoken.[123] People even come from the land of the Chichimecs[124] to be in a place where they can be safe.

Quiroga spends the day observing his creation. He watches the men tend to the orchards and the crops, while the women weave. As in Mexico, everything appears to betoken humility.[125] The people are deferent, and realise now that a single, omnipotent God sits above them in judgement of their sins (and that the earthly representative of this God is Bishop Quiroga). Everywhere he looks, Quiroga sees harmony, perfection, and an expression of the divine will; it is almost as if he looks with his mind rather than with his eyes.

His routine is abstemious in the extreme. He eats sparingly, and sleeps only a little just before dawn.[126] He hardly ever undresses when

*See below, ch. 13, pp. 241–3.

resting, except when needing to change his shirt.[127] He embodies the monastic restraint and devotion which he seeks to instil among his beloved Purépecha. When it comes to baptism, his whole being is transported with joy, his eyes brimful with genuine emotion,[128] which this time he allows himself to feel, as with the holy water he casts out and cleanses the impure idolatries of the Indians, and brings them to salvation. It is a personal, and deeply spiritual triumph; a heavenly reprise of the territorial conquests made by Cortés and Guzmán.

Beauty is everywhere to be seen in this world order that he is creating – in the community, in the Purépecha's growing Christianity, and in the land.

At dusk in Santa Fe de la Laguna the wispy clouds hang low over the earth, their thin line of grey broken only in a few places where the vanishing sun dyes the sky apricot and honeysuckle. Midges dance over the grassy marshes, buzzing here and there like motes of dust. Torches flare up from the villages that cluster around the lake shore, and a crescent moon filters its light through the gathering darkness as the shadows of the hills merge with the night.

Once upon a time, just a few years ago, the Purépecha dreamt, as the world slept.

ELEVEN

The landing was a rocky one. Cruising down from the mountain heights, I felt myself returning to normality with alarming speed. I did not break up on entering the atmosphere, although the pollution made me think twice about it. Nor did I develop a sunny halo about my neck; I was not going to follow in the footsteps of Juan Diego, that was for sure.

Instead, as I veered towards Santa Fe de la Laguna, the dusty corrugated iron roofs of the settlement took shape, the small plaza became clearer, and the blue and olive colours of Lake Pátzcuaro rippled out towards the west. For a worrying moment I thought that I might head-butt the village church, but I managed to avoid it, and skated to a stop beside one of the stone benches in the plaza.

I had come back to earth.

I dusted myself down. The handful of vendors – all Purépecha women – maintained their equanimity as they waited for people to buy their goods. One woman had a pail full of milk (which she sold by the mug), another a bag of grain (which she sold by the scoop), another a table set out with cigarettes (which she sold by the fag). A fly-bitten dog hobbled around the edge of the plaza, scavenging for rotting orange peel. Santa Fe was still; the girdle of poverty embraced it.

Looking around, I saw that no one was paying me any attention, in spite of my brash arrival. Alien incomers were clearly run-of-the-mill. So I made my way onto one of the stone benches and sat there awhile, brooding.

I was in trouble. I had set out from S—— with much highfalutin talk about the perfect society; but Juan Diego had punctured my hot air, and deflated me so much that I no longer knew whether idealism was a positive force, even if wedded to the sort of realism that he had encouraged me to adopt.

Still, the recollection of Juan Diego's rapid and unexpected canonisation cheered me. Something was, after all, better than nothing, and a saint – even a false one – was a step up from deluded idiots like myself. In spite of the headlong rush towards a future which filled people with unease, life still lived – cascaded.

Looking around, I realised that there was doubtless much more to Santa Fe de la Laguna than what I saw. The village was unfettered by busyness and hence could lap up the waves from the lake, and the emotional legacies of the past. The people moved slowly, within themselves. The women had their hair parted in the middle, trailing in pigtails. The men wandered beneath wide-brimmed hats, deferring to one another as they passed.

The village breathed; it was alive, as the lake had once been for the Purépecha.

Looking up, I realised that a group of children had gathered and were staring at me as if I really had been an alien. They pointed and giggled and then were overtaken by shyness.

'Hello,' I said, trying to reach out to them in spite of our differences (I was not planning to abduct them; I had no spacecraft, after all).

One of them – the oldest of the boys, as it appeared – stepped forward, his face bright with excitement and nerves.

'Hello,' he said. 'Have you come from the heavens?'

'In a manner of speaking,' I answered.

'And you've brought perfection, of course?' he asked.

'Well, no. Perfection's not something that I really believe in any more. It's been shown up to be a hollow ideal, and so now, like most other people, I've lost my idiosyncrasies and seem to believe in nothing.'

The boy broke up into fits of giggles, and was joined in his laughter by his peers. Their faces parted into joy, delight, and disbelief. They slapped one another and, when no one else was available to be slapped, slapped the stone of the bench beside me.

'I don't believe it,' their spokesperson said in the end. 'A white man comes from far away, and he doesn't claim to have the answers to all our problems.'

'He doesn't claim to bring us perfection,' said a young girl. 'Or even token handouts.'

'He hasn't got any useless information to share with us,' said a little boy.

They turned to slap one another again in mirth. Then their leader turned to me with a wry smile on his face.

'That's really a first,' he told me. 'We'll all be happy that you've come to our village, now – seeing as you don't want to bother us with perfection.'

They turned and ran off as quickly as they had come, and I felt drab. For I was left staring into the emptiness of the village, where little moved, and there was no engine to disturb the peace. The sun shone; songbirds filled the plaza with their tales of woe, which to me sounded like harmonies.

I stood up, and stretched my upper body, deciding to take a stroll around the village. I could sense that it was a poor place, that there were more signs of decay than of vitality, as the paving crumbled, the dust spiralled into the cracks of the buildings, the elderly people sat stoically, watching, still; yet I hoped to find something here that would satisfy my inquisitiveness, as curiosity was virtually the only desire that I had just then. My quixotic flights of fancy had done away with my cravings, so that I was not hungry; I no longer craved power, which was just as well, as there was no power to be had here, little food, and any lust that I might have wished to sate would have required such naked violation that it would have been inhuman.

'You feel all this,' a voice said sadly behind me, just as I was on the point of beginning my walkabout, 'yet you say you believe in nothing.'

Wheeling around, I saw one of the Purépecha traders. She had set aside her mug of milk and was eyeing me suspiciously.

'When did I say that?'

'To the children,' she said, in slow and measured Spanish.

'Oh the children,' I said, taking a step back, and trying to get my bearings.

'Don't get me wrong,' she went on, avoiding eye contact. 'I'm impressed that you haven't got any foolish ideas about perfection, that you've recovered a sense of normality – but I'm still worried that you don't believe in anything.'

'Well,' I said hurriedly, 'if the truth be told, none of us believes in much any more except the satisfaction of our desires. But surely even that's better than nothing.'

At that she shook her head sorrowfully, and looked past me into the middle distance, 'Oh no,' she said softly, 'no it isn't. For in our community we've long held that until you learn to see something other than your own personal satisfaction as valuable, you'll be a danger to the entire natural order – people (for once) included.'

I stared at her goggle-eyed. In my patronising way I had expected little in the way of chat among the Purépecha of Santa Fe, and I had certainly not expected my recent history of pontificating to continue unchecked. Juan Diego – San Juan, as they were calling him – had said it clearly enough: I needed to recapture a sense of realism. What was more, I knew that in Cervantes's book Don Quixote's speeches and ideas had developed a greater ring of sanity and truth as his adventures had worn on, so that in a funny way I could remain quixotic and become sensible at the same time.

So the last thing I wanted was another far-fetched escapade to include in my account, particularly as I had yet to distinguish what was true from what was false in what I planned to include. And what was more, I had not spoken to this woman, or even told her what I was thinking about. Yet she knew. This ageing crone, whose face was creasing into folds, whose black-and-blue shawl was threadbare, whose legs were swollen, could read me easily.

'A danger to the natural order?' I asked weakly, in the end.

'Oh yes,' she said. 'What with all those desires to satisfy just so as to feed your pride. The lust, the hunger, the fury! Oh, we see it all on TV, we can't avoid it – and all I can say is, it's no wonder there's so much misery.'

'I'm sorry,' I said. 'I didn't ask for this psychological breakdown, or rather your breakdown of my psychology. I can't cope with this.'

She appeared to be unmoved by my protest, and returned to stirring her bucket of milk with one hand, flicking her pigtails with the other.

I got up and left her, walking quickly away from the shrubbery in the middle of the plaza towards the sanctuary of the side streets. As I went, I passed a striking mural, which had been painted on the building beneath the plaza's western arcades. Members of the community were depicted adopting various strident poses, their portraits filled with colour. The slogans declaimed: 'This community says "Enough"'; 'Return our communal lands to us.'

Passing by the mural, I toured the village, trying to work up the excitement which I had had when I had embarked on this journey in S——: so this was Santa Fe de la Laguna, I told myself, trying to stir up a false sense of meaning, the home of Utopia, the cradle of togetherness, the place where fantasies of perfection had been supplanted by its reality! Of course, with its excessive poverty, I recognised that the modern world would not have called this place a success; but then Quiroga – who himself had shunned personal wealth – would surely have looked at it differently! Things were not as bad as the old woman, with her lecture on the satisfaction of desires, had made out.

Turning the corner of a street in the village, I found her walking straight towards me.

'What?' I said, shrinking back (and wondering whether it was in fact she, and not I, who was the alien in Santa Fe). 'I've already said I've had enough. Why have you followed me here?'

'The satisfaction of desires!' she blurted out, ignoring me. 'I've already told you that that's the root of your problem. Which ones do you have in mind now?'

Of course I was used to her insights into my inner thoughts by now, but I still felt confused. I looked at her, and she looked back, bunching her shawl into her hand, so that the blue and black lines of the fabric merged into a colourful blur, and somehow mirrored the lines of her face. There was a sense of resolution in her, besides the dignity and humility which went unsaid.

'Which desires do I have in mind right at this minute?' I asked.

'Yes.'

I thought for a moment, but again felt that my acquisitive urges had abated, and were not troubling me in Santa Fe de la Laguna.

'Well,' I answered eventually, 'oddly enough, and in spite of everything that you've said, I'm relatively content just now.'

The old woman burst into laughter at this. Her ebony hair glittered in the sunlight; her jowls juddered with her mirth, and for a moment I wondered if the skin might separate from the chin and reveal a younger, more radiant incarnation.

'Content?' she asked eventually, in high-pitched mockery. 'Surely not.'

'Oh but I am,' I insisted, emboldened by her doubts. 'There's nothing that I really want. I'm just happy with myself for the time being.'

She cackled again, and then sidled up to me. 'Of course,' she said, 'I know you're lying. Even if you're not hungry or craving sexual fantasies, there is one desire that you haven't let go of.'

'What's that?' I asked, with dread.

'Fame,' she said. 'Oh yes, here in Santa Fe we've watched all those programmes that give people instant fame on TV.'

'What's that got to do with me?'

Her dark-brown, watery eyes blinked in astonishment for a moment. Then she smoothed her hand across her forehead and spoke.

'Well,' she said, 'it's obvious that you wouldn't use up so much time and money to come here if you didn't believe that it would be worth your while, and know that when you go home everyone will fall at your feet and say how brilliant you are.' She paused, perhaps noting that I had said nothing to stop her. 'And of course,' she continued, her eyes escaping my gaze and falling back towards the earth, where they seemed to find their strength, 'that's when the desires that you appear to be managing to suppress will come into their own, and you'll truly be able to sate your hunger and your lust. Oh yes, then you'll devour the dishes of red meat that get proffered to you at exclusive soirées, followed by the women who fling themselves at you not because of who you are, but because of what you represent.'

'What I represent?' I echoed.

She was silent for a moment, before raising her head; a light seemed to come upon her eyes then, and burnt into me. Afraid that it was fury, I looked aside.

'Yes,' she said then, with sadness. 'That's the way with people like you, and of course it's the absolute death of anything that might be called creativity, for people are pressured into producing what is expected of them and not what derives from their truest feelings about their lives. So just you come back here in a few years' time, and I'll show you how revolting you've become – how all your idealism has turned to fat, your creativity to junk produced to order, your youth to degeneration.'

She turned and walked off with measured dignity into the dust.

'Wait!' I called after her, dismayed at the increasing reality of my situation. 'That's not fair.'

She glanced back at me: 'I don't care if it's fair or not. Is it true?'

I said nothing – my mouth opened; my voice cut into a whimper. Then I shrank back and went to sit on the cracked pavement.

'You people, you've come a long way,' the old Purépecha woman said then, returning to me as I sat there. 'I don't deny that. In the past fifty years, you've learnt what it means to be ashamed, and that's something; but you've still got a long way to go. I mean, take yourself, for instance – what are you doing here anyway?'

'I've come in search of Don Vasco de Quiroga and his Utopia,' I said.

'What on earth for, when it was just a figment of his imagination?'

'Well,' I said heatedly, 'I wouldn't agree with you there. He did his best, I'm sure of that. Besides, I've discovered a family connection between myself and Quiroga. One branch of my own family were called de Paz, a hispanicisation of their old Hebrew surname before the forced conversions of Jews in 1492 – and de Paz was the surname of Quiroga's notary when he first came here to Michoacán, a man who must have been a relative of my own forebears.'

'And what of it?' she asked.

'Well,' I said, 'it's obvious that we all have a share in this old Utopia. Everyone in Michoacán, and more people than you'd believe around the world, had a stake in what went on here. And so I've set myself the task of trying to decipher what that might have been.'

'Of course you have,' she said sarcastically. 'And did you think you'd find Don Vasco's perfection, and not some delusion that you yourself had created?'

'I suppose...'

Yet in spite of everything that I'd said, I was not sure what I supposed. I sat there pathetically, caking my trousers in dust, and my delusions in reality. For all the spuriousness of my familial connection with Quiroga's utopias, there was nothing perfect about poverty, or bitterness – and far less about me. How had I dared to have so many ideals when my own soul had been warped by the desire for acclaim, and the self-immolation which that represented? That desire alone was enough to scupper any right I had to preach to others about art, about truth, about the perfect world. Until I shed the self-aggrandisement which went with utopianism, my views would be redundant, and I would remain a fantasist; I would never have a handle on my emotions, which would always appear to me as parentheses to the reality that I sought to portray.

Without normality, I saw, remembering San Juan's imprecations, there was no hope for idealism.

I spent some time lost in my thoughts before I realised that the Purépecha woman had not gone. The songbirds were still cheeping in the plaza, and the apparent harmonies of their music gradually called me back to this place, this time, and the urgent need to address the present and nothing else.

'Come,' she said then. 'Come with me. If you're really in search of Tata Vasco, I've got something to show you.'

Turning calmly, she led the way round the dusty back streets of the town, passing slender peach trees green with unripe fruit, and bursts of oranges in the broader trees beside them, until we entered the courtyard of the old hospital. Here there were more fruit trees, and the air remained compressed by birdsong. The patio was occupied by groups of Purépecha men who were sweeping it clean with improvised brushes made of twigs. They glanced at us before continuing steadfastly with their work.

To the side of the patio was a covered walkway that gave on to a row of dilapidated buildings. The old woman beckoned me towards one of them, and opened the door with a rusty key.

'This is the museum,' she said, gathering up her shawl again.

'Museum?' I asked.

'Yes,' she said, ushering me inside. 'Oh I know that someone like you, who comes from one of the world's rich countries, thinks that our way of life is a museum piece in itself, something that can be categorised and objectified, so that you can persist in the illusion that we are not actually people like you, people who have the same rights and needs as you do.'

She came to a stop. Through the windows we could hear much activity, for the cleaning of the patio was continuing; glancing outside, I saw that people were now arriving with huge bouquets of flowers in apparent preparation for a wedding.

'I'm sorry,' she said. 'I've drifted off the point, rather. But in here, if you ignore me, you'll find things that are really worthy of being put up for public display. For this is the repository of belongings and furniture and everything that Tata Vasco, the founder of this community, once used.'

My interest piqued, I began to examine the small room. There was an old writing desk, a leather chair of the type which I knew to exist in the library of Salamanca's university, and other, smaller trinkets. I picked up letter-knives, small caskets, seals. So these were the objects that Don Vasco had used himself! These were the precious things that he had touched with his very hands! This was the quill with which he had written, holding it in his ink-stained fingers! These objects would tell me so much about him – of that there was no doubt, I thought.

Then I sat down rather heavily on an upturned cardboard box, and stared at it all vacuously.

'Of course,' I said to her, 'this is all fascinating.'

'Fascinating?' she asked.

'Yes,' I said. But I could not really explain what I meant, and sensed that the amazement I felt at being in a room filled with so much history was the product of an emotion which I had yet to explore.

'Why?' she asked eventually. 'Why is it fascinating? Because of the fame that you hope it will bring you?'

'No, I'm not interested in any of those fantasies now,' I replied. 'What I think is of desperate importance is recovering the truth that idealism can relate to reality. We don't have to communicate as if in a farce, through some ludicrous updating of the mythology of *Don*

Quixote, in order to understand that, and any writer who tells you that we do is a bigger fraud than I am. And it's my feeling that something of this truth is hinted at in these objects that belonged to Don Vasco. They show how real he was.'

I did not know where to begin an explanation, though. Certainly I had not imagined that, in this remote place, I would engage anyone in a serious discussion of the unravelling of the social fabric. Yet there was something in the old Purépecha woman's piercing eyes, and her shrewd guidance of our talk, that suggested otherwise.

'Oh,' she said then, 'we keep these things because we feel we ought to. But we rarely look at them ourselves.'

'No,' I said.

'But I'm sure it's different in your country,' she said. 'You must love your history, since everything's a triumph for you.'

I looked up wildly, hurt by this barb, but she had turned to face out of the window, and was admiring the flowers that her people continued to bring.

Of course, in this small, dusty room, surrounded by a collection of ancient objects from Europe, in a culture increasingly overrun by modern European ways, everything that I represented was bound up in the sort of brash triumphalism that usually leads people to want to vomit.

'Our history is a triumph,' I repeated. I had no answer, and sensed that in fact I might soon be sick myself. Yet how could I share my shame at this truth with someone who was hurt by it far more than I was? I continued to look at her profile, as she took in the bustle in the patio, and my eyes felt as if they might almost be brimful.

Then she turned her gaze to meet mine. We said nothing as we watched one another; and a moment later, without understanding quite how, or why, I felt my idealism, and my feelings, beginning to return.

Yes, perhaps perfection was a false reflection of the mind, and undiluted idealism generally led to delusions and dystopia; but if you could equate that idealism to the belief that there was something valuable in what was external to the individual, and to the individual's desires – then utopianism was perhaps not so doom-laden as San Juan had led me to believe, and it might even return from fantasy to the province of the everyday.

'It's true,' I said then, 'our history books are filled with triumphalism; but at the same time, it's not entirely straightforward. For if you take the world that I come from, it cannot get enough of its history at the moment. There are countless documentaries on great war leaders, insignificant war leaders, secret histories, obscure figures in hitherto unrecognised political movements. Some cultural commentators say that the tie-in books that accompany these television programmes are replacing the novel as the fullest expression of the zeitgeist – as the locus of great literature, whatever that might be.'

'I see,' she said, continuing to watch me gently.

'But actually,' I went on, 'I wonder whether what is going on is not something rather different. For it's well known that, as people get older and start to feel as if most of their active life is behind them, they reminisce.' I looked at her to ensure that she was listening. 'Well,' I said, 'it seems to me that our society's present obsession with history is in fact an unconscious expression of its growing sense of impending ecological or military catastrophe. For, make no mistake, people feel in their bones that the way in which life is lived at the moment (in the West) cannot outlive the twenty-first century, and is likely only to be overturned by some terrible event; and this impression means that they shrink from the future, and its meaning, and turn instead to the past.'

I finished with a rush of blood to the head, and the old Purépecha woman sat there silently, watching me. The stillness of the world beyond this room, this museum – its silence, and surface gentleness – was such a contrast to the fury of my thoughts that for a moment I was quiet. A dove came to perch upon the window ledge, and darted its head about in all directions, almost in a frenzy, as if it was absorbing some of the wasted energy of my diatribe; then it flew off, vanished.

'You're funny,' she said then.

'Funny?'

'Yes,' she said. 'You say that your ancestor was called de Paz – "of Peace". Yet your words are filled with anger, and I can't see that you're going to find contentment for as long as that's the case, or anything that you might call emotional truth.'

The voices of the men in the courtyard pierced through the outer wall of the museum. To me, their strange language sounded as musical as the birdsong.

'Emotional truth,' the old woman said now, gently shaking her head. Her gaze was milky as she looked at me, filled with a global sadness. 'Of course, we've learnt from talking to the gringos who've come here that that's one of the very things that is still to be uncovered among you.'

'Among us?' I asked.

'Yes,' she said. 'For, as long as you ignore the violated origins of your mental categories, and as long as you blind yourself to those through overloads of information and desire, your core of emotional distress will remain undisturbed.'

'Overloads of information and desire?' I asked her.

'Yes,' she said. 'Even though we here live so far from all that, it filters through to us on the TV, which allows us to sense the shaping of consciousness that is going on in your world. And though the information revolution is but the latest manifestation of the will to blind humanity to that past, the mass appeal to human urges that accompanies it is part of the same process – and its clothes are junk food, pornography, video games, anything which can appeal to inner rage.'

Everything she said seemed so sensible, reasonable. She was the absolute opposite of the fat old hag I had met in Seville, and of all the distractions I had endured since then.

'And how can we divest ourselves of that?' I asked, realising belatedly that she might be able to point me in the right direction.

'You must talk to the parish priest about that,' she said, then. 'Come on, I'll show you the way,' she said abruptly, moving away from me now, and forcing me to leave the museum, which I relinquished with sadness.

She shuffled back out onto the patio, and I followed her. The cracked slabs of stone were cleaner than they had been before. The flowers that people had brought for the wedding sprawled about the aisle of the church, the entrance, lay in garlands by the pews, ensuring that the place was now filled with colour. Even though there was such stillness, there was also a sense of joy, and of reverence, just through the flowers.

There was no full moon to worship, but the world still turned, and people's impending happiness – such as it was – was enough.

'We are going to have a wedding today,' the old woman said unnecessarily, brushing her hand across her dark skin. 'Perhaps you will come.'

'Me?' I asked, with surprise.

'Yes,' she said. 'For even though you are a foreigner, you can be one of us.'

One of the men called over to her, and she left to talk with him. I sat down on the side of the covered walkway, beside the museum, and watched. The sun had risen higher in the sky now, and the colours were sharp. The birds still sang. A dog barked in the stillness, and was answered by a flurry of cockerels. All at once I felt a tremendous welling of happiness. This did not all have to come to an end, and in fact would go on – if we believed in it rather than in ourselves.

That, I realised, was the core of my new idealism.

The old woman came back towards me. She looked bashfully past my eyes, as if aware of how strange we each appeared to the other. 'The priest lives in the old building beside the church,' she said. 'I'm sure he'd like to see you, if he's got time before the wedding.'

I raised myself, and walked slowly back out under the arch of what had once been Quiroga's hospital. I felt sad when I looked at the vicarage, whose old pink stones were glowing in the morning sunlight, cracking with decay. But then I tried to banish that emotion as I knocked on the thick double doors.

They were opened almost at once by the priest of Santa Fe de la Laguna, who was an enormously tall albino.

'Come on, come on,' he said impatiently, bustling me into the hallway. 'I've been waiting for you, it seems like for ages. We haven't got long.'

Somewhat surprised, I followed him through to the sitting room. The priest sat me down in a deep armchair. Then, with a great flapping of limbs, he placed himself opposite me on a hard wooden bench. Crossing one gangling leg over the other one, he smoothed his shock of white hair with his left hand, and stared at me excitedly.

'Padre Franciso de la Fuente de la Paz at your service, *caballero*,' he said.

'De la Paz?' I asked.

'Of course,' he said. 'We're all at peace here in Quiroga's Utopia.'

'At peace?'

'Of course,' he said. 'But let's talk about that later. What really concerns me is whether you're prepared for what's to come.'

'What's to come?'

I wasn't sure that I wanted anything more to be 'coming', for I felt as though I had been through quite a lot just lately. In fact, I needed a rest, perhaps even a sabbatical from existence, and I certainly did not like the look of the mania that I sensed in the priest. I'd had enough of all that sort of thing.

'Well,' he said, 'of course, we'll all have to pull together – in this Utopia that you're planning.'

There was something in his crazed manner that reminded me of the old man in S——, and for a moment, in fact, I wondered if it wasn't him in disguise; but then the priest turned his reddish eyes onto me, and I realised that they weren't those of the madman who had set me on my way to utopian adventures.

'How do you know that I'm a utopian?' I asked him, then.

'Well, you've come to Santa Fe,' he said, 'you're obsessed by Quiroga, and you claim some absurd connection to that very first expedition. So that's quite enough for me to see you as a spiritual brother, even if you're an athiest, which is quite likely in this day and age. That's why I was so willing to take up this posting after all. Quiroga's story is a fascinating one, and not without its resonance for our own time, if you're someone like me, who's crazy (about utopias).'

'That's my belief too,' I said, deciding that this was the best answer to the priest's medley of confusion.

'But of course, we utopians have a great problem now,' he said excitedly, crossing his legs with great clumsiness, 'particularly if, like you and me, *caballero*, we believe in peace.'

'A problem?'

'Well, two, in fact,' he said, leaning back and settling into the exchange. 'The first is that no one believes in idealism. But the second is this: utopian societies are born of poverty, so that the need to pull together and to work for each other, to have a really strong communal framework rather than a group of atomised individuals, is most apparent in societies where there is not any great wealth.'

'That's true,' I said, glad that I could agree wholeheartedly this time. 'You can still see that here today, in the dusty streets of your parish, Santa Fe de la Laguna. And that's why Quiroga was so sure that he had found the proper testing ground for More's ideas in New Spain – because of the humility of the people, and the absence among them of a desire for possessions.'

The priest smiled at me. He stood up now, and began to pace up and down the room – he was so tall that he had to stoop, but this did not seem to concern him.

'Agreed, *caballero*,' the priest said, settling deeper into his own world with every sentence. 'At the same time, the problem that the modern world faces is this. There's no doubt that it's presently galloping through resources at an enormous rate, so that within your lifetime, if not within mine, there will be severe shortages. But at the same time, instead of trying to develop an atmosphere in which people are happy to co-operate with one another, and put their communities ahead of their own self-interest – the sort of society which will be able to pull together when the moment of shortage arrives, as it inevitably will – every particle of the cultural framework seeks to accentuate people's individualism. And if you ask me, that's a recipe for impending social disaster.'

'Of course,' I said, grasping his point (but trying to keep our worlds separate). 'It must be.'

'For if people are goaded into seeing their desires as the main focus of their existence,' he continued, stopping by the window and looking longingly towards the flowers which were gathering by the church, 'they inevitably turn in on themselves, and become more individual. How can they see the world as an end in itself, as something sacred, after all, when they are encouraged to see it simply as a playground for their urges? How can they, *caballero*?'

'I see,' I said, thinking of Juan Diego. 'No, they can't. They can't see it as sacred.'

'Of course not,' the priest said, slicing through the air with the side of his hand. 'And the present consumer economy can only operate if it appeals to those desires, those urges, so that people need things and buy them. But as the time approaches when resources evaporate, people – having been led down the road towards individualism – may yet be unable to shift their consciousness into the collective framework that is required in times of shortage.'

'So what you're saying,' I said slowly, 'is that it's the very dependency on desire-satisfaction which not only drives the economy, but is also driving us towards social and ecological disaster. For society is becoming atomised and a stranger to the sort of co-operation that enables impoverished communities – such as ours will be before too long – to survive.'

'Absolutely,' he said.

I looked up at the towering figure of the priest, and saw in his eyes at once idealism, passion and a sliver of unabashed madness. As if to confirm my impression, he now walked over to a bookshelf, selected a book, and balanced it on his head.

'Excuse me,' he said. 'It's for my posture.'

'Posture?' I asked.

'Yes,' he said.

'Oh no!' I said with dread. 'It's not *Don Quixote* is it?'

'No,' he said, beginning to pace up and down with the book perched on his hair. 'It's only Plato's *Republic*, and we all know now that that's worthless. Now where were we?'

'Togetherness,' I said, trying to keep my feet firmly on the ground, where they would, doubtless, soon be joined by his book.

'Oh yes,' he said. 'Well we've got that here. Santa Fe's even more together than I am, which isn't saying much, of course. But without the faith in the divine, I wonder if it wouldn't all fall apart fairly quickly.'

'You mean without the Church?'

'Of course,' he said, stopping sharply and leaving Plato's *Republic* oscillating alarmingly on his head. 'The Church is vital, especially in these days of the survival of the fittest.'

'You're a Darwinian?' I asked, failing to keep the surprise from my voice.

'Of course,' he said. 'The pope recognised Darwin's theory just a few years ago. And it makes sense when you look at the Church, for what is Christianity but the fittest religion of all, Islam included, not that I'd say that if I went to the Middle East?'

At first I was disgusted by his faith – using an anti-religious doctrine such as Darwinism to justify his prejudices appalled me. But then my disgust fell away, as I recalled what the old Purépecha woman had said about how important it was to believe in something external to yourself.

The priest did, at least, believe in something. It was a start.

'But how can we address these urges that our society appeals to?' I asked, then. 'How can we begin to deal with that issue, when time is running out and we've only just addressed the problem of information, and that with the help of a saint, even if he was one who didn't carry a book on his head and was granted his miracle in the time of Quiroga?'

'A saint?' he asked.

'San Juan. San Juan Diego.'

The priest raised his eyes to the heavens, and intoned with great emotion: 'The new Quiroga!'

'Well,' I said then, 'no one's gone as far as that yet. After all, we both know that saints are two a penny, but there's only one Don Vasco.'

'Yes,' the priest said then, disregarding me, and beginning to pace around again, keeping his back taut and the *Republic* evenly balanced. 'Yes, how can we address this?' He knotted his brow for some moments, and then went on: 'The point seems to me to be that, as San Juan said to you, before we can address the crucial question of ecology, we have to address the way in which every aspect of our mental framework tends to destroy it. He's dealt with information, so he must be a saint; but the fact remains that, as I've said, our culture also plays on our desires and encourages us to sate them rather than to structure our behaviour so that they do not obsess us. And while that's the case, I'm afraid that there's not much point in addressing the protection of the environment, since the deepest subconscious desire of all would appear to be – from all the evidence, which is surely now mounting up beyond dispute – to destroy it.'

I was baffled by this litany of half-truths, wisdom and make-believe, and did not know what to suggest, particularly when the priest began to bear down on me with the *Republic* teetering threateningly overhead. All I was looking for was a good subject for a thumbnail character sketch that would slot easily into my narrative, and iron out the structural inconsistencies that I felt mounting up without end. This man wasn't helping at all.

'So what do you suggest?' I asked pathetically.

'Well it's obvious,' he said, wheeling around. 'We need to foment an unconscious shift away from destruction as a target of our will, and refocus it instead on peace, and on contentment. If we could manage that, then the appeal of the desires would begin to diminish, and we would have made a start. For with that, individualism would lessen, and the possibility of rediscovering communities would open up again. And, of course, once the will is not focused on urges, it might be possible to see the world as something which is an end in itself – or even sacred.'

'Well,' I said, 'that's not going to be very popular, far less possible. Because the appeal to the desires is the engine of capitalism, and therefore of everything that modern society holds dear.'

'Absolutely,' he said again. 'That's why it's so important. And though I can understand your pessimism, I do believe that if we address information overload first, as San Juan suggested, then the shift of collective atmosphere to more positive targets might be more plausible, as there will be fewer things to clutter the consciousness with junk and thereby distract it from the sanctity of the world.'

He stopped talking and stared at me from the middle of the room. If anything his eyes seemed redder and his hair whiter than before. In fact, for a moment, I wondered if he was really human, especially when he now twisted up one of his legs, bent it 180 degrees at the knee so that the toe was by the hip, and began to scratch his belly with it. The fact that we both had ancestors with the same surname began to seem extremely alarming, and I decided that perhaps I had better keep quiet about this in future, especially if I wanted people to believe that the vestiges of madness were his and his alone, and that my idealism was grounded in utmost good sense.

'Excuse me,' he said, then, 'I'm double jointed.' He scratched hard for a while, and then put his limb away – hurriedly, as if it was something to feel guilty about – before looking askance at me. 'Come over here a moment,' he said then. 'Come here, and hear me out.'

I was deeply sceptical by then; nevertheless I stood up and walked over to join the priest by the window. He was looking out over the patio, where the Purépecha people were preparing their great celebration with joy, and tenderness. The patio was now spotless; the flowers continued to multiply; but the old woman who had shown me the museum was nowhere to be seen.

The priest glanced at me out of the corner of his eyes and put an avuncular hand on my shoulder. Then, facing me, he began to bring his thoughts to a head.

'Let's get rid of this, for starters,' he said, dispensing with the *Republic* and tossing it back over his head so that it crashed to the floor. 'Then let's look at where Utopia can go from here.'

The fact was, he began, this interconnection between poverty and functioning utopias, which we had been discussing, was essential; and, of course, it was no accident, he continued, that the nineteenth-century face of utopianism – or ideal societies, at any rate – had been adopted by Marxism. That wasn't to say that Marx had seen himself as utopian. In fact, he had seen utopians as reactionary and bourgeois, people who idealised the old property relations through a false picture of the agricultural paradise.[1]

Nevertheless, the priest continued, much of what Marx wrote was an industrialised echo of previous utopian thought. Like More, he had seen private property as the root of all evil,[2] despising the bourgeoisie's 'icy water of egotistical calculation',[3] much as More and Campanella had been wary of individualism. The fact was, the priest said, the locus of exploitation in the nineteenth century had shifted from the serfs who were booted off the land following the beginning of enclosures and the advance of livestock raising – pitied by More[4] – to the hell of the newly industrialised cities. Hence, it was not surprising that it was through the newly emergent class of the industrialised proletariat that idealism should be given its voice.

'That's all very well,' I said now, 'but no one's interested in Marx any more. Marxism's utterly discredited. You're not going to bring about a shift in the collective unconscious with an appeal to an old fogey like him.'

Particularly not when you're a double-jointed madman who walks about with books on his head, I felt like adding – but just managed to restrain myself (after all, it was not so very long since I had been behaving just as strangely as him).

'No of course not,' the priest answered. 'But back in the nineteenth century – and even more recently than that, although sometimes it's hard to believe it – these ideas were all the rage.'

The fact was, he went on, that, following Marx, the late nineteenth century saw a veritable glut of utopian novels, all beginning with Butler's *Erewhon*.

It was interesting to note, the priest said, that even as late as 1872, when *Erewhon* had been written, the original utopian conceit of travelling to an unknown land had still been alive, and Butler had written of this unknown country in the southern hemisphere as being wildly beautiful[5] – much like utopias are supposed to be. None of the Erewhonians were rich,[6] and, like Utopia, the country was 'highly cultivated, every ledge being planted with chestnuts, walnuts, and apple-trees'.[7] Like More, Butler had used merciless satire to make his point: bad luck was immoral and illness was a criminal offence, while thieving was perceived as an illness, so that one Erewhonian merchant was in need of company during his convalescence as he had just 'recovered from embezzling a large sum of money under singularly distressing circumstances'.[8] In place of hypochondriacs, Erewhon was full of 'valetudinarians', 'who ma[d]e themselves exceedingly ridiculous by their nervous supposition that they [we]re wicked, while they [we]re very tolerable to people all the time'.[9]

In fact, in many ways Butler had been the true inheritor of More and Swift, said the priest, with Erewhon being an anagram of 'nowhere' and thus a different version of More's not-place, and Butler writing of many far-from-perfect practices, such as of 'prophets' who claimed actually to know what they said they knew, thereby stopping people from thinking,[10] and the educational system which discouraged people from thinking for themselves.[11] But Butler's real point, quite apart from all this satire, was to drive home the dangers of the remorseless expansion of machinery, which had been cast aside as museum pieces in Erewhon – he feared 'the ultimate development of mechanical consciousness'[12] and the 'extraordinary rapidity with which [machines we]re becoming something very different'.[13]

So you see, the priest told me, the fact was that, like Marx, Butler's work reflected the atmosphere of the times; and that was the case of other utopian works of that period, such as the books by William Morris and Edward Bellamy. They both used the premise of time travel, with their narrators waking up in the future when everything was 'perfect'. In Morris's case, this involved the transformation of society into a socialist paradise where 'the sacred rights of property'[14] had been done away with, work was the key to fulfilment,[15] everybody did some agricultural work,[16] and nationhood and decision-making had been devolved to local groups.[17] For Bellamy, by contrast, the growing accumulation of capital in vast corporations was solved by the consolidation of these few businesses into one giant state capital monopoly, which conducted all business 'in the common interest and for the common profit',[18] meaning that money had now been disposed of,[19] there was sexual equality, work was nation-serving rather than self-serving, and people could all retire at the age of forty-five.[20]

'And so,' said the priest, turning away from the window at last and returning to his perch on the hard bench, 'as you see, idealism remained strong throughout the nineteenth century. It was just its focus that shifted, as society itself shifted following the industrial revolution. That of course was the real utopian context of Marx's ideas, and the motor behind the growth of communism.'

'And what's that got to do with us today?' I asked.

'Well,' the priest said, 'what was important to many of these writers was the change of consciousness. Marx talked of the need to formulate a communist consciousness,[21] and Butler worried about machines developing consciousness – perhaps a forerunner of your concern about the mechanisation of human consciousness. And what's most essential of all now is to engineer a shift in *our* consciousness – and in our unconscious. And that's why, just like its predecessors in the nineteenth century, any good utopian book today has got to take account of both the contemporary social reality and reveal an emotional picture that is not reduced to a footnote. Forget the lies of politicians, tell it how it really is, and the unconscious might realise what it needs to become.'

'What it needs to become?' I asked weakly, aware that he was so deranged that he had no idea of what this contemporary reality might consist.

'Yes: first, cut down information overload; second, work with the new consciousness which this creates to foment a new atmosphere in which people pull back from their urges, and by doing so turn more towards communities; and third, thereby foster greater emotional respect for the environment, and put that changed perspective to work in restructuring our relationship with the planet. And that's about as much utopianism as we'll be able to stomach, particularly if, like me, you've been living here for thirty years and have yet to see perfection in anything but the Church, which shows how pathetic you must be, so that if my surname wasn't de la Fuente de la Paz I would have given up long ago.'

With that, he came to a stop. He stood up from the bench with decision, bounding with the enthusiasm of a young man.

'Where are you going now?' I asked him.

'Can't you see?' he said. 'I've got a wedding to perform. And you're invited.'

'But wait,' I said. 'You can't just rush off. Your ideas are full of problems. For one thing, they offer nothing practical, and purely address the emotional and psychological roots of all our problems.'

'Precisely,' he said, 'that's what's so good about them. It's about time we grasped the importance of the emotional and psychological roots of the present situation.'

'And for another thing,' I said, 'anyone who reads your litany of vague generalisations won't take any of it seriously. After all, it's not even clear whether you expect anyone to respond to your suggestions or not, or if you want them to. Your thoughts are masked by a deceptive structure so that you can pretend that anything's true, and can claim that you believe in whatever suits you.'

'Absolutely,' he said, 'and in that way the structure's precisely reflective of our current social atmosphere, where a person's belief at any one time is just a function of their immediate social imperative.'

'And what's more,' I said, 'it's not a structure that I can take seriously, even though I'm quite likely to write about it, since you're an interesting character. It's too much of a hybrid.'

'Again,' he said, 'a reflection of our atmosphere, which has so many sources of information. And besides, none of this is my problem,' he added, flexing his knees at the joint. 'You're the writer here, so you're the one who's going to have to make it credible. What's more, everyone has to live with their own consciences – if they still have them – so they can read all this just as they want to, as biography, historical reconstruction, polemic or fictional satire. I really don't care.'

Without waiting for me any longer, he tore through the door and left for the church. Watching him go, I felt a great sense of relief. The room seemed calmer, more manageable now that he had gone; I felt that the good sense that San Juan had called for was now within my grasp.

Getting up, I went after the priest, following him out into the patio, which was now crushed full of people awaiting the bride and groom.

The Purépecha had come dressed in all their finery. The women wore multicoloured shawls, and the men wore their best suits, and leather shoes and hats. Colour mixed with stillness, dignity, peace. The flowers sparkled, and held the attention of everyone as they reflected the sparkle of the sun, which had now reached its zenith.

I waited at the back of the throng, aware that I was an outsider, as the priest marched through the people and entered the church. He walked down the aisle, and then said a word to the bridegroom, who was by far the smartest man there, his buttonhole a spray of petals.

The priest bent over now, and picked up one of the petals from the buttonhole, before allowing it to fall through his fingers to the floor. Then he walked up to the altar, and turned to face the Purépecha congregation.

His white hair glowed in the stillness; no one said a word.

After a few minutes of hushed waiting, I was aware of a stirring behind me. Turning round, I was staggered to see the old woman who had guided me round the museum of Don Vasco. She was dressed in silk, her dress reaching down to the floor, her hair a riot of flowers, her arms laden down with bouquets. The wrinkles had gone from her face, and she was suddenly young again.

She was the bride.

I gasped as she approached me. She winked, and passed me by with a smile. Then she was engulfed by her friends, and their flowers. I could not see her amidst all the colour, as the sea of people closed behind her and swallowed her up, protecting her from my vision.

I could see nothing, but the elation that filled Santa Fe was palpable. At last I felt the weight of my feelings lightening, as I became more conscious of them.

Soon I heard the joyous tones of the priest – doubtless taking a leaf out of the behaviour of Don Vasco – as the wedding ceremony began.

Gradually the colours of the flowers subsided; the petals had fallen down to earth again, and began to mix in with the mulch below.

Looking up at the burning sun, I had a fleeting glimpse of the feelings that Quiroga might have gone through as he worked to build his own world here. He had travelled tirelessly around his vast diocese, preaching, communing, praying.

My body felt empty. I sensed that I had to wander away from this ceremony, and explore the rest of Michoacán, if I were to join him at last.

TWELVE

The renowned work of the hospitals rapidly spreads outwards, irradiating through Michoacán like the strands of a spider's web whose centre is Santa Fe de la Laguna.

Though Santa Fe is the utopian heartland, Quiroga's idealism percolates through his diocese via a network of smaller institutions known as *hospitales de la concepción*.* Eventually, every town in Michoacán will have one of these places, where the ill and the poor may be tended to and fed, and the Holy Sacraments can be administered.[1] Within a radius of just a few leagues of the town of Chilcota, for instance, even the tiny hamlets of Acachuen (with no more than twenty people), Guanastao (twenty-five people) and Mascuaro (fifteen people) will all have their own hospital by 1579.[2] Near the settlement of Sirandaro, down in the thick heat towards the Pacific Ocean, 'there are hospitals in every neighbourhood'.[3] By the end of the seventeenth century, there will be 264 of them in Michoacán.[4]

These smaller hospitals are not entire functioning communities – unlike Santa Fe de la Laguna – but they are community centres which instil the utopian ideal, and are run according to the same principles as the pueblo-hospital.[5] Goats and sheep are kept by every hospital,[6] while each town grows maize and wheat for their hospital's granary,[7] and the local craftspeople – the farriers, carpenters and others – all work there on certain days.[8] These hospitals have a small chapel and space to lodge passing travellers[9] – in More's *Utopia*, after all, people could travel wherever they wished provided they did a day's work – while the running of the institution is in the hands of the Purépecha, with the priests having no official function.[10] Local townspeople take it in turn to do the hospital's work, with a team of five married couples cleaning the house and the clothes, cooking the food and nursing the

*It seems significant that the hospital in Madrigal was also dedicated to Santa Maria de Ia Concepción – see above, ch. 2, p. 28.

sick; these people eat the hospital's food if they are poor, or their own food if they are better off.[11]

However, while Quiroga is the main motor of this growing network,[12] his energies are not inexhaustible. Even he could not found every single hospital in every single town, and for his idealism to be made real, he needs helpers (utopianism requires togetherness, after all); and so, in these early years, his allies have been the Franciscan mendicants. Even before he accepted the bishop's mitre last year, the mendicant friar Juan de San Miguel was working in the Purépecha's lakeland, congregating the Indians in settlements around Pátzcuaro, and further away, in the subtropical paradise of Uruapan.[13] Just three years ago, in 1536, the Indians were 'reduced' in Tzintzuntzan and other neigh-bouring towns,[14] so that the network of *hospitales de la concepción* could begin to expand. These hospitals will continue to be founded by the Franciscans – and other mendicants – throughout Quiroga's lifetime, although some will also be built by the local *encomenderos*.[15]

Often, however, before the Purépecha gather around these smaller hospitals, they come down from the hills to Santa Fe de la Laguna, which is the most famous hospital of all. Once they have learnt the appropriate ideas there, they return to the areas from which they have come to build their own slice of perfection.

In Santa Fe, the Purépecha find solace from the terrors they have recently been subjected to by Nuño de Guzmán and the *encomenderos*. Fear is a watchword for their world just now, with so many unexpected terrors and reverses assailing them that it is difficult to see how the primordial beauty of the world can be returned to them – how life can recover its wholeness. Yet in Santa Fe, they find that they are all so well treated, fed, clothed and housed, that they themselves spread the word,[16] telling others in detail of everything that they have seen: 'how they [have] been received by the wonderfully kind bishop, how they [have] been lodged and fed, how they [have] received the rudiments of Christian education, and how they [have] been ideally settled in groups, according to age, sex and condition'.[17] Quiroga himself composes hymns for them, which are sung in their own language and which melt their hearts with emotion, so that people often break into tears[18] at the joy of Christian faith, at their salvation, at the blinding heavenly sunlight (and at their recollection of the horrors of conquest, at how fear now impales their environment).

Crowds of Purépecha are constantly breaching the green hills that ring Lake Pátzcuaro, funnelling down towards Santa Fe as if drawn by some irresistible physical force, a magnet, a sign. They arrive stark naked, their skins glistening in the watery sunlight, or they come with their private parts covered by animal hides.[19] Quiroga's spirit is lacerated when he hears how these people have been used to sleeping out in the open, or in caves, eating raw meat,[20] without justice or God. And so, he concentrates himself on ensuring that this will never happen again in his diocese.

The Purépecha are quickly so smitten with the way of life in Santa Fe that, when they go hunting, they return to him with offerings of the deer that they have caught.[21] He also organises contests of archery to entertain them, giving away live pigs as prizes,[22] and reminding them at the end of the competition that life consists of spiritual as well as material arrows – with divine, and not material, ends.[23]

During this first year of his episcopacy, Quiroga is utterly absorbed in the development of his project; and so it is no surprise to him that his ideals are soon mirrored by a heavenly vision. Late one night, he has a dream of a beautiful, impressive man bringing him a child, and asking him to baptise it; of course, this child represents the people in Quiroga's own diocese, and it is presented to him by God.[24] He prays that he may be able to fulfil this dream and create a state of heaven on earth for the Purépecha.

All his energies are directed towards his hospitals and his vision of a republic for the Indians. He gives the Spanish settlers short shrift, and feels that his Utopia is a very necessary counterbalance to their dissolute lives. Yes, wealth creation is important in civil society, but it is worthless without some non-material idealism to go with it; and in fact, were it not for his cherished hospitals, he might soon find life impossible, knowing as he does that his work is but a fraction of what is needed.

For the Purépecha continue to starve and die in spite of his good intentions. Some of them are still up in the hills,[25] or lurking in caves, like the necromancers of Salamanca, resisting the tide of Christian truth, of progress. They are still backward and impoverished. They are still terrorised by the forces that represent Spain in this New World, where the desire of most people is to get rich quick, and the colonists live anxiously, hoping that if not this year then the next they will have the resources with which to return to the Old World.[26]

By rights, of course, the Spaniards should be content in Michoacán, for these are some of the most fertile lands in all New Spain,[27] so that if the colonists could only content themselves with what the peoples in Old Castile are contented, 'there would be no happier people on earth'.[28] But the colonists' lives are shredded by this desire to amass enough money never to have to work again, and by the ludicrous fantasy that this alone will make them happy, and safe, and free, rather than chaining them to a new, and fiercer, network of desires. Impaled by impossible and self-obsessed dreams, and by their fear of failing to realise them, they become bitter, but it is this very bitterness that drags them ever deeper into their self-obsession, and the Purépecha ever deeper into slavery.

So whatever Quiroga does, greed and short-termism still plague the lives of the Indians, plunder their world and will continue to plunder it, rendering his work piecemeal at best. In truth, to some of the settlers his idealism appears laughable, pathetic, and indicates a refusal to take account of the basic historical processes that are involved in living.

Faced with this wall of opposition, the bishop entrenches himself still further in his idealist mentality. If 'they' call idealism absurd, and claim to be pragmatists, *he* will be more idealistic, and recognise that *they* are his enemies. Yes, his enemies might call themselves pragmatists, but their pragmatism does not involve biting the hand that feeds them; it involves humiliating it, wrenching it off, devouring it, so that soon there may be no hands left.

If 'they' want to pick a fight with him, they will find that he is more than willing to stand up for his beliefs.

Quiroga's obstreperousness was by now well known. The protests of the Cabildo of Mexico and the Spanish settlers of Michoacán had not deterred him from setting out on what he thought was the correct course in his pueblo-hospitals.* This obstinacy was something that he developed into an art form over the course of the rest of his life, entering into prolonged battles with the Bishops of Mexico and Guadalajara over the boundaries of his diocese, with the *encomenderos* of Michoacán and with the Franciscan missionaries in his see, and embarking on interminable legal battles that lasted for decades. Like a good utopian, he knew that he was right, and that 'they' were wrong.

However, while this stubbornness can seem indicative of the fact that Quiroga's project – and its motor – were not as 'perfect' as is made out, a different interpretation suggests itself for his running battles with other Spaniards in the New World: the colonial project was so destructive and self-interested that anyone who spent his life fighting most of those involved in it cannot have been too bad.

*See above, ch. 8, pp. 141–2 and ch. 10, pp. 178–9.

In New Spain as a whole, divisiveness was acute by the late 1530s. For while the infighting between the conquistadors in the 1520s had perhaps gradually ebbed away under the Second Audiencia – albeit, the government of New Spain was still in the dark as to much of what went on[29] – it had been replaced by fears of contamination by the Jewish and Moorish 'plague', and indeed with wider questions concerning the faith of the Indians. These had developed in the late 1520s with the burning in Mexico of the 'judaisers' Hernando de Alonso and Gonzalo de Morales in 1528, and gathered pace throughout the 1530s under the watchful eye of Bishop Zumárraga.*

The Inquisition had been active in Mexico as early as 1523,[30] although it had taken several years for the first burnings to occur. Once Zumárraga arrived, however, the inquisitorial trials gathered pace, and the bishop had active correspondence on issues concerning the 'purity of the faith' in Panuco and Tasco, as well as in Mexico,[31] with his initial concern being over Islam and Judaism. The burnings of 1528 were followed in 1530 by information about 'various individuals, children of burnt people,† or those who had been reconciled‡ by the Inquisition in Spain, and were therefore prohibited from being in New Spain';[32] then, in 1532, Ruy Díaz was tried for blasphemy, and information was given about the dubiousness of his *limpieza*.§[33]

It was in 1536, however, that the most severe inquisitorial trials began. Again, Jews and Moslems played a part. Hernán Nuñez from Seville was accused of saying, while playing cards in Mexico, that 'if there were Moors [Moslems] in this land he would become a Moor'.[34] Alonso Ávila was accused of 'keeping a cross under his desk and putting his feet on top of it'.[35] Jorge González and Gonzalo Ecija –

---

*See above ch. 7, p. 116. Indeed, one is struck by the parallels between this experience and that of Spain in the fifteenth century, where the civil wars of the 1460s and 1470s only ended just prior to the formal establishment of the Spanish Inquisition by Ferdinand and Isabella in 1481. In Mexico, the bloody infighting which had come to a head during Cortés's absence in Honduras from 1524–6 was followed by the burnings in 1528 and the expansion of the Inquisition in the 1530s.

†*Quemados* in Spanish.

‡I.e. they had accepted their 'heresy' and had reconciled themselves to the Church on fulfilling certain penalties – which varied from case to case.

§This literally means 'cleanliness'. However, in sixteenth- and seventeenth-century Spain the term had a meaning which is impossible adequately to translate into English. At this time, there was an obsession with '*limpieza*' among the Castilian nobility, which involved having no Jewish or Moorish blood and being an 'old' Christian. Religious orders and posts of civil authority were barred from those who could not show themselves as having *limpieza*, and this obsession remained virtually undiluted into the eighteenth century.

both merchants – were said to have been hiding in Mexico after having been accused by the Inquisition in Spain.[36] By now, however, Zumárraga's focus of attention was shifting to the Indians, and many of the Mexica were tried themselves; for instance, there was the accusation of 'Tacatetle and Tanixtetle, Indians who when baptised were respectively called Alonso and Antonio, neighbours of Tanacopan, for being idolaters and sacrificers following their gentile rites and customs'.[37]

This induction of the Indians into the inquisitorial process was highly controversial. Many held that the Indians, as recent converts to Catholicism, could not be tried by the Holy Office.[38] However, Zumárraga did not hold this view, perhaps remembering that few people had invoked this argument to protect the forced Jewish converts to Christianity against the Inquisition in the fifteenth century. The late 1530s saw gathering evidence that the Indians were reverting to their devilish religion, and there were several trials of Indians – and African slaves – accused of witchcraft.[39] The culmination of all this came in 1539, with the trial and the burning of the Cacique of Texcoco, Don Carlos,[40] whose active encouragement of the local religions was jeopardising christianisation.

In Michoacán, however, Zumárraga's inquiries into the faith had few parallels. In all these early years of the Spanish colony, only one case emerged from Quiroga's see, that of Gonzalo Gómez in 1536, for being a judaiser.[41] Indeed, the inquisitorial cases from Michoacán are notable for their extreme infrequency during Quiroga's life, with just one later case from Valladolid in 1562 of a woman, Isabel Vera, accused of casting spells.[42] If Quiroga did have Jewish blood on his mother's side,* this might explain the lack of inquisitorial activity; but the absence of trials of faith also supports the evidence of the many Spanish chroniclers who claimed Michoacán to be the most Christian of all the provinces of New Spain, and confirms that Quiroga – who, as bishop, was the Inquisition's representative in the see – directed his energies towards the welfare of the Indians, instead of embarking on needless witch-hunts of Spanish 'heretics'.

That Quiroga's position was now in strong opposition to that of his old friend Zumárraga is confirmed by a litigious argument which developed between them at this time as to the boundaries of their dioceses. The row centred over land in Querétaro, where there were rich haciendas that were claimed as part of their sees by each bishop.[43]

*See above, ch. 2, p. 24.

Of course, both men wanted a share of the tithes for their own dioceses, but Quiroga's case was perhaps the least grasping, as none of his *hospitales de la concepción* – which were by now expanding rapidly – paid any tithes.

The first Viceroy of New Spain, Antonio de Mendoza, was now in Mexico, and had declared that the disputed land belonged to Zumárraga's see; but Quiroga responded by firing off letters of excommunication to the owners of the haciendas, which put them in a tricky position: either they had to pay two tithes, or they would be excommunicated.[44] In November 1538, Quiroga suggested that the Viceroy and the Audiencia should resolve the controversy, and on 3 October 1539 – just a few months after the burning of Don Carlos of Texcoco – Charles V wrote to Quiroga demanding that he accept Mendoza's original ruling 'and that there [should] be no new legal case or any difference whatsoever'.[45]

Charles's language implies that by now the Spanish court had a good grasp of what a tough customer the Bishop of Michoacán could be. However, Quiroga was in no mood to back down. The legal case rumbled on through the 1540s, and Quiroga again sent letters of excommunication to the ranchers Juan de Burgos and Juan de Soria[46] in 1541. Only in 1544 did the *gran pleito* between the two bishoprics finally begin to be heard, but the case would remain disputed into the 1580s, although it was eventually resolved in favour of Michoacán.

Quiroga's battle with Zumárraga is open to many interpretations. The legal case over the haciendas was certainly grounded in economics, for Quiroga was still spending all of his salary on the work of the hospitals, and so of course his bishopric needed as much income as possible. It is also true that, convinced that his project was divinely inspired, he doubtless wanted his jurisdiction to extend as far as possible.

However, while these suggestions embrace some of the answers, Quiroga's stance is best viewed in relation to the Bishop of Mexico's expansion of the Inquisition. Quiroga held that the best way to lead the Indians to salvation was to show them good works,* and so the burning of one of their caciques as an 'example' would surely not have met with his approval. Believing as he did that More's book and his enactment of it were divinely inspired, the prospect of some of his see falling into Zumárraga's zealous hands would have troubled him after this, and so he sought to avoid it.

*See above, ch. 10, p. 184.

Quiroga was not alone in his view. Zumárraga's punishment of Don Carlos of Texcoco eventually led to his being stood down as chief inquisitor of Mexico in 1543. Well before this time, however, Quiroga's struggles against his fellow Spaniards had intensified still further.

The divine purpose of God is, of course, unerring. Satan, however, is a playful devil, and the legions of his followers are capable of throwing the severest obstacles into the path of perfection. Sometimes, when the Most Illustrious Bishop of Michoacán considers the state of the world, it almost appears difficult to see the agency of God, so many are the fingerprints of these devils.

The wheel of the seasons has turned again, so that he has now been consecrated for one year. Again, it is the rainy season. Don Vasco stands on the veranda of the chapel of Santa Fe, leaning on its wooden supports. A chill wind sweeps down from the thick clouds where he knows the mountains to stand, buffeting the houses with icy rain. Few people have ventured outside since the downpour began earlier this afternoon, although Quiroga glimpses one or two canoes pitching across the bay. Eaves guide the raindrops down to the muddy streets, so that they can dig their own channels and cascade towards the lake where the rain dances scatterfoot across the water.

This is a time of signs. With the rain teeming down, it is as if the Flood may come again to cleanse humanity of its sinners. For a moment, Quiroga imagines his humble lodgings taking wings, as it were, soaring onto the surface of Lake Pátzcuaro; as the waters rise, the land is drowned, the world begins again – perfection is born.

– Don Vasco.

His dreams are interrupted by his companion, Cristóbal Cabrera. Quiroga turns to look at the young man, who has so recently shared in his vision of the young child.

– It is getting late, Don Vasco, and you will catch an illness outside.

– Perhaps, Cristóbal. But my own bodily illness does not concern me.

The young man will learn, he feels. Cristóbal comes from Burgos,[47] where the cold rains of Michoacán are inconceivable. This is his first winter in the diocese, and the newly ordained cleric spends his time shivering inside, longing for the baking heat of his childhood. He stands there now, inviting Quiroga inside:

– Don Vasco, there is nothing you can do about it.

No, there is nothing to be done. Quiroga ducks under the lintel, and sits down ponderously on a stiff leather chair. He has laboured so hard to build his hospitals, in both Mexico and Michoacán, working himself almost to the point of exhaustion only for his work to be undone by the colonists – and in particular by the *encomendero* Juan de Infante.

Two days ago, on 27 September 1539, Infante arrived in Michoacán to claim the *barrios de la laguna*, the neighbourhoods near Lake Pátzcuaro that Quiroga has earmarked for his communal societies. Infante has come with the legal authority of the Spanish Crown and the reluctant blessing of the Audiencia; there is little, it would seem, that Quiroga can do to stop this vulgar triumphalism, the victory of greed over idealism.[48]

– Tell me truly, Cristóbal, he says now, running his hand tiredly across his face. Infante has no just claim to the lands, has he?

– None, Don Vasco.

No, of course he has not. Quiroga knows that he has done everything in his power to make his experiment a success, given the constraints of the earthly sphere.

A year ago, on 21 June 1538, he strove to put the pueblo-hospital on a sure footing. Don Pedro Cuiniarángari and his wife Inés drew up a bill of sale for certain lands to the pueblo-hospital and its founder, giving the utopian experiment an all-important legal stamp.[49] But now all this is threatened by the cupidity of Infante.

Everyone knows the *encomendero* to be a loathsome individual. He is a young upstart, barely thirty years of age![50] During the time of Nuño de Guzmán (who, at long last, is rotting in jail – evidence that the hand of God is long, and His memory eternal), Infante stole various towns in the region of Lake Pátzcuaro, claiming that his wife was the daughter of Charles V.[51] He was one of the accusers of Tzintzicha, the *cazonci*, at his 'trial', and, with Juan de Alvarado and Juan Villaseñor Cervantes, he was one of the cabal of Spanish thugs who took advantage of the chaos caused in Michoacán by the death of Tzintzicha to bring off a land-grab.[52] Years of legal arguments followed with the Audiencia in Mexico as to Infante's entitlements in Michoacán, but he has recently returned from Spain with royal authority to make good his legal claim to the settlements by the lake. Two appeals from Don Pedro Cuiniarángari have been rejected by the Audiencia in Mexico, and Infante has now come to take possession of the twenty-five lakeside settlements – a claim which, if realised, will destroy Quiroga's Utopia.

– We cannot allow this pig to be victorious, Cristóbal, the bishop says in the end. He will undo everything that we have sought to build.

– But we cannot stop him, Don Vasco. He has legal authority, and we have none.

– That is true, Cristóbal. And yet, would you not agree with me that the authority of our Lord is more weighty than that of any court on earth?

– That goes without saying, Don Vasco.

– Then as this Utopia is a work of God, we are entitled to do everything in our power to prevent the will of God from being usurped by the failings of human institutions.

– The will of God, Don Vasco?

Quiroga sees that his companion is wary. Yet the bishop is the mouthpiece of the Lord in Michoacán, and he has an intuition as to what the divine realm seeks here on earth. It does not wish for the people to be broken and their souls to rot, the land to be ruined, the earth destroyed; no, it seeks for the people to be saved, and the land to be worked, so that perfection can exist in reality as well as in dreams. Infante does not share his heavenly vision, but his mind is corrupt, depraved, chained to earthly desires – if he will not soar, heavenbound, at least he must not be allowed to prevent the Purépecha from doing so.

Quiroga stands up, and begins to pace across the room.

– Remind me, Cristóbal. Remind me of what we have done so far to prevent Infante from taking our land.

– What have we not done, Don Vasco? Cristóbal asks. We have arranged for the case to be put for two months in the city of Mexico, fighting Infante's claim. In the last week you have urged the Indians to discuss how to resist the implementation of Infante's authority. You have even spoken at the meeting of their council to press this on them.[53] You have fomented the deep feeling among the people here that what Infante pretends is not divine justice, but human injustice.

It is true, Quiroga thinks. He has worked tirelessly to prevent Infante from realising his ends, yet it all seems to have been in vain. Quiroga knows that the atmosphere among the Indians is riotous, and that there could be terrible consequences if Infante has his way.[54]

Yet perhaps that fury could be channelled to a positive end, he thinks, towards justice rather than rebellion. The people are tired of being exploited, they are sick of this new empire. They are ready to fight to protect the Utopia that they have been building, but that fight does not have to be bloody. Indeed, the threat of force may prove to be enough to overturn the forces of oppression.

– We have done everything possible, Don Vasco, Cristóbal says now.

– No, Cristóbal. We have done much to stop this from happening, but we have not done everything in our power.

Quiroga does not sleep that night. Instead he sits by his old desk – brought by sea from Castile – and reads in the pale glow of candlelight. He ploughs through works by Gerson, Lucian, Budé, so that by morning his eyes are tired with the strain.

But even then he does not rest. There is no time to rest, he calls to Cristóbal, when the world must be saved! So that day he rides ceaselessly across the land, talking to the Purépecha, planning the resistance, plotting.

By the evening of 30 September, everything is ready to safeguard his dream of the world.

On the morning of 1 October 1539, Juan de Infante left Tzintzuntzan together with his receptor and his court-appointed executor Andrés Juárez, and travelled along the shore of Lake Pátzcuaro to take possession of the *barrios de la laguna*. Though aware that Bishop Quiroga had done everything in his power to make things difficult, Infante did not see that anything could stop them now.

The previous day, Quiroga had met with Andrés Juárez and told him that all he sought was to prevent Infante and Juárez from provoking riots by exceeding their rights, thereby putting their own lives and those of many others into jeopardy.[55] However, Juárez had warned Quiroga that he would have to take responsibility for any public disturbances, and Infante had then presented him with the royal decree, giving him ownership of the twenty-five lakeside settlements. If the bishop kept his word now, as they rode out to take the *barrios*, everything would pass off peacefully.

Yet as the men spurred on their horses, they noticed that an uneasy quiet had settled across the lakeland. The teams of Purépecha who were usually to be seen threshing hay in the fields, or fishing in the lake, had vanished. There was no smoke rising from the roofs of the houses of Santa Fe de la Laguna in the distance, no high-pitched voices calling to one another across the smoky, chill morning. It was as if the two men were riding through a land peopled by ghosts, a land in which the bloodiest dreams of the conquistadors had been realised.

They had travelled no great distance when they were passed by Bishop Quiroga riding a mule, and eleven Spaniards riding on horseback, all of them carrying lances. There were also three churchmen mounted on horses, who bore swords tucked into their belts.[56] Faced by the threat of force, Infante and Juárez reined in their mounts and began to fight their corner.

During the long legal battle that followed, rolling on interminably, with a review in Madrid in July 1552[57] and a case brought against Tzintzuntzan by Infante's son following the *encomendero*'s death in 1574, the Infante party claimed that Quiroga and Don Pedro Cuiniarángari had gone to the *barrios de la laguna* on the night of 30 September, forcing people to flee.[58] This was confirmed by Toribio of Quisquaro, a Purépecha, who said that they had all been made to go to Quiroga's burgeoning settlement at Pátzcuaro.[59] Infante even claimed that some people had been killed in the flight, although this seems extremely unlikely.

This explained the emptiness that Juan de Infante and his sidekicks found all around them, as they looked at the green hills, and the still waters of Lake Pátzcuaro. The air was disturbed by nothing but birdsong. Where were the people whom he sought to dominate now? This was not what Infante had imagined at all, and he began to feel uneasy.

Steeped in the legalistic practices of their age, the two groups of colonists began to communicate in writing. Infante again argued that any public unrest would be down to Quiroga, but Quiroga countered that his duty was to see whether the possession of the settlements could be carried off without riots, and he did not believe that it could. Juárez then commanded the eleven laymen to turn back or face a large fine, warning that the clerics would be charged as laymen, as they came bearing arms. Three people turned back, but everyone else remained there.[60]

By and by, the party continued riding on towards the settlements that Infante coveted. They had gone a little further when the Spaniards accompanying Quiroga told Infante that 6000 Purépecha and Chichimec Indians were waiting further up the road in ambush, and that they would kill him, and him alone. Infante made one further protest, but then his cowardice got the better of him, and he turned back with Juárez and Quiroga.[61]

His receptor continued, however, to see what threat there really was up ahead. One of Quiroga's servants spurred his horse and rode on to the place at which the ambush was alleged to be laid, so that when the receptor arrived all he found was many Indians sitting in apparent peace among the cornfields and the rocks. The terror represented by

Infante had receded, and so the army had willingly disbanded without a shot being fired or a stone being thrown, ultimately achieving their aims through non-violence; nevertheless, Infante's receptor later testified that he thought it was the servant who had told the warriors to disband at the last minute.[62]

All this, of course, was outrageous behaviour on Quiroga's part. The authority of the Council of the Indies and the Audiencia of Mexico – both of which had upheld Infante's claim – was unquestioned. Whether or not Quiroga had incited the Purépecha to kill Infante, there was no doubt that he had actively encouraged them to show their disobedience to the prevailing order. He had entered the meeting of the Purépecha council and urged them to defend themselves, and he had told them that, if Infante were successful in his claim, they should abandon the lakeside villages and move to Pátzcuaro, where he lived.[63]

Some of Quiroga's motivations in this stand-off were probably similar to those of his confrontation with Zumárraga. Pouring so much money into all his hospitals and exempting them from paying tribute as he was,[64] his bishopric was feeling the pinch, and he needed as much land under his direct jurisdiction as possible, both to balance the books and to maintain the work of the hospitals. In a letter of 1543, he constantly referred to the poverty of the church in Michoacán, calling himself the 'first husband of a terribly poor and needy church',[65] as being 'poor and attacked from all sides',[66] and recounting how six or seven priests had come to Pátzcuaro, but did not want to stay there 'with the bishop and his church being so poor'.[67] He was doubtless also genuinely concerned about the fate of the Purépecha in the hands of an unscrupulous *encomendero* such as Infante.

Nonetheless, it is difficult to see that Quiroga would have taken his rebellion against legal authority so far without two elements: his belief in the divine inspiration behind his work, and the support of the Crown. By this time, he had managed to obtain royal protection for his hospitals, in a royal decree issued by the Spanish Crown on 16 June 1536,[68] in which the authorities had praised Quiroga for having 'made two hospitals of poor Indians of the land and [having] gathered them there', noting that they were 'well informed in the matters of our Holy Catholic faith'.[69]

Quiroga's victory turned out to be only partial. In spite of the many obstacles, Infante was not someone to leave this matter lightly, and he returned to Mexico, where he enlisted the support of Viceroy Mendoza. On 23 October 1539, the Audiencia recommended that

Mendoza return with Infante to settle the argument,[70] and Infante eventually took possession of the towns, ejecting those Purépecha who opposed him.[71]

However, the matter did not end here. The following years saw legal suits filed by both parties in this conflict, which was a battle not only for the land, but for an entire worldview. The 1552 review in Madrid favoured Quiroga, ordering Infante to give up his land to Pátzcuaro, with Quiroga accusing Infante of being disgracefully greedy, shipping the Indians of his lands off to the mines forty leagues away.[72] According to Quiroga, 'many other conquistadors ... desire to have just a sixth part of the number of Indians and towns held by Juan Infante, without including the *barrios de la laguna*'.[73] Still the Infante party did not give up; but in the case finally brought by Infante's son in the 1570s, the Council of the Indies ruled that the settlements belonged to Tzintzuntzan, and that was the end of the matter.[74]

The legacy of all these lawsuits was distrust. Quiroga felt ever more embattled, and his view that – in life – he was assailed from all sides was nothing less than the truth. Following on from the cases of Zumárraga and Infante, there quickly came the polemic over the transferral of the capital of Michoacán from Tzintzuntzan to Pátzcuaro.

This first year as Bishop of Utopia has really been full of upheavals. Even prior to being formally appointed bishop Quiroga was aware of the problems of Tzintzuntzan,[75] and it has not taken long since his arrival last year for him to decide that the capital of his see has to move. For, though this place has long been at the heart of the Purépecha empire, it will not do as the centre of Quiroga's vision.

Tzintzuntzan, he holds, is in 'a deep valley full of ravines ... it is surrounded by a lake ... there is a sickly and bad breeze there ... because of which many people fall ill with headaches'.[76] If the capital remains here, Quiroga has argued in written depositions, 'the town will have to be split into two neighbourhoods on the dry slopes of the valley, and the people from the lower neighbourhood will only come up to the church with much labour'.[77] Furthermore, there is no clean spring, and the residents survive by drawing water from bad wells.[78]

For some time, now, he has had his eyes turned towards the area called Pátzcuaro, three leagues south-west of Tzintzuntzan around the lake. Pátzcuaro has never been an important spot in the eyes of the Purépecha, being a small settlement with no more than ten or twelve houses[79] that they see as simply an outlying neighbourhood of Tzintzuntzan, and certainty not a place fit to be at the heart of empire.

Yet if an empire can be overturned, surely its heart can also be transplanted, its soul reconstituted; and certainly there is much in favour of Pátzcuaro, as far as Quiroga can see, not least its beauty. Although a minor settlement, it used to be a place of leisure for the ruling caste of the Purépecha.[80] The surrounding hills and woods are busy with brilliantly coloured birds,[81] which flit from tree to tree and fill the world with the colour that staves off melancholy, so that it is no wonder that Pátzcuaro means 'place of happiness' in Purépecha,[82] or that the Mexica call this place Huitzitzila, the 'place of the birds'.[83] These are surely good omens for his work, in a world that is filled with signs, if only people will listen to them.

He has been up to Pátzcuaro many times. The place nestles in the cradle of gently sloping hills, where the forests are thick and sprawling with mosses and ferns, and the rocks of the forest floor shine like fur beneath the rains. To the west, one hill rises sheer from the plain in which Lake Pátzcuaro stretches out into a milky haze, drizzled with islands and steeped in an apparent peace. There are many horses, more than in other provinces, for Michoacán will be the equine capital of New Spain in the sixteenth century.[84] So already, after less than two decades of colonisation, the scene is pastoral in the Spanish mould: herds of cattle spread out in the meadows by the lakeside, grazing amid wild flowers, while beyond them are the green ears of cornfields. At twilight, sun gilds the clouds, and birds hum in the stillness; the waters of the lake fold into a scarlet silence; the hills to the west, towards Uruapan, fall back into darkness; and Pátzcuaro withdraws into its sheath of shadows and dreams.

Yes, it is a beautiful place, and Quiroga will never lose his vision of beauty as central to his Utopia. Beauty is not just in the world around them, but in the love of God, in the mind as free of fear;* and this is what he finds in Pátzcuaro, where the steep hills of Tzintzuntzan are absent, and the thoughts can be free of the fear that is so readily engendered in the present atmosphere.

---

*The interconnection of fear and beauty in the minds of the American colonists is exemplified by an early seventeenth-century account of Peru. The anonymous author – probably a crypto-Jew – explains that boa constrictors 'do no harm and move very slowly, and this is why they are called boas'. *Boa* meaning 'beautiful' or 'good' in Portuguese, there seems to be a connection between this naming of the snake and the fact that it poses no threat to people. See *Descripción del Virreinato del Perú* (anonymous author), ed. Boleslao Lewin (Rosario, Universidad Nacional del Litoral, 1958), p. 23.

This place must be his capital. It has many good springs, lush woods that will provide excellent fuel, the air is healthy, and there are fertile orchards, copses and fish.[85] Already, last September, he was agitating for the city to be moved. By the end of the year, he had built his own house in Pátzcuaro and traced out the Spanish neighbourhood there.[86] Then, just a few weeks ago, he received a letter from Charles V saying that he could move the cathedral to Pátzcuaro if he wished.[87] As the decade draws to a close, and the struggle with Infante rumbles on, Quiroga begins to oversee the transplant of the see from Tzintzuntzan, and plans the huge cathedral which he intends to be at the heart of his community.[88]

Naturally, not just any cathedral will do. Just as the Spaniards in Mexico needed to build a city that was even more impressive than that of the Mexica, so Quiroga wishes to construct something that will be greater than anything the Purépecha have seen, a monument to God's coming to the New World. After all, what is an empire without architectural enormity to exemplify its qualities and impose its will? Seville needed its cathedral, Mexico needed its ostentation, and Pátzcuaro needs something similar.

Quiroga's idea is to have the cathedral built in a semicircle which is divided into five naves, in each of which mass can be preached in a different Mesoamerican language.[89] The house of God is modelled on St Peter's Church in Rome, and on the new cathedral that Quiroga saw erected in Granada when a young man, and will be so vast as to be something 'never before seen in this land',[90] so that when it is finished it will be like the eighth wonder of the world.[91] The bishop's mind is filled with the cathedral in Seville, his last sight of the Old World, a monument which was built in part to remind the Moors that God really was great, and that their defeat really was permanent. The same must now go for the Purépecha, for do not the Indians share the tendency of the old infidels, the Jews and Moslems, whose beliefs encourage them to desire only the good things of this world, 'without recalling those of the heavens'?[92]

Of course, Quiroga knows that where the ideas of heaven are concerned, the devil's envoys on earth will always be obstructive. So the complaints of the *encomenderos* about his plan are only to be expected. Even the long and vicious arguments he has had with some of the Franciscan mendicants do not surprise him, and rekindle his determination never to give way.[93] Nevertheless, the bishop has been dismayed to see that the Purépecha have been equally unhappy about his moving of the capital to Pátzcuaro. The children of Tzintzicha, the nobles, Don Pedro Cuiniarángari and the Purépecha council have all protested to him about the plan,[94] and some of them have even taken up arms as if to threaten him.[95]

Quiroga cannot help but give a wry smile when he remembers this, for only the godless could believe that they could threaten the divine will. Do they not realise that the old religion, and the old customs which went with it, have been defeated? They should be happy with the move, for is not Pátzcuaro 'the door to the heavens',[96] the way by which the heathen gods of the Purépecha come and go from the earthly sphere? As a sop to *their* obstinacy – and in recognition of the fact that there are many facets to conversion – he is building the cathedral on the site of the old sacred stones in Pátzcuaro. Yes, the old religion is finally to be destroyed, but the geography of the Purépecha cosmos will live on.[97]

The roads between Tzintzuntzan and Pátzcuaro are filled with the Purépecha as they carry out Quiroga's plan. The organ, the bell, the pews, the confessional chambers – all of them must be dismantled and carried to the site of the new cathedral,[98] where meanwhile the immense labour of construction continues. As the work on the site unfolds, 14,000 people gather from all over Michoacán to live here,[99] and the town swells beyond all memory. The diseases may have attacked the Purépecha remorselessly, and greatly reduced them in number, but in Quiroga's capital the population soars, as they dig the foundations, erect the wooden skeleton on which the cathedral will be constructed, carry the masonry, toiling for the love of God.

The Purépecha work long days. Their bodies are bent beneath huge burdens, spawn rivers of sweat. The capital of his see is witnessing a glut of activity, and Quiroga finds that the sight reminds him of the frenzy of construction in Seville and Mexico; but that is the way of empire, which – like his *hospitales de la concepción* – radiates outwards from the centre. Seville is the richest city in Spain, and so it is natural that the building should have begun there; but now that it has spread to Mexico, and Pátzcuaro, the networks of Christian justice are touching every corner of the world. This global reach is surely part of God's plan, that everyone should be touched by His law before the Day of Judgement.

That day is drawing near, the bishop feels, and there is no time to lose. This monument must be raised up tall, magnificent, indestructible to everything except messages sent from the heavens. The Purépecha must be brought to perfection on earth.

By night, in the Purépecha neighbourhoods, however, there is much sadness and fear. The people light fires in the patios of their adobe homes, to remind them of the cult of fire that used to govern their cosmology.[100] The monstrous task that the bishop has allotted to them opens wounds of resentment.[101] He says that he is here to help them, and yet all he does is give them work in the same spirit as do the *encomenderos*.

Ah yes, says Quiroga, but the work you do for them is solely for their own profit, whereas the cathedral is a work for God, and for your souls. I reap no benefit, I gain no gold from it, I do it all for you. Yes, I do it all for you.

Gradually, the new city takes shape. The cathedral rises slowly. The central nave is the first to be completed, but as the years pass, the rest of the work will become more and more difficult. The soil here is not strong, and the cathedral is so immense that its walls begin to crack.[102] By the 1550s the project will have to be abandoned, and restricted just to the central nave.[103]

On the outskirts of the city, meanwhile, orchards of apple, pear, quince and peach trees are planted.[104] There are fields of wheat and barley, and a quarry is opened nearby where white stone can be mined.[105] By and by, the memories of Tzintzuntzan, the bitterness of the move, the recriminations, will fade into the hills where only the forest can feel them.

So the natural world absorbs the unspoken distress without complaint, even though it knows that eventually it too, like the Purépecha, will reap the bitter emotional harvest that has been sown in the New World; but for the time being, the trees say nothing, the birds still fly, the coyotes and pumas retreat further into the wilderness, which is still there for them, and will still be there one hundred, two hundred years hence (but not for ever).

This will be a slow death, for everyone but the Purépecha.

THIRTEEN

At times, it is difficult to grasp the meaning of the world's change of direction.

Here, the Purépecha think, we were at peace with ourselves. Yes, we fought against other peoples to secure their hearts and sacrifice them to our gods, but the hills were cloaked with mists that breathed, trees that spoke, animals that represented the sacred core of the earth. We fished and we farmed, we trod the footpaths that snake through our forests, we pulsed out our lives almost without being aware of how we lived. There were many of us in our family.

Now here comes the bishop, though, the representative of the heavens. He is a pale slip of a man who seems never to smile. His fellows are the bearded devils who whip us to work in the mines that are opening up every year now, in Santa Clara and Tlapujalma, Charo and Ozumátlan.[1] Then there are the slave drivers who call themselves the gods of the land, and bring over their ravenous livestock, spreading them across our territory like a four-legged army so that they consume its grass like wildfire.[2] And what do we get in return for our work in the fields of the new gods of the land? Instruction in the worship of the Chief God to whom they all answer!*

Ah, says the bishop, and it is this for which we should be so grateful. He tells us that this is our salvation, that our previous ways have bathed us in sin. He says that man is made in the image of God, but who is this God? Is it the incarnation of our *cazonci*, perhaps, fallen into the realm beyond the water? Is it our very own Curicaveri? And why must God be like a person, when the sacred essence of life is all-encompassing?

Sublimating humanity at the expense of its fellow species could cost us the earth, the Purépecha feel intuitively, as they perceive the bishop's

*This was the bargain of the *encomienda* – Indian labour for instruction in Christianity. See above, ch. 5, p. 83.

idols – those sticks his acolytes have lashed together, the portrait of the Doleful Woman.

It is difficult for them to grasp this unfamiliar divinity, even when the new gods of the land force-feed them with its nature; how much harder to understand the new world. The bishop has made it plain that the old ways must be consigned to the pit of oblivion, but this is almost to say that the Purépecha must become different creatures altogether, as if they have been invited to throw off their primordial essence and adopt a new one; and while there are always some people who are willing to prostitute themselves for future gains, there are many who are crushed by the demand.

The people go to the mines where they scrape out the base metals that consolidate conquest.[3] They work as labourers, building the colonists their new cities, sometimes having to hammer the stonework with other stones because of the lack of tools.[4]

Then they retreat to their homes, as if eviscerated, their spirits raddled with distress. Weakened physically by the hard work of the *encomiendas* and the mines, and culturally by the imperious new force, they sit around the villages of Michoacán, overcome by lassitude. Their eyes empty, their limbs flop disconsolately by their sides, their bellies gnaw with hunger, and yet they eat sparingly. It is as if they have nothing to live for, and so they may as well depart this life at the first opportunity; for the soul has been ripped out of their world, and all that is left to it is its bare materials, which the Spanish are busily exporting.

In 1545, another epidemic strikes New Spain. The faces of the Indians burst with blood all across the Viceroyalty. The life force streaks down their faces to stain the earth, falling into a nothingness so lasting that it feels as if it may never be disturbed once this catastrophe has ended. In Tlaxcala, 150,000 people die; in Cholula, 100,000.[5] In Michoacán, the results are no less acute: nine tenths of the population pass away.[6]

Village after village sees its people evaporate, steaming up to join the volcanic clouds in the heavens. Souls fall by the wayside, and the human world empties, to be replaced by scavenging vultures and dogs, parasites who grow fat on the blood of others. In thirty years' time, the effects of the epidemic will still be apparent, and indeed the events of 1545 will come to be seen as the starting point for the ruination of Michoacán.[7] In Pátzcuaro, the population will have fallen from 14,000 to 5000.[8] In smaller towns of the sierra such as Xiquilpa, there will be just one twelfth of the number of people that there used to be.[9] Down by the coast the population of Epatlan will have dropped from 500 to ten, and in Cuxquaquautla from 400 to five;[10] meanwhile, these fifteen people 'live in illness, most of them suffering from a sickness of wounds that look like ulcers that come out in the legs, in the arms and across the body'.[11]

For those who endure, as for all holocaust survivors, their remaining battle is with their consciences. Perhaps like the priest of Tzintzuntzan just twenty years ago, they have had dreams about a coming apocalypse, have imagined how they might escape, to the hills, across the water, far away; but once they survive they recognise that perhaps living is harder than dying, especially when the vector of the world is destruction. They must ask what they have done to merit continued existence, when almost all of their companions have left them. For, of course, they would much prefer to be with their families, in peace, rather than in a world destroyed by the triumvirate of fear, illness, and innovative weaponry.

At least, now that there are so few of them left, the new culture is easier to bear; their own deepest beliefs easier to bury. Perhaps, indeed, the bishop has it right, and the answer to all this lies with the will of God.

In fact, the Purépecha now see, the reason for their health in old times and their weakness today must be that, because they were heathens in the past and their souls were food for the devil, God was kind to them and postponed their deaths; but now that they are Christians, God simply finds their souls in good condition and takes them away.[12]

Such is the mercy of the God of the Spanish; yea, He will seek out Satan wherever he is on earth, and punish his followers, even if this means smoking out civilisation itself in the flames of justice, of the Inquisition, of the Black Death!

The bishop retains his equanimity through the terrible fields of the dead. He finds that the meaning of the epidemic of 1545 is transparent: this really is the 'end time', the point from which all must be prepared for the Second Coming. Even as he visits the homes of the villagers, and finds their corpses resting beside one another, he loses none of his faith. The newly founded *hospitales de la concepción* have proved their worth in the midst of the sickness, dealing with up to 400 sufferers at a time without cracking under the burden.[13] Surely the people will see that he labours only for their salvation, and come to the flock in even greater numbers, once the divine curse has passed.

So even the decimation of his diocese strengthens the bishop's belief in his creations. Just two years ago, on 1 May 1543, the Emperor Charles V became patron of Santa Fe de la Laguna,[14] something that cemented the bishop's strength of purpose. The mass deaths of the Purépecha are a great sadness of course, but they will not deflect him. God's triumph will be on earth, as it is in heaven, and so there is no need to consider what it means when an entire people, and their cosmology, wither into nothingness. Species are created by God, and He can take them away! It is not for men to consider the motivations behind the will of God, nor His actions.

Yet among the Purépecha all is sadness, not the joy of God.

Their cacique Don Pedro Cuiniarángari has died from the sickness. Most people are buried just as well as the survivors can manage – before the scavengers can pick at them, if possible – but the governor must be given a proper send-off; and so the funeral mass in the unfinished cathedral at Pátzcuaro is suitably solemn, arranged by the bishop, whose eyes have cried themselves out.

An image of the Doleful Woman is decked in flowers and borne on the shoulders of four people into the nave, who are surrounded by many others, all of them carrying thick candles. Inside the cathedral there are more garlands of flowers, whose petals sparkle.[15] The clouds close overhead, and the light is snuffed out. The town is silent. The last representative of the old Purépecha order is accompanied into the vault of mystery.

Don Pedro is to be succeeded as governor by Don Antonio Cuitzimengari,[16] a man in the mould that the bishop seeks to encourage. He can speak Hebrew, Greek, Latin, Spanish and Purépecha,[17] and has been tutored at the newly finished school of San Nicolás in Pátzcuaro, which the bishop has founded to instruct people in truth.[18]

The funeral procession wends its way up the nave, to the rustling of feet, polite coughs, the acquiescent silence of a people at its end.

In Pátzcuaro's makeshift Temple of God, the bell tolls.[19]

Around three years after the 1545 epidemic came to an end, Quiroga travelled to Spain, probably arriving some time in the summer or early autumn of 1548.[20] This was not the first time that he had attempted to return to Europe, for in 1543 he had sailed from Veracruz for the Council of Trent, to which all Catholic bishops who could make it had been summoned by the Pope[21] – the ship in which he was travelling had started to founder, and had been forced to return to port.[22] In 1548, however, there were no such problems, and Quiroga spent at least five years in Spain, probably based in Madrid.[23]

Although this is among the most obscure periods of Quiroga's life,[24] the purpose of his visit was certainly manifold. For one thing, he wished to obtain royal privileges for his pueblo-hospital:[25] the Indians of the two Santa Fes were now freed of the obligation to offer 'personal services' in the mines or farms, something that they kept until the late eighteenth century,[26] and the crown gave additional land to Michoacán's pueblo-hospital, where vines and olive trees were planted.[27] Also related to the defence of his hospitals was Quiroga's legal battle against Juan de Infante, and his desire to win back the *barrios de la laguna* for his utopian project* – something he was also successful in doing.

However, two other important strands of his visit were his developing feuds, with the Spanish settlers of Michoacán on the one hand, and with the Franciscan friars on the other.

His arguments with the settlers centred around their desire to move the capital of Michoacán from Pátzcuaro to Guayangareo, or Valladolid, as the Spanish called it.† This went back to 1540, when Viceroy Mendoza had come to Michoacán and visited Tiripetío. The Spanish settlers had set about lobbying him to move the capital, and Mendoza had sympathised.[28] About thirty Spaniards had decamped en masse to Guayangareo,[29] demanding that Quiroga go there to administer the sacraments to them.

Having just transferred the capital from Tzintzuntzan to Pátzcuaro, this was obviously something to which Quiroga was strongly opposed. He wrote a long letter to the Crown objecting to Guayangareo, which was situated in a 'barren plain and uninhabited and very windy and empty of people and far from firewood and water',[30] a place where in the middle months of the year it almost never stopped raining.[31] He added that he had spent all his salary on developing Pátzcuaro, where there would be no problem about administering sacraments.[32] It was not his fault that the Spanish had fled to Guayangareo, when 'they were not being chased by the Moors who wanted to capture them, nor were they under threat from an arm of the sea which was about to drown them in the cathedral, nor were they so many that they did not fit inside the said cathedral'.[33]

Quiroga saw the move of the settlers as designed deliberately to undermine his authority. The argument confirmed his feeling that his vocation was with the Purépecha, and in saving their souls, rather than with the Spanish, most of whom he probably thought were beyond

*See above, ch. 12, p. 223.
†Now known as Morelia.

recall. In his mind they were now – like so many – cast into the camp of 'the enemy'. In his letter, he underlined that he was very poor,[34] and that he had spent all his income on good works – he could not afford to move to Guayangareo.

Nevertheless, the matter did not end here. The residents of Guayangareo held that his journey to Spain was made 'following up on a legal case which he had brought against us, based on our request for the administering of the sacraments'.[35] They said that Quiroga had lost the case in Mexico, and so took it to the Council of the Indies in Spain. In Quiroga's mind, of course, this was all related to the protection of the Purépecha, and his concentration on their welfare instead of on the Spanish – in other eyes, though, it could reflect his growing litigiousness and his sense that he was always in the right.

The same was true of his cases against the Franciscans. His power struggle with the mendicants went at least as far back as 1539, when, at the first Church Council of Mexico, the bishops of New Spain had implied that monasteries were founded more for the welfare of the mendicants than for the benefit of the *naturales*.[36] In a subsequent letter of 1540 signed by Quiroga and Zumárraga, the bishops had protested at the number of friars in the colony.[37]

By the time that Quiroga travelled to Spain, the dispute was becoming ugly. In the first letter he received whilst in Madrid, he heard from the caciques and canons of Pátzcuaro that the friars were bribing the Purépecha to go to their masses rather than to those in the churches.[38] The friars were also demanding more and more labour from the Indians to erect their monasteries, and indeed the Franciscans were by now controversial in many parts of the region, accused in Yucatán of whipping the Indians to get them to do as they wanted.[39] The Franciscans retorted, however, that Quiroga was not one to talk, and that his cathedral was a 'Babylon' in which 'the lives of many poor people are wasted, who die working on that useless task ... the Indians have no need of closed churches, let alone one with five naves'.[40]

Quiroga's cathedral was indeed a vast undertaking that could never be completed;[41] but at the same time, this was only one cathedral, whereas the Franciscans sought to build numerous monasteries. In fact, the truth appears to be that Quiroga was right to fear the effect of this in conjunction with the ongoing works demanded by the Spaniards at Guayangareo; though his own record was not without blemishes, his fights against the Spaniards and the friars do seem to have been motivated by genuine concern for the Purépecha.

Early in 1549 – now in Spain – he received news from the Purépecha caciques of the settlers' demands in their new town of 'Valladolid'. Viceroy Mendoza – who was particularly taken with the spot – was demanding that the Purépecha build a house fit for a Roman Emperor.[42] They were also being forced to build opulent homes for the royal officials, and a butcher's.[43] Canoe-loads of Purépecha were being brought in from virtually the whole province to do the work,[44] and the people of Pátzcuaro were so busy building the town and digging the drains[45] that they had no time to sow their own crops.[46] The situation was so bad that, two months later, Quiroga heard that the people of Pátzcuaro were leaving for the towns belonging to Juan de Infante, where they hoped things would be better.[47] Three Indians had died in the work at Valladolid,[48] the caciques told him, and 'God knows how much pain and sadness and labour has come to us because of your departure from your see'.[49] As far as the Purépecha were concerned, Quiroga was on their side.

Viceroy Mendoza, however, did not see himself as an exploitative man. In February 1548, at roughly the time that Quiroga was sailing for Spain, he had founded his own pueblo-hospital, Santa Fe del Río, about twenty leagues north of Lake Pátzcuaro.[50] Santa Fe del Río must – given the public arguments between the two men at this time – have been seen by Mendoza as a rival to Quiroga's work, something that would show that it was not only Quiroga who had the interests of the Indians at heart. Despite this initial divisiveness, however, the two institutions would eventually come to be governed together,[51] and Santa Fe del Río would also be taken under royal protection.[52]

While in moments of quiet Quiroga may have seen Mendoza's pueblo-hospital as a complement to his own work, he was not fooled by such 'charity'. People were far from happy at Santa Fe del Río, and late in 1556 an Indian from the town called Roque Robles Roldán would drown himself in the nearby river,[53] in spite of being comparatively wealthy, the owner of cattle, mares and a saddle[54] – a testament both to the fact that old beliefs lived on (the gods lay in the water), and that Mendoza's new hospital was not an unmitigated good.

All these developments in his diocese troubled Quiroga deeply. In 1551, Mendoza declared Valladolid the capital of Michoacán, but shortly afterwards he left New Spain to be Viceroy of Peru, and was replaced by Luis de Velasco. Perhaps this gave Quiroga renewed hope, and in June 1552 he returned his attentions to the Franciscans, asking Velasco to allow no new Franciscan monasteries to be built in his see.[55] This request was repeated in March 1553,[56] drawing up the battle lines for the last decade of his life – the battles that he would fight for 'his' Indians and 'his' view of perfection after his long-awaited return from Spain.

Quiroga's critics have seen his litigiousness at this time as a reflection of his own 'repressive rationality',[57] and of the fact that he *knew* that he was in the right.[58] There is an element of truth in this and, of course, a lack of self-criticism is one of the defining elements of utopian founders. However, when one reads the protests of the caciques at the new workload imposed by the Spanish in Valladolid, and independent accounts of the behaviour of the Franciscans, it is perhaps fairer to see these legal cases as the product of a man who had an obsession both with the law and with the welfare of the Purépecha as he saw it.

This will not save Quiroga in the eyes of many – after all, the road to Hell is paved with good intentions – but, when combined with the growing evidence of the strength of the social systems that he put in place, it will begin to rescue his idealism from the critical flames of pragmatism.

During Quiroga's absence, the epidemic's scars heal slowly. Whole villages are abandoned,[59] and homes fall into disrepair, as weeds, lizards, snakes and spiders reclaim the world from the Purépecha. The dead are buried, so that only the emotional violations of the living remain desperate for an outlet. These scars will have to find new channels down which to pour themselves, else they have the potential to remain dormant for decades, centuries, before erupting with untold destructiveness.

For the Purépecha, reconciliation comes from music and dance and disguise, all of which they loved long before the coming of the Spanish. Should not everyone heal their traumas through releasing their burdens in the whirl of dance and forgetting? The essence of dance and sound is to refract the world's complexity and recast it in a human vision, after all. It is pure celebration, a vehicle without which a society wastes away.

So the energies that have clotted up the thoughts of the Purépecha burst out into the world, in all directions, and then dissipate; but had they remained still, there would have been no way of redirecting their anguish other than through people, and the world. In Michoacán, they often dress up in a myriad of disguises, and then ride out to greet visitors, playing tricks on one another, pretending to be Chichimec Indians with bows and arrows, or performing masked dances that hark back to the ways of their ancestors.[60] They laugh and shriek, wheel around on their horses and doff their hats to the startled Spaniards, greeting the coming night, bidding farewell to the sunlight as it clutches the skyline with blushes and then obsidian.

Their energy is also channelled into making musical instruments, so that as they work they can heal the widening rift they sense between themselves and the world through the same sounds and movements. Farriers and masons work in time to music and dance, striking the iron or the stonework to the beat of a tambourine,[61] as if feeling that harmony abides in the unity of movement, sound and labour. It is in this way that the masons of Pátzcuaro have built their fountain, which has eight large pipes, six of which depict Indians, one an eagle and one a lion that releases water through a shield clasped close to its chest.[62] The rushing of the fountain's water echoes through the surrounding woods with the birdsong, recalling the musicality with which the fountain was built, with which the people live: the brocade that glitters in Michoacán's soul.

Quiroga's diocese quickly becomes famous across New Spain for its musicians.[63] It will soon be said that no Spaniards are more dexterous or able in 'the science and art of music'.[64] Even away from the fountain, Pátzcuaro is filled with musicians and singers.[65] Quiroga will ensure that the finest musical instruments are imported from Toledo to instruct and complement those which are made in the workshops of his see. The organ that he has brought over will encourage Purépecha organists,[66] and, by the early seventeenth century, one of them will put all the Spanish organists to shame at a recital in Mexico.[67]

The musical flowering of Michoacán is symptomatic of the emphasis that Quiroga has placed on developing the crafts of the Purépecha. Following the principles of More's *Utopia*, where everyone does the work to which they are most suited, he has laid down that all the people in his diocese should have a particular craft speciality. So as well as the makers of musical instruments, there are highly skilled carpenters who make cupboards, desks and frames. There are tailors, farriers, cobblers, and people who make devotional icons. Bells are made here, and copper objects; there are painters, and others who portray images using brilliantly coloured feathers.*[68]

---

*Many of these crafts are still practised in Michoacán today – 'feather art' is growing in popularity again, with workshops held around the state, while Santa Clara remains famous for its copper.

Quiroga's emphasis on this is vital to Michoacán. Not only has he encouraged each person to have a trade, but he has tried to develop specialities in each town in order to avoid encouraging the profit motive[69] and unnecessary competition.[70] So in Jarácuaro, musical instruments are made, while Tzintzuntzan and Santa Fe de la Laguna specialise in ceramics. Copper is smelted in Santa Clara and wooden furniture is made in Cuanajo.[71] Markets have been instituted in different towns of each region for different days,[72] and Quiroga has been the main engine of all these developments, frequently writing to Europe for more materials in one of the various crafts which he has fomented.[73]

Of course, the Purépecha have long been fine craftspeople, and it is not that Quiroga has invented these skills among them.[74] As with the togetherness needed for a successful Utopia, so the Purépecha already have the artistic talents which blossom in Quiroga's network of craft communities. Indeed, the success of these communities is founded in the artistry of the Purépecha,[75] and their joy at expressing their spirit through the crafts encouraged by the Bishop of Utopia.

With this wide network of crafts, Michoacán is famous for its good living and order, and in comparison to the rest of New Spain it really is a paradise. Elsewhere in the Viceroyalty, religion takes on widely different forms. There are Lutherans from northern Europe,[76] atheists,[77] and others who maintain a hidden form of Judaism: in Mexico during a game of cards, Francisco Tejera spits on a crucifix and says, 'Curse whoever drew you!'[78] The Indians and the Africans cast spells, meanwhile, as do the immigrants from the Canary Islands.[79] People use holy relics for fortune telling[80] and to see if people love them.[81] The mendicant friars sleep with Indians and mestizas, and openly have children.[82] Bigamy is rife,[83] and it is not surprising that the famous Bishop of Chiapas, Bartolomé de las Casas, has written despairingly that the Church is so downtrodden in Mexico that he might as well be in Germany among the new Protestants.[84]

It is precisely this breakdown that Quiroga fears, and that has guided his institutions of the pueblo-hospitals and the crafts in the towns. Even in Michoacán, the Spanish remain uneducated and a barrier to progress, with many of them being illiterate.[85] Nevertheless, he feels that his see really is different, and so he should see eye to eye with the Bishop of Chiapas on many things.

But circumstances will soon dictate otherwise.

Quiroga's stay in Spain dragged on much longer than he had probably intended. For one thing, Charles V was then occupied in far more weighty matters than the rights of worthy projects in distant Mexico. The Emperor was now facing a crisis following his failed assault on the Duke of Guise at Metz in December 1552. This led to his withdrawal from Germany, and paved the way for his final abdication from the Crown at Brussels in October 1555, and the succession of his son Philip in 1556; the problems of Philip's reign, including the secession of the Low Countries and the beginning of the eighty-year war between Spain and the United Provinces of the Netherlands, were beginning.

Quiroga, meanwhile, was catching up with his extended family. While in Spain, he doubtless met his nephew, Gaspar de Quiroga, who would soon become Archbishop of Toledo. Through Vasco, the Quirogas were a family now known for their work in the overseas colonies and, following the unification of the kingdoms of Spain and Portugal in 1580, one Fernão de Quiroga would work for the crown in Santiago, Cape Verde, and become the first parish priest at the settlement of Cacheu, in what is today Guinea-Bissau, while at the same time another member of the family, Pedro, took a posting in Peru.[86]

Although he caught up with his family, like the Emperor, Vasco did not find things easy. While he lobbied the court for the rights of 'his' Purépecha, his body showed signs of stress. In Madrid, he fell ill, and became bedridden.[87] Bleeding and feverish, his fellow clerics urged him to accept a gentler posting in Spain, and not to return to the New World;[88] but Quiroga remained adamant. He was, he said, 'in the best disposition ... for rounding up cattle'[89] – that is, for dismissing the arguments of his enemies. As long as he lived, he said, he would ensure that there was good grazing for his lambs and sheep – the Indians.[90]

Fighting his corner, he began to send out feelers to a new religious order which had sprung up in Spain at this time, the Compañia de Jesús – the Jesuits. The founder of the Jesuits, Ignacio de Loyola, was from Arévalo, near Madrigal, and Quiroga tried to persuade him to despatch missionaries to Michoacán.[91] Recognising that some mendicants were needed to carry out his work, but loathing the ones that he found himself saddled with, Quiroga doubtless felt that the Jesuits would be an improvement on the Franciscans. Furthermore, the Jesuits were by now the sole religious order not to have a statute of *limpieza* to discriminate against those with Jewish or Moorish blood, something of which Quiroga – with his own possible mixed origins, and his belief in converting through good deeds – seems to have approved.[92]

Perhaps also he sensed that the Jesuits shared his own brand of idealism. Although the first Jesuits did not arrive in Michoacán until after Quiroga's death, they would be instrumental in furthering the work of the *hospitales de la concepción*. Writing during the terrible epidemic that struck New Spain in 1576, a Jesuit priest, Juan Sánchez Vaquero, wrote that Quiroga's hospitals meant that 'the province of Michoacán was one of those that suffered least from the plague'.[93] It is quite possible that the Jesuits were spurred by witnessing how Quiroga's hospitals worked towards the founding of their famous utopian missions in Paraguay, which began to take shape in 1609.[94]

Quiroga's other main concern at this time was his position on the famous dispute at Valladolid between Bartolomé de las Casas and Juan Ginés de Sepúlveda regarding the status of the Indians. The Valladolid dispute unfolded in 1550 and 1551, its importance recognised by all to be immense: for this was one of the only moments in history when an empire paused to consider the justice of its actions,[95] perhaps sensing that it was on the brink of an enterprise which – once fully undertaken – would be irreversible.

Sepúlveda's team held that force could be used to overcome the many difficulties faced in converting alien peoples to Christianity; Las Casas's, that force had to be opposed as a matter of principle. The question cut to the heart of the nature of empire: how should the most powerful nation of the world go about recasting it in its own image?

Implicit in the debate – even in the camp of the 'doves' – however, was that the conversion itself was imperative.[96] The world would only be a good place when it was made as God and the Spanish decreed. The accent on the debate fell, then, on whether military or peaceful means were the best way of achieving such vital international uniformity.

The Indians are rebelling?

Said the Sepúlveda camp: they are ungrateful, shameless barbarians, who do not recognise the greatness of our gift to them. They only understand one language – War! – so let us teach them through it.

Said the Las Casas camp: they are rebelling *because* we are oppressing them. Let us show them peace, and give them justice, food, and health. Then they will embrace our teachings.

Only a very few people said: let them have their own teachings.*

---

*But even this camp did exist. In the early seventeenth century, one Adrian Suster, a Lutheran in Mexico, would be tried by the Inquisition for declaring that 'every nation

This, then, was a debate that cut to the heart of morality, raising issues that would not be aired again for over 400 years. Although present in Spain, Quiroga was not invited to Valladolid, however, something that irritated him profoundly.[97] Hurt and slighted, he responded by opposing Las Casas,[98] and composed *De Debellandis Indis*, a torpid work on the question of 'just wars' and the Indians, which held that the Pope and the Castilian Crown had the duty to subjugate those Indians not yet subjugated, and so had the right to make war.[99]

Quiroga's position on the Valladolid debate has often surprised his champions. How could someone who worked so tirelessly to defend the Purépecha oppose Las Casas, who held that any war opened against the infidels was repugnant to the teachings of Jesus?[100] It was not as if the party fighting against 'just war' on the Indians came solely from the extremity of society: on a trip from Rome to Bologna, Las Casas's opponent Sepúlveda had himself witnessed a protest from aristocratic students at a convent, who held that any war, including one waged in self-defence, was contrary to the Catholic religion.[101] Conscientious objectors were increasingly widespread; Quiroga's supporters find it difficult to accept that their hero was in the opposite camp from them.[102]

However, the truth is that Quiroga's position was in no way out of keeping with his personality. His earlier 'Información en Derecho' had not argued against war on the Indians per se, but had tried to set out limits to its brutality and emphasise its purpose.[103] Quiroga also worried that the dispute threatened the rights of the Spanish in the Indies, and thus, by extension, his work in Michoacán.[104] However, perhaps most important in understanding Quiroga's personality – and that of all utopians – is that he probably felt threatened by Las Casas.

The Bishop of Chiapas was, after all, a leading light in the movement for Indian rights, and had been a utopian long before Quiroga. His first work outlining a way to save the Indians had been written as early as 1516,[105] he had led a move to convert through peaceful means and not through war at Verapaz in Guatemala in 1535, and had pressured the Spanish Crown to adopt the Leyes Nuevas which prohibited the *encomienda* – albeit only temporarily – in 1542.

For Quiroga, who – like Las Casas – saw his work as of divine importance, this must all have appeared as a direct personal challenge.

(*cont*) would find salvation by keeping the laws of the faith which they professed'. See *Historía del Tribunal del Santo Oficio de Ia Inquisición en México* by José Toribio Medina (Santiago de Chile, Imprenta Elzeviriana, 1905), p. 138.

Furthermore, just like him, Las Casas was an argumentative man liable to believe that he was always in the right. Threatened and provoked by Las Casas's personality – so much like his own – being snubbed at the seminal conference at Valladolid was the last straw. *De Debellandis Indis* was probably a work inspired as much by envy as by conviction, and perhaps this is why its legal grasp is deemed by some to be unsteady.[106]

As for the Valladolid debate itself, there was never an adequate resolution. The judges each gave their own opinions – some of them several years later[107] – but no policy was changed following the debate.[108] This time, the great match between the militarists and the pacifists ended in a draw. Both sides claimed victory.

But in New Spain, the *encomienda* persisted; the conquest extended. The only defence against them was the collectivism found in the hospitals, where Quiroga's creations were the embodiment of the argument that the way forward was through peace – whatever his embittered arguments with Las Casas might have suggested.

Even during the absence of Quiroga, his pueblo-hospital at Santa Fe de la Laguna remains the nexus of all that is good for the Purépecha. This is the cornerstone of the network of *hospitales de la concepción* and of the craft towns. It is no wonder that Viceroy Mendoza copied it at Santa Fe del Río, for he saw how the people of Michoacán have reverence for Santa Fe, and are attracted to anything that bears its name.

Now that the pueblo-hospital has been at work for twenty years, its way of life has settled into a routine. Quiroga has only felt able to leave his see for so long because he knows that the institution will be able to function without him. Although his ordinances declare that the pueblo-hospital is overseen by a rector, appointed by Quiroga himself for three-year periods,* all the main authorities come from among the Purépecha.[109]

The town is divided into four neighbourhoods, each of which puts forward candidates to be the principal of the community; there is then a secret ballot among the whole pueblo-hospital, and the principal is elected for three or six years.[110] Councillors are elected by each neighbourhood, following the same process, and the elected members then appoint the other officials who will help them in their work.[111]

---

*After Quiroga's death, the rector was appointed by the rector of Quiroga's Colegio de San Nicolás in Pátzcuaro.

The officials meet every third day – or more often if necessary – and two heads of family are present to witness the meetings, with the composition of these witnesses changing with each meeting.[112] As well as overseeing the running of the pueblo-hospital, the officials are charged with visiting the land and renewing the boundary posts each year.[113]

Although these electoral procedures are not the same as those in More's *Utopia*,* they instil the same democratisation among the Purépecha that existed in Utopia. Furthermore, away from officialdom, a visitor from the European Renaissance would find that it is virtually impossible to distinguish Quiroga's society from Thomas More's dream.

The building block of the pueblo-hospital is the 'familia',[114] which More called the 'family'.[115] These are buildings in which people live together, with between eight and twelve married men in each house; as in Utopia, when there are too many people in a house, a new familia must be started.[116] Patriarchal hierarchies of the type envisaged by More are the norm here too, for in these households women obey their husbands, and young people their elders, with the oldest grandfather being the most respected.[117] People work every day – six hours daily or three full days per week remaining the norm, as in Santa Fe de México[118] – and only miss work if they are ill.[119] Distribution of the harvest is made according to the needs of each family, with any leftovers being kept for charity towards the needy,[120] so that all the poor are looked after, the 'orphans, students, widows, widowers, old men and women, the healthy and the sick, the crippled and the blind'.[121] To avoid lack of food, up to twice the amount required for the people of the pueblo-hospital is planted each year; when the community is sure that there will be no shortage, the remainder is distributed among the poor.[122]

Outside the town of Santa Fe de la Laguna, there are farms in the country, whose workers come from the towns of the hospital. There are between four and six married couples working in each farm, looking after the cattle and the poultry that are raised there;[123] these farms are smaller than those proposed by More, who had forty people at each farm.[124] Exactly as in *Utopia*, however, these people work in the country for two years, and can stay longer if they obtain the permission of the rector and the councillors.[125] The oldest married couple stay on at the end of the two years, with the man acting as the

*See above, ch. 3, p. 44.

overseer and instructing the newcomers as to how the farm works.[126]

On the farms there are ducks, turkey and chickens, as well as sheep and cows, goats, pigs and oxen.[127] There are also large orchards in which 'every type of fruit tree from both Castile and this country' are planted.[128] There are hemp and flax, as well as maize, wheat and barley.[129] Some of the workers on the farms quarry stone, others cut wood, others harvest grain.[130] People from the town occasionally come out to the farms to relax, with the permission of the rector and the councillors, but – as in Utopia – they have to help out with the work when they are there.[131]

Quiroga has imparted the same hunger for work as that which More described among the Utopians. People should work 'with great willingness, because the work required will be little'.[132] The philosophy is the same as that in the book that has inspired him: 'Wherever you are, you always have to work. There's never any excuse for idleness.'[133]

This communal, agrarian lifestyle – like the music and dance – is of course deeply suited to the Purépecha. They have long been farmers* and, while the Spanish have introduced some new crops, the rhythms of life in Santa Fe are easy for them to absorb. It is also traditional among them to have more than one family living in a house,[134] and to have a public distribution of grain after the harvest.[135] Even Quiroga's institution of the same clothes for the whole community – white cotton shifts whose uniformity will lead to the end of 'envy and arrogance ... dissent and discord'[136] – is not too hard to come to terms with, since it retains equality, while differentiating from the pre-Cortesian era when most of them went naked.[137]

The Purépecha can relate to the Bishop, at least. Like the Mexica, they understand his obsession with divinity, and the fact that every aspect of the world of the hospitals revolves around religion; and so, as they can find no security in this world, they refer back to the Christian crutch that Quiroga has brought them. They love Saint Peter, for he was a fisherman, just like them, and their old men enjoy dressing up as the Disciple with a large fishing net; other saints, too, are portrayed with fish.[138]

The fish, the sense of faith and the immanence of the divine in Quiroga's Michoacán – all this makes them feel that they can recover the true sacredness of the world. They have only to intersperse a few of their own customs among those brought over by the Bishop, they

*See above, ch. 10, p. 173.

sense, and the world may yet be saved. Yes, his is not their tradition, but it gives them hope. It was not Quiroga who let loose the torrent of destruction of the conquest, after all. His work is just an attempt to alleviate the suffering that it has brought them.

And so visitors to Michoacán are impressed by the depth of Christianity that they find here. The famous Motolinía has himself recently visited the state, and was so impressed by what he found that he 'left giving thanks to the Lord, saying that among the *naturales* of New Spain, there was not a half or even a third part of the Christianity that there was in the province of Michoacán'.[139]

Quiroga's creations are blossoming, feeding off one another – but this depends perhaps more on the Purépecha's character traits than on their bishop. For Utopia is certainly easier to found in a place where people are used to working together, and so the Purépecha have taken to Quiroga's – and More's – ideals like no one else; and it is just as well that there are some vestiges of continuity in their lives, when so much has changed so quickly for them: for Michoacán has now been taken over not only by the Spanish, and their crops and animals, but by the strange ebony people that the Spanish have brought with them to do their bidding.

In Pátzcuaro – as in all of New Spain by now – African slaves are often to be seen, bought and sold among the settlers and the *encomenderos* to do everything from overseeing the mines to collecting tithes. So in 1550 a black slave agrees to help Pedro de Figueroa collect tithes in Colima;[140] in May 1551 the Purépecha governor Don Antonio de Cuitzimengari himself asks for help in recovering an escaped black slave called Bernardo;[141] in April 1552 a black slave called Juan is sold in Pátzcuaro for 160 pesos.[142] By now, escaped African slaves are living as bandits near the mines of Tornacustla.[143] They are stevedores in Veracruz and miners in Zacatecas. They work as blacksmiths, tailors, carpenters and servants in every city, and as herdsmen and mine overseers.[144]

The Purépecha watch fearfully as another new people comes into their country. They understand that the Africans, too, suffer at the hands of the white gods of the land, but they have no conception of where they can have come from.* What – a place where the deserts

---

*At this early point in the history of the transatlantic slave trade, most African slaves came from Senegambia, via Cape Verde. In the first half of the sixteenth century, three-quarters of the slaves in Peru came from 'the Guinea of Cape Verde', and the very first slaves to be brought to Mexico had come via Cape Verde. Cortés himself contracted for slaves to come from Cape Verde, and most of his slaves came from the

are oceans, shells are currencies, gold dust is scrabbled from the mother earth at the insistence of those whose eyes light up with the intensity of lust, possession, abdication of self-control? That is a place that they could relate to, even though it is so distant; but they wonder what sort of emotions are produced as its peoples are taken across the ocean – and if there is only destruction there, too. Is that the universal rule for the world in human hands?

Perhaps there is no answer to redress those feelings except through living. The Purépecha stand aside from these strange people, melt away into their homes, shrinking from the terrifying world beyond their villages, where the woods are still thick, their branches gathering overhead like arches in the vault of an eternal cathedral. The trees have not all been uprooted for the sake of economic expansion. Birdsong remains strong, outshining the noise of the towns in the valleys. Humanity, indeed, seems to have been left far behind, floundering in the wake of whatever it means to be alive, consumed by its inalienable passions. As traditions melt away and are replaced by an expanding, increasingly global faith (that of the God of Quiroga, of course), nature seems to have mutated into its antithesis.

peoples of the coasts of Senegambia and the Upper Guinea Coast. See Hugh Thomas (1997), op. cit., pp. 101, 116, 117. Also Philip D. Curtin (1975), op. cit., p. 13.

FOURTEEN

The woods were still thick, their branches gathering overhead like arches in the vault of an eternal cathedral. The trees had not all been uprooted for the sake of economic expansion. Birdsong remained strong, outshining the noise of the towns in the valleys. Humanity, indeed, seemed to have been left far behind, floundering in the wake of whatever it meant to be alive, consumed by its inalienable passions. As traditions melted away, and were replaced by an expanding, increasingly global faith (that of the market, of course), nature seemed to have mutated into its antithesis.

So, setting off from Santa Fe and leaving the Purépecha wedding behind me, I marched along the shore of the lake for hours until I cut into thick woodland to the north.

The air was fresh, untaxed. Butterflies fluttered like the eyelids of the forests, keeping watch. The riverbanks bloomed with orchids. Moss sprang up behind me as I walked, feigning that I had never touched it. Creepers trailed everywhere, fallen tresses that covered the rocks scattered across the earth.

Perhaps the longing for self-destruction was a natural universal, I thought as I walked, absent-mindedly treading on snails and tearing branches loose from their trunks. The world had given birth to humanity, after all, and as a species we had become a repository of destructiveness to be directed back at the world. Yes, the forests, the flowers, the animals, the birds – none of them could live with us; or rather, we had developed too much intelligence to live with them.

I walked on. After a time, I paused at a stream to drink. I knelt down by a rock pool and gulped at the water. I picked at some wild berries and stuffed them into my mouth.

Soon I continued. Clouds reared up in the curves of the skyline, promising an afternoon storm. The rain came thick and prolonged, gushing down long into the night. I sheltered in the hollow of a rotting pine, and continued the next morning. Then I scaled minor peaks, delved through further expanses of forest, and stopped to rest on tree trunks which I shared with beetles and lizards.

At midday I came to a village, and found a group of Purépecha gathered about a pair of old mules. I bought some avocados from them, and then one of the women who had sold me the fruit accompanied me a little way as I advanced into the forest. When I asked her her name, she told me that she was called Patricia.

Patricia wanted to know where I was going.

'I don't know,' I told her, admiring her tightly knotted plaits.

She smiled shyly. 'There's a mountain just ahead,' she said. 'You get a great view from up there.'

'Perhaps I'll go there then,' I said. 'It sounds as good as anywhere.'

Patricia sized me up for a moment, and the two of us cut a strange picture there in the woods, two balls of energy in the endless tangle of greenery.

'Well,' she said eventually, turning on her heel and leaving me, 'good luck, *señor*.'

I went on and, sure enough, as she had said, the woodland soon bunched into a rocky hillside.

Encouraged, I started up the bottom of a steep-sided ravine, clawing at loose stones, which came away in my hands. My feet sent dust spiralling into the forests as I stumbled up, until after about twenty minutes I had reached the top.

As soon as I got to the summit, though, I ploughed on down the far side into more thickets. Here I launched myself into creepers, thorns, saplings, remorselessly knocking them out of my path even though they stabbed me. Not once did I pause to consider if there might be a better path. I had even forgotten where it was that I wanted to get to: Utopia existed, of that I was certain, and Quiroga's utopian paradigm had existed right here, but how the two coincided was a deeper question and one that I stubbornly refused to answer; I had a book to finish, after all, and nuanced positions would not help me get it over and done with.

Utopia was a heaven on earth, and yet Quiroga had believed in a divine heaven above – the two paradises were rivals, and perhaps could never be reconciled; still, Quiroga had sought both, and in doing so he had uprooted the world of the Purépecha and recast it in his own 'perfect' image, as if that sort of dogmatic idealism could be beneficial; what was I doing, then, looking for the perfection that I no longer believed in, in the temperate jungles of Michoacán?

I did not answer this question. This was the course that I had set at the beginning, almost by accident, and I was going to see it through, however much pain, madness or exhaustion it brought me.

After I had been advancing in this fruitless way for an hour, I heard the sound of someone chopping wood in the distance. By now it was mid-afternoon, and I was thirsty. Reorienting myself, I struck towards the sound, hoping to find some water. Soon enough I came upon a clearing where a tall, broad, northern European man was hacking at a cedar with a blunt axe.

His arms moved like cylindrical machines, back in a great arc towards the heavens and then down into the twisted fibres of the bark. I could see that he was deeply immersed in his work and unaware of my presence; nevertheless I could not hold out for long. I walked straight up to him and asked him for some water.

'Water?' he asked, standing up and wiping the sweat from his forehead. 'There'll be none of that left once I've finished here.'

'What do you mean?' I asked, taken aback. 'What are you doing?'

'Well,' he said, resting contentedly on the handle of his axe, 'I've set myself the task of uprooting this entire forest. Once I've done that, all the topsoil will be blown away, it'll silt up the rivers, and they'll all disappear soon enough, just as they have in the Sahara.'

He seemed very pleased with himself. When I asked him to explain, he pointed out that this was merely the most pragmatic way of carrying on. The trees were interfering with the economy, causing great problems when they burst into flames and money had to be spent extinguishing the fires that resulted. It would be far easier just to cut them down and have no fires or trees at all, particularly as that would dispense with the need for having rivers in the first place, since the trees would no longer be there to give rise to the fires that the water was used to extinguish.

'I see,' I said. 'And you call that pragmatic and efficient?'

'Absolutely,' he said. 'It's the most efficient form of economics that you can imagine. If something is practical it can't be idealised, and there's nothing more practical than good old-fashioned manual labour, even if no one really values that any more and society or its upper hierarchy in fact despises those who still have to earn a living through physical exertion. So anyhow, all around the world, even as we're speaking here, armies of people just like me are attacking the trees as best we can, for we all know that idealising anything is a bad idea, and where nature's concerned it's even worse.'

'I see,' I said, feeling deeply alarmed. I looked closely at him, and saw that he seemed possessed by a messianic glow, so that his words overshadowed the sounds of insects and birdsong that still echoed from the further reaches of the forest. But I was not going to stand for this sort of silliness any longer; I was now the voice of reason, and memories of Juan Diego and quixotic lunacy had been revealed for the bad dream in which they had doubtless existed. 'But don't you think,' I went on, 'that if you all cut the trees down so that there are none left to absorb carbon dioxide, the world may heat up to such a point that life comes to an end?'

'Oh no,' he said, laughing at me as if I were insane, 'it can't do that. That's not the purpose of our pragmatism.'

'But,' I persisted, 'that's surely what will happen.'

'Oh no,' he said again, 'it can't.'

Aware now that I was dealing with a dogmatic ideology – one that was so deep-rooted as to claim not to be one – I told him that he hardly appeared to me to be a beacon of pragmatism: if he were really pragmatic, I said, he would stop cutting down the trees.

'Oh no,' he said, ignoring me, 'I'm pragmatic all right.'

'But,' I said, 'by refusing to acknowledge any challenge to your view of yourself, you've turned what you call pragmatism into an ideology – a fantasy that is about as realistic as some trumped-up account of a modern-day utopian and his adventures; and so for all the fantasy I've got in mind, if anyone reads about this, they're bound to wonder which of us is telling the truth after all.'

He laughed, waving his free hand in an arc in the air as if to emphasise how funny he found me, and told me that, by definition, pragmatism was not an ideology, so that I was just plain wrong. I replied that he could define things just as he pleased, but that it still seemed to me that his economic pragmatism was indeed an ideology, and all the more insidious for pretending not to be. For in fact it masqueraded as the sole answer to the problem of living in the twenty-first century, percolating every pore of the planet's fabric, and was thus in a sense the most dominant form of ideology that the world had ever seen: the archetype of the rigid, delusional utopianism that the supposedly non-ideological West now professed to despise.

He burst into an even louder peal of laughter when I had finished. 'You are funny,' he said. 'These are just not ideological times, particularly where the environment is concerned, so I'm not even going to take you seriously, and in fact I'm going to dismiss your ludicrous ecotopia as just a hippy nonsense, provided that you don't do anything silly like try to gain influence or power through the democratic process, in which case you can be sure I'll bug your telephone, particularly if you do something subversive like become involved with an ecological party.'

Recognising the maniac for what he was, I did not argue with him any longer. We were alone in the forest, after all, and I realised that if I began to object, and indulged in a non-violent protest against his indiscriminate murdering of trees, he might just get rid of me then and there, particularly as we were in the middle of the jungle, and everyone knew that these tropical countries were inhabited by dangerous criminals who blew people away for $100 or less, so that no one would bat an eyelid if that was what happened to me. Once his urge to destroy had been let loose, why should it stop at trees when there were whole peoples, species, worldviews ripe for destruction? Was not this multiplicity of cultural ways deeply inefficient? Wasn't it just the most pragmatic solution to make them all alike?

We stood looking at one another for some moments. Gradually, my senses expanded to take in the sounds of the forest, the colours of the flowers, the lengthening shadows cast by the trees; the strength of the sunlight was just beginning to decline, and I realised that I ought to press on and find a good place to stop for the night. I was through with adventuring, and wanted a comfortable bed where I could begin to weld all these experiences into an attractive narrative.

I repeated my request for some water, and he passed me his hip flask with bad grace. After I had drunk, I thanked him, and was about to go on my way when he asked me what my own reasons were for being there.

'Well,' I said, I've come to look into Vasco de Quiroga and the Utopia that he built here.'

'Utopia!' he scoffed. 'And *you* berate *me* for being ideological!'

I explained that I shared his concern about ideologies. However, I went on – echoing Juan Diego – it seemed to me that a distinction could be drawn between ideology and idealism. An ideology was dogmatic. Idealism, however, tended to centre ethical frameworks in the good of society as a whole, rather than in self-interest, and its results could not be predicted; while sometimes it overlapped with ideology – and Quiroga was perhaps a case in point – it could still produce beneficial effects. A world without idealism, reduced to an ideology of self-interest, was a world that would ultimately go nowhere.

'Nowhere,' he said. 'That's Erewhon by another name, and I wouldn't want to end up there.'

'Well,' I said, 'at least we're agreed on that. But now I'd better be on my way, for if I'm not careful I'll end up having to spend the night here, and this is as close to nowhere as anywhere else.'

He laughed and picked up his axe, preparing to take another swing at the tree. I saw that his eyes were fixed on the matter in hand, limpid, clear, strong; he retained his dignity even as he chopped, showing that it could still be reclaimed and put in its rightful place at the centre of his being.

Turning on my heel, I walked back the way that I had come. With the sun having fallen quite low, the light was brighter, but it did not penetrate as far down as it had done earlier on. The ground was now a lattice of shadows, where the moss straggled across the green rocks and the lizards ducked beneath them, and dead leaves curled up and appeared to merge into one another.

Unconsciously, I found myself aiming for the high ground (I had always been morally narcissistic), and soon recognised some of the marks that I had passed on my way from the Purépecha village. Perhaps I had had enough of this solitary tramping, for I decided to make for that place and try to pass the night there. I climbed back up to the hill that Patricia had guided me towards, and then clung to the bottom of the ravine as I made my way back down the other way. Soon I heard the sounds of village life, and knew that I was nearly there.

It was dusk when I arrived. The villagers stared at me as rigidly as they had done earlier that morning when I had bought the avocados. They objectified my clothes, my spectacles, my knapsack with their disinterested gaze, and I felt as if I was a museum piece. I was beginning to regret my return until I saw Patricia waving happily at me.

'Why have you come back?' she asked me.

'I got lost,' I said, throwing out the half-truth in a mumble.

She invited me to come back for dinner, and I happily accepted her invitation. I followed her to her basic, four-square adobe home, and she introduced her husband, Don Ambrosio, and her children Florencia and Juan Vasco. We cut open the avocados that I had bought from her and she made guacamole, which we spread onto some tortillas.

Then everyone ate dinner, sitting around the table in silence.

'What are you doing here, *señor*?' Patricia asked me, when we had finished the meal.

'Well,' I said calmly, 'I've come here to look for Utopia, and inquire into the meaning of the communities founded by Vasco de Quiroga.'

'Ah!' she said, turning away with a smile. 'Tata Vasco.'

She pronounced the name with reverence, I noticed fondly.

'Yes,' I said. 'For though utopianism is deeply unpopular today, long before I came to Michoacán I had this feeling that in fact you could not make a generalisation about idealism – at any rate – and that although people are rightly suspicious of anyone who claims to have "the answer", some measure of idealism can be good for society – and may in fact prove to be the only way of safeguarding what's left of the world.'

'I see, *señor*,' said Patricia. 'And you thought Tata Vasco could give you a clue as to that.'

I agreed. Although it was getting dark outside, and the children were staring at me as though I had been not only a museum piece but one struck down with rabies at that, I carried on, knowing that at last I had stopped tilting at windmills, and was making sense. I said that it had seemed to me that the testament to Quiroga's beneficial idealism could still be found in Michoacán, for it was here that some of the institutions that he had founded were still in existence – the Colegio de San Nicolás in Morelia, for instance – and that the craft specialisation which he had instituted was still cherished in many villages around the sierra, with Santa Clara still having copper artisans and Paracho its guitar-makers.

When I had finished speaking, I was greeted with silence. The children were giggling at something or other – not me, of course – and I listened to them and the rustling of chickens out in the yard. A flurry of yelps burst out as some puppies fought one another, and soon I wondered if my words had really meant anything to the family.

Patricia rose, and silently offered me a glass of water, which I accepted; but looking at her husband, I could not help feeling that Don Ambrosio was appraising me with a flicker of mockery. In fact, he had hardly said a word since my arrival.

'Well, *señor*,' he said now, wiping his lips with a threadbare handkerchief, his eyes darting hither and thither, 'you can see that we admire your Tata Vasco. Look at the name we have given our son: Juan Vasco.'

'Yes,' I said quickly, 'I had noticed.'

'Unlike others,' Don Ambrosio went on in a monotone, 'we respect Tata Vasco deeply. We try to live in togetherness, as he would have wished. We try to maintain the use of our hands, and have trust in God. And that's all a person can do today!' he ended with a wheezing cough. 'Yes, that's all a person can do.'

'And what do you think about Tata Vasco?' I asked, turning to the couple's son.

He was a slight child, with straggly hair and impenetrable black eyes.

'I think you're odd,' Juan Vasco said, ignoring the question. 'Very odd.'

'Perhaps I am,' I said, 'but one of the things I've learnt since I became a utopian is that that often goes with the territory.'

'That's as may be,' said Juan Vasco, 'but at least you should go and be odd somewhere else – back in your own country.'

'But what do you think about your namesake, the Utopian of Michoacán?' I persisted.

'He was born, he lived as a Christian, he died,' he said. 'And that's about it.'

Soon, the two children went out to play. They ran in circles, chasing one another, and then tumbled onto the ground and tussled together like the puppies. Behind me, I heard Patricia sweeping the dust from the earthen floor. That was one task, I realised, that would never be completed.

'So in spite of everything you've come across, you're still an idealist,' Don Ambrosio said to me now, rolling a cigarette with a piece of old newspaper.

'Yes, *señor.*'

'You're trying to save the planet with your green politics,' he said, tamping down the tobacco.

'Something like that.'

'Well,' he said, 'good luck.'

He stood up and laughed bitterly, before walking out of the empty doorway into the twilight.

'Husband!' Patricia called out. 'Don't burden our guest with your own worries.'

She set to her housework again. I glanced at them both – her intense, methodical sweeps of the floor, and his receding back – and then stood up quickly.

'No, wait,' I said, following Don Ambrosio outside. 'I can understand your frustration, even pessimism, but things aren't as negative as you imagine,' I told him when I had joined him. 'We've already dealt with the issues of information overload and the surfeit of desires. We've accepted the need to channel the collective unconscious into together-ness, not interpersonal rivalry. And so we can genuinely turn to the root problem of the environment, without the need to ignore its emotional origins – and not before time.'

But Don Ambrosio ignored me. He stooped down and scrabbled around in the dust with a sharp knife, digging for something.

'What are you looking for, *señor*?' I asked.

'The roots.'

'Where are they?'

'In Africa, and beyond. Perhaps we began to sense that when those ebony slaves first came over with the Spanish, but now we feel it beyond dispute.'

He turned his back on me and continued to dig. In Africa! But that was impossible to imagine when we were here in Michoacán. What – a place where the deserts were oceans, shells were once currencies, gold dust was scrabbled from the mother earth at the insistence of those whose eyes lit up with the intensity of lust, possession, abdication of self-control: was there only destruction there, too?

I sat down.

'Ah!' said Don Ambrosio with triumph. He prised some more of the dust up with his knife and emerged with a buried stick of dynamite. 'That was what we were looking for,' he said.

'Looking for?' I echoed. It was darker with every minute, and I could only see his outline, but I sensed that his eyes had become possessed by a strange frenzy, as if he had been suddenly taken over by something entirely alien to him.

'Yes,' he said stiffly, as if trying to imitate me. 'Yes, yes! And now you can just set fire to all the forests, rather than have to pretend that you need to cut them down for economic reasons.'

'Set them on fire, *señor*?' I asked, bewildered at his sudden pessimism.

'Get it all over with now!' he shouted. 'Burn, destroy, pillage, loot, possess! Rape, despoil, contaminate, desecrate! Express it all! Get it all out in the open! All that bottling up of emotions, matured lovingly over centuries in the European aristocracy, oh it's now the best of vintages! All the vileness, the rage, the self-loathing you've stored inside you! Get it out! Won't that make you feel good?'

'Good?' I asked weakly.

'Come on!' he shouted. 'What are you waiting for? Come on! I know how your world operates. Time is money, money is comfort, comfort is boredom! Let's all get bored before this life gets interesting again!'

I could tell that Juan Vasco knew about oddness. Indeed, the two children had not stopped playing during their father's outburst, and were steadfastly ignoring him.

'Come on,' Don Ambrosio said again wildly, grasping me by the hand and marching me out of the village, on into the forest, into the night.

'But *señor*, where are we going?' I protested, following along with the force of his hand, and glancing back at the receding comforts of the village lights.

'We're going towards the truth,' he said. 'The truth and nothing but the truth. It's all coming out now in the forests, because you can't trust a lawyer to help you.'

'From Africa?' I asked softly.

'Yes,' he said, 'from Africa.' He walked on a little way until he had reached a clearing, and then stopped to face me. 'Look,' he said, handing me some matches and the dynamite, 'here you are. Now get on with it – we haven't got a moment to lose. It's the easiest way.'

I looked at the surrounding trees, whose trunks loomed tall in the darkness. They were gnarled, their bark bunched into fists, their branches still stretched out in apparent health – blocking out the starlight, and leaving us to our own devices. It would have been so easy to burn it all to ashes there and then, but yet I held back.

'I can't,' I said in the end, turning to him.

'Why on earth not?' he demanded. 'You and your ilk have been pretty good at it up to now.'

'I can't!' I wailed then, taking a step back from him and feeling my eyes well with tears. I dropped the dynamite and the matches to the floor and felt the supreme emptiness of my desires.

For some time my body shook electrically with sobs. A door had opened somewhere inside me, and I had dreamed of a different world entirely.

'Why are you so upset?' he asked now. 'What's so valuable about these trees anyway? Who cares about the animals and plants that live in them? The hellfire of flames is too good for them, even if that is today's answer to the Inquisition, and nature's the one on trial for resisting our unshakeable faith in the economy!'

He stooped down and picked up the dynamite and the matches himself now, stalking off further into the forest.

'No!' I shouted. 'No!'

I ran after him and grabbed his shoulder. 'Wait, *señor*. We can save this.'

'How?' he asked.

'By going back to the beginning.'

'The beginning?' he asked. 'And where was that, then?'

The beginning of all this destruction was in Africa – I saw that now. That was what he had been trying to get me to say.

'I understand,' I said weakly. 'I understand.'

We sat down on two opposite tree stumps, watching one another warily. The darkness pressed in all about us; bats brushed past our faces.

'Do you?' he asked, more gently, as if he had never intended me to burn down the forest, and all this had been a charade to get me to unveil a genuine emotional realism.

'Yes, *señor*,' I said.

We listened to the birdsong fill our ears for a moment. Overhead, the leaves stirred in a gentle breeze. At last, I felt ready to begin my story:

'Several millennia ago, as Europe crawled slowly out of the Ice Age, the Sahara was not the desert that it is today. It was fertile, filled with lakes, an earthly paradise for wild animals and for people.[1] Ancient rock paintings suggest that this fertility continued until the end of the fourth millennium BC and there were still elephants, rhinoceroses, giraffes, hippopotami and crocodiles.[2] Over the course of the next two thousand years, though, the desert gradually took over, and these animals separated to north and south. Hannibal's Carthaginian elephants were probably the vestiges of this great lost wealth of animals from what is now the world's largest desert.[3]

'Naturally, the people who had been forced out to live in the bitter cold of the European Ice Age resented those who all the while had lived in the comparative ease of what was then the fertile heart of Africa. These northerners shivered, and lived off blubber and beneath hides and skins. Their souls suffered a terrible pounding, and those who emerged were utterly different at the end of their collective experience. Furthermore, these survivors had two pathologies which arose from their terrible suffering in the northern wastes: firstly, that they would never experience such cold again, and secondly, that they would hate anyone who had lived in the warm climates during their pain and had doubtless banished them into their suffering in the first place.

'As time moved on, the balance of power shifted. The difficulty of surviving the Ice Age meant that the northern Europeans were fearsome warriors, hungry and powerful for conflict and comfort. They advanced, expanded, conquered, and developed their technologies; and as they did so, they began to fulfil their pathological need for heat. When they discovered oil, they were able to transform that desire into a mass form of combustion, heating up the world, and frying their collective unconscious memory of the terror of the Ice Age. So, they had suffered from being frozen, and their persecutors had been comfortably warm: they would all fry now, they would all burn in heat! The world itself would combust! Those formative cultural memories would be boiled dry!

'And so their way of life had to become dependent on the one thing that could heat up their surroundings. Oil became the most valuable commodity, the basis of the world economy, and in the main their conflicts would eventually be directed at securing more of it.

'Now, at an early point in all these developments, they had adopted a religion whose origins themselves lay in Africa. Jesus had been a Jew, and the Jews had an uncomfortably large number of ancient African customs, including circumcision and the belief in a single overarching and all-powerful God.[4] The Old Testament, indeed, read like an account of the doings of the ancestors, another African trait. The Jewish people even had a creation myth, the Garden of Eden, which – although it was often thought to refer to Arabia – could be read as harking back to an exodus from the tropical jungles of Central Africa, or even the Sahara: an earthly paradise, a place where, as the first words of Genesis revealed, light was tropical – day and night – and the subtler shades of the temperate zones did not exist.

'The second pathology now began to express itself. The Jews were an unconscious reminder of the hot countries beyond the Sahara. They could be forcibly converted, torched, expelled. Then, when the voyages of discovery laid Africa bare to European eyes, as it were, in the fifteenth century, the process could be continued – expanded.* The peoples who had prospered while northern Europeans had shivered in their glaciers – they would work now. They would work to heat up the world even more. They would suffer as the slaves of those who had suffered before them. Natural justice would be implemented, the deepest collective urges satisfied. The world's broken circle would be made whole.

'But unfortunately, the process never stopped. The combustion continued, the punishment of others accelerated. The old, deep-seated

---

*The role of the anti-Semitic attitudes developed in Spain in the fifteenth century for future race prejudice in Africa and the Americas was crucial. In a document of 1627 regarding the status of the 'white Europeans' of Cape Verde, the exact same language was used to differentiate the whites from the blacks as was previously used to differentiate Christians from Jews – whites were '*limpio*' (clean), while the black 'neophytes' were '*nouos christãos*' (new Christians) (see António Brásio (1968–78), op. cit., vol. V, p. 199). In the Americas, similarly, by the end of the eighteenth century, scribes were erroneously transcribing '*judíos*' instead of '*indios*', exemplifying how the same category of prejudice was directed to both peoples – see *Los Judíos Bajo la Inquisición en Hispanoamérica* by Boleslao Lewin (Buenos Aires, Editorial Dedalo, 1960), pp. 61–62.

urges demanded more victims, more heat. They did not want to be laid to rest. When peace was secured they demanded more – War!

'But the earth was not an endless sponge for the unrequited emotions of some of its people. Gradually, it fragmented. Its ecosystems started to implode. It soon became obvious that, unless all the passions could finally be laid bare, brought out into the open, and thus put to rest, the planet itself would be sacrificed to their needs.

'And so, as a new millennium dawned, and some shred of hope became apparent in the people who had emerged from the Ice Age – through a partial sense of self-realisation – it became clear that if we could not give those ancient urges their own burial over the course of the next generation, we would have destroyed ourselves altogether – or rather, they would have destroyed us.'

I had spoken calmly, without any maudlin emotions: the words had come from a well that I had never tapped before.

I felt unbearably relieved by what I had said. I lay down on the forest floor then, stretching my legs out into the moss. The relief elided into a sense of utter exhaustion. For so long I had been trying to lay bare my feelings as to this world, its sanctity, and the danger that threatened it. Now that I had done so, I felt calm; empty.

I closed my eyes, accepted the darkness, and slept deeply, forgetting in an instant that I was so far from home – or even Utopia – and that Don Ambrosio was by my side.

When I woke it was dawn. The first things I saw were Don Ambrosio's two eyes, peering into me as if I had been an inanimate object.

'Ah, *señor*,' he said kindly. 'I'm so glad to see you return from sleep.'

I sat up. Blinking hard, I tried to recollect how I had got here.

'Did you sleep well?' he asked.

'Yes,' I said.

He stretched out a hand to me and I stood up unsteadily. Having spent so long lying down, I felt the blood rush to my head. A sudden wave of passion overcame me, but this passed soon enough. The morning was fresh, vivid, real. The night before, and the quixotic events that had dogged me over the previous weeks, seemed more and more incredible.

We began to walk back towards the village, which was stirring into the morning.

'Tata Vasco,' Don Ambrosio said softly, 'he had his own views on the soul.'

'Well of course,' I said. 'He believed in it passionately.'

'But only in the human soul as an expression of divinity,' Don Ambrosio said. 'Of course the old Purépecha had a much grander vision of divinity and the sacred essence – one that encompassed every element of being.'

'So what do you think, *señor*?' I asked him. 'Do you think Tata Vasco destroyed that old vision with his own idealism, or that he was simply trying to make the best of a ghastly situation?'

Don Ambrosio chuckled softly, and we walked on in silence for a moment. The path cut through the gathering brightness of the forest, and the sunlight flickered. Animals rustled through the undergrowth, rushing as far away from us as possible.

'I think that both are true,' he said eventually. 'Tata Vasco thought that his idea was right, so he uprooted what he found. But at the same time, his idealism was better for us than were the other Spaniards who came with him, who answered only to their urges.'

'Some idealism is better than none?' I asked.

'But yes!' he cried. 'Yes!' He stopped to face me, and his eyes glittered like stars. 'Some idealism is better than none, even if it's just reduced to altruism directed at the planet as a whole. Provided that it doesn't go off the rails, some idealism is better than none.'

'Provided that it doesn't go off the rails ...' I echoed.

I sensed that my idealism had done just that, and wondered if any of the things that I remembered as happening to me on this utopian quest had been real. The man in S——— had warned me right at the outset that delusions beckoned in the narrative that I would create, and certainly, my quixotic experiences had been so bewildering that I found it impossible to judge the reliability of my memories. But if the truth value of my stories was indeterminate, and I had just been seeking out a clever narrative structure, could my purported views on idealism be valid?

'Of course,' Don Ambrosio muttered then, 'it's all too easy for idealism such as yours to be derailed. Those wells of fantasy beckon. But at the same time, the richest truth of all is in feelings, and not in the bald evocation of events. And so even if fantasy masquerades as truth, I think it can be legitimate, provided that it reveals emotional honesty.'

'I agree with you,' I replied with a swell of relief. 'And in that sense even the greatest fantasy can appear real – as any economic pragmatist will tell you. In a way, it doesn't matter if the account is true or false. It's what you turn it into that counts.'

Ahead we could see the morning cooking fires of the village now, sparkling through the trees. A dog barked in the stillness, smelling our approach.

'But you know what people will say,' I went on then. 'The pragmatists, as they like to call themselves. They will say that an idealism which is just reduced to the sort of altruism we've described is so watered down – with so few concrete pillars – that it's meaningless.'

'Well,' said Don Ambrosio, 'for centuries now people have been putting forward various versions of idealism filled with practical suggestions, and look where it's brought us to: the brink. Perhaps, instead, if we can express the deep-rooted emotional causes of this situation, and come to terms with them, a genuine pragmatism will follow of its own accord.'

We fell silent as we walked through the village. Don Ambrosio was greeted by the villagers, and I melted into his shadow. We walked a little way along the dusty track and then went into his home, where Patricia was preparing breakfast.

'Ay, husband!' she said as soon as she saw us, taking her hands out of some maize flour. 'Where have you taken our guest, that you have spent the night in the open?'

'We have been talking about this and that,' he said.

'We went off into the forest,' I added, 'and then I slept.'

'Like a little child!' she exclaimed, her mothering instinct straight to the fore. 'Like a little child!'

'I was tired,' I added. 'Very tired. I've found that this whole business of Utopia isn't half as straightforward as I'd imagined, and that trying to pin it down can be utterly exhausting – particularly if you've got an imminent publishing deadline and you're worried that your book is a meaningless expression of your own insanity.'

'But you've found what you were looking for in Michoacán?' she asked a little anxiously. 'Among the Purépecha?'

'Yes,' I said. 'Yes I think so. And I don't think it's as insane as all that. In fact, I've come to believe that you don't have to be crazy to be an idealist, and that even if the narrative that results from idealism is incredible, it can take consciousness of its own confused, fragmentary, sacred being through emotional truth.'

'That's wonderful,' she said, turning back to her work preparing the tortillas. 'And you've got nothing left to do?'

'I've finished my inquiry,' I said.

I closed my eyes, and tried to reflect on everything. Yes, surely I had finished on both counts.

On the psychological level, now that the destructive emotion had been expressed, it could at last fall into nothingness: perhaps, indeed, this was the origin of the great tiredness that I felt now, the sense that I had fought a tremendous battle almost without being aware of it, and that it had finally come to an end.

As far as Quiroga went, I had followed him from birth to death, from Spain to Mexico, and come to my own conclusions. He had been a difficult, combative character, someone who had believed that he was always in the right. This was of the essence of old-style utopianism – the dogmatic ideology that came of a separation of people from the world around them. Yet, at the same time, the institutions that he had founded through his idealism had had a great influence, not only in the way that they had endured in Michoacán, but in Mexico as a whole. Two of the leaders of Mexico's independence movement, Hidalgo and Morelos, had come from Michoacán, while the *ejido* system of communal land ownership – which had been the mainstay of the rural economy in Mexico after the Mexican revolution – had been instigated by Lázaro Cárdenas, also from Michoacán, and had had many similarities to Quiroga's utopian communes.

Idealism did not have to be negative, even though the political classes now believed that it was all played out. A little shot of it in our collective, withering arm, could indeed revive us.

'That's wonderful,' Patricia said, interrupting my daydream. 'You must be so relieved to have finished.'

'Well I am,' I said slowly. 'For although it's unfashionable, I'm still an idealist. Even though the twentieth century was really a time of dystopianism as far as the literature was concerned, I haven't been put off.'

'Dystopianism?'

Feeling an urge to unburden myself of it all, I talked to Patricia about the work of twentieth-century writers of utopian literature. Even Aldous Huxley and Ursula Le Guin – neither of them entirely despairing about idealism – had recognised that there were two sides to the utopian coin. Although Huxley thought that his *Island*[5] represented the possibilities of Utopia, he also saw that the controlling forces of society could produce something as soulless as his *Brave New World*;[6] and though Le Guin depicted Anarres – an ecotopian planet – in largely positive terms, she recognised that 'the complexity, the vitality, the freedom of invention and initiative' had been thrown away there.[7]

Other authors, though, I said to Patricia, had had no problems with depicting the horrors of a state of mass-control, as 'ideal states' were seen to be. Yevgeny Zamyatin, whose work had preceded Huxley's *Brave New World*, had satirised the utopian goal of 'the endless equalization of all creation'.[8] Arthur Koestler had summarised the prevailing view, when he wrote that in 1920, 'one believed that the gates of Utopia stood open, and mankind stood on its threshold',[9] but that twenty years later, the question had to be asked: 'Where was the Promised Land? Did there really exist any such goal for this wandering mankind?'[10]

The roots of this disillusion, I finished, were clearly in the experiences of the twentieth century, in places such as the Soviet Union; yet this outright rejection of idealism seemed to me to be too easy. Perhaps Le Guin had it right when she said that brotherhood 'begins in shared pain'.[11] For it had been among the Purépecha in the sixteenth century, as Quiroga found their suffering to be immense, that he had also found fertile ground to recover the togetherness of the Purépecha community.

Now, as the Earth's resources began to disappear, the same fertile ground would exist in our lifetimes. For all that the pragmatists disputed it, the twenty-first century would be one of utopianism and togetherness – given the disappearance of the Earth's resources, it would have to be. Therefore it would be one where shared values would reassert themselves, and the triumph of individualism would be shown to have been fleeting. In spite of everything, this really was a moment of optimism.

'What do you think about that, husband?' Patricia said softly, turning to Don Ambrosio.

'Time will be the judge,' was all he said.

Then he stood up and poured two glasses of water from a pitcher. He offered me one, and we drank quietly, our gulps the only noise in the kitchen other than the smooth pats of the maize flour as Patricia laid the tortillas on a tray and baked them over the fire.

We ate shortly afterwards. Beans were mixed with the chillies and tortillas, and we all consumed our breakfast without ceremony. When we had finished eating, Florencia asked me to read her a morning story, and so I squinted at an old children's book as she lay on the mattress that she shared with Juan Vasco. The little boy thought this was all far too childish, though, and skulked around outside, waiting until we had finished.

After I had finished, Don Ambrosio suggested that we go outside for a cigarette.

'But I don't smoke, *señor*,' I said.

'That doesn't matter,' he replied. 'Just come and talk to me anyway.'

We wandered out of the house and stood in silence for a while. Don Ambrosio held a small bag in his left hand, and the cigarette with his right. The rings of smoke gradually drifted up, mingling with the woodsmoke from people's homes, and diluting the strength of the morning sunlight.

'What's in the bag, Don Ambrosio?' I asked him by and by.

'Ice,' he said.

'Ice?'

'We're going to bury it,' he said, 'and perform the last rites of that story you told.'

'Bury the ice?'

'Yes,' he said. 'Put it back to work in the earth, and then its power may be directed in a beneficial way and not towards unending destruction.'

He turned and beckoned me to follow him round to the back of his house. Then he squatted down beside the earth and signalled that I should dig. I scratched away for some minutes, like a chicken searching for grain, until I had excavated a reasonable hole.

'Is this really necessary?' I asked him.

'Yes,' he said. 'There is great power in symbolism. If we could just accept the seeds of our feelings by burying the ice, by denying large corporations access to the land of the indigenous peoples like the Purépecha, by taxing aviation fuel, or even by writing off all the debt of the African nations and symbolically recognising the historical roots of Europe's relationship with that continent – then much could still be achieved by way of laying these hellish feelings to rest.'

'It would not cost so very much,' I said.

'It would not cost the Earth.'

I laid the ice carefully in its grave, and then covered it. It was cold outside, and I did not want to remain out there for much longer.

'Shall we go in to have some tea?' he asked.

'Yes,' I said. 'Let's do that.'

We walked back towards the doorway, and for a moment I hovered outside.

'I'll just be a moment,' I said to Don Ambrosio.

He left me there to listen to the village as it awoke from what seemed to be an eternal sleep. Looking about myself, the sharpness of every sensation convinced me that, at last, what I saw was all true. The quixotic journey that I had been propelled into by the old man in S—— was over. I was my own person now, in spite of my belief in the merits of togetherness, and the book that I would write would have to reflect that. By fusing fact and fantasy, I would seek to mirror the gradual process of awakening, distortion and non-categorisation that was overtaking this postmodern world, which, like my book, needed to take consciousness of how its own story had been wrought, and could only do so by concentrating on the emotional level and by disregarding any other apparent truth.

In this small Purépecha village the daylight crept up on the houses, clutching them fondly to its chest. Shadows of foxes darted about, sniffing for a way to get at the chickens. Moths whirred past, flitting off into the trees on their unknown journeys. There was stillness, calm, the breath of forgiveness from the woods of our passing there. Down in the empty meadows, in the brooks babbling ceaselessly through the day, in the caves and on the distant hills, the world breathed more easily.

I felt happy.

Then I let the feeling go – let everything go – and stood alone with my conscience. It was time to wake up, I knew, so I turned and went inside.

FIFTEEN

The daylight creeps up on the houses, clutching them fondly to its chest. Shadows of foxes dart about, sniffing for a way to get at the chickens. Moths whirr past, flitting off into the trees on their unknown journeys. There is stillness, calm, the breath of forgiveness from the woods of his passing there. Down in the empty meadows, in the brooks babbling ceaselessly through the day, in the caves and on the distant hills, the world breathes more easily.

Quiroga feels happy.

Then he lets the feeling go – lets everything go – and stands alone with his conscience. It is time for the world to wake up, so he turns and goes inside.

Soon it will be dawn. He sits on one of his three chairs that have been carved from walnut trees,[1] staring out as Pátzcuaro is reclaimed by daylight. The town did not change much during his absence in Spain, and it has not taken long to get used to life in the New World again. The tiles of the houses gleam red with the dawn light; soon the streets will be filled with carts, wrapped in a shroud of dust shaken free from the masonry; the Purépecha will pass by his dwelling, their faces downcast, absorbing the cracks between the cobbles that crisscross over the 'place of happiness'.

Quiroga enters the small oratory beside his bedchamber, and prays steadfastly to an image of the Virgin, which has been erected behind a gold cross.[2] His body moves slowly, like a mechanical cog cranking into place, ready for its holy labours. He is getting old now, but his vision remains pure.

– Holy Mother, bless this world, and all who live in it. May we be worthy of your Divine Grace, and that of Your Son, our Father, blessed in Heaven. May this benighted people be raised up to be worthy to Your eyes. May this world be deemed fit for Heaven on Earth. May it be reclaimed by Your divine perfection.

When he has finished, he washes his face with a pitcher of water brought from the fountain and dresses in one of his coarsely woven shirts.[3] Then he eats some maize bread with his servant. His routines change little between Spain and New Spain, and this steadfastness bridges the two worlds – Utopia as it is on Earth, and as it will be in Heaven.

He steps outside again. A mist of movement clings to Pátzcuaro as the Purépecha begin to work, and the friars shuffle barefoot around the streets, supervising the construction of the Templo de Compañía just across from the cathedral and the Colegio de San Nicolás. The Spanish settlers stand idly beside one another, talking to the vagrants who are passing through en route to the mines of Guanajuato and Zacatecas.[4] Quiroga stares at the travellers: they will not be allowed to haul off some of his Purépecha to do their greedy work for them, he will see to that![5]

His target this morning is the Colegio de San Nicolás. The school is finished now and is currently one of the focal points for his earthly dreams. He shuffles through the entrance, beneath the coat of arms, and stands in one of the covered walkways that surround the patio. The courtyard bursts with flowers and twists of greenery, as if presenting a homily to the students on the bounties of nature. The roofs over the walkways are propped up with wooden pillars, and the shutters guarding the classrooms have been wrought in the old Mudéjar style that reminds him of Madrigal. Behind the patio is the long refectory, and then a smaller courtyard where the students can draw water from a well. The lintels above each doorway are carved with heraldic symbolism from Spain, with the same rough workmanship that graced the font in which both he and Isabella, the Catholic Queen, were baptised – in a different century; when they belonged to a different world.

Ah, Madrigal! Of course, when in Spain, he returned there, to the church of San Nicolás in which his parents are buried,[6] and the streets which he once rode through at the beginning of his life's voyage. Yet he had developed a growing sense of the melancholy of the lookout towers surrounding his home town, surveying the plain to protect against an enemy that was no more, but lived on stubbornly in the psyche. The narrow alleys and streets were no longer as animated as they had been in his childhood; they were emptier, sadder, so that it was almost as if they had thrived on that threat. The thrill of the child's world had launched itself out into Castile, Africa, the Americas, but that joy had gradually become dissipated, almost as if life itself had withered on the vine.

The axis of the old country is of course shifting. Soon, in 1561, Philip II will found the Spanish capital definitively in Madrid, and Quiroga's home town will slip into the world of the forgotten. Perhaps that is the way with empires as their centres move across plains, mountain ranges, oceans, and worlds disintegrate even as the threat to imperial survival is sustained.

Eventually, everything is forgotten, Quiroga feels, rooting about in his memory. He finds that his mind wanders as he gets older, refusing to be chained to the material world. His recollections are like chaff discarded from a harvest, blown into the eddies of his identity and alighting incomprehensibly, just as they choose to, stirring up his feelings so that he cannot ignore them. Here, as they settle on his childhood, he wonders if it can be a coincidence that the motors of the triumph of the Church both in Spain and in New Spain were brought to Divine Grace in that same font, in that small town in the heart of Castile.[7]

No, every trajectory has a divine purpose; Madrigal's former greatness, and its growing lethargy, remind everyone of how the most powerful people and cities are made but of dust, and return, sooner or later, to their origins.

That morning, he stands in the shadows watching the students of San Nicolás set about their morning tasks, repeating the lessons of their teachers by rote, reading learned works even at mealtimes as they feed their hunger with bread, fruit, fish.[8] The students of theology are all Spanish, and under the age of twenty; the Purépecha teach them their own language, and learn Spanish in return.[9] Everyone studies for free:[10] the Spaniards are admitted because of the great shortage of priests in New Spain,[11] the Purépecha because of the hard work they put in to the building of the school in the 1540s.[12] It is a mingling of the races, the first step on the road to the painful *mestizaje* of the Mexican nation and, Quiroga feels, towards the genuine Christian emancipation of the Purépecha.

As the morning wears on, he takes his leave of the school. It is not yet hot, and the streets are awash with Indians talking to Spaniards, entering the workshops of the saddlers and farriers. Down by the plaza some of the settlers are bragging extravagantly to one another, toying with the handles on their swords. The air is filled with the smells of smoke, rotting vegetables, the innards of animals split open in the butchers' stalls; the atmosphere mixes the harsh sounds of Spanish with the musical lightness of the Purépecha language, in which every change of tone gives a change of meaning.[13]

As he walks past the stalls, Quiroga comes cross a group of Purépecha who have already fallen into a drunken stupor, something that reminds him of the painful necessity of educating these people as swiftly as possible. Glugging their way through pitcher after pitcher of pulque, he knows that some of them are often to be seen sprawled over the cobbles, like animals, or tearing at each other in their brutishness.[14] Even their governor, Don Antonio Cuitzimengari, is a well-known drunkard, someone who has often had to be reprimanded by the civil authorities.[15]

Quiroga himself has berated Don Antonio:

– What! Have you no shame, Don Antonio, to go drinking yourself into oblivion in the face of God? What is it that you want so greatly to forget? There is nothing to be ashamed of, Don Antonio, no sin which God will not pardon. The deepest hatred can be repaired, the deepest gulf from the earth patched up. You must just confess it openly, freely, without artifice, and peace will be yours! That is the role of the confessional, is it not? – to sanction the basest urges felt in the human breast with divine forgiveness.

But Don Antonio had been as quiet as the night, his gaze skulking by the ground, muttering half-formed apologies in Spanish.

– Can you not recover the grace of existence? (Quiroga had found the silence of the Purépecha cacique deeply frustrating.) Can you not find a way to the heart of God? And if not faith, surely you can at least recover a sense of your dignity! Surely you can see that festering in your own urges, requiting the most deracinated freedoms in your debauchery, is no way to happiness! If you cannot have faith in God, can you not at least have faith in yourself, in the world?

Of course, Don Antonio had made promises, but Quiroga has yet to see them fully realised. That is the divine struggle epitomised, he feels now, as he watches the layabouts with distress. No matter how rigid the rules of a society, no matter how divine, people remain individuals, and do not allow that individuality to surrender itself entirely. His society is defined by strict parameters, and yet these Indians cannot be prevented from getting drunk. Sinfulness, pride, individuality, will never be done away with; and so what is important is to set up parameters which allow both the society and the individual to thrive, sacrificing neither one to the other. This is why he has written in the past of the danger of trying to cure all ills with the same solution.*[16]

*See above, ch. 10, p. 183.

For himself, however, he is in no doubt as to what the solution is. The cassock must be donned; the prayers must be read; the lessons imparted and absorbed.

He returns to his dwelling and dresses himself in one of his two threadbare cassocks.[17] The streets of Pátzcuaro have emptied as the afternoon has pressed upon them, but he has a service to give in the cathedral. Even though only one nave has been completed, that is better than nothing. He walks imperiously through the streets, his heart thrilling in its journey through the order which he has created.

Soon after his return from Spain in 1554, Quiroga travelled to Mexico for the Church Council. Present were all the bishops of New Spain, including the new Bishop of Mexico, Alonso de Montúfar. In many ways the council was not accompanied by auspicious omens: the Bishop of Oaxaca, Juan de Zárate, actually died as it was in session,[18] and the council also banned Indians from being ordained as priests in the colony, a retrograde step that would have serious consequences for the future nature of the Church in Mexico.[19]

By this point the bishops were all wary of the mendicant orders. The council decreed that mendicants should not hear confession unless they had a legal licence,[20] and that no monastery could be built without permission.[21] They were also troubled by the general quality of the priests who came over from Europe, passing decrees that priests should not play cards or dice, go to gambling houses or lend money to people,[22] and that they should carry no weapons either.[23] The clerics were clearly still in fear of this unfamiliar continent, and armed themselves against it with the crutches of violence and dissolution that they knew from old Spain.

In Michoacán, meanwhile, Quiroga's struggles with the mendicant orders went from bad to worse. His cathedral had created a controversy, and was something which the Franciscans and Augustinians could always point to if he criticised them. They stirred up resentment among the Purépecha, and so, also in 1555, the caciques of Tzintzuntzan took a case against Quiroga to the court at Mexico about the work that they had done on the cathedral.[24] With the continuation of legal cases brought against Quiroga by some of the most powerful people in the colony – including Cortés's son, Martín, later in his life – the Bishop of Michoacán's defence of his hospitals and his ideals remained deeply unpopular.

That year, another mendicant friar to begin preaching among the

Purépecha was Miguel de Gornales, who had arrived in New Spain aged twenty-eight. He had learned the language of the Purépecha within eighty days, and had achieved great things before falling ill and dying suddenly. Juxtaposing his life with that of Quiroga, the friar Gerónimo de Mendieta wrote that 'the early death of the saintly youth accuses the long and bad life of the sinner'.[25] Or, as Viceroy Velasco said to the ageing Quiroga on the death of Martín Sarmiento de Hojacastro, second Bishop of Tlaxcala: 'Great are the mysteries of our Lord, sire, who takes those whom He ought to leave (as we see it), and leaves behind those whom He ought to take.'[26]

As the 1550s progressed, things did not get any easier for Quiroga. The struggle with the Franciscans and the Augustinians for the hearts and minds of the Purépecha became more difficult for him to win as he got older. In 1558, Don Bartolomé, a Purépecha elder from Tzintzuntzan, complained against him for taking the land of Santa Fe de la Laguna, and Quiroga had to repeat the arguments of twenty years before, concerning the holy nature of the pueblo-hospital and the fact that it was under royal protection. The hospital was necessary for the sustenance of those who lived there, and served as an example for everyone else.[27]

Nonetheless, the expansion of the mendicant orders continued unchecked. In 1559, Quiroga complained that the Augustinians had gone in violently to Tacamalca and built a new church without his permission, wanting 'to strip the very pastor of his parishioners'.[28] The friars were 'so dangerous ... that even just looking at them may be enough for them to complain and denounce us to everyone'.[29] The Tacamalca case turned very nasty: an unruly mob formed by Quiroga's ally Pérez Gordillo Negrón set fire to the houses of the Augustinians, and six friars nearly burnt to death with their homes.[30] A similar thing occurred at Calimaya in a dispute over land between the diocese and the friars, and this time one person did die.[31]

Clearly, things could not continue like this, and yet Quiroga was in no mood to compromise. Later in 1559, he complained to Bishop Montúfar about the work of a Franciscan friar, Maturino Gilberti, and Gilberti's translation of doctrine into the Purépecha language without his permission.[32] On 6 April 1560 Montúfar banned Gilberti's work from being circulated.[33] This argument led to the biggest showdown of all with the Franciscans.

In January 1561, Gilberti travelled to Mexico to give evidence in the case. His allies in the order joined forces with him, and on 20 February Luis de Anguis wrote to Philip II in Spain denouncing the

Bishop of Michoacán. Quiroga, he said, had hardly been in the see for three years ever since his ordination,[34] and if he had not been so severe with the friars there would not have been all these arguments:[35] in fact, people were so used to arguing here that not a day passed without a legal case being brought.[36] The cathedral, meanwhile, was an absurd waste of money 'which [would] never be finished as long as there [we]re people on this earth'.[37] The Bishop's acolytes, he said, formed themselves into a mob who directed their actions solely at recovering what was in the hands of the friars.[38]

None of this went down very well with Montúfar and Quiroga, of course, who had long been suspicious of the friars. Later that year they accused the Franciscans, Dominicans and Augustinians of abusing the Indians and usurping their rightful jurisdiction as bishops. Quiroga wrote that the mendicant orders beat and flogged the Indians, and even clapped them in irons when they did not obey orders.[39] In February 1563, Gilberti would retaliate with a pamphlet accusing Quiroga of equal mistreatment of the Purépecha, through the cathedral at Pátzcuaro, the work demanded at the hospitals, and the charity he asked them to give to the Chichimecs.[40]

With the benefit of 450 years of hindsight, these opposite views are slightly easier to reconcile than they were in the heat of the disagreements. Quiroga had indeed spent long periods away from his see, but this was – as he saw it – to protect his work among the Purépecha, fighting in Spain for royal protection of his hospitals, and securing their lands in the courts in Mexico: his frequent trips to Mexico were a reflection of the number of cases that settlers brought against him, resentful of his concentration on the Purépecha.[41] Meanwhile both groups were probably guilty of exacting too much labour from the Purépecha – the Franciscans with their monasteries and Quiroga with his cathedral; but, as has been pointed out before, Quiroga's was only one cathedral.*

Nevertheless, the sight of such a blatant power struggle is unsavoury. Quiroga – as his position on the Valladolid debate had shown – was not against the concept of 'just war' per se, but believed that sometimes 'perfection' (as he saw it) could only be achieved through struggle: he would not give way to the mendicants without a fight. The messianic idealism that had characterised his early work as an *oidor* in Mexico had transformed itself into something harder. Confronted by the violence of both religious and temporal colonisation, it had not proved

*See above, ch. 13, p. 233.

itself innate and untouchable, but rather had performed the difficult elision that reality so often seems to require of idealism.

In 1562, Don Antonio Cuitzimengari falls ill in Pátzcuaro. His years of drinking, confusion, forgetfulness draw around his features; his face smoothes itself of its lines and prepares to return to its earthly rest. He retires to his deathbed, there to consider the nature of this strange life of his, during which all certainties have been uprooted, and the nature of good and evil has been rewritten.

Outside, a fresh sunlight clutches the walls of the Spanish houses. The water bursts from the stone fountain in the plaza, its splashes broken only occasionally as people fill their buckets. Oxen low as they rumble into the town, and the carts which they haul creak uncertainly with the produce being brought to the market. Don Antonio lies there, falling in and out of delirium, listening to the chanting of the students from San Nicolás: *Deo gratia, Pater nostrum.*

Six leagues away in Tiripetío, Quiroga hears of Don Antonio's sickness. He often retires here to spend time in a bare cell which is reserved for him there, where he lives the life of a monk.[42] The news arrives in the evening from Pátzcuaro, and Quiroga spends the night in prayer for Don Antonio's soul.

– Yes, Lord, he drank a great deal, and could be debauched. But he was also a good scholar who learnt Latin and our own script.[43] He tried to accommodate himself to Your ways, and I believe he learnt a great deal. He read Erasmus and Ptolemy,[44] and understood the classics. Spare him Hellfire and Purgatory, Lord. Spare him the suffering of the world.

It is a long night. The bats flit past the shuttered windows, calling to one another like spirits from the beyond. Of course he – Quiroga – will not be immune from their wiles, and eventually will join Don Antonio in his passage beyond the darkness of the planet's eternal night. What will his life, his good intentions, his immutable aspirations count for then?

He sleeps poorly. In the morning, he steps outside to take in the work that he has instigated. The *hospital de la concepción* of Tiripetío is one of the biggest in Michoacán, made of lime and stone. Its infirmary accommodates up to fifty people, and is reached by a stone staircase from the downstairs area.[45] One of the patios is filled with orange trees, and the other is sown with vegetables; there are looms here for weaving the shifts of the Purépecha or the habits of the friars.[46]

Quiroga stands in the courtyard, preparing himself to travel by mule[47] to Pátzcuaro. The sunlight gilds the green hills behind the town, and floods the oranges in the orchard with brilliance. Everything seems to shine that morning, as he mounts his mule and rides back to the city with just his page for company.[48] The rooftops, the leaves, the water meadows by the lake – they all sparkle. The hills rise about him as if they are runways, giving Don Antonio's soul a guiding path on its heavenbound journey.

As they near Pátzcuaro, groups of Purépecha cluster about them, and Quiroga talks to them calmly, but without forced jocularity. This is a serious time, heralding a move towards the light for Don Antonio – for us all! Pray intensely. Believe in perfection. Seek the answers to your questions. Do not be fooled by material comfort.

The hollow of Pátzcuaro clutches Quiroga's settlement to its heart. Birds duck beneath the eaves of the houses as the Bishop rides into the town and ties up his mule outside the home of Don Antonio. Crowds of Purépecha have clustered about the entrance, their bodies wrapped in white, as if they themselves were corpses wrapped in their own burial shrouds, preparing the way for the funeral of their entire culture.

This must not be entered into lightly, this endtime. Everyone must consider what it means for humanity to be cast in such a dangerous position, on the brink of the earthly abyss. Everyone must seek reconciliation, and consciousness of their feelings.

Quiroga stoops as he enters the home – his height has always given his neck a bowed quality. He exchanges greetings with the family of the dying man, with the Spaniards who are there, the scribe Hernando Gutierrez, Cristóbal López, Alonso Gómez and Miguel Cuara.[49]

– How is Don Antonio? Quiroga whispers.

– He is nearly in the arms of the Lord, a priest replies. He will soon be taken.

Quiroga crosses himself. The atmosphere in the room is almost like that of a crypt: cool, silent, pensive. Don Antonio lies swaddled in a coarse blanket, sweating profusely. His eyes are cloudy, misted over with sadness at this life and at his departure from it. Quiroga moves forward slowly, and sits in a chair by his bedhead.[50]

– Don Antonio.

– Yes, *señor*.

– How are you doing, Don Antonio?

– I am very sick, *señor*. Even now, I am in the hands of God.

Yes, Quiroga sees, it is true. But then we are all in the hands of God at every moment of our lives, and fate is our constant judge! Is

Don Antonio's sickness any more terminal than that of fallen Man, or of the imperfect world? No, we live as invalids and die as sinners! Yet while we live, we must strive to reverse our natural condition as far as we can, to transcend our innate barbarism. We must all seek to be like the Apostles, and disguise the true nature that lies buried at the roots of our fractured emotions.

That is why we must have religion, Quiroga thinks. And that is why the school of San Nicolás is so essential – so that the Truth may be propagated!

– Don Antonio, he says.

– Yes, *señor*.

– Give us the stone wall inside which we have built the school of San Nicolás. You know it is a holy work.

There – he has said it. The school had been built within land belonging to Don Antonio, and he has always held that the cacique will relinquish that land on his death. It is for the good of God, of the Earth, of the Purépecha.

– I cannot, Don Antonio replies. That belongs to my children.

– Don Antonio, this is a work of God.

Yet Don Antonio does not reply. A minute, two minutes pass, and the old man is wheezing, panting, his eyelids closed as if by the very effort of keeping alive what is his. Flies buzz around the room, and his struggle for life seems to have got even more intense.

– Don Antonio, Quiroga says again.

But the cacique now turns his face and pushes it stubbornly against the wall.

– Very well, Quiroga says. It seems that you are really very sick. It is of no matter. We are already in possession of the wall.

Don Antonio turns his head slowly to face the bishop.

– Well, *señor*, if Your Holiness is already in possession, why do you ask me for my approval?

Then his gaze slips away into the distance.

There is no point in staying any longer when the man is so sick, Quiroga feels. He has asked him for the wall because he wanted to respect Don Antonio's right to have an opinion, even though (as everyone knows) it is God's opinion that counts. He knows that his is a divine struggle, and so everything is permitted to secure its success.

But that does not mean that Quiroga will not ask others – such as Don Antonio – to agree with him.

Outside, the town still moves through its daily routines. People swap goods, mule trains pass through with saddlebags of minerals.

The smell of rotting fruit lingers in the air, companion to a deceptive calmness on the point of no return.

Two days later, Don Antonio Cuitzimengari dies, his soul arcs into the water of the living being, on the other side.

The last years of Quiroga's life passed with a mixture of emotions.

Though the royal protection of his precious pueblo-hospitals remained secure, Philip II became increasingly impatient with God's representative in Michoacán. On 24 June 1560 he wrote to Quiroga: 'We have been told that you do not want to ordain any friar from any religious order ... because of your passionate disagreement with the said friars.'[51] Quiroga's true colours were evident for all to see, because Philip went on to point out that this did not prevent him from ordaining 'many *mestizos* and other people born in that country'[52] – something which went against the spirit if not the letter of the 1555 Church Council's decree on the ordination of Indians.

Two years later, on 11 July 1562, tiring of Quiroga's obstinacy where the mendicants were concerned, Philip bypassed him and wrote straight to the Audiencia in Mexico. He had heard, he said, that Quiroga often threatened the Augustinians, saying that he would strip them of their monasteries in his diocese, even though the Crown itself had ordered their construction.[53] Philip ordered the Audiencia to ensure that Quiroga did not do this.[54]

Quiroga tried not to let any of this affect him. He continued to travel about his diocese by mule, accompanied by just a secretary and a page,[55] visiting the sierra and the area by the Pacific coast. In 1561 he ordered a church to be built in Silao; in 1563 he supervised the construction of a hospital in Barahona.[56] Towards the end of that year, though, another wave of death swept across Michoacán in the form of a smallpox epidemic.[57] Quiroga watched as many more of his people melted away into the heavens. Feeling under attack from the Crown and the friars, the combination of the epidemic and the virulent pamphlet that was now circulated against him by Maturini Gilberti* was difficult to take.

Perhaps he sensed that he was weakening. Towards the end of 1564 he made preparations to draw up his will; it was finally signed by him in January 1565. This fascinating document emphasised what Quiroga saw to be his twin triumphs in life: the pueblo-hospitals of Mexico and Michoacán, and the school of San Nicolás in Pátzcuaro. Quiroga

*See above, p. 271.

left his library of 626 books – a considerable number at that time – to San Nicolás.[58] He also stressed the shortage of priests, and said that he wanted many to be trained in the school.[59]

Much of his will, however, was devoted to the utopian hospitals. In case anyone should be in doubt, he stressed: 'I founded and personally endowed, from my own wages, two Hospitals ... for poor Indians and wretched people, pupils, widows, orphans and twins which it was said were killed by their mothers as their great poverty and misery meant that they could not bring them up'.[60] He made it clear that though he had personally paid for the property of the hospitals, the Indians had also worked hard and 'ha[d] helped and [we]re helping'.[61] All the property of the hospitals should be left to the institutions themselves, which should never be changed to something else, as 'with great difficulty would it be possible to come across a more pious or better work in these parts, since in it almost all possible types of hospitality are found'.[62]

Quiroga's pride in the 'hospitality' of his pueblo-hospitals is easy to understand when they are compared to the rest of New Spain. In his eyes, here the people were fed and clothed and housed, they were given work, they were settled in civil society, and they were instructed in a faith that could redeem them. This was a prototype for a welfare state with a difference, where people were both rescued from penury and given the tools with which to build a better life – in Santa Fe, and throughout Michoacán, as the craft specialisation became established, charity became self-help. Of course, the Purépecha customs had to be diluted – this was a conquest, after all – but this was as close to a model for 'just colonisation' as existed in the sixteenth century.[63]

The first months of 1565 saw Quiroga steadily begin to weaken. Tradition has it that he went off on a final farewell tour of his diocese before expiring in Uruapan on 14 March 1565;[64] recently, however, some have argued that he in fact died in his beloved Pátzcuaro, as is testified by a document from the cathedral there.[65] Like all mortals, he died without having done everything that he would have wished; but at least he had the impression that something had been accomplished.

One of the best barometers of the impact of the utopian communities among the Purépecha was their readiness to stand up for their rights. In 1581, just sixteen years after Quiroga's death, a priest wrote: 'If they feel oppressed by their *corregidores* or vicar or by anyone at all, within four days they present themselves before the Viceroy or the Bishop and demand justice, with as much liberty as if they had been Spaniards.'[66] They were quite happy to go to the homes of the *corregidores*, and present their petitions in writing or in *laminas*, seeking redress through the legal process.[67] Quiroga's hospitals had instilled a sense of civil rights that his people never lost – something that is surely apparent in the origins of Hidalgo, Morelos and Cárdenas in Michoacán.*

By the end of the sixteenth century, the hospitals of Santa Fe in both Mexico and Michoacán had settled down into the routine which they would maintain throughout the colonial period. In his will, Quiroga had put the hospital of Santa Fe de México under the jurisdiction of the diocese of Michoacán,[68] a move that symbolised the extent to which he had moved on from his first utopian project as *oidor*. Trying to take advantage of this following Quiroga's death, the Council of Mexico sought to regain control of Santa Fe in 1572, claiming that few people went there to be cured;[69] but this attempt was denied in 1574, and by 1582 the annual income of the hospital was 3,500 pesos.[70]

In Michoacán, Santa Fe de la Laguna was recognised as autonomous. Its crops were used for the sustenance of the people of the pueblo-hospital and for the students of San Nicolás.[71] By 1599, the judge Vazquez de Tapia applauded the settlement, saying that any Indian who wanted to find refuge could do so there, and that it was an 'admirable' place.[72] His account suggests that the pueblo-hospital worked according to Quiroga's ordinances, with the people rotating their work on the farm just as More and Quiroga had required.[73] By the seventeenth century, the rectors of the Mexican Santa Fe came from Michoacán,[74] and the Mexican pueblo-hospital was prosperous, owning over 400 sheep and producing an annual surplus of 59 bushels of wheat.[75]

Quiroga's ordinances remained the rubric for the hospitals through-out the colonial period. They were referred to for guidance when difficult questions arose,[76] and they still set the tone for daily routines; in 1650 in Michoacán, for instance, there were still two keys to the granary, one held by the rector and the other by the Purépecha.[77] Even by 1766, Moreno claimed that the role of the hospitals founded by Quiroga had changed little.[78] It was only with new laws in the 1850s that did away with common land ownership, and nationalised ecclesiastical property, that the ordinances of Quiroga's hospitals finally fell into abeyance.[79]

*See above, ch. 14, p. 261.

For Quiroga, who was deeply aware of the transience of earthly endeavours, the endurance of his hospitals would have been bitter-sweet. He had longed for them to be an earthly answer to paradise, a protection for his beloved Purépecha. The fact that they lasted for 300 years after his death represents a triumph of sorts; but that they ultimately failed to vanquish the avaricious forces against which he had designed them as protection would have given him little comfort.

The last testament has been sealed. Its wax congeals slowly about the parchment, like a clotted wound that will scar and then heal, slowly revealing the meaning of his life's work – whatever that might be.

The Bishop is ill! He is sick! He is in the arms of God!

He can hear his people scampering about in the streets, as the word goes around, and is carried by horsemen and muleteers off into the sierra. Ah, these Purépecha, they love their horses and are among the finest riders in New Spain.[80] They are even excellent at bullfights.[81] He can hear the hooves drumming off along the cobbles, striking the stones with the frenzy of a blacksmith's hammer, moulding the land to its desired shape.

The hooves hammer in his head. He feels the blood rising inside him, as if to pour out and smother his work. His head drums like the beats of those devilish dances that they refuse to give up entirely. The percussion mounts inside his thoughts until it feels that it must spill out, bursting like a pustule of the pox and covering everything in fire.

So much blood! The murder of the Purépecha, the pustules of the pox, the stains of the earth. How much of this is the blood of a just war, and how much the fulfilment of a rage that boils inside him as if he were a vat on a fire? But Jesus bled for us, of course, and so we must be prepared to bleed for Him on occasion. The pox could even be just recompense for our sinfulness! And the will of God is not something that we can protect ourselves against.

Thoughts coalesce in their violent madness; the blood boils out.

He is raging! His complexion is discoloured! He is not far from Paradise!

Yes, he can hear them. They are disconsolate at his passing. What will the world mean when he is no longer there? What will his life have meant? Oh, he can imagine the torrent of questions pouring through their minds as the word spreads down the streets of each town of his see. The Bishop! The Bishop! The Bishop is leaving us!

At that he feels calmer, more reconciled to his end. The fits come and go, and occasionally the fire seems to ebb; it will not consume him just yet. He calls his page and says that he wishes to see his earthly perfection one last time, before seeing its match in heaven.

– Arrange the litter, he says. It is time for me to bid farewell to my country.

The litter is an old one,[82] but it will still function. It is attached to two mules,[83] and Quiroga is carried out on his last tour of the diocese.

The hills move in the light, twisting as if at any moment ready to adopt the forms of angels. But no! The angels are up in the clouds, and their trumpets are sounding loudly. Or is that the dancing and the wailing of the Purépecha in the flyblown villages of his see, as they bid him farewell? Oh it is all such confusion; his thoughts race round one another like flies in the evening and it is impossible to see where they might rest.

The days are clear and chill. The light is resolute. He rests in his litter as the mules take him from one village to the next, staring emptily at the passing meadows, forests, orchards and fields of crops. Oh it is all planted, harvested, ripe for development, beautiful in its essence if only it could be seen as such; but of course none of this is in the image of God – that is the privilege of Man.

He circles the lake. The fishermen haul in their nets as a mark of respect; the women stop pedalling their looms. They are all dressed in white like the clouds, the heavens, the perfection to come.

Oh, it is all so obvious now! He feels its proximity to his life, its immanence. There is no need to doubt, when Paradise is so near at hand.

The circle is drawn tight, as the litter returns to Pátzcuaro. He lies down in his bedchamber and at once his blood begins to boil again in his head. The most respected among the Spaniards and the Purépecha gather to witness his departure.

– I am going, he whispers gently, when the fits ebb. But I will never leave entirely.

God bless this land and its people. They have been so greatly affected as the end time draws near; stricken by war and disease and exploitation. They deserve only the best in the life to come, if – as appears to be Your will, Oh Lord – this earthly realm is no longer worthy of salvation.

The blood rises to his head again, reaching heavenwards, like his soul – accompanying those countless Purépecha who have gone before him. His face draws white, mirroring the glow in his spirit as he soars, light-headed. He can see the brilliance now, it is within his grasp. Everything is crystal clear; everything is granted its own piece of heaven. He can finally acknowledge all that his life has meant to him: every moment of his existence, every feeling that has arisen.

The last, blinding awareness is all over in a flashing fury.

The Bishop lies inert on his bed.

Beneath him, the world is still spinning, spinning without end, waiting to join him in heavenly glory.

God bless this land and its people with earthly perfection.

God bring us peace.

NOTES

PREFACE

1. *The Open Society and its Enemies* by Karl Popper (London, Routledge, 1945, 2 vols), vol. I, pp. 141–2.
2. *The Guardian Review*, p. 8, 16 March 2002.
3. *Good Places and Non-Places in Colonial Mexico: The Figure of Vasco de Quiroga (1470–1565)* by Fernando Gómez (London, University Press of America, 2001), p. 3.

CHAPTER ONE

1. *Four Essays on Liberty* by Isaiah Berlin (Oxford, Oxford University Press, 1969), p. 32.
2. *Utopia* by Thomas More, translated by Paul Turner (Harmondsworth, Penguin Books, 1965; first published 1916).
3. *Utopia* (1965), op. cit., p. 27.
4. Ibid., p. 102.
5. Ibid., p. 10.
6. Ibid., p. 106.
7. For more details see Felipe Tena Ramírez, *Vasco de Quiroga y Sus Pueblos de Santa Fé en los Siglos XVIII y XIX* (Mexico, Editorial Porrúa, 1977), p. 168.
8. *Island* by Aldous Huxley (London, Flamingo, 1994; first published 1962), p. 160.
9. Ibid., p. 90ff.
10. Cit. Sybille Bedford, *Introduction to Brave New World*, in *Brave New World* by Aldous Huxley (London, Chatto & Windus, 1984; first published 1932), p. xviii.

CHAPTER TWO

1. For more details on John II of Castile, see *The Rise of the Spanish Empire in the Old World and in the New* by Roger Bigelow Merriman (New York, The Macmillan Company 1918–1934, 4 vols.), vol. II.
2. Santa Maria de la Concepción, a hospital founded by Quecn Mary of

Aragón, John II's first wife, in 1443. The ordinary hospitals in Michoacán were subsequently called '*hospitales de la concepción*' by Quiroga.

3. *The Ingenious Hidalgo Don Quixote de la Mancha* by Miguel de Cervantes Saavedra (London, Penguin Books 1999; first published 1604–1615), p. 600.

4. At this time, Granada was the capital of Spain's silk trade – see *Trade and Business Community in Old Castile Medina del Campo 1500–1575* by Falad Hassan Abed Al-Hussein (Norwich, University of East Anglia, unpublished PhD thesis, 1989), p. 55.

5. See Yitzhak Baer, *A History of the Jews in Christian Spain* (Philadelphia, The Jewish Publication Society of America, 1966; 2 vols., tr. Louis Schoffman), vol. II, p. 247.

6. Again, the sizes of these communities can be calculated from the tax information for 1488–1491 – see *Documentos Acerca de la Expulsión de los Judíos*, ed. Luis Suárez Fernández (Valladolid, Ediciones Aldecoa, 1964), pp. 64–70 for the tax figures for Avila, Arévalo, Medina del Campo and Madrigal. It is interesting to note that, even after 1492, the area remained a hotbed of crypto-jewry – in the 1520s, an African slave in the Canaries testified that his masters, the Núñez family, often travelled to the fairs of Medina del Campo, where they would stay at the house of an old woman who seemed to know them well, and whose eldest daughter was intimate with one of the Núñezes; en route to the fair, the family spoke in a strange language which the slave had never heard – probably Hebrew – and refused to eat pork. See *Jews in the Canary Islands, Being a Calendar of Jewish Cases Extracted from the Records of the Canariote Inquisition of the Marquess of Bute* by Lucien Wolf (London, The Jewish Historical Society of England, 1926), p. 34.

7. In reality the exodus of the Jews from Iberia had been in progress ever since 1391. After this pogrom – which flared up across the peninsula – it is estimated that a third of the Jews fled, a third converted, under force, and a third remained with their faith (see Haim Beinart, in *The Converso Community in 15th Century Spain*, pp. 425–56 of Barnett (1971), vol. I). Following the 1492 expulsion order, approximately 200,000 fled to Portugal, North Africa and the Ottoman Empire. For more information see e.g. Yitzhak Baer (1966) op. cit., *The Marranos of Spain* by B. Netanyahu (New York, American Academy for Jewish Research, 1966) and *The Sephardi Heritage* (ed. R. D. Barnett, Valentine, Michell & Co., London, 1971, 2 vols.).

8. See *El Real Colegio de San Nicolas de Pátzcuaro* by Francisco Miranda Godinez (Cuernavaca, Centro Intercultural de Documentación, 1967), p. 11.

9. Ibid.

10. Ibid, p. 10.

11. For more details on the Quiroga family crest, see *Los Escudos de Don Vasco de Quiroga* by Armando Mauricio Escobar Olmedo (Morelia, 1999).

12. See *Vasco de Quiroga: La Utopía en América* by Paz Serrano Gassent (Madrid, Historia 16, 1992), pp. 7f.

13. See Armando Mauricio Escobar Olmedo (1999), op. cit., p. 50.

14. For more on the economic crisis in Spain 1502–1508, see *Emigración Española a las Indias* by Luis Aranz (Santo Domingo, 1979), cit. Hugh Thomas, *The Conquest of Mexico* (London, Hutchinson, 1993), p. 58 n. 19. For more on the failed harvests of 1503–1504, see Roger Bigelow Merriman (1918–34) op. cit., vol. II.

15. *Memorias del Reinado de los Reyes Católicos* by Andrés Bernáldez (Madrid, Real Academia de la Historia, 1962), p. 342.

16. Ibid.

17. Ibid.

18. See *A Social and Religious History of the Jews* by Salo Wittmayer Baron (New York, Columbia University Press, 1969), vol. XIII, p. 75.

19. See *Recuerdo de Vasco de Quiroga* by Sílvio Zavala (Mexico, Editorial Porrúa, 1987), p, 252. Talavera had also been one of the pioneers of introducing printing to Castile, and it is highly possible that this connection with the Quiroga family had born fruit in the young Vasco's fascination for books and learning; see *Linaje Judío de Escritores Religiosos y Místicos Españoles del Siglo XVI* by José-Carlos Gómez-Menor, pp. 587–600 of *Judíos. Sefarditos. Conversos: La Expulsión de 1492 y sus Consecuencias*, ed. Ángel Alcalá (Valladolid, Ámbito Ediciones, S.A., 1995), p. 596.

20. *Criterios Inquisitoriales Para Detectar al Marrano: los Criptojudíos en Andalucía en los Siglos XVI y XVII* by María de los Angeles Fernández García, pp. 478–502 of Ángel Alcalá (1995), op. cit., p. 480.

21. The cosmopolitan nature of the fairs as early as 1450 is mentioned in the *Crónica de Don Álvaro de Luna, Condestable de Castilla, Maestre de Santiago*, vol. II of *Colección de Crónicas Españolas*, ed. Juan de Mata Carriazo (Espasa-Calpe, Madrid, 1943, 7 vols), p. 252. See also *Las Antiguas Ferias de Medina del Campo* by Cristóbal Espejo and Julian Paz (Valladolid, La Nueva Pincia, 1908) pp. 37–8.

22. See Cristóbal Espejo and Julian Paz (1908), op. cit., p. 30.

23. Ibid., p. 41.

24. Fintan B. Warren, *Vasco de Quiroga and his Pueblo-Hospitales of Santa Fe* (Washington, Academy of Franciscan American History, 1963).

25. Francisco Miranda Godinez (1967), op. cit., p. 8.

26. *La Historia Verdadera de la Conquista de la Nueva España* by Bernal Diaz del Castillo (Madrid, Información y Revistas S.A., 1984, 2 vols; first published 1568), vol. II, p. 385. Sílvio Zavala also cites a document from 1555 saying that Quiroga is then '*sesenta*' (sixty) – although he suggests this as a misprint for '*setenta*' (seventy). See *Ensayo Bibliográfico en Torno de Vasco de Quiroga* by Sílvio Zavala (Mexico, Colegio Nacional, 1991).

27. *Hernán Cortés: Conqueror of Mexico* by Salvador de Madariaga y Rajo (London, Hodder & Stoughton, 1942), p. 23.

28. Francisco Miranda Godinez (1967), op. cit., p. 16.

29. *Crónica de Enrique IV* by Mosén Diego de Valera – vol. IV of de Mata Carriazo (1943), op. cit., p. 160.

30. Ibid., p. 5.

31. Ibid.

32. *Crónica de los Reyes Católicos* by Fernando del Pulgar – vols. V and VI of Mata Carriazo (1943), op. cit.; vol V, p. 224.

33. *Imperial Spain: 1469–1716* by J. H. Elliott (Harmondsworth, Penguin Books, 1970; first published 1963), p. 21.

34. Another indication of Spain's obsession with its hybrid past is in the Statutes of *'limpieza de sangre'* – or 'cleanliness of blood' – which became commonplace in the sixteenth century. Albert A. Sicroff has shown how these created such an atmosphere of fear, suspicion and intrigue that they contributed to the decline of Spanish institutions and fed emigration to the New World. See *Los Estatutos de Limpieza de Sangre: Controversias entre los Siglos XV y XVII* by Albert A. Sicroff, tr. Mauro Armiño (Madrid, Taurus Edicions, 1985).

35. *Spain Under the Habsburgs* by John Lynch (Oxford, Basil Blackwell, 1964; 2 vols.), vol. I, p. 27ff – these converts were known as Moriscos, and were eventually expelled in 1609.

36. Fintan B. Warren (1963), op. cit., p. 27.

37. *La Vida Estudiantil en la Salamanca Clásica* by Luis Cortes Vázquez (Salamanca, Ediciones Universidad de Salamanca, 1985), p. 15.

38. Ibid.

39. *Viaje por España y Portugal en los Años 1494 y 1495* by Jerónimo Münzer, tr. and ed. by Julio Puyol (Madrid, Tip. De la 'rev. de Arch, Bibl. y Museos', 1924), p. 140.

40. See *Vasco de Quiroga, Jurista y Defensor del Derecho del Indio Frente a la Encomienda* by Humberto Aguilar Cortés, in *Juegos Florales Conmemorativos del V Centenario del Natalicio de Don Vasco de Quiroga* (Morelia, Talleres Gráficos del Gobierno del Estado de Michoacán, 1971).

41. Jerónimo Alcalá Yañez in *El Donador Hablador*, part I, chapter I, cit. Luis Cortes Vázquez (1985), op. cit., p. 40.

42. Luis Cortes Vázquez (1985), op. cit., p. 42.

43. Ibid., p. 45.

44. 'The Pretended Aunt' by Miguel de Cervantes Saavedra, pp. 25–36 of *Spanish and Portuguese Short Stories* (London, Senate, 1995), p. 28.

45. See *The Spiritual Heritage of the Sephardim* by Solomon David Sassoon, pp. 1–28 of R. D. Barnett (1971), op. cit., vol. I, p. 14. Sassoon points out that the earliest cities in Europe to have universities were those to have direct or indirect contact with the Arab world – the largely medical schools of Salerno and Montpellier (near to North Africa and Aragón), followed by Paris, with its contacts with semi-Arab Barcelona, and Oxford, which came under French influence. The Jews, who were important figures in the civilisation of Al-Andalus, were 'the principal medium through which Moorish civilization was permanently impressed upon Europe' (S. P. Scott, *Moorish Empire in Europe*, cit. Sassoon, p. 14).

46. This reveration of the book is again something which is not unconnected to Spain's Moorish heritage – Solomon David Sassoon (1971), op. cit., cites the case of King Hakam II of the Caliphate (961–76), who sent

'agents to every city in the East to obtain rare books, [and] built up a library of no less than 400,000 manuscripts' (p. 3). This sort of collection was far ahead of anything comparable in other parts of Europe, and in fact the beginnings of the expansion of learning in Europe can be traced to the reconquest of Toledo from the Moors in 1085; thereafter, the twelfth and thirteenth centuries saw teams of Jewish and Moorish translators employed to render classical works of antiquity – which had been lost to Christian Europe for centuries – from Arabic into Latin, including works by Aristotle, Averroes and Euclid; see *Los Judíos Españoles* by José Torroba Bernaldo de Quirós (Madrid, Suc. De Rivadeneyra, 1967), pp. 58–9, and *Función Cultural de la Presencia Judía en España Antes y Después de la Expulsión* by José-Luis Abellán, pp. 395–407 of Ángel Alcalá (1995), op. cit., p. 398.

CHAPTER THREE

1. Thomas More (1965), op. cit., p. 69.
2. *The Life of Thomas More* by Peter Ackroyd (London, Chatto & Windus, 1998), p. 167.
3. Thomas More (1965), op. cit., p. 131.
4. Ibid., p. 40.
5. Ibid., p. 70.
6. Ibid., p. 71.
7. Ibid., p. 80.
8. Ibid., p. 73.
9. Ibid.
10. Ibid., p. 74.
11. Ibid., p. 76.
12. Ibid., p. 84.
13. Ibid., p. 83.
14. Ibid., p. 118.
15. *The First Social Experiments in America: A Study in the Development of Spanish Indian Policy in the Sixteenth Century* by Lewis Hanke (Cambridge Mass., Harvard University Press, 1935), p. 9.
16. Thomas More (1965), op. cit., p. 86.
17. Ibid., p. 89.
18. Ibid., p. 79.
19. For more on Erasmus, More and humanism see, e.g., *More's Utopia: The Biography of an Idea* by J. H. Hexter (New York, Harper & Row, 1965; first published 1952), p. 52; *Thomas More* by R. W. Chambers (London, Jonathan Cape, 1935), p. 122; *Don Vasco de Quiroga: Educador* by Saul Lemús Gomez (Morelia, Universidad Vasco de Quiroga, 1997), p. 25ff; *Erasmus: A Study of His Life and Ideals* by Preserved Smith (New York, Harper and Brothers, 1923); *Erasmus: His Life Works and Influence* by Cornelis Augustijn, tr. J. C. Grayson (Toronto, University of Toronto Press, 1991).

20. See *Utopía y Contrautopia en el Quijote* by J. A. Maravall (Santiago de Compostela, Editorial Pico Sagro, 1976), p. 28ff.
21. See *Erasmo y España* by Marcel Bataillon, tr. Antonio Alatorre (Mexico, Fondo de Cultura Económica, 1950).
22. *A Dialogue of Comfort Against Tribulation* by Thomas More, ed. P. E. Hallett (London, Burns, Oates & Washbourne, 1937), p. 169.
23. Thomas More (1965), op. cit., p. 65.
24. Ibid., p. 66.
25. Ibid.
26. Ibid., p. 130.

CHAPTER FOUR

1. According to the Venetian ambassador to Spain, Andrés Navajero – see *Viajes Por España de Jorge de Einghen, del Barón León de Rosmithal de Batna, de Francisco Guiccardini y de Andrés Navajero*, ed. Antonio Maria Fabié (Madrid, Academia de la Historia de Madrid, 1879), p. 273.
2. Navajero writes: 'I saw in Seville many things from the Indies, and I ate the roots which are called potatoes.' Navajero (1879), ibid., p. 274.
3. AGI, Indiferente 737, N8. These sorts of shortages were not new to Seville – fifty years before there had been such a lack of meat in the city that according to a cédula of Ferdinand and Isabella of 19 January 1480, 'to supply the butchers fifteen and twenty horsemen travel by land to the neighbouring communes and right up to the frontiers to look for and bring back cattle, and it is a great effort to find them and bring them back'; see Luis Suárez Fernández (1964), op. cit., p. 164.
4. *Carta Inédita de Hernán Cortés* in *Colección de Documentos Para la Historia de México*, ed. Joaquín García Icazbalceta (Mexico, Libreria de J. M. Andrade, 1858, 2 vols – hereafter Icazbalceta), vol. 1, p. 471.
5. *Carlos V y el Pensamiento Político del Renacimiento* by J. A. Maravall (Madrid, Instituto de Estudios Politicos, 1960), p. 184.
6. Chapter XVI of *De Solicitanda Infidelium Conversione* by Cristóbal Cabrera, pp. 107–58 of *Don Vasco de Quiroga y Arzobispado de Morelia* (Mexico, Editorial Jus, 1965).
7. Many of the first who sailed for the Indies were Jews and Moslems escaping the Inquisition. On 13 July 1559, for instance, the Spanish Crown was urging its bishops in the Indies 'to inform themselves about the Lutherans, Muslims and Jews who are in their dioceses, to punish them and to make them return to Spain' – AGI, Indiferente 427, L.30, f.95v–96v.
8. AGI, Indiferente 1961, L.2, f20v–21v.
9. AGI, Indiferente 737, N.27.
10. AGI, Patronato 276, N4, R276.
11. *Sevilla en el Imperio (Siglo XVI)* by Santiago Montoto (Sevilla, Nueva Librería Vda. de Carlos García, 193?), p. 20.
12. 'The Conquest' by Hugh Thomas (in Warwick Bray (2002)), p. 79.

13. *Mexican Architecture of the Sixteenth Century* by George Kubler (New Haven, Yale University Press, 1948; 2 vols.), vol. II, p. 312.

14. Maria de los Angeles Fernández García in Ángel Alcalá (1995), op. cit., p. 481.

15. See *Vasco de Quiroga: Utopia y Derecho en la Conquista de America* by Paz Serrano Gassent (Madrid, Fondo de Cultura Economica de Espana, 2001), p. 17.

16. *A Compleat History of the Present Seat of War in Africa, Between the Spaniards and the Algerines* by J. Morgan (London, W. Mears, 1632), p. 11.

17. Ibid., p. 15.

18. *L'Économie de l'Empire Portugais aux XVe et XVIe Siècles* by Vitorino Magalhães Godinho (Paris, S.E.V.P.E.N, 1969), p. 149.

19. Ibid., p. 829. Mina gave 120,000 cruzados of revenue in the time of João II, in comparison to 126,000 cruzados from all other sources.

20. Miguel de Cervantes Saavedra (1999), op. cit., p. 592.

21. Fintan B. Warren (1963), op. cit., p. 17.

22. Oran had been a repository of information from the Empire of Mali for almost 100 years. In the 1450s, Prince Henry the Navigator of Portugal wrote that he had heard from a merchant in Oran about the war between two rivals in the Mali empire. See *Documentos Sôbre a Expansão Portuguesa*, ed. Vitorino Magalhães Godinho (Lisboa, Editorial Gleba, 1945; 3 vols), vol. I, p. 84.

23. *La Domination Espagnole à Oran* by Paul Ruff (Paris, Ernest Leroux, 1900), p. 12.

24. *Vasco de Quiroga en Africa*, ed. J. B. Warren (Morelia, Fimax Publicistas, 1998); see also Fintan B. Warren (1963) op. cit. The Jewish community in Tlemcen had been founded from scratch following the flight of 1391, and had itself lived through a period of turmoil in 1467, when there had been many forced conversions and Jews had actually sought refuge back in Spain – an indication of how difficult things were for them. See *A History of the Jews in North Africa* by H. Z. (J. W.) Hirschberg (Leiden, E. J. Brill, 1974), pp. 386–9.

25. J. B. Warren (1998) op. cit., p. 124.

26. Andrés Bernaldez (1962), op. cit., p. 258.

27. J. B. Warren (1998) op. cit., p. 74.

28. For a full account of the sack of Rome, see *The Emperor Charles V: The Growth and Destiny of a Man and a World Empire* by Karl Brandi, tr. C. V. Wedgwood (New York, Harvester Press, 1980; first published 1939).

29. *Fragmentos de la Vida y Virtudes del Ilustrísimo Señor Dr. Don Vasco de Quiroga* by Juan Joseph Moreno (Mexico, Imprenta del Real y Más Antiguo Colegio de S. Ildefonso, 1766), p. 6.

30. Fintan B. Warren (1963), op. cit., p. 18.

31. *Aristotle and the American Indians: A Study in Race Prejudice in the Modern World* by Lewis Hanke (London, Hollis and Carter, 1959), pp. 5ff.

32. *Lo que Hispanoamérica Perdió: El Impacto de la Expulsión en su Atraso Cultural y Económico* by Mario Cohen, pp. 434–54 of Alcalá (1995), op. cit., p. 446 –

the banning of books 'which have profane and fabulous material, and false histories' was promulgated in royal cedulas of 1532 and 1543.

33. *Los Esclavos Indios en la Nueva España* by Sílvio Zavala (Mexico, El Colegio Nacional Luis González Obregón, 1968), p. 16.

34. AGI, Mexico 1088, L.1. f.225v–226v. The maravedi was another symbol of how deeply Iberia depended on the Muslim world for its heritage; its name was a hispanicisation of the coins struck in North Africa in the twelfth century, the 'morabeti'. Alfonso VIII began to strike the coins in Toledo in 1173, and they were known as 'morabeti d'Alfonsi'. See Vitorino Magalhães Godinho (1969), op. cit., p. 131.

35. *México a Través de los Siglos* by Alfredo Chavero (Mexico, Ballescá y Compañía, 1888), vol. II, p. 173.

36. *Documentos Inéditos del Siglo XVI Para la Historia de México*, ed. Mariano Cuevas (Mexico, Editorial Porrúa, 1975; first published 1914), p. 9 – a letter from Zumárraga to the Council of the Indies of 28 March 1531.

37. Tony Judt, *On 'The Plague'*, in *New York Review of Books, Vol. 48, no. 19*, p. 6.

38. Andrés Navajero (1879), op. cit., p. 266.

39. Santiago Montoto (193?), op. cit., pp. 168–75.

40. *El Teatro en Sevilla en Los Siglos XVI y XVII* by José Sánchez Arjona (Madrid, Establecimiento Tipográfico de A. Alonso, 1887), pp. 28–9.

41. Ibid., pp. 45–6.

42. Santiago Montoto (193?), op. cit., p. 40.

43. Andrés Navajero (1879), op. cit., p. 271.

44. Cervantes gives an excellent description of the galleys of the era (of which he had personal knowledge) in *Don Quixote de la Mancha*; Miguel de Cervantes Saavedra (1999), op. cit., pp. 916–18.

45. Nicolaus Von Popplau's account in *Viajes de Extranjeros por España y Portugal en los Siglos XV, XVI y XVII*, ed. Javier Liske (Madrid, Casa Editorial de Medina, 1878), p. 43.

46. Galleons were very new sailing vessels at this time, having recently replaced the caravels, which were of Portuguese origin. It is known that they were in operation by 1529, when Diego Ribero, Charles V's cosmographer, depicted several full-rigged galleons in his *Carta Universal*. Classic galleons had three masts and a bowsprit – see *Cogs, Caravels and Galleons: the Sailing Ship 1000–1650*, ed. Robert Gardiner (London, Brasseys, 1994), p. 102.

47. When Magellan sailed in 1519 aboard *La Victoria*, these hills were thronged with people according to the chronicler of the voyage, Pigafeta – *Tradiciones de Sevilla: Santa María de la Victoria* by Manuel Ruiz del Solar y Azoriaga (Sevilla, Lib. é Imp. de Izquierdo y C.a, 1897).

CHAPTER FIVE

1. *The Conquest of New Spain* by Bernal Díaz del Castillo, tr. J. M. Cohen (Harmondsworth, Penguin, 1963), p. 107 – hereafter BDC.

2. Ibid.

3. Ibid.

4. Ibid., p. 108.

5. Ibid., p. 122.

6. *Historia General de las Cosas de Nueva España* by Bernardino de Sahagún (Madrid, Alianza Editorial, 1988, 2 vols.), vol. II, p. 811 – also known as the Florentine Codex (hereafter FC).

7. *Historia de los Indios de la Nueva España* by Fray Toribio de Benavente (Motolinía) (Madrid, Historia 16, 1985; first written, 1536), p. 249. 'In the Mexican countryside nature reclaimed her territory, covering magnificent monuments in vegetation' – 'Introduction' by Eduardo Matos Moctezuma and Felipe Solís Olguín to *Aztecs*, ed. Warwick Bray (London, Royal Academy of Arts, 2002), p. 18.

8. BDC, p. 37.

9. *Horribles Crueldades de los Conquistadores de México* by Fernando de Alva Ixtlilxochitl, p. 22 (Mexico, Imprenta del Ciudadano Alejandro Valdés, 1829; first published c. 1608) – hereafter HC.

10. As the Mexica initially saw the Spanish ships – vol. II, p. 118 of *The General History of the Things of New Spain* by Fr. Bernardino de Sahagún, tr. Charles E. Dibble and Arthur J. Anderson, 12 vols., (New Mexico, University of Utah, School of American Research, 1952–).

11. BDC, p. 45.

12. Lewis Hanke (1959), op. cit., p. 5.

13. BDC, p. 87.

14. Ibid., p. 123.

15. Ibid.

16. Ibid., p. 405. For a full description of the conquest of Mexico, the classic account is W. H. Prescott's *The Conquest of Mexico* (Phoenix, 2001; first published 1845). Hugh Thomas's brilliant *The Conquest of Mexico* (London, Hutchinson, 1993) has superseded it in recent years.

17. A letter from the Imperial Crown of 22 October 1523 talks of the forts of Veracruz needing 'artillery, which until now they have not been provided with, and without which they are in great danger' – *Epistolario de la Nueva España 1505–1818*, ed. Francisco del Paso y Troncoso (Mexico, Antigua Librería Robredo, de José Porrúa e Hijos, 1934; 24 vols. – hereafter ENE), vol. I, p. 57.

18. Narváez had been sent by Velazquez from Cuba to capture or kill Cortés, who was suspected of disregarding his orders. For a fuller description of the events surrounding Cortés, Narváez and Diego Velazquez, see Hugh Thomas (1993) or BDC.

19. Hugh Thomas (1993), op. cit., p. 153. The fear with which the dogs were held can be gauged by the statement of the Mexica to the people of Michoacán when trying to forge an alliance of the two former enemies against Cortés: the Mexican ambassadors talked of 'the great destruction which the dogs were wreaking among the Indians' (*'el gran destrozo que los perros hacían en los indios'*) – *Crónica de Michoacán* by Pablo Beaumont (Mexico, Talleres Gráficos de la Nación, 1932, 3 vols.; first published 1826), vol. II, p. 11.

20. FC, vol. II, p. 846. Says Sahagún: 'This plague killed an infinity of people (*gente sin número*).'

21. Ibid.

22. BDC, p. 122.

23. *Michoacán and Eden: Vasco de Quiroga and the Evangelisation of Western Mexico* by Bernardino Verastique (Austin, University of Texas Press, 2000), pp. 101–102; also *The Millennial Kingdom of the Franciscans in the New World: A Study of the Writings of Gerónimo de Mendieta (1525–1604)* by John Leddy Phelan (Berkeley, University of California Press, 1956), pp. 8, 17, 25.

24. *Carta al Capítulo General de Tolosa* by Juan de Zumárraga, in vol II, pp. 300–302 of *Don Fray Juan de Zumárrga*, ed. Joaquín García Icazbulceta (Mexico, Editorial Porrúa, 1947; 4 vols. – hereafter Z).

25. According to Francisco de Terrazas, Cortés's butler, in a letter to Cortés of 30 July 1529. Letter 76 of ENE, vol. I.

26. The use of Indians to ferry goods from ship to land was permitted by the Crown in a letter from Toledo of 4 December 1528. See *Colección de Documentos para la Historia de la Formación Social de Hispanoamérica 1493–1810*, ed. Richard Konetzke (Madrid, Consejo Superior de Investigaciones Científicas, 1953; 2 vols. – hereafter CDH), vol. I, p. 116.

27. *Ordenanzas de Buen Gobierno Dadas por Hernando Cortés Para Los Vezinos y Moradores de la Nueva España* (Madrid, José Porrúa Turanzas, 1960; first written 1524), p. 12.

28. Letter from Rodrigo de Albornoz to Charles V, 15 December 1525 – *Colección de Documentos para la Historia de México*, ed. Joaquín García Icazbalceta (Mexico, Librería de J. M. Andrade, 1858; 2 vols. – hereafter Icazbalceta), vol. I, pp. 484–511.

29. AGI, Mexico 1088, legajo 2, f.27r–30v – a letter from Queen Isabel dated 20 March 1532 in which she says that the officials of the Casa de la Contratación have sent the seeds and plants which the *oidores* asked for.

30. Letter of 27 March 1531 to Charles V – Z, vol. II, pp. 265–67.

31. Hugh Thomas (1993), op. cit., p. 131.

32. Rodrigo de Albornoz in a letter to Charles V, 1 March 1533. Vol. II, letter 131, of ENE.

33. BDC, pp. 92–3.

34. Lewis Hanke (1959), op. cit., p. 14: 'A Spaniard of ten years' experience in America [said] that he had seen ... Spanish gentlemen sowing the fields [of Honduras] "with their own hands", a scene he had never witnessed before.'

35. Ibid., p. 16.

36. Cit. Sílvio Zavala, *Servidumbre Natural y Libertad Cristiana – Según los Tratadistas Españoles de los Siglos XVI y XVII* (Buenos Aires, Peuser S.A., 1944).

37. Lewis Hanke (1935), pp. 1–4. In 1835, Barbara Anne Simon wrote a book entitled *The Ten Tribes of Israel Historically Identified with the Aborigines of the Western Hemisphere*. Also a subscriber to the view that there were Jews in the Americas before 1492 is José Monin, in *Los Judíos en la América Española* (Buenos Aires, Biblioteca Yavne, 1939), pp. 24–5.

38. For more information on this case – which many historians now believe to have been so fabricated that the child may not even have existed – see, e.g., Yitzhak Baer (1966), op. cit., vol. II, p. 370ff. Also *Los Judíos en la España Moderna y Contemporánea* by Julio Caro Baroja (Madrid, Ediciones Istmo, 1978; first published 1963, 3 vols.). Caro Baroja argues that such cases may have taken place, but they were symptomatic of black magic, and not of Judaism, which roundly condemned them (vol. I, p. 188).

39. Bernardino Verastique (2000), op. cit., p. 99.

40. Ibid., p. 101.

41. John Leddy Phelan (1956), op. cit., p. 18.

42. Rodrigo de Albornoz in a letter to Charles V, 1 March 1533 – ENE, vol. II, letter 131.

43. Zumárraga described Mexico thus in a letter to Cortés of 13 December 1530 – Z, vol. IV, p. 105.

44. Letter of 7 August 1529 – ibid., vol. II, p. 99.

45. *Historia de la Nación Mexicana* by Mariano Cuevas (Mexico, Talleres Tipográficos Modelo, 1940), p. 174.

46. BDC, p. 106.

47. Motolinía (1985), op. cit., p. 247.

48. Ibid., p. 249.

49. Ibid., p. 244.

50. Ibid., p. 245.

51. Ibid., pp. 249–50.

52. *Cartas de Relación Enviada a Su Majestad*, in *Historia de Méjico* by Hernán Cortés, ed. Manuel del Mar (New York, White, Gallaher & White, 1828 – hereafter CR), p. 58.

53. BDC, p. 135.

54. In *Philosophiae Sagacis*, Frankfurt, 1605, lib. 1, c. 11, vol. x 110, cit. Hugh Thomas (1993), op. cit., p. 296.

55. CDH, p. 117; Motolinía (1985) wrote of the Spanish settlers: 'They ensure that they are served and feared as if they were absolute natural lords, and never do anything except make demands, and however much they are given they are never content' (p. 70).

56. CDH, p. 117.

57. Ibid., p. 118; see also Motolinía (1985), p. 70.

58. The words of Roger Casement as he travelled through King Leopold's Congo in the first years of the twentieth century – *The Black Diaries: An Account of Roger Casement's Life and Times with a Collection of his Diaries and Public Writings*, ed. Peter Singleton-Gates and Maurice Girodias (New York, Grove Press, 1959), p. 153; cit. Adam Hochschild in *King Leopold's Ghost* (London, Macmillan, 1998), p. 202.

59. Ixtlilxochitl makes this point repeatedly – see HC, op. cit., pp. 31–2.

60. Ibid.

61. See ENE, vol. II, Letter 122, p. 231 – a notarised testimony of the *oidor* Salmerón of 12 December 1532, sent to the royal court.

62. Z, vol. II, p. 238.

63. Ibid.
64. Motolinía (1985), pp. 72–3.
65. Ibid.

CHAPTER SIX

1. Miguel de Cervantes Saavedra (1999), op. cit., p. 74.
2. Ibid., p. 84.
3. Ibid., p. 85.
4. *Utopía y Contrautopia en el 'Quijote'* by José Antonio Maravall (Santiago de Compostela, Editorial Pico Sacro, 1976), p. 20.
5. Ibid., p. 169.
6. Miguel de Cervantes Saavedra (1999), p. 943.
7. *Realistic Utopias: The Ideal Imaginary Societies of the Renaissance 1516–1530* by Miriam Eliav-Feldon (Oxford, Clarendon Press, 1982), p. 2.
8. Ibid., p. 3 – examples include Leon Battista Albertis (1452) and Leonardo (1487).
9. Ibid., p. 11.
10. *Republic* by Plato, tr. G. M. A. Grube (Indianapolis, Hackett Publishing Company, 1992).
11. *The City of the Sun* by Thomas Campannella (London, Journeyman Press, 1981; first published 1623), p. 21.
12. Ibid.
13. Ibid., p. 27.
14. Ibid., p. 34.
15. Ibid., p. 61.
16. Ibid.
17. See Yitzhak Baer (1966), op. cit., for a full account of this process.

CHAPTER SEVEN

1. Motolinía (1985), op. cit., p. 227.
2. Zumárraga's letter to Charles V of 27 August 1529. See vol II, p. 191 of Z.
3. Ibid.
4. Letter of 15 December 1525 from Albornoz to Charles V – see p. 488 of vol. II of Icazbalceta.
5. See pp. 84–116 of *Land and Society in Colonial Mexico: The Great Hacienda* by François Chevalier, tr. Alvin Esutis (Berkeley, University of California Press, 1963).
6. Motolinía (1985), op. cit., p. 227.
7. Alfredo Chavero (1888), op. cit., vol. II, p. 187.
8. Nicolaus von Popplau (1878), op. cit., p. 36.
9. Alfredo Chavero (1888), op. cit., vol. II., p. 187.
10. *El Conquistador Anónimo: Relación de Algunas Cosas de la Nueva España, y de la Gran Ciudad de Temestitán México* by 'Un Compañero de Hernán Cortés'

(Mexico, Alcancia, 1938; first published 1556 – hereafter ECA) p. 43.

11. Ibid.

12. *Mythes et Rituels du Méxique Ancien Préhispanique* by Michel Graulich (Brussels, Palais des Academies, 1987), p. 66.

13. One of the reasons why so many of the Mexica were willing to die in the siege was that they believed that those who went to heaven were those who were killed in war or those who had died in the hands of their enemies – Sahagún (1988), op. cit., vol. I, p. 222.

14. HC (1829), op. cit., p. 43.

15. Ibid., p. 48.

16. Ibid., p. 49. It is important to note, though, that estimates of number are notoriously unreliable in this period. Hugh Thomas (1993) suggests that the real figure was 100,000 dead.

17. Ixtlixochitl suggests that there were over 100,000 houses, whereas before there had been 60,000 – even if the figures are wrong, the proportions are probably correct. HC, op. cit., pp. 55–60.

18. Motolinía (1985), op. cit., p. 71.

19. This detail in a royal cedula of 22 June 1531 – *Documentos Inéditos Relativos a Hernán Cortés y su Familia*, vol. XXVII of *Publicaciones del Archivo General de la Nación* (México, Talleres Gráficos de la Nación, 1935), p. 22.

20. *Colección de Documentos Inéditos Relativos al Descubrimiento, Conquista y Organización de las Antiguas Posesiones Españolas de América y Oceania, sacados de los Archivos del Reino y muy especialmente del de Indias*, ed. Joaquín F. Pacheco, 42 vols. (Madrid, J. M. Perez, 1868 – hereafter CDI), vol. XII, pp. 520ff.

21. Motolinía (1985), op. cit., p. 72.

22. See letter 76, vol. II of ENE, from Francisco de Terrazas to Cortés dated 30 July 1529 – this information on p. 140.

23. BDC (1963), op. cit., p. 214.

24. *Poesía Lírica Azteca* by A. Garibay (Mexico, Bajo el Signo de 'Abside', 1937), p. 39; cit. *The Daily Life of the Aztecs on the Eve of the Spanish Conquest* by Jacques Soustelle (Weidenfeld & Nicolson, London, 1961; tr. Patrick O'Brian), p. 241.

25. ECA (1938), op. cit., p. 19.

26. BDC (1963), op. cit., p. 215.

27. CR (1828), op. cit., p. 107.

28. ECA (1938), op. cit., p. 42.

29. Ibid.

30. CR (1828), op. cit., p. 160.

31. *The Aztecs' Search for the Past* by Leonardo López Luján (in Warwick Bray, ed. (2002)), p. 22.

32. Ibid.

33. 'Cosmovision, Religion and the Calendar of the Aztecs' by Alfredo López Austin (in Warwick Bray, ed. (2002)), pp. 32, 34.

34. Ibid., p. 36.

35. ECA (1938), op. cit., p. 42.

36. BDC (1963), op. cit., p. 215.

37. ECA (1938), op. cit., p. 18.
38. CR (1828), op. cit., pp. 96–7.
39. ECA (1938), op. cit., p. 39.
40. BDC (1963), op. cit., p. 233.
41. Ibid.
42. ECA (1938), op. cit., p. 40.
43. Jacques Soustelle (1961), op. cit., pp. 33–4.
44. BDC (1963), op. cit., p. 232.
45. CR (1828), op. cit., p. 148.
46. BDC (1963), op. cit., p. 235.
47. CR (1828), op. cit., p. 147.
48. BDC (1963), op. cit., p. 234.
49. FC (1988), op. cit., vol. I, p. 362.
50. Ibid., p. 230.
51. *El Teatro de Nueva España en el Siglo XVI* by José Rojas Garcidueñas (Mexico, Sep/Setentas, 1973; first published 1935), pp. 17–24.
52. FC (1988), op. cit., vol. I, p. 91.
53. Ibid., vol. I, p. 85.
54. Ibid., vol. I, p. 95.
55. Ibid., vol. I, p. 365.
56. Ibid., vol. I, p. 366.
57. Ibid., vol. I, p. 374.
58. Ibid., vol. I, p. 366.
59. *Historia de la Literatura Nahuátl* by A. Garibay (Mexico, Editorial Porrúa, 1953; 2 vols.), vol. I, p. 43; cit. Jacques Soustelle (1961), op. cit., p. 240.
60. George Kubler (1948), op. cit., vol. I, p. 190.
61. Ibid.
62. Jacques Soustelle (1961), op. cit., p. 2.
63. Ibid., p. 6.
64. Motolinía (1985), op. cit., p. 77.
65. Ibid., p. 71.
66. HC (1829), op. cit., p. 84ff.
67. Ibid.
68. In Zumárraga's letter to Charles V of 27 August 1529; Z, op. cit., vol. II, p. 227.
69. Ibid., p. 189.
70. Mariano Cuevas (1940), op. cit., p. 169.
71. Z, op. cit., vol. II, pp. 191ff.
72. Alfredo Chavero (1888), op. cit., vol. II, p. 175.
73. J. H. Elliott (1970), op. cit., p. 64.
74. ENE, op. cit., vol. II, p. 36 – letter 91.
75. Icazbalceta, op. cit., vol. II, p. 503 – letter of 15 December 1525 from Albornoz to Charles V.
76. Letter of Quiroga to the Consejo de las Indias of 14 August 1531, CDI, vol. XIII, p. 422.

77. *The Hummingbird and the Hawk* by R. C. Padden (Columbus, Ohio State University Press, 1967), p. 232.
78. Cristóbal Cabrera, chapter XIX (1965), op. cit.
79. R. C. Padden (1967), op. cit., p. 253.
80. *The Just War in Aquinas and Grotius* by Joan D. Tooke (London, SPCK, 1965), pp. 23–4.
81. Cortés says that there were over 400 temples in Cholula, which was the religious centre of the region before the Spanish, and which contained the biggest temple in the empire of the Mexica. CR (1828), op. cit., p. 92.
82. These are Quiroga's words. See p. 64 of vol. II of ENE, op. cit.
83. For more on Erasmus's influence on Quiroga, see *The Politics of an Erasmian Lawyer* by Ross Dealy (Malibu, Undena Publications, 1976).
84. The Christian meaning of the term 'polis', which was the basis of Quiroga's ideal of republics, was of spiritual perfection prompted by fear of an apocalypse – Bernardino Verastique (2000), op. cit., p. 124.
85. Sílvio Zavala – the great Mexican historian who first made the connection between Quiroga and More – subsequently discovered Zumárraga's copy of *Utopia*, which may well have been the only copy in Mexico, and quite possibly provided Quiroga with his first taste of More. See p. 5 of *Sir Thomas More in New Spain: A Utopian Adventure of the Renaissance* by Sílvio Zavala (London, The Hispanic and Luso-Brazilian Councils, 1955).
86. FC (1988), op. cit., vol. I, p. 219.
87. Cit. Albert A. Sicroff (1985), op. cit., p. 340.
88. Hugh Thomas (1993), op. cit., p. 161.
89. Ibid., p. 455; with unusual honesty, he had admitted that 'at the same time it brings us both honour and profit: things which very rarely can be found in the same bag'.
90. *Probanza Hecha en la Villa Segunda de la Frontera*, Icazbalceta, op. cit., vol. I, p. 447.
91. Hugh Thomas (1993), op. cit., p. 168.
92. *Los Esclavos Indios en la Nueva España* by Sílvio Zavala (Mexico, El Colegio Nacional Luis González Obregón, 1968), p. 30.
93. Ibid., p. 31.
94. For more on this conflict, see Dealy (1976), op. cit., pp. 11–12.
95. George Kubler (1948), op. cit., vol. I, p. 13.
96. Painted by Christoph Weiditz, the only portrait of Cortés ever done from life.
97. Almost a year later, the Audiencia would write to the Crown that they were still beset by complaints from the Indian vassals of Cortés in these towns. See ENE, vol. II, p. 124.
98. FC (1988), op. cit., book X.
99. The god Quetzalcoatl was said to have lived there. See Hugh Thomas (1993), op. cit., p. 474.
100. The palace had been granted to the Audiencia by a royal cedula of 12 July 1530. The possession of the palace was confirmed again by a cedula of 30 April 1532.

101. Letter of Quiroga to the Consejo de las Indias of 14 August 1531, CDI, vol. XIII, p. 427.

102. *The Slave Trade* by Hugh Thomas (London, Picador, 1997), pp. 122–3.

103. The words of Fernández de Oviedo regarding Santo Domingo in the 1530s – cit. Hugh Thomas (1997), op. cit., p. 103.

104. Alfredo Chavero (1888), op. cit., vol. II, p. 189.

105. ENE, vol. II, p. 17, a letter from Oidor Salmerón to the Crown of 27 February 1531.

106. Alfredo Chavero (1888), op. cit., vol. II, p. 189.

107. Ibid.

108. Thomas More (1965), op. cit., p. 69; E. W. Palm notes the connection between the situation of Tenochtitlan and that of Utopia in *Tenochtitlan y la Ciudad Ideal de Dürer* (Journal de la Société des Américanistes, Paris, vol. XL, pp. 59–66).

109. Thomas More (1965), op. cit., p. 73.

110. Ibid.

111. Hugh Thomas (1993), op. cit., p. 477 fn. 64.

112. Thomas More (1965), op. cit., p. 69.

113. Ibid., p. 80.

114. R. W. Chambers (1935), op. cit., p. 142.

115. *Tractatus de Immortalitae Animae* by Pomponazzi, cit. R. W. Chambers (1935), op. cit., p. 135.

116. Thomas More (1965), op. cit., p. 120.

117. Ibid.

118. This was Erasmus's marginal note in his own copy of the book – cit. J. H. Hexter (1965), op. cit., p. 45.

119. Ibid., p. 46.

120. ENE, vol. II, p. 181, a letter from the *oidores* to the Crown of 5 July 1532.

121. ENE, vol. I, p. 152, a letter from the Crown to Diego de Ordaz of 24 August 1529.

122. CDI, vol. XLI, pp. 92–3 – a letter from the Audiencia to the Crown of 14 August 1531.

123. Letter of Quiroga to the Consejo de las Indias of 14 August 1531, CDI, op. cit., vol. XIII, p. 424.

124. Ibid.

125. These authors are all cited by Quiroga in 'Información en Derecho' (CDI, op. cit., vol. X, pp. 333–516) – hereafter IED.

126. Letter of Quiroga to the Consejo de las Indias of 14 August 1531, CDI, op. cit., vol. XIII, p. 423.

127. Letter from Rodrigo de Albornoz to Charles V, 15 December 1525, Icazbalceta, op. cit., vol. I, p. 500.

128. Ibid., vol. I, pp. 498–9.

129. Letter of Quiroga to the Consejo de las Indias of 14 August 1531, CDI, op. cit., vol. XIII, p. 424.

130. Ibid.

131. Ibid., p. 421.
132. Ibid., p. 422.
133. Ibid.
134. Ibid., p. 424.
135. Ibid.
136. Ibid., p. 425.

CHAPTER EIGHT

1. FC, op. cit., vol. II, p. 846.
2. ENE, op. cit., vol. I, p. 126, a letter of 10 July 1529 states: 'This great city of Tenuxtitan [*sic*] is all surrounded by water,' and that the nearest piece of land is a quarter of a league distant – but on some sides of the city is up to 2 leagues away.
3. Ibid., vol. I, p. 58ff.
4. Ibid., vol. II, p. 736.
5. Ibid., vol. II, p. 737.
6. Motolinía (1985), op. cit., p. 75.
7. Ibid.
8. Vasco de Quiroga, IED, op. cit., p. 483.
9. This censure was so strong that, as Jacques Soustelle put it, 'one has the feeling that the Indians were very clearly aware of their strong natural inclination to alcoholism, and that they were quite determined to work against this evil, and to control themselves'; Soustelle (1961), op. cit., p. 156.
10. FC, op. cit., vol. I, p. 238.
11. Ibid., vol. I, p. 239.
12. Ibid., vol. I, p. 349.
13. Ibid.
14. This is how Quiroga was referred to in the *residencia* against him taken in 1536 – *Testimonio del Proceso de Residencia*, in *Don Vasco de Quiroga: Documentos* (ed. Rafael Aguayo Spencer) (Mexico, Talleres Gráficos 'Acción Moderna Mercantil' 1939), p. 412.
15. *Crónica de la Orden de N.P.S. Augustin en las Provincias de la Nueva España* by Juan de Grijalva (Mexico, 1924; written 1624), p. 56.
16. *Requerimiento* of Quiroga to the governors of Mexico and Santiago-Tlatelolco, 19 March 1534 – in *Vasco de Quiroga y sus Hospitales Pueblos de Santa Fe* by J. B. Warren (Michoacán, Editorial Universitaria Morelia, 1977), p. 187.
17. Ibid., p. 176.
18. Ibid., pp. 178–9.
19. Ibid., p. 179.
20. Motolinía (1985), op. cit., p. 104.
21. J. B. Warren (1977), op. cit., p. 183.
22. Ibid.
23. Ibid.

24. HC, op. cit., p. 76.
25. FC, op. cit., vol. I, p. 208. This is, rather, the codex's description of Quetzalcoátl and his vassals – however, since Mexican popular mythology came to identify Quetzalcoátl with the Europeans, and since Sahagún began to compile these stories several decades after the conquest, the identification is fairly secure.
26. J. B. Warren (1977), op. cit., p. 176, 180.
27. Ibid., p. 176.
28. Ibid.
29. Ibid., p. 181.
30. Fintan B. Warren (1961), op. cit., p. 57.
31. Juan de Grijalva (1924), op. cit., p. 56.
32. A letter from the Audiencia of 3 November 1532, for instance, states that Quiroga does not sign as 'he was not found present when the time came to sign off this sheet' – ENE, op. cit., vol. II, letter 120.
33. Fintan B. Warren (1963), op. cit., p. 46.
34. Ibid., p. 50.
35. Juan de Grijalva (1924), op. cit., pp. 54–5.
36. Fintan B. Warren (1963), op. cit., p. 43.
37. Ibid., pp. 43–4.
38. Ibid., p. 44.
39. ENE, op. cit., vol. II, p. 218.
40. For instance, the letter of Hernando de Cantillería of 5 June 1532, saying that he has been thirteen years in the conquest and that 'I humbly beg in remuneration for all my service that I should be apportioned Indians in the general parcelling out of the land, so that I can sustain myself, my wife, my children, weaponry and horse.' ENE, op. cit., vol. II, letter 108.
41. ENE, op. cit., vol. III, letter 155.
42. Ibid., vol. II, p. 185.
43. Fintan B. Warren (1963), op. cit., p. 55.
44. Ibid.
45. Pablo Beaumont (1932), op. cit., vol. II, p. 259.
46. Ibid., p. 57.
47. IED, p. 335.
48. Pablo Beaumont (1932), op. cit., vol. II, p. 166.
49. Rafael Aguayo Spencer (1939), op. cit., p. 418.
50. Ibid., p. 421.
51. Ibid., p. 418.
52. Ibid., p. 417.
53. Ibid., p. 419.
54. Ibid., p. 420.
55. Ibid., p. 440.
56. J. B. Warren (1977), op. cit., p. 182.
57. Ibid., p. 181.
58. Rafael Aguayo Spencer (1939), op. cit., p. 414.
59. Ibid., p. 413.

60. Ibid.

61. Ibid., p. 417.

62. Ibid., p. 433.

63. Pablo Beaumont (1932), op. cit., vol. II, p. 169.

64. Juan de Grijalva (1924), op. cit., p. 54.

65. Ibid., p. 55. This figure is also cited by Juan de Joseph Moreno in his 1766 biography of Quiroga (p. 22).

66. From the *Reglas y Ordenanzas Para el Gobierno de los Hospitales de Santa Fe de México y Michoacán* in Rafael Aguayo Spencer (1939), p. 249.

67. Ibid., p. 254.

68. As Quiroga would put it: 'Today there are so many Montezumas to sustain in this country that I don't understand how they can be supported'; IED, p. 367.

69. Motolinía (1985), op. cit., pp. 68, 70.

70. Rafael Aguayo Spencer (1939), op. cit., p. 249.

71. *Don Vasco de Quiroga: Taumaturgo de la Organización Social* by Rafael Aguayo Spencer (Mexico, Ediciones Oasis, 1970), p. 30.

72. *Don Vasco de Quiroga (Protector de los Indios)* by Francisco Martín Hernández (Salamanca, Publicaciones Universidad Pontificia Salamanca, 1993), p. 97.

73. Rafael Aguayo Spencer (1939), op. cit., p. 254.

74. Juan de Grijalva (1924), op. cit., p. 56. This spring was still well known in the late nineteenth century, but has now been swamped by the modern suburb of Santa Fe.

75. Juan Joseph Moreno (1766), op. cit., p. 21.

76. Juan de Grijalva (1924), op. cit., p. 55. De Borja appears to have been appointed in 1535.

77. Ibid.

78. From the '*Reglas y Ordenanzas Para el Gobierno de los Hospitales de Santa Fe de México y Michoacán*', in Rafael Aguayo Spencer (1939), op. cit., p. 258.

79. Juan de Grijalva (1924), op. cit., p. 55.

80. Juan Joseph Moreno (1766), op. cit., p. 22.

81. Ibid., p. 56.

82. Jacques Soustelle (1961), op. cit., p. 95.

83. Ibid., p. 142.

84. *Zumárraga and the Mexican Inquisition: 1536–1543* by Richard E. Greenleaf (Washington, American Academy of Franciscan History, 1961), p. 43. See also *Pueblos-Hospitales y Guatáperas de Michoacán: Las Realizaciones Arquitectónicas de Vasco de Quiroga y Fray Juan de San Miguel* by Juan B. Artigas (Mexico, Universidad Nacional Autónoma de México, 2001), p. 23. On similarities between the *pueblos-hospitales* and the traditional life of Michoacán, see Paz Serrano Gassent (2001), op. cit., pp. 214–5.

85. *The Spiritual Conquest of Mexico* by Robert Ricard, tr. Lesley Bird Simpson (Berkeley, University of California Press, 1966), p. 29.

86. R. C. Padden (1967), op. cit., p. 251.

87. FC, op. cit., vol. II, p. 815.

88. Fintan B. Warren (1963), op. cit., p. 45.
89. Ibid.
90. Testimony of Juan de San Román in the *residencia* – Rafael Aguayo Spencer (1939), op. cit., p. 450ff.
91. Juan Joseph Moreno (1766), op. cit., p. 19.
92. Juan de Grijalva (1924), op. cit., p. 57.
93. Francisco Martín Hernández (1993), p. 94.
94. Fintan B. Warren (1963), op. cit., pp. 49–50.
95. Jacques Soustelle (1961), op. cit., p. 128.
96. FC, op. cit., vol. II, p. 538.
97. Ibid., vol. I, p. 383.
98. Ibid., vol. I, p. 384 – '*el que curiosamente mira a la mujer, adultera con la vista*'.
99. Ibid.
100. IED, p. 337.
101. Ibid., p. 467.
102. Ibid., p. 482.
103. Ibid., p. 363.
104. In a royal cedula of 20 February 1534 – see CDH, op. cit., vol. I, pp. 153–9; also Sílvio Zavala (1968), op. cit., for a good elucidation.
105. IED, p. 333.
106. Ibid., pp. 370–1.
107. Ibid., p. 494.
108. Ibid., p. 493.
109. Ibid., p. 511.
110. Ibid.
111. Ibid.
112. Juan de Grijalva (1924), op. cit., p. 81.
113. Ibid.
114. Ibid.
115. IED, p. 358.
116. Ibid., p. 364.

CHAPTER NINE

1. As late as the seventeenth century, the settlers in Portugal's North Atlantic colony of Cape Verde were using textiles – *barafula* – as the principal means of exchange, simply because of the lack of metal for coinage: see *Atlantic Islands: Madeira, the Azores and the Cape Verdes in Seventeenth Century Commerce and Navigation* by T. Bentley Duncan (Chicago, University of Chicago Press, 1972), p. 223, and *Monumenta Misionaria Africana: África Ocidental* by Antônio Brásio (Lisboa, Agência Geral do Ultramar, 1968, 5 vols) vol. IV, pp. 507–8. Meanwhile, in Senegambia, silver dollars did not become common currency until the 1720s: see *Economic Change in Precolonial Africa: Senegambia in the Era of the Slave Trade* by Philip D. Curtin (Madison, University of Wisconsin Press, 1975), pp. 264–5.

2. *Republic* by Plato, book VI, 509d–511e, tr. G. M. A. Grube (Indiana, Hackett Publishing Company, 1992).

3. *New Atlantis* by Francis Bacon, in *Three Early Modern Utopias*, ed. Susan Bruce (Oxford, Oxford University Press, 1999), p. 177.

4. Ibid.

5. Ibid., p. 185.

6. Ibid., p. 173.

7. *Gulliver's Travels* by Jonathan Swift (Harmondsworth, Penguin, 1985; first published 1726).

8. *Utopia and the Ideal Society: A Study of English Utopian Writing 1516–1700* by J. C. Davis (Cambridge, Cambridge University Press, 1989), p. 15.

9. *Introduction to The Social Contract and Discourses* of Jean-Jacques Rousseau by G. D. H. Cole (London, J. M. Dent, 1961; first published 1913), p. ix.

CHAPTER TEN

1. *Relaciones y Memorias de la Provincia de Michoacán, 1579–1581*, eds. Álvaro Ochoa and Gerardo Sánchez (Morelia, Universidad Michoacana de San Nicolás Hidalgo, 1985), p. 44.

2. Ibid.

3. Pablo Beaumont (1932), op. cit., vol. II, p. 34.

4. *Relación de las Ceremonias y Ritos, Población y Gobierno de los Indios de la Provincia de Michoacán* (Madrid, Imprenta de la Viuda de Calero, 1869 – hereafter known as *Relación*), p. 67. This crucial document as to the customs and history of the Purépecha prior to the conquest was written in around 1540 by a Franciscan missionary who had clearly already spent some time in Michoacán – the author of the *Relación* has never been identified with certainty.

5. Ibid.

6. Ibid., p. 14.

7. Beaumont (1932), op. cit., vol. II, p. 6.

8. *Relación*, op. cit., p. 14.

9. *The Conquest of Michoacán: The Spanish Domination of the Tarascan Kingdom in Western Mexico, 1521–1530* by J. Benedict Warren (Norman, University of Oklahoma Press, 1985), p. 10ff.

10. These details are known from the drawings which accompanied the original 1541 version of the *Relación*.

11. Bernardino Verastique (2000), op. cit., p. 13 – this was in the 1470s.

12. *Relación*, op. cit., p. 15.

13. Ibid., p. 16.

14. Álvaro Ochoa and Gerardo Sánchez (1985), op. cit., p. 40.

15. Ibid., p. 182.

16. A priest writing in 1581 says: 'Before the plague I counted 3,500 taxpayers in one town of whom more than 500 were older than 80 or 90' – ibid., p. 183.

17. *Relación*, op. cit., p. 16.
18. Ibid., p. 20.
19. Álvaro Ochoa and Gerardo Sánchez (1985), op. cit., p. 51.
20. Known from the illustrations of the *Relación*.
21. *Relación*, op. cit., p. 41f.
22. Álvaro Ochoa and Gerardo Sánchez (1985), op. cit., p. 40.
23. Bernardino Verastique (2000), op. cit., p. 33.
24. All this known from the illustrations of the *Relación*.
25. *Relación*, op. cit., p. 50.
26. Ibid.
27. Ibid.
28. Ibid., p. 51.
29. Bernardino Verastique (2000), op. cit., p. 17.
30. Ibid., p. 17.
31. *Relación*, op. cit., p. 24.
32. Ibid., p. 22.
33. Ibid., pp. 22–3.
34. Ibid., p. 15.
35. Ibid., p. 17.
36. All this known from the illustrations of the *Relación*.
37. *Relación*, op. cit., p. 68.
38. Pablo Beaumont (1932), op. cit., vol. II, p. 7.
39. Hugh Thomas (1993), op. cit., p. 472.
40. Pablo Beaumont (1932), op. cit., vol. II, p. 7.
41. Ibid., p. 14.
42. Ibid., p. 17.
43. J. Benedict Warren (1985), op. cit., p. 148.
44. Bernardino Verastique (2000), op. cit., p. 80.
45. Ibid., p. 81.
46. J. Benedict Warren (1985), op. cit., p. 233.
47. Beaumont (1932), op. cit., vol. II, pp. 187–8.
48. Ibid., vol. II, p. 193ff.
49. See e.g. Juan Joseph Moreno (1766), op. cit., p. 33.
50. See 'Vasco de Quiroga, Jurista, y Defensor del Derecho del Indio Frente a la Encomienda' by Humberto Aguilar Cortés (in *Juegos Florales Conmemorativos del V Centenario del Natalicio de Don Vasco de Quiroga* (Morelia, Talleres Gráficos del Gobierno del Estado de Michoacán, 1971) by Humberto Aguilar Cortés et al.), p. 12.
51. The date of Quiroga's expedition is confirmed by a letter from the *ayuntamiento* of Granada in Michoacán, dated 3 September 1534, writing that 'ten months ago' Quiroga came to Michoacán (see ENE, op. cit., vol. III, p. 158) – and also his later *residencia* (see above, ch. 8, p. 143), taken in February 1536. Fray Francisco de Bolonia, for instance, Guardian of the Monastery of Tzintzuntzan, gave evidence that Quiroga first went to Michoacán 'two and a half or three years ago' – see Pablo Beaumont (1932), op. cit., vol. II, p. 166.

52. ENE, op. cit., vol. II, pp. 180–2 – dated 5 July 1532.
53. Juan Joseph Moreno (1766), op. cit., pp. 33–5.
54. Quiroga's words from his *residencia* – see Pablo Beaumont (1932), op. cit., vol. II, p. 162.
55. Rafael Aguayo Spencer (1939), op. cit., p. 436.
56. Ibid.
57. Pablo Beaumont (1932), op. cit., vol. II, p. 166; see also Juan Joseph Moreno (1766), op. cit., p. 34.
58. Juan Joseph Moreno (1766), op. cit., p. 34.
59. Pablo Beaumont (1932), op. cit., vol. II, p. 166.
60. ENE, vol. III, p. 158.
61. Ibid., vol. III, p. 169.
62. Rafael Aguayo Spencer (1970), op. cit., p. 48.
63. Rafael Aguayo Spencer (1939), op. cit., p. 428.
64. Ibid., p. 429.
65. Ibid., p. 430.
66. Bernardino Verastique (2000), op. cit., p. 94. The post had originally been offered to Fr. Luis de Fuensalida, who had declined.
67. Pablo Beaumont (1932), op. cit., vol. II, p. 365.
68. '*El dicho Señor electo primer obispo, hizo presentación cuyo tenor por su prolixidad no va aqui inserto.*' AGI, Legajo 67–23, cajón 5, estante 47 – cit. Nicolás León in *Vasco de Quiroga: Grandeza de su Persona y Su Obra* (Morelia, Universidad de San Nicolás Hidalgo, 1984; first published 1904), pp. 265–6.
69. *Documentos Inéditos Referentes al Ilustrísimo Señor Don Vasco de Quiroga*, ed. Nicolás León (Mexico, Antigua Librería Robredo de José Porrúa e Hijos, 1940), p. 17.
70. Juan Joseph Moreno (1766), op. cit., pp. 154–5; this story originates from Quiroga's *residencia*, and the evidence of Alonso Rodríguez (see Rafael Aguayo Spencer (1939), op. cit., p. 448).
71. Ibid.
72. Warwick Bray (2002), op. cit., p. 419.
73. Álvaro Ochoa and Gerardo Sánchez (1985), op. cit., p. 60.
74. Nicolás León (1940), op. cit., p. 13.
75. Álvaro Ochoa and Gerardo Sánchez (1985), op. cit., p. 60.
76. Alonso Ponce, travelling in 1584, wrote of his interpreter falling in at a bad ford – see *Relación Breve y Verdadera de Algunas Cosas de las Muchas que Sucedieron al Padre Fray Alonso Ponce en las Provincias de la Nueva España, Siendo Comisario General de Aquellas Partes* by Alonso Ponce (Madrid, Imprenta de la Viuda de Calero, 1873; 2 vols), vol. I, p. 526ff.
77. FC, vol. II, p. 682.
78. Ibid.
79. Ibid.
80. Álvaro Ochoa and Gerardo Sánchez (1985), op. cit., p. 61; also *Anales del Museo Michoacano* by Nicolás León (Morelia, Imp. y Lit. del Gobierno en la Escuela de Artes, 1888), p. 47.

81. *La Batalla por la Libertad: Bartolomé de Las Casas y Vasco de Quiroga* by Marco Antonio López López (Morelia, Ediciones Preparatoria Rector Hidalgo, 1993), p. 36.
82. Pablo Beaumont (1932), op. cit., vol. II, p. 169ff.
83. Bernardino Verastique (2000), op. cit., p. 33.
84. Ibid.
85. Robert Ricard (1966), op. cit., p. 37.
86. Bernardino Verastique (2000), op. cit., p. 135.
87. Rafael Aguayo Spencer (1970), op. cit., p. 59; Francisco Miranda Godinez (1967), op. cit., also mentions the celebrations on Quiroga's return.
88. *Grandeza de Michoacán* by Rodolfo Jasso Espinoza (Mexico, Talleres Gráficos de B. Costa-Amic, 1969), p. 68.
89. Thomas More (1965), op. cit., p. 31.
90. This interpretation is in *Recuerdo de Vasco de Quiroga* by Sílvio Zavala (Mexico, Editorial Porrúa, 1987), p. 66.
91. IED, op. cit., p. 364.
92. Rafael Aguayo Spencer (1970), op. cit., p. 215.
93. Having said this, it is also true that there were cultural similarities, which of course to an outsider would have seemed more pronounced. Alfredo López Austin writes that Mesoamerican cosmography had 'an ancient tradition shared by farmers from very different ethnic groups', and that there was a certain set of core ideas which allowed them to perceive situations in a similar way. See *Cosmovision, Religion and the Calendar of the Aztecs* by Alfredo López Austin in Warwick Bray (ed.) (2002), op. cit., p. 31.
94. Fernando Gómez (2001), op. cit., p. 50.
95. *The Humanism of Vasco de Quiroga's 'Información en Derecho'* by Anthony Pagden in *Humanismus und Neue Welt*, ed. Wolfgang Reinhard (Bonn, Deutsche Forschunggemeinschaft, 1987), p. 134.
96. Ibid., pp. 135–6.
97. Hugh Thomas (1997), op. cit., p. 98; *Fray Bartolomé de las Casas, a la luz de la moderna crítica histórica* by Angel Losada (Madrid, Editorial Tecnos, 1970), p. 206.
98. Hugh Thomas (1997), op. cit., p. 98.
99. IED, op. cit., p. 398.
100. Ibid., p. 389.
101. 'El Pátzcuaro de Don Vasco: un modelo de integración étnica y cultural' by Francisco Miranda in *Vasco de Quiroga: Educador de Adultos* by Francisco Miranda and Gabriela Briseño (eds.) (Pátzcuaro, Crefal-Colmich, 1984), p. 79.
102. This is, for instance, the argument in *The Politics of an Erasmian Lawyer* by Ross Dealy (Malibu, Undena Publications, 1976).
103. Alonso Ponce (1873), op. cit., vol. II, p. 2.
104. Álvaro Ochoa and Gerardo Sánchez (1985), op. cit., p. 92.
105. Ibid.
106. Juan de Grijalva (1924), op. cit., p. 217.

107. Ibid.

108. Rafael Aguayo Spencer (1939), op. cit., p. 430.

109. Ibid., p. 424 – the evidence of Francisco Castilleja.

110. Ibid., p. 440.

111. Alonso Ponce (1873), op. cit., vol. I, p. 525.

112. Nicolás León (1984), op. cit., p. 121.

113. Juan de Grijalva (1924), op. cit., p. 118.

114. That he did eventually learn enough Purépecha to speak to the Indians is argued by Luis Gonzalez y Gonzalez in *Humanistas Novohispanos de Michoacán* (Morelia, Universidad Michoacana de San Nicolás de Hidalgo, 1982), p. 14.

115. Francisco Martín Hernández (1993), op. cit., p. 116.

116. Ibid.

117. Rafael Aguayo Spencer (1939), op. cit., p. 440 – evidence of Alonso Rodríguez.

118. IED, op. cit., p.509.

119. Ibid., p. 386 – '*todo lo de esta tierra que depende de la conservación de ellos se acaba*'.

120. Rafael Aguayo Spencer (1939), op. cit., p. 447.

121. Ibid., p. 449.

122. Ibid., p. 446.

123. Many witnesses of the *residencia* concur about this.

124. Rafael Aguayo Spencer (1939), op. cit., p. 429 – the evidence of Ramiro, a Purépecha cacique.

125. Ibid., p. 424 – the evidence of Francisco Castilleja.

126. Cristóbal Cabrera, chapter XIX (1965), op. cit.

127. Ibid.

128. Ibid., chapter XVI.

CHAPTER ELEVEN

1. 'The Communist Manifesto' by Karl Marx, pp. 221–46 of *Karl Marx: Selected Writings* (ed. David McLellan) (Oxford, Oxford University Press, 1972), p. 240.

2. 'The theory of the Communists may be summed up in the single sentence: Abolition of private property.' Ibid., p. 233.

3. Ibid., p. 223.

4. Thomas More (1965), op. cit., pp. 46–7.

5. *Erewhon* by Samuel Butler (London, Heron Books, 1969; first published 1872), p. 8.

6. Ibid., p. 58.

7. Ibid., pp. 58–9.

8. Ibid., p. 74.

9. Ibid., p. 92.

10. Ibid., p. 278.

11. Ibid., p. 209.

12. Ibid., p. 221.
13. Ibid., pp. 226–7.
14. 'News From Nowhere' by William Morris (pp. 41–230 of *News From Nowhere and Other Writings*, ed. Clive Wilmer: London, Penguin, 1993; first published 1890), p. 91.
15. Ibid., p. 81.
16. Ibid., p. 224.
17. Ibid., p. 117ff.
18. *Looking Backward: 2000–1887* by Edward Bellamy (Mineola NY, Dover Publications, 1996; first published 1888), p. 27.
19. Ibid., p. 41ff.
20. Ibid., p. 30.
21. Karl Marx (1972), op. cit., p. 176ff.

CHAPTER TWELVE

1. Alonso Ponce (1873), op. cit., vol. I, pp. 524–5.
2. Álvaro Ochoa and Gerardo Sánchez (1985), op. cit., pp. 67–73.
3. Ibid., p. 139.
4. This is the estimate of Ramón López Lara in *Los Hospitales de la Concepción*, in *Vasco de Quiroga: Educador de Adultos*, eds. Francisco Miranda and Gabriela Briseño (Pátzcuaro, Crefal-Colmich, 1984), p. 21. However, it must be said that even this figure may not do justice to the enormous spread of hospitals evidenced in the parish breakdowns. For the sixteenth century, Lynn M. Gomez estimates that there were at least 132 such communities in Michoacán – see *Vasco de Quiroga: Otro Punto de Vista* by Lynne M. Gomez, pp. 414–35 of *Revista Comunidad* (August 1975), p. 426.
5. Juan de Grijalva (1924), op. cit., p. 218.
6. Ibid.
7. Ibid., p. 219.
8. Ibid.
9. Ramón López Lara (1984), op. cit., pp. 119–20.
10. Ibid., p. 120.
11. Ibid., p. 119.
12. Juan de Grijalva (1924), op. cit., p. 218. Beaumont argued that Quiroga had had too much of the credit for the founding of the hospitals, and that the real energy behind them had come from Fray Juan de San Miguel (Beaumont (1932), op. cit., vol. II, p. 360, vol. III, pp. 151–2). However, this is not borne out by early sources, such as those published in Ochoa and Sánchez from 1579–81 – one informant states specifically of the hospitals that the inventor of them was Don Vasco de Quiroga (p. 45). See also *Relación de los Obispados de Tlaxcala, Michoacán, Oaxaca y Otros Lugares en el Siglo XVI*, ed. Joaquín García Icazbalceta and Luis García Pimentel (Mexico, Casa del Editor, 1904), which has a document dated 1573 saying of Michoacán that 'all of them [the towns] have hospitals in the main

town in the area and in those surrounding it, most of which were made and founded by Bishop D. Vasco de Quiroga' (p. 55).

13. Pablo Beaumont (1932), op. cit., vol. II, pp. 313, 360.

14. Ibid.

15. Álvaro Ochoa and Gerardo Sánchez (1985), op. cit., p. 73ff on the hospitals of Xiquilpa, all founded by Franciscans; ibid., p. 196, on the hospital of Tiripetío, founded by Juan de Alvarado, brother of the famous conquistador who accompanied Cortés.

16. Cristóbal Cabrera (1965), op. cit., ch. XVI.

17. Ibid.

18. Ibid.

19. Ibid., ch. XVII.

20. Ibid.

21. Ibid.

22. Ibid.

23. Ibid.

24. Ibid., ch. XVIII.

25. As late as 1555, the Church Council convened in Mexico – at which Quiroga was present – complained that it was very inconvenient that the Indians were 'so spread out, and separated from one another by the fields, woods and hills, where many of them live like beasts'; *Concilios Provinciales Primero, y Segundo, Celebrados en la Muy Noble, y Muy Leal Ciudad de México, Presidiendo el Illmo. y Rmo. Señor D. Fr. Alonso de Montúfar, en los años de 1555 y 1565*, ed. Francisco Antonio Lorenzana (Mexico, Imprenta de el Superior Gobierno, 1769), p. 147.

26. Álvaro Ochoa and Gerardo Sánchez (1985), op. cit., p. 186 – the Spanish are *'inquietos esperando que si no este año sino este otro tendrán con que se yr a España'*.

27. Ibid.

28. Ibid.

29. R. C. Padden (1967), op. cit., stresses this point, citing a 1531 order of a census to see who was paying tribute, which had still not been carried out by 1567 (p. 237). The *oidores* were not even permitted to know what had been called for by Montezuma's old tribute rolls (p. 234).

30. See Alfonso Toro's introduction to his *Los Judíos en la Nueva España, selección de Documentos del Siglo XVI, correspondiente al Ramo de la Inquisición* (Mexico, Talleres Gráficos de la Nación, 1932), p. xxiv.

31. Ibid., p. xxvii. Toro writes that Zumárraga exercised his function with 'fanatical zeal' – *'con celo de fanático'*.

32. Ibid., p. 94. New converts to Christianity were repeatedly barred from emigrating to the New World – see above, ch. 4, p. 61.

33. Ibid.

34. Ibid., p. 98.

35. Ibid., p. 101.

36. Ibid., pp. 99–100.

37. Ibid., p. 98.

38. Richard E. Greenleaf (1961), op. cit., p. 14.
39. Alfonso Toro (1932), op. cit., p. 103.
40. Ibid., p. 108.
41. Ibid., p. 94.
42. Ibid., p. 133.
43. Pablo Beaumont (1932), op. cit., vol. III, p. 95.
44. Nicolas León (1904), op. cit., p. 32.
45. Pablo Beaumont (1932), op. cit., vol. III, p. 127.
46. Ibid., vol. III, p. 123.
47. Cristóbal Cabrera, Quiroga's constant companion between 1539 and 1545 was born in Burgos in the 1510–20 decade. See *Don Vasco de Quiroga y Arzobispado de Morelia* (Mexico, Editorial Jus, 1965), p. 107ff.
48. On 30 June 1539, Infante had presented a letter from the Council of the Indies to the Audienca in Mexico, giving him title to the *barrios de la laguna*. Although the Audiencia had been furious, they had little option in the end but to back his claim. Full accounts of the Infante affair are given in Fintan B. Warren (1963), op. cit., and Bernardino Verastique (2000), op. cit.
49. Fintan B. Warren (1963), op. cit., p. 87.
50. Infante lived from *c.* 1506–1574 – see *La Vida Michoacana en el Siglo XVI: Catálogo de los Documentos del Siglo XVI del Archivo Histórico de la Ciudad de Pátzcuaro*, ed. Rodrigo Martínez Baracs and Lydia Espinoza Morales (Mexico, Editorial Fuentes, 1999).
51. Nicolas León (1984), op. cit., p.325; the claim of caciques from Michoacán in a letter of 1549.
52. *Michoacán Histórico y Legendario* by Jesús Romero Flores (Mexico, Costa-Amic Editor, 1971), p. 35.
53. Fintan B. Warren (1963), op. cit., p. 94.
54. Ibid., p. 95.
55. Ibid.
56. Ibid., p. 96.
57. Ibid., p. 99.
58. Ibid., p. 95.
59. Ibid., p. 96.
60. Ibid.
61. Ibid., p. 97.
62. Ibid., p. 98.
63. Ibid., p. 95.
64. As late as 1682, documents complained about the tributes demanded from the hospitals, 'because from time immemorial they have not paid any' ('*porque an estado de tiempo immemorial a esta parte en no pagarla*'). See AAM, Santa Fe de la Laguna, Legajo 1, no. 37.
65. Nicolas León (1984), op. cit., p. 10.
66. Ibid.
67. Ibid., pp. 22, 27.
68. Ibid., p. 5.

69. Ibid.
70. Bernardino Verastique (2000), op. cit., p. 130.
71. Ibid.
72. Pablo Beaumont (1932), op. cit., vol. III, p. 277.
73. Ibid., p. 277.
74. Ibid.
75. A royal cedula of 20 September 1537 says that Viceroy Mendoza had informed the Spanish court that Quiroga was already considering how and where to build the cathedral – Pablo Beaumont (1932), op. cit., vol. II, p. 364.
76. Nicolas León (1984), op. cit., p. 300.
77. Ibid., p. 301.
78. Ibid.
79. Pablo Beaumont (1932), op. cit., vol. II, p. 370.
80. Ibid.
81. Ibid.
82. Ibid. Another theory has it that the original name of Pátzcuaro was 'Tzacapu-Hamacutin Pátzcuaro', meaning 'the site of the stone that signals the entry to paradise' – *Don Vasco de Quiroga y la Ciudad de Pátzcuaro* by Antonio Arriaga Ochoa (Mexico, Editorial Libros de México, 1978), p. 27.
83. Ibid., p. 371.
84. *La Nobleza Indígena de Pátzcuaro en la Época Virreinal* by Delfina Esmeralda López Sarrelangue (Mexico, Universidad Nacional Autónoma de México, Mexico, 1965), p. 75.
85. Nicolas León (1984), op. cit., p. 302.
86. *El Pátzcuaro de Don Vasco: un modelo de integración étnica y cultural* by Francisco Miranda, pp. 77–96 of Francisco Miranda and Gabriela Briseño, eds. (1984), op. cit., p. 85ff.
87. Pablo Beaumont (1932), op. cit., vol. II, p. 371ff. The letter was dated 26 June, so Quiroga is unlikely to have received it before November 1539.
88. Juan Joseph Moreno (1766), op. cit., says that Quiroga lived for a year in Tzintzuntzan before embarking on moving the cathedral to Pátzcuaro. Beaumont suggests this means that the transfer of the cathedral must have taken place 1539–40.
89. George Kubler (1948), op. cit., vol. II, p. 309.
90. *História de la Provincia de San Nicolas de Tolentino* by Diego Basalenque (Mexico, Tip. Barbedillo y Comp., 1886; first published 1673), p. 449.
91. Ibid.
92. *História Eclesiástica Indiana* by Gerónimo de Mendieta (Mexico, Antigua Librería, 1870; written c. 1595), p. 513 – '*los demas bienes temporales (que eran lo que los indios deseaban, como el pueblo de los judíos, sin acordarse de los del cielo)*'.
93. Miranda suggests that Quiroga's decision to move the see to Pátzcuaro was behind the running feud he later developed with the Franciscans;

Francisco Miranda (1984), op. cit. – see also below, ch. 13, p. 233 and 15, pp. 269–71.

94. Delfina Esmeralda López Sarrelangue (1965), op. cit., p. 61.
95. Ibid.
96. Ibid., p. 66.
97. Bernardino Verastique (2000), op. cit., p. 94.
98. Pablo Beaumont (1932), op. cit., vol. II, p. 370.
99. Álvaro Ochoa and Gerardo Sánchez (1985), op. cit., p. 115.
100. *Las Primeras Juntas Eclesiásticas de México (1524–1555)*, ed. Cristóforo Gutiérrez Vega (Roma, Centro de Estudios Superiores, 1991), p. 265. A meeting of 1539, at which Quiroga was present, stated that the Indians were not to have 'fires by night or day in front of crosses or patios, because this used to be their custom in their idolatry'.
101. As late as 1555, the Purépecha nobles complained of all the suffering that the people underwent due to the change of city. See Delfina Esmeralda López Sarrelangue (1965), op. cit., p. 61ff.
102. Diego Basalenque (1886), op. cit., p. 449.
103. George Kubler (1948), op. cit., vol. II, p. 309.
104. Álvaro Ochoa and Gerardo Sánchez (1985), op. cit., p. 115ff.
105. Ibid.

CHAPTER THIRTEEN

1. From 1539 onwards, these mines were opened up across Michoacán. See Pablo Beaumont (1932), op. cit., vol. III, p. 70.
2. The 1540s saw a rapid growth in the quantity of all types of cattle in Michoacán. Ibid., vol. III, pp. 62–3, 71.
3. See Mario Cohen, in Alcalá (1995), op. cit., p. 448; also Vitorino Magalhães Godinho (1969), op. cit., pp. 479–83.
4. Álvaro Ochoa and Gerardo Sánchez (eds.) (1985), op. cit., pp. 191–2: '*yo lo e bisto estar martillando con una piedra en obras de yglesias por no tener picos ... esto se hazia en muchas partes.*'
5. Gerónimo de Mendieta (1870), op. cit., p. 515.
6. The estimate of the chronicler Alonso de la Rea – cit. Delfina Esmeralda López Sarrelangue (1965), op. cit., p. 72.
7. Pablo Beaumont (1932), op. cit., vol. III, p. 141.
8. Álvaro Ochoa and Gerardo Sánchez (eds.) (1985), op. cit., p. 115; see also *Anales del Museo Michoacano* by Nicolas León (Morelia, Imp. y Lit. del Gobierno en la Escuela de Artes, 1888–90; 3 vols), vol. II, p. 42.
9. Álvaro Ochoa and Gerardo Sánchez (eds.) (1985), op. cit., p. 73.
10. Ibid., p. 89.
11. Ibid.
12. This was the unanimous view of the people of Tiripetío – ibid., p. 183.
13. Juan Joseph Moreno (1766), op. cit., p. 72ff.
14. Ibid., p. 58.
15. Juan de Grijalva (1924), op. cit., p. 220.

16. Nicolas León (1888), op. cit., vol. II, p. 172.
17. Ibid.
18. For a full account of the school of San Nicolas, see Francisco Miranda Godinez (1967), op. cit. The building of this school probably got under way c. 1542.
19. Ibid.
20. The precise dates of Quiroga's stay in Spain are unclear. Pablo Beaumont, citing an Indian source, says that he stayed from 1547 to 1554 (vol. III, p. 300); Nicolas León (1984), op. cit., p. 158, cites a document of 1555 from Pátzcuaro which supports this. However, a letter from the canons and caciques of Pátzcuaro, dated 12 March 1549, claims to have received Quiroga's letter telling of his safe arrival only on 6 January 1549, implying that he had arrived in the summer of 1548 at the earliest (see Nicolas León (1984), op. cit., p. 314). Quiroga was frequently in Mexico for legal cases, and so perhaps the 1547–54 gap refers to his absence from Michoacán, rather than to his presence in Spain. In her introduction to Vasco de Quiroga: La Utopía en América (Madrid, Historia 16, 1992), Paz Serrano Gassent argues that he was in Spain between 1548 and 1553 (p. 14).
21. Tata Vasco: A Great Reformer of the Sixteenth Century by Paul L. Callens (Mexico, Editorial Jus, 1959), p. 65ff.
22. Nicolas León (1904), op. cit., p. 53.
23. Fernando Gómez (2001), op. cit., p. 182.
24. Paz Serrano Gassent (1992), op. cit., p. 14.
25. Cristóbal Cabrera, op. cit., says that his main reason for returning to Spain was to argue for the Indians – chapter XVIII; Juan Joseph Moreno (1766), op. cit., also mentions the privileges (p. 67).
26. Juan Joseph Moreno (1766), op. cit., p. 67.
27. Ibid.
28. Historia del Colegio Primitivo y Nacional de San Nicolás Hidalgo by Julián Bonavit (Morelia, Universidad Michoacano, 1958), p. 37ff.
29. Nicolas León (1940), op. cit., p. 14.
30. Ibid., p. 13.
31. Ibid.
32. Ibid., p. 11ff.
33. Ibid., p. 14; the last phrase doubtless being a barbed reference to their poor attendance at church.
34. Ibid., p. 22.
35. Icazbalceta, vol. II, p. 244.
36. Cristóforo Gutiérrez Vega (1991), op. cit., p. 277.
37. Ibid., p. 288.
38. Nicolas León (1984), op. cit., p. 309.
39. In Yucatán, for instance, one Francisco Hernández complained about the 'Franciscan friars who whipped, maltreated and charged tributes to the Indians'. Alfonso Toro (1924), op. cit., p. 123.
40. Ibid., p. 161.

41. One of the letters that Quiroga received in 1549 would have confirmed this to him, as his sources told him that neither lime nor stones was being brought for the building works except that which was brought by cart. Nicolas León (1984), op. cit., p. 307.
42. Ibid., p. 309.
43. Ibid.
44. Ibid., p. 308.
45. Much was made of the distance of the city from water sources, and of the backbreaking work in digging canals. This is supported by the evidence of a traveller in the 1580s, who wrote that the water has to be brought from 'far from here, by way of a canal' – Alonso Ponce (1873), op. cit., vol. I, p. 530.
46. Nicolas León (1984), op. cit., p. 317.
47. Ibid., p. 323.
48. Ibid., p. 324ff.
49. Ibid., p. 324.
50. AAM, Santa Fe de la Laguna, Legajo 2, no. 6.
51. By 1650, the rector of the two institutions was expected to spend half of the year in each one – AAM, Santa Fe de la Laguna, Legajo 1, no. 108.
52. AAM, Legajo 1, no. 9.
53. AHP, Caja 1, Expediente 34, Hoja 246A.
54. Ibid., 248A–250A.
55. Pablo Beaumont (1932), op. cit., vol. III, p. 294.
56. Ibid.
57. Fernando Gómez (2001), op. cit., p. 182.
58. *Empire's Children: The People of Tzintzuntzan* by George M. Foster (Mexico, Imprenta Nuevo Mundo SA, 1948), p. 18.
59. Alonso Ponce (1873), op. cit., vol. I, p. 532, describes travelling past ghost towns.
60. Ibid., vol. II, p. 4; vol. I, p. 529. That the Church was aware that these dances referred to old customs is apparent through a chapter of the 1555 Church Council in Mexico, which stated: 'The Indians of these parts are very inclined towards dances and celebrations ... they tend to mix in some things with the bitter taste of the old ways into these dances.' Francisco Antonio Lorenzana (1769), op. cit., p. 146.
61. Ibid., vol. I, p. 525 – in Acambaro, Ponce saw farriers 'to the sound of a tambourine, hammering and working iron very slowly, the masons were dancing and working stone to the sound of another'.
62. Ibid., vol. I, pp. 532–3.
63. Ibid., vol. I, p. 532.
64. Diego Basalenque (1886), op. cit., p. 125.
65. Álvaro Ochoa and Gerardo Sánchez (eds.) (1985), op. cit., p. 118.
66. By the latter part of the sixteenth century, even small towns might have one or two Purépecha organists – ibid., p. 63.
67. Ibid., pp. 124–5.
68. Ibid., pp. 450–1.

69. Quiroga's distrust of the profit motive is underlined in *Vasco de Quiroga's 'Regula Ubi Commodum'* by Ross Dealy (Bologna, Societá Editorice Il Mulino, 1978), where Dealy points to Quiroga's phrase in his 'Información en Derecho', '*regula ubi commodum*', which he applies to the institution of slavery – where there is no profit, there is no reason that there may be damage.

70. *Michoacán Histórico y Legendario* by Jesús Romero Flores (Mexico, Costa-Amic Editor, 1971), p. 78.

71. *Ideas Utópicas de los Evangelizadores en América* by Higilio Alvarez Constantino (Morelia, Ediciones del Comité de Festejos del LIII Aniversario de la Fundación de la Escuela Normal Urbana Federal, 1968), p. 2ff.

72. Ibid.

73. Personal communication from Sr Armando Mauricio Escobar Olmedo on a letter in AGI requesting examples of art using feathers to be sent out to Michoacán.

74. George M. Foster (1948), op. cit., pp. 10, 130.

75. Higilio Alvarez Constantino (1968), op. cit., p. 31.

76. Ibid., pp. 47–9.

77. That God and nature were the same was the opinion of Pedro de la Torre, a doctor in Veracruz, in 1551. Alfonso Toro (1924), op. cit., p. 119.

78. Ibid., p. 192.

79. Ibid., pp. 100, 103.

80. José Toribio Medina (1905), op. cit., p. 94.

81. Ibid., p. 138.

82. Ibid., p. 13.

83. Ibid., pp. 36, 50.

84. Ibid., p. 13.

85. On 9 January 1550, Miguel de Espinosa agreed to teach his neighbour in Pátzcuaro Pedro Díaz Gordillo to read and write, in exchange for 30 gold pesos, two shirts, a horse, some leather sandals, some boots and two pairs of shoes – see Rodrigo Martínez Baracs and Lydia Espinosa Morales (1999), op. cit., p. 35.

86. *Os Portugueses nos Ríos da Guiné: 1500–1900* by Antonio Carreira (Lisboa, Litografia Tejo, 1984), p. 40; also Antonio Brásio (1963), op. cit., vol. III, p. 407. Pedro was commissary in Cuzco of the Inquisitional tribunal of Lima around 1580. See *Historia del Tribunal del Santo Oficio de la Inquisición de Lima (1569–1820)* by J. Toribio Medina (Santiago de Chile, Imprenta Gutenberg, 1887; 2 vols), vol. I, p. 134.

87. *Vasco de Quiroga et Bartolomé de las Casas* by Marcel Bataillon, pp. 225–38 of his *Études sur Bartolomé de las Casas* (Paris, Centre de Recherches de l'Institut d'Études Hispaniques, 1965), p. 226.

88. Cristóbal Cabrera, op. cit., chapter XIX; Cabrera says that this request came from the Chancellor and the Patriarch of the Indies.

89. Marcel Bataillon (1965), op. cit., pp. 226–7.

90. Cristóbal Cabrera, op. cit., chapter XIX.

91. Paz Serrano Gassent (1992), op. cit., p. 16.
92. Juan Blazquez Miguel (1988), p. 139. They did not introduce a statute until 1592; but, curiously, were the last of the religious orders to lift the restriction, as late as the 1920s.
93. Cit. Ramón López Lara (1984), op. cit., p. 125.
94. For more details on the Paraguayan missions, see *A Vanished Arcadia* by R. B. Cunninghame-Graham (Century, London, 1988; first published 1901) and *The Lost Paradise* by Philip Caraman (London, Sigwick & Jackson, 1975). The collectivism, the envy inspired in neighbouring colonies by the collectives, and the religious underpinning of the communities are all similarities between the work of Quiroga in Michoacán and that of the Jesuits in Paraguay.
95. Angel Losada (1970), op. cit., p. 247; also Hugh Thomas (1997), op. cit., p. 96.
96. Angel Losada (1970), op. cit., p. 247.
97. In a letter to his friend Bernal Díaz de Luco, he complains that he had not been 'called or named or taken heed of as an expert witness' – Marcel Bataillon (1965), op. cit., p. 227.
98. Ibid., pp. 227–8.
99. Ibid., p. 233ff.
100. Angel Losada (1970), op. cit., p. 271.
101. Ibid., p. 249.
102. So Zavala, for instance, tried to dispute that Quiroga had even been the author of the *De Debellandis Indis (En Busca del Tratado de Vasco de Quiroga, de Debellandis Indis, in Historia Mexicana, vol. XVII, no. 4, 1968)*.
103. *Don Vasco de Quiroga y su Tratado de Debellandis Indis* by Benno Biermann, pp. 193–7 of *Recuerdo de Vasco de Quiroga* by Sílvio Zavala (Mexico, Editorial Porrúa, 1987), p. 195.
104. Ibid., p. 196; Paz Serrano Gassent (1992), op. cit., p. 29.
105. Angel Losada (1970), pp. 103–22; also *El Padre las Casas y la Defensa de los Indios* by M. Bataillon and A. Saint-Lu (Barcelona, Editorial Ariel, 1976), pp. 10–15. There were also a few striking similarities between the two programmes, such as limits to the working day and rules on holidays.
106. Fernando Gómez (2001), op. cit., pp. 182–205.
107. Lewis Hanke (1959), op. cit., p. 40ff; in 1557, a note was sent to Melchor Cano saying that all judges had given their opinions except for him.
108. Ibid.; also Angel Losada (1970), op. cit., pp. 286–7.
109. Ramón López Lara (1984), op. cit., p. 120.
110. From the *Ordenanzas* in Rafael Aguayo Spencer (1939), op. cit., p. 259.
111. Ibid.
112. Ibid.
113. Ibid., p. 255.
114. Ibid., p. 258.
115. Thomas More (1965), op. cit., p. 80.
116. Rafael Aguayo Spencer (1939), op. cit., p. 258; Thomas More (1965), op. cit., p. 80.

117. Rafael Aguayo Spencer (1939), op. cit., p. 254; Thomas More (1965), op. cit., p. 126 on the respect of wives for husbands and children for elders, and pp. 82–3 on the respect accorded to the old.

118. Rafael Aguayo Spencer (1939), op. cit., pp. 249–50.

119. Ibid., p. 250.

120. Ibid.

121. Ibid.

122. Ibid., pp. 256–7.

123. Ibid., p. 255.

124. Thomas More (1965), op. cit., p. 70.

125. Rafael Aguayo Spencer (1939), op. cit., p. 255; Thomas More (1965), op. cit., p. 71.

126. Rafael Aguayo Spencer (1939), op. cit., p. 255.

127. Ibid., p. 256.

128. Ibid.

129. Ibid.

130. Ibid.

131. Ibid., p. 259; Thomas More (1965), op. cit., p. 84.

132. Rafael Aguayo Spencer (1939), op. cit., p. 250.

133. Thomas More (1965), op. cit., p. 84.

134. George M. Foster (1948), op. cit., p. 9.

135. Bernardino Verastique (2000), op. cit., p. 33.

136. Rafael Aguayo Spencer (1939), op. cit., p. 258.

137. Álvaro Ochoa and Gerardo Sánchez (1985), op. cit., p. 40.

138. Alonso Ponce (1873), op. cit., vol. II, pp. 2–3.

139. Nicolas León (1984), op. cit., pp. 314–15.

140. Rodrigo Martínez Baracs and Lydia Espinoza Morales, eds. (1999), op. cit., p. 35.

141. Ibid., p. 36.

142. Ibid., p. 38.

143. Hugh Thomas (1997), op. cit., pp. 103–4.

144. Ibid., p. 121–2.

CHAPTER FOURTEEN

1. *A History of West Africa* by J. D. Fage (Cambridge, Cambridge University Press, 1969; first published 1955), p. 13.

2. *Ancient Ghana and Mali* by Nehemiah Levtzion (New York, Africana Publishing Company, 1980; first published 1973), p. 5.

3. Ibid.

4. For similarities between Judaic practices and those of various West African peoples, see *Hebrewisms of West Africa: from Nile to Niger with the Jews* by Joseph J. Williams (London, George Allen & Unwin, 1930). See also *La Découverte de l'Afrique au Moyen Âge: Cartographes et Explorateurs* by Charles Bourel de la Roncière (vol. V of *Mémoires de la Société Royale de Géographie d'Égypte Publiés Sous les Auspice de Sa Majesté Fouad Ier, Roi*

d'Égypte – Cairo, Institut Français d'Archéologie Orientale, 1924).

5. Aldous Huxley (1994), op. cit.

6. Aldoux Huxley (1984), op. cit.

7. *The Dispossessed* by Ursula Le Guin (London, Victor Gollancz, 1999; first published 1974), pp. 146–7.

8. *We* by Yevgeny Zamyatin, tr. Bernard Guilbert Guerney (London, Jonathan Cape, 1970; first published 1924), p. 23.

9. *Darkness at Noon* by Arthiur Koestler (London, Hutchinson, 1973; first published 1940), p. 128.

10. Ibid., p. 183.

11. Ursula Le Guin (1999), op. cit., p. 54.

CHAPTER FIFTEEN

1. This information from his will – see Nicolas León (1904), op. cit., pp. 75–103 for Quiroga's will; pp. 103–4 for his possessions.

2. Ibid. Quiroga possessed two images of the Virgin, and a gold cross.

3. Ibid. Quiroga had two of these shirts.

4. Michoacán was a popular stopover en route to the rich mines of the North – see e.g. AHP, Caja 1, Expediente 33, 242A, which talks of the many people passing through. See also Rodrigo Martínez Baracs and Lydia Espinosa Morales (1999), op. cit., p. 46.

5. The Purépecha were often kidnapped by wandering settlers in this way – see AHP, Caja 1, Expediente 33, 242A–B.

6. This information as to the burial of his parents – and indeed the fact that Quiroga comes from Madrigal – is only known from Quiroga's will; see Nicolas León (1904), op. cit., p. 86.

7. *The Penguin History of Latin America* by Edwin Williamson (London, Penguin Press 1992), pp. 100, 113 – Williamson argues that Quiroga's hospitals pioneered the christianisation of the Mesoamerican peoples through organised settlements.

8. Julián Bonavit (1958), op. cit., p. 12.

9. Juan Joseph Moreno (1766), op. cit., p. 51 – the Church Council of 1555 banned Indians from being priests; hence, they could not learn theology in Quiroga's school.

10. Julián Bonavit (1958), op. cit., p. 10.

11. Ibid.

12. Nicolas León (1904), op. cit., p. 81 – the will of Quiroga.

13. The extent of this becomes apparent in Maturino Gilberti's famous *Arte de la Lengua Tarasca de Michoacán* (Mexico, Tipografía de la Oficina Impresora del Timbre, 1898; first published 1558) – the simple change of emphasis made '*vérani*' mean 'to go outside', while '*veráni*' meant 'to cry' (p. 17); or '*vehpáni*' 'to extinguish a candle or light' while '*vepáni*' meant 'to go crying' (p. 15).

14. So in June 1556 the Alcalde Mayor had to take a case against 'various

drunk Indians of the city [of Pátzcuaro]' (AHP, Caja 1, Expediente 30, Hoja 193).

15. AHP, Caja 1, Expediente 42, Hoja 280; Don Antonio was criticised for being 'full of vices' (*por ser vicioso*), and was stripped of his office for a year by the civil authority, Alonso Carrillo.

16. IED, op. cit., p. 364.

17. Nicolas León (1904), op. cit., pp. 103–4.

18. Francisco Antonio Lorenzana (1769), op. cit., p. 36.

19. Ibid.

20. Ibid., p. 54.

21. Ibid., pp. 92–3.

22. Ibid., p. 118.

23. Ibid., p. 125.

24. Nicolas León (1940), op. cit., p. 35.

25. Gerónimo de Mendieta (1870), op. cit., p. 716.

26. Ibid., p. 684.

27. AAM, Hospital de la Laguna, Legajo 2, no. 43.

28. Nicolas León (1984), op. cit., p. 272.

29. Ibid.

30. *Documentos Inéditos del Siglo XVI para la História de México*, ed. Mariano Cuevas (Mexico, Editorial Porrúa, 1975; first published 1914), p. 261.

31. Ibid.

32. *Libros y Libreros en el Siglo XVI*, ed. Francisco Fernández del Castillo (Mexico, Fondo de Cultura Económica 1982; first published 1914), p. 5.

33. Ibid., p. 7.

34. Mariano Cuevas (1975), op. cit., p. 254.

35. Ibid., p. 255.

36. Ibid.

37. Ibid., p. 262.

38. Ibid., p. 263.

39. Cit. Robert Ricard (1966), op. cit., p. 244.

40. Francisco Fernández del Castillo (1982), op. cit., pp. 25–7.

41. Paz Serrano Gassent (1992), p. 14ff.

42. *Tata Vasco: A Great Reformer of the 16th Century* by Paul Callens (Mexico, Editorial Jus, 1959), p. 96.

43. Álvaro Ochoa and Gerardo Sánchez (1985), op. cit., p. 184.

44. AHP, Caja 131, legajo 3 – this is a very interesting document from Francisco de Mendoza, a bookseller in Mexico who claimed to be owed 30 gold pesos by Don Antonio Huitzimengari, and listed the books which the cacique had bought.

45. Ibid., p. 196.

46. Ibid.

47. Juan Joseph Moreno (1766), op. cit., p. 142.

48. Ibid.

49. Delfina Esmeralda López Sarrelangue (1965), op. cit., pp. 308–12.

50. Ibid. for this detail and the following exchange between Quiroga and Don

Antonio; from the testimony of the scribe, Hernando Gutiérrez, who witnessed this event.

51. Pablo Beaumont (1932), op. cit., vol. III, p. 406.
52. Ibid.
53. Ibid.
54. Ibid.
55. *Noticias para Formar la Historia y la Estadistica del Obispado de Michoacán* by José Guadalupe Romero (Mexico, Imprenta de Vicente García Torres, 1862), p. 11.
56. Nicolas León (1984), op. cit., p. 170.
57. Pablo Beaumont (1932), op. cit., vol. III, p. 420.
58. Nicolas León (1904), op. cit., p. 97.
59. Ibid., p. 75.
60. Ibid., p. 84.
61. Ibid., p. 85.
62. Ibid., pp. 85, 95.
63. Paz Serrano Gassent (1992), op. cit., p. 23.
64. Juan Joseph Moreno (1766), op. cit., p. 144.
65. Francisco Miranda Godinez (1967), op. cit., p. 191.
66. Álvaro Ochoa and Gerardo Sánchez (1985), op. cit., p. 141.
67. Ibid.
68. Nicolas León (1904), op. cit., p. 91.
69. Fintan B. Warren (1963), op. cit., p. 112.
70. Ibid., pp. 114–15.
71. Nicolas León (1904), op. cit., p. 77.
72. AAM, Santa Fe de la Laguna, Legajo 2, no. 48.
73. Ibid.
74. See e.g., AAM, Santa Fe de México, Legajo 1, no. 2 – November 1633; the new rector of this hospital has come from the church in Valladolid.
75. Ibid; also AAM, Santa Fe de México, Legajo 1, no. 8.
76. E.g., AAM, Santa Fe de México, Legajo 1, no. 100–1633.
77. AAM, Santa Fe de la Laguna, Legajo 1, no. 108.
78. Juan Joseph Moreno (1766), op. cit., p. 66.
79. Felipe Tena Ramírez (1977), op. cit., p. 168.
80. Delfina Esmeralda López Sarrelangue (1965), op. cit., p. 75.
81. Ibid.
82. Nicolas León (1904), op. cit., p. 103.
83. Ibid.

SELECT BIBLIOGRAPHY

PRIMARY MATERIAL (UNPUBLISHED)

Morelia, Mexico: Arquivo del Arzobispado de Michoacán (in footnotes: AAM)
Santa Fe de la Laguna, Legajos 1–3.
Santa Fe del Río, Legajos 1–2.

Pátzcuaro, Mexico: Archivo Histórico de Pátzcuaro (in footnotes: AHP)
Caja 1, 1530–1570.

Sevilla, Spain: Archivo General de las Indias (in footnotes: AGI)
Escribanía, 159B
Indiferente 421, legajo 11, f. 148r
Indiferente 427, legajo 30, f. 95v–96v
Indiferente 737, no. 8
Indiferente 737, no. 27
Indiferente 1961, legajo 2, f. 20v–21v
Justicia, 148, ramo 3
Justicia, 155, ramo 2
Justicia 173, no. 1, ramo 2
Justicia 200, no. 2, ramo 1
Justicia 204, no. 3, ramo 3
Justicia 279, no. 2
Justicia 1019, no. 2, ramo 1
Lima 565, legajo 2, f. 270v
Mexico 1088, legajo 1 bis., f. 45v–49r
Mexico 1088, legajo 1, f. 226–227v
Mexico 1088, legajo 2, f. 27r–30v
Mexico 1088, legajo 2, f. 75v–76v
Mexico 1088, legajo 3, f. 184
Patronato 74, no. 2, ramo 1
Patronato 175, ramo 13
Patronato 251, ramo 23
Patronato 276, no. 4, ramo 276
Patronato 277, no. 3, ramo 38
Patronato 284, no. 1, ramo 238

PRIMARY MATERIAL (PUBLISHED)

On Vasco de Quiroga

Aguayo Spencer, Rafael (ed.), *Don Vasco de Quiroga: Documentos* (Mexico, Talleres Gráficos 'Acción Moderna Mercantil' 1939).

Cabrera, Cristóbal de, 'De Solicitanda Infidelium Conversione' (Various (1965), pp. 107–158).

León, Nicolas (ed.), *Documentos Inéditos Referentes al Ilustrísimo Señor Don Vasco de Quiroga* (Mexico, Antigua Librería Robredo de José Porrúa e Hijos, 1940).

——: *El Libro de Doctrina Cristiana* (Mexico, 1928).

Mendieta, Gerónimo de, *Historia Ecclesiástica Indiana* (Mexico, Antigua Librería, 1870; written *c.* 1595–96).

Quiroga, Vasco de, 'Carta del Licenciado Quiroga, Oidor de la Audiencia de Santo Domingo, al Consejo de Indias, Sobre la Venida de Aquel Obispo a la Presidencia de Dicho Tribunal, y Sobre Otros Asuntos' (Pacheco (1868), vol. 13, pp. 420–29).

——: 'Información en Derecho' (Pacheco (1868), vol. 10, pp. 333–516).

——: 'Reglas y Ordenanzas para el Gobierno de los Hospitales de Santa Fe de México y Michoacán' (in Aguayo Spencer (1939)).

——: 'Testamento' (in Aguayo Spencer (1939)).

Various, 'Litigio Sobre la Isla de Tultepec' (in Aguayo Spencer (1939)).

——: 'Testimonio del Proceso de Residencia' (in Aguayo Spencer (1939)).

Warren, Fintan B. (ed.), *Vasco de Quiroga en Africa* (Morelia, Fimax Publicistas, 1998).

——: *Vasco de Quiroga y sus Hospitales Pueblos de Santa Fe* (Michoacán, Editorial Universitaria Morelia, 1977).

On Mexico and the Indies

Anonymous, *Descripción del Virreinato del Perú* (ed. Boleslao Lewin) (Rosario, Universidad Nacional del Litoral, 1958).

Anonymous, *Relación Breve y Verdadera de Algunas Cosas de las Muchas que Suciedieron al Padre Fray Alonso Ponce en las Provincias de la Nueva España, Siendo Comisario General de Aquellas Partes* (Madrid, Imprenta de la Viuda de Calero, 1873, 2 vols; written *c.* 1584).

Anonymous, *Relación de las Ceremonias, Ritos, Población y Gobierno de los Indios de la Provincia de Michoacán* (vol. LIII of *Colección de Documentos Inéditos para la Historia de España* (Madrid, Imprenta de la Viuda de Calero, 1869)).

Archivo General de la Nación, *Documentos Inéditos Relativos a Hernan Cortés y su Familia* (Mexico, Talleres Gráficos de la Nación, 1935, vol. XXVII).

Benavente, Fray Toribio de (Motolinía), *Historia de los Indios de la Nueva España* (Madrid, Historia 16, 1985; written 1536).

Carreño, Alberto María (ed.), *Don Fray Juan de Zumárraga: Documentos Inéditos* (Mexico, Editorial Jus, 1950).

Cortés, Hernando, *Cartas de Relación Enviadas a Su Majestad* in *Historia de Méjico by Cortés*, ed. Manuel del Mar (New York, 1828, White, Gallagher & White).

——: *Ordenanzas de Buen Gobierno Dadas por Hernando Cortés Para los Vezinos y Moradores de la Nueva España* (Madrid, José Porrúa Turanzas, 1960; published 1524).

Cuevas, Mariano (ed.), *Documentos Inéditos del Siglo XVI Para la Historia de México* (Mexico, Editorial Porrúa, 1975; first published 1914).

Díaz del Castillo, Bernal, *The Conquest of New Spain*, tr. J. M. Cohen (Harmondsworth, Penguin, 1963).

——: *La Verdadera Historia de la Conquista de la Nueva España* (Madrid, Información y Revistas SA, 1984).

El Conquistador Anónimo, *Relación de Algunas Cosas de la Nueva España y de la Gran Ciudad de Temestitán México* (Mexico, Alcancía, 1938; first published 1556).

Fernández del Castillo, Francisco (ed.), *Libros y Libreros en el Siglo XVI* (Mexico, Fondo de Cultura Económica, 1982; first published 1914).

Gilberti, Maturino, *Arte de la Lengua Tarasca de Michoacán* (Mexico, Tipografía de la Oficina Impresora del Timbre, 1898; first published 1558).

Grijalva, Juan de, *Crónica de la Orden de N.P.S. Augustin en las Provicias de la Nueva España* (Mexico, 1924; written *c.* 1624).

Icazbalceta, Joaquín (ed.), *Colección de Documentos, Para la Historia de México* (Mexico, Librería de J. M. Andrade, 1858–1866, 2 vols).

——: *Don Fray Juan de Zumárraga* (Mexico, Editorial Porrúa, 1947, 4 vols; first published 1881).

——: *Nueva Colección de Documentos Para la Historia de México* (Mexico, Antigua Librería de Andrade y Morales, Sucesores, 1886, 3 vols).

Icazbalceta, Joaquín and García Pimentel, Luis (eds.), *Relación de los Obispados de Tlaxcala, Michoacán, Oaxaca y Otros Lugares en el Siglo XVI* (Mexico, Casa del Editor, 1904).

Ixtlilxochitl, Fernando de Alva, *Horribles Crueldades de los Conquistadores de México* (Mexico, Imprenta del Ciudadano Alejandro Valdés, 1829; written *c.* 1608).

Konetzke, Richard (ed.), *Colección de Documentos para la Historia de la Formación Social de Hispanoamérica 1493–1810* (Madrid, Consejo Superíor de Investigaciones Cientificas, 1953, 2 vols.)

Lorenzana, Francisco Antonio (ed.), *Concilios Provinciales Primero, y Segundo, Celebrados en la Muy Noble, y Muy Leal Ciudad de México, Presidiendo el Illmo. Y Rmo. Señor D. Fr. Alonso de Montúfar, en los años de 1555 y 1565* (Mexico, Imprenta de el Superior Gobierno, 1769).

Ochoa, Álvaro and Sánchez, Gerardo (eds.), *Relaciones y Memorias de la Provincia de Michoacán, 1579–1581* (Morelia, Universidad Michoacana de San Nicolás de Hidalgo, 1985).

Pacheco, Joaquín F. (ed.), *Colección de Documentos Inéditos Relativos Al Descubrimiento, Conquista y Organización de las Antiguas Posesiones Españolas de América y Oceanía, sacados de los Archivos del Reino, y muy especialmente del de Indias* (Madrid, J. M. Perez, 1868, 42 vols).

Paso y Troncoso, Francisco del, *Epistolario de Nueva España* (Mexico, Antigua Librería Robredo, de José Porrúa e Hijos, 1934, 24 vols).

Sahagún, Fray Bernardino de, *Historia General de las Cosas de Nueva España* (Madrid, Alianza Editorial, 1988, 2 vols.; finished *c.* 1580).

Toro, Alfonso, *Los Judíos en la Nueva España Selección de Documentos del Siglo XVI, correspondientes al ramo de la Inquisición* (Mexico, Talleres Gráficos de la Nación, 1932).

'Varias Relaciones Antiguas', *Historia de los Mexicanos por Sus Pinturas* (Icazbalceta (1886), vol. 3).

Vila Vilar, Enriqueta and Sarabia Viejo, Ma. Justina (eds.), *Cartas de Cabildos Hispanoamericanos – Audiencia de México (Siglos XVI y XVII)* (Sevilla, Escuela de Estudios Hispano-Americanos, 1985).

On Spain, North Africa and the Atlantic

Anonymous, *Crónica de Don Álvaro de Luna* (vol. II of Mata y Carriazo (1943)).

Bernáldez, Andres, *Memorias del Reinado de los Reyes Católicos* (Madrid, Real Academia de la Historia, 1962).

Brásio, António, *Monumenta Missionaria Africana: África Ocidental* (Lisboa, Agência Geral do Ultramar, 1968–78, 5 vols).

Cervantes y Saavedra, Miguel de, *The Ingenious Hidalgo Don Quixote de la Mancha*, tr. John Rutherford (London, Penguin, 1999).

——: 'The Pretended Aunt', pp. 25–36 of *Spanish and Portuguese Short Stories* (London, Senate, 1995; written in 1590s).

Chacón, Pedro, *Historia de la Universidad de Salamanca* (Salamanca, Ediciones de la Universidad de Salamanca, 1990; written 1569 – ed. Ana María Caralias Torres).

Fabié, Antonio María (tr. and ed.), *Viajes por España de Jorge de Einghen, del Baron Leon de Rosmithal de Blatna, de Francisco Guicciardini y de Andres Navajero* (Madrid, Librería de los Bibliófilos, 1879).

Liske, Javier (ed.), *Viajes de Extranjeros por España y Portugal en los Siglos XV, XVI y XVII* (Madrid, Casa Editorial de Medina, 1878).

Magalhães Godinho, Vitorino (ed.), *Documentos Sôbre a Expansão Portuguesa* (Lisboa, Editorial Gleba, 1945, 3 vols).

Mata y Carriazo, Juan de (ed.), *Colección de Crónicas Españolas* (Madrid, Espasa-Calpe, 1943, 7 vols).

Morales, Baltazar de, *Dialogo de las Guerras de Oran* (Córdoba, Francisco de Cea, 1593).

Morgan, J., *A Compleat History of the Present Seat of War in Africa, Between the Spaniards and Algerines* (London, W. Mears, 1632).

Münzer, Hieronymus, *Viaje Por España y Portugal en los Años 1494 y 1495*, tr. and ed. Julio Puyol (Madrid, Tip. de la 'Rev. de Arch., Bibl. y Museos', 1924).

Pulgar, Fernando del, *Crónica de los Reyes Católicos* (vols. V and VI of Mata y Carriazo (1943)).

Suárez Fernández, Luis (ed.), *Documentos Acerca de la Expulsión de los Judíos* (Valladolid, Ediciones Aldecoa S.A., 1964).

Valera, Mosén Diego de, *Crónica de Enrique IV* (vol. IV of Mata y Carriazo (1943)).

SECONDARY MATERIAL (GENERAL)

Abed Al-Hussein, Falad Hassan, *Trade and Business Community in Old Castile Medina del Campo, 1500–1575* (University of East Anglia, unpublished PhD thesis, 1989).

Abellán, José Luis, 'Función Cultural de la Presencia Judía en España Antes y Despues de la Expulsion' (in Alcalá (1995)).

Aguayo Spencer, Rafael, *Don Vasco de Quiroga: Taumaturgo de la Organización Social* (Mexico, Ediciones Oasis, 1970).

Aguilar Cortés, Humberto, et al., *Juegos Florales Conmemorativos del V Centenario del Natalicio de Don Vasco de Quiroga* (Morelia, Talleres Gráficos del Gobierno del Estado de Michoacán, 1971).

Aguilar Cortés, Humberto, 'Vasco de Quiroga, Jurista y Defensor del Derecho del Indio Frente a la Encomienda' (in Aguilar Cortés et al., 1971).

Aguirre Medrano, Fidel, *Historia de los Hospitales Coloniales de Hispanoamérica* (New York, Editorial Arenas, 1992, 3 vols).

Alcalá, Angel, (ed.), *Judios. Sefarditos. Conversos – La Expulsión de 1492 y sus Consecuencias* (Valladolid, Ámbito Ediciones S.A., 1995).

Alvarez Constantino, Higilio, *Ideas Utopicas de los Evangelizadores en América* (Morelia, Ediciones del Comité de Festejos del LIII Aniversario de la Fundación de la Escuela Normal Urbana Federal, 1968).

Antuña, Melchor M., *Sevilla y sus Monumentos Arabes* (Escorial, Imprenta del Real Monasterio, 1930).

Arriaga Ochoa, Antonio, *Don Vasco de Quiroga y la Ciudad de Pátzcuaro* (Mexico, Editorial Libros de Mexico, 1978).

Baer, Yitzhak, *A History of the Jews of Christian Spain*, tr. Louis Schoffman (Philadelphia, The Jewish Publication Society of America, 1966, 2 vols).

Barnett, R. D. (ed.), *The Sephardi Heritage: Essays on The History and Cultural Contribution of the Jews of Spain and Portugal* (London, Valentine, Mitchell & Co., 1971, 2 vols).

Basalenque, Diego, *Historia de la Provincia de San Nicolás de Tolentino* (Mexico, Tip. Barbadillo y Comp., 1886; first published 1673).

Bataillon, Marcel, *Erasmo y España: Estudios Sobre la Historia Espiritual del Siglo XVI*, tr. Antonio Alatorre (Mexico, Fondo de Cultura Económica, 1950).

——: 'Vasco de Quiroga el Bartolomé de las Casas', pp. 225–38 of *Études sur Bartolomé de las Casas* (Paris, Centre de Recherches de l'Institut d'Études Hispaniques, 1965).

Bataillon, Marcel and Saint-Lo, André, *El Padre Las Casas y la Defensa de los Indios*, tr. Javier Alfaya and Bárbara McShane (Barcelona, Editorial Ariel, 1976).

Baudot, Georges, *Histoire et Utopie au Mexique: Les Premiers Chroniqueurs de la Civilisation Mexicaine (1520–1569)* (Toulouse, Privat ed., 1976).

Beaumont, Pablo, *Crónica de Michoacán* (Mexico, Talleres Gráficos de la Nación, 1932, 3 vols; first published 1826).

Beinart, Haim, 'The Converso Community in 15th Century Spain' (in Barnett (1971)).

Benitez, Fray Jesus Miguel, *Madrigal de las Altas Torres: Monasterio de Nuestra Señora de Gracia* (León, Edilesa, 1998).

Berdan, Frances, 'Aztec Society: Economy, Tribute and Warfare' (in Bray (2002)).

Blazquez Miguel, Juan, *Inquisición y Criptojudaismo* (Madrid, Ediciones Kaydeda, 1988).

Bonavit, Julián, *Historia del Colegio Primitivo y Nacional de San Nicolás Hidalgo* (Morelia, Universidad Michoacana, 1958).

Bourel de la Roncière, Charles, *La Découverte de l'Afrique au Moyen Âge: Cartographes et Explorateurs* (vol. V of *Mémoires de la Société Royale de Géographie d'Égypte Publiés Sous les Auspice de Sa Majesté Fouad Ier, Roi d'Égypte* – Cairo, Institut Français d'Archéologie Orientale, 1924).

Brandi, Karl, *The Emperor Charles V: The Growth and Destiny of a Man and a World Empire*, tr. C. V. Wedgwood (New York, Harvester Press, 1980; first published 1939).

Bravo Ugarte, José, *Inspección Ocular en Michoacán* (Mexico, Editorial Jus, 1960).

Bray, Warwick (ed.), *Aztecs* (London, Royal Academy of Arts, 2002).

Callens, Paul L., *Tata Vasco: A Great Reformer of the Sixteenth Century* (Mexico, Editorial Jus, 1959).

Caraman, Philip, *The Lost Paradise* (London, Sidgwick & Jackson, 1975).

Caro Baroja, Julio, *Los Judíos en la España Moderna y Contemporánea* (Madrid, Ediciones Istmo, 1978; first published 1963 – 3 vols).

Carreira, Antonio, *Os Portugueses nos Rios da Guiné: 1500–1900* (Lisboa, Litografia Tejo, 1984).

Chavero, Alfredo, *México a Traves de los Siglos* (Mexico, Ballescá y Compañía, 1888).

Chevalier, François, *Land and Society in Colonial Mexico: The Great Hacienda*, tr. Alvin Esutis (Berkeley, University of California Press, 1963).

Cohen, Mario, 'Lo que Hispanoamérica Perdió: El Impacto de la Expulsión en su Atraso Cultural y Económico' (in Alcalá (1995)).

Cortés Vázquez, Luis, *La Vida Estudiantil en la Salamanca Clásica* (Salamanca, Ediciones Universidad de Salamanca, 1985).

Cuevas, Mariano, *Historia de la Nación Mexicana* (Mexico, Talleres Tipograficos Modelo, 1940).

Cunninghame-Graham, R. B., *A Vanished Arcadia* (London, Century, 1988; first published 1901).

Curtin, Philip D., *Economic Change in Precolonial Africa: Senegambia in the Era of the Slave Trade* (Madison, University of Wisconsin Press, 1975).

Dealy, Ross, *The Politics of an Erasmian Lawyer* (Malibu, Undena Publications, 1976).

——: *Vasco de Quiroga's 'Regula Ubi Commodum'* (Bologna, Societá Editrice Il Mulino, 1978).

Duncan, T. Bentley, *Atlantic Islands: Madeira, the Azores and the Cape Verdes in Seventeenth Century Commerce and Navigation* (Chicago, University of Chicago Press, 1972).

Elliott, J. H., *Imperial Spain: 1469–1716* (Harmondsworth, Penguin, 1970; first published 1963).

Escobar Olmedo, Armando Mauricio, *Los Escudos de Don Vasco de Quiroga* (Morelia, Michoacán, 1999).

Espejo, Cristóbal and Paz, Julian, *Las Antiguas Ferias de Medina del Campo* (Valladolid, La Nueva Pincia, 1908).

Fage, J. D., *A History of West Africa* (Cambridge, Cambridge University Press, 1969; first published 1955).

Fernández, Fidel, *Fray Hernando de Talavera: confesor de los Reyes Católicos y primer arzobispo de Granada* (Madrid, Biblioteca Nueva, 1942).

Fernández García, María de los Ángeles, 'Criterios Inquisitoriales Para Detetctar al Marrano: Los Criptojudíos en los Siglos XVI y XVII' (in Alcalá (1995)).

Foster, George M., *Empire's Children: The People of Tzintzuntzan* (Mexico, Imprenta Nuevo Mundo SA, 1948).

Galaviz de Capdevieille, Ma. Elena, *Rebeliones Indígenas en el Norte del Reino de la Nueva España (Siglos XVI y XVII)* (Mexico, Editorial Campesina, 1967).

Gallegos Rocafull, José M., *El Hombre y el Mundo de los Teólogos Españoles de los Siglos de Oro* (Mexico, Editorial Stylo, 1946).

García Zurdo, Antonio, *Madrigal de las Altas Torres, Cuna de la Hispanidad* (Madrigal de las Altas Torres, Institución 'Alonso de Madrigal', 1961).

Gardiner, Robert (ed.), *Cogs, Caravels and Galleons: The Sailing Ship 1000–1650* (London, Brasseys, 1994).

Garibay, Angel María, *Historia de la Literatura Nahuátl* (Mexico, Editorial Porrúa, 1953, 2 vols.)

——: *La Poesía Lírica Azteca* (Mexico, Bajo el Signo de 'Ábside', 1937).

Gómez, Fernando, *Good Places and Non-Places in Colonial Mexico: The Figure of Vasco de Quiroga (1470–1565)* (London, University Press of America, 2001).

Gómez, Lynne M., 'Vasco de Quiroga, Otro Punto de Vista' (in *Revista: Comunidad*, pp. 414–35, August 1975).

Graulich, Michel, *Mythes et Rituels du Méxique Ancien Préhispanique* (Brussels, Palais des Academies, 1987).

Greenleaf, Richard E., *Zumárraga and the Mexican Inquisition: 1536–1543*, (Washington DC, Academy of American Franciscan History, 1961).

Guadalupe Romero, José, *Noticias para Formar la Historia y la Estadística del Obispado de Michoacán* (Mexico, Imprenta de Vicente García Torres, 1862).

Gutiérrez Vega Cristóforo, *Las Primeras Juntas Eclesiásticas de México (1524–1555)*, (Roma, Centro de Estudios Superiores, 1991).

Hanke, Lewis, *The First Social Experiments in America: A Study in the Development of Spanish Indian Policy in the Sixteenth Century* (Cambridge Mass., Harvard University Press, 1935)

——: *Aristotle and the American Indians: A Study in Race Prejudice in the Modern World* (London, Hollis and Carter, 1959).

Haring, C. H., *The Spanish Empire in America* (New York, Oxford University Press, 1947).

Herrejón Peredo, Carlos, 'Dos Obras Señaladas de Don Vasco de Quiroga' (in Various (1965)).

———: 'Vasco de Quiroga: Educación y Socialización del Indígena' (in Miranda, Francisco and Briseño, Gabriela (1984)).

Hirschberg, H. Z. (J. W.), *A History of the Jews in North Africa*, tr. M. Eichelberg (Leiden, E. J. Brill, 1974).

Jarnes, Benjamin, *Don Vasco de Quiroga: Obispo de Utopía* (Mexico, Colección Carabela, 1942).

Jasso Espinosa, Rodolfo, *Grandeza de Michoacán* (Mexico, Talleres de B. Costa-Amic, 1969).

Kirchoff, Paul, *La Relación de Michoacán Como Fuente para la Historia de la Sociedad y Cultura Tarascas* (Madrid, Aguilar, 1966).

Kubler, George, *Mexican Architecture of the Sixteenth Century* (New Haven, Yale University Press, 1948, 2 vols).

Leddy Phelan, John, *The Millennial Kingdom of the Franciscans in the New World: A Study of the Writings of Gerónimo de Mendieta (1525–1604)* (Berkeley, University of California Press, 1956).

Lemús Gomez, Saul, *Don Vasco de Quiroga: Educador* (Morelia, Universidad Vasco de Quiroga, 1997).

León, Nicolas, *Anales del Museo Michoacano* (Morelia, Imp. y Lit. del Gobierno en la Escuela de Artes, 1888).

———: *Don Vasco de Quiroga: Grandeza de Su Persona y Su Obra* (Morelia, Universidad Michoacana de San Nicolas Hidalgo, 1904; 1984 edition with documentary supplement).

León Portilla, Miguel, 'Aztec Codices, Literature and Philosophy' (in Bray (2002)).

Levtzion, Nehemiah, *Ancient Ghana and Mali* (New York, Africana Publishing Company, 1980; first published 1973).

Lewin, Boleslao, *Los Judíos Bajo la Inquisición en Hispanoamérica* (Buenos Aires, Editorial Dedalo, 1960).

Liebman, Seymour B., 'The Secret Jewry in the Spanish New World Colonies 1500–1820' (in Barnett (1971)).

———: *The Inquisitors and the Jews in the New World: Summaries of Procesos 1500–1810, and Bibliographical Guide* (Coral Gables, University of Miami Press, 1974).

López Austin, Alfredo, 'Cosmovision, Religion and the Calendar of the Aztecs' (in Bray (2002)).

López Lara, P. Ramón, 'El Oidor' (Various (1965)).

López López, Marco Antonio, *La Batalla por la Libertad: Bartolomé de las Casas y Vasco de Quiroga* (Morelia, Ediciones Preparatoria Rector Hidalgo, 1993).

López Lujan, Leonardo, 'The Aztecs' Search for the Past' (in Bray (2002)).

López Sarralangue, Delfina Esmeralda, *La Nobleza Indigena de Pátzcuaro en la Época Virreinal* (Mexico, Universidad Nacional Autónoma de México, 1965).

Losada, Angel, *Fray Bartolomé de las Casas – a la luz de la moderna crítica histórica* (Madrid, Editorial Tecnos, 1970).

Lynch, John, *Spain Under the Habsburgs* (Oxford, Basil Blackwell, 1964, 2 vols).

MacKay, Angus, *Spain in the Middle Ages: From Frontier to Empire, 1000–1500* (London, Macmillan, 1977).

Madariaga y Rajo, Salvador de, *Hernán Cortés: Conqueror of Mexico* (London, Hodder & Stoughton, 1942).

Magalhães Godinho, Vitorino, *L'Économie de l'Empire Portugais aux XVe et XVIe Siècles* (Pairs, S.E.V.P.E.M., 1969).

Maravall, José Antonio, *Carlos V y el Pensamiento Político del Renacimiento* (Madrid, Instituto de Estudios Políticos, 1960).

Martín Hernández, Francisco, *Don Vasco de Quiroga: Protector de los Indios* (Salamanca, Publicaciones Universidad Pontífica de Salamanca, 1993).

Martínez Baracs, Rodrigo and Espinosa Morales, Lydia (eds.), *La Vida Michoacana en el Siglo XVI: Catálogo de los Documentos del Siglo XVI del Archivo Histórico de la Ciudad de Pátzcuaro* (Mexico, Editorial Fuentes, 1999).

Matos Moctezuma, Eduardo and Solís Olguin, Felipe, 'Introduction' (in Bray (2002)).

Mena, José María de, *Las Leyendas y Tradiciones de Sevilla* (Sevilla, Talleres-Escuela de Tipografía del Sanatorio de Niños Lisiados 'Jesus del Gran Poder', 1968).

Merriman, Roger Bigelow, *The Rise of the Spanish Empire in the Old World and the New* (New York, The Macmillan Campany, 1918–34, 4 vols).

Miranda, Francisco, 'El Pátzcuaro de Don Vasco: Un Modelo de Integración Étnica y Cultural' (in Miranda, Francisco and Briseño, Gabriela (1984)).

——: *El Real Colegio de San Nicolás de Pátzcuaro* (Cuernavaca, Centro Intercultural de Documentación, 1967).

Miranda, Francisco and Briseño, Gabriela, *Vasco de Quiroga: Educador de Adultos* (Pátzcuaro, Crefal-Colmich, 1984).

Monín, José, *Los Judíos en la América Española, 1492–1810* (Buenos Aires, Biblioteca Yavne, 1939).

Montoto, Santiago, *Sevilla en el Imperio (Siglo XVI)* (Sevilla, Nueva Libreria Vda. De Carlos García, 193?).

Morales García, Rogelio (ed.), *Epistolario Patzcuarense: Fé, Humanismo, Solidaridad* (Morelia, Ediciones Michoacanas, 1999).

Moreno, Juan Joseph, *Fragmentos de la Vida y Virtudes del Illustrissimo Sr. Dr. Don Vasco de Quiroga* (Mexico, Imprenta del Real y Más Antiguo Colegio de S. Ildefonso, 1766).

Navarrete Pellicer, Sergio, 'La Población Tarasca en el Siglo XVI' (in Paredes Martínez (1997)).

——: 'La Tecnología Agricola Tarasca Del Siglo XVI' (in Paredes Martínez (1997)).

Netanyahu, B., *The Marranos of Spain, from the late XIVth to the early XVIth century according to contemporary Hebrew sources* (New York, American Academy for Jewish Research, 1966).

Nieto Manzo, Rafael, 'Don Vasco de Quiroga, Benefactor de la Raza Purépecha y Precursor de la Salud (in Aguilar Cortés et al., 1971).

Padden, R. C., *The Hummingbird and the Hawk: Conquest and Sovereignty in the Valley of Mexico 1503–1541* (Ohio, Ohio State University Press, 1967).

Pagden, Anthony, 'The Humanism of Vasco de Quiroga's "Información en Derecho"', pp. 133–142 of *Humanismus und Neue Welt*, ed. Wolfgang Reinhard (Bonn, Deutsche Forschunggemeinschaft, 1987).

Palm, E. W., *Tenochtitlan y la Ciudad Ideal de Dürer* (Paris, Journal de la Société des Américanistes, 1951, vol. XL, pp. 59–66).

Paredes Martínez, Carlos (ed.), *Historia y Sociedad: Ensayos del Seminario de Historia Colonial de Michoacán* (Morelia, Instituto de Investigaciones Históricas de la Universidad Michoacana de San Nicolás Hidalgo, 1997).

Paredes Martínez, Carlos, 'El Mercado de Pátzcuaro y los Mercaderes Tarascos en los Inicios de la Época Colonial' (in Paredes Martínez (1997)).

Prescott, W. H., *The Conquest of Mexico* (London, Phoenix, 2001; first published 1845).

Ricard, Robert, *The Spiritual Conquest of Mexico*, tr. Lesley Bird Simpson (Berkeley, University of California Press, 1966).

Rodríguez y Fernández, D. Ildefonso, *Historia de la Muy Noble, Muy Leal y Coronada Villa de Medina del Campo* (Madrid, Imprenta de San Francisco de Sales, 1903–1904).

Romero Flores, Jesús, *Michoacán Histórico y Legendario* (Mexico, Costa-Amic Editor, 1971).

Ruff, Paul, *La Domination Espagnole à Oran* (Paris, Ernest Leroux, 1900).

Ruíz del Solar y Azoriaga, Manuel, *Tradiciones de Sevilla: Santa María de la Victoria* (Sevilla, Lib. é Imp. de Izquierdo y C.a, 1897).

Sánchez Arjona, José, *El Teatro en Sevilla en los Siglos XVI y XVII* (Madrid, Establecimiento Tipográfica de A. Alonso, 1887).

Sassoon, Solomon David, 'The Spiritual Heritage of the Sephardim' (in Barnett (1971)).

Serrano Gassent, Paz, *Vasco de Quiroga: La Utopia en América* (Madrid, Historia 16, 1992).

——: *Vazco de Quiroga: Utopía y Derecho en la Conquista de Americá* (Madrid, Fondo de Cultura Económica de España, 2001).

Sicroff, Albert A., *Los Estatutos de Limpieza de Sangre: Controversias Entre los Siglos XV y XVII*, tr. Mauro Armiño (Madrid, Taurus Ediciones, 1985).

Solís Olguín, Felipe, *Art at the Time of the Aztecs* (in Bray (2002)).

Soustelle, Jacques, *The Daily Life of the Aztecs on the Eve of the Spanish Conquest*, tr. Patrick O'Brian (London, Weidenfeld & Nicolson, 1961).

Tena Ramírez, Felipe, *Vasco de Quiroga y Sus Pueblos de Santa Fe en los Siglos XVIII y XIX* (Mexico, Editorial Porrúa, 1977).

Thomas, Hugh, *The Conquest of Mexico* (London, Hutchinson, 1993).

——: *The Slave Trade* (London, Picador, 1997).

——: 'The Conquest' (in Bray (2002)).

Tooke, Joan D., *The Just War in Aquinas and Grotius* (London, SPCK, 1965).

Toribio Medina, José, *Historia del Tribunal del Santa Oficio de la Inquisición de Lima (1569–1820)* (Santiago de Chile, Imprenta Gutenberg, 1887, 2 vols).

——: *Historia del Tribunal del Santo Oficio de la Inquisición en México* (Santiago de Chile, Imprenta Elzeviriana, 1905).

Vajda, Georges, 'La Philosophie Juive en Espagne' (in Barnett (1971)).

Various, *Humanistas Novohispanos de Michoacán* (Morelia, Universidad Michoacana de San Nicolás de Hidalgo, 1982).

Various, *Don Vasco de Quiroga y Arzobispado de Morelia* (Mexico, Editorial Jus, 1965).

Verastique, Bernardino, *Michoacán and Eden: Vasco de Quiroga and the Evangelization of Western Mexico* (Austin, University of Texas Press, 2000).

Vilanova, Antonio, *Erasmo y Cervantes* (Barcelona, Consejo Superior de Investigaciones Científicas Instituto 'Miguel de Cervantes' de Filología Hispanica, 1949).

Warren, Fintan B., *Vasco de Quiroga and His Pueblo-Hospitales of Santa Fe* (Washington, Academy of American Franciscan History, 1963).

Warren, J. Benedict, *The Conquest of Michoacán: The Spanish Domination of the Tarascan Kingdom in Western Mexico, 1521–1530* (Norman, University of Oklahoma Press, 1985).

Williams, Joseph J., *Hebrewisms of West Africa: From Nile to Niger with the Jews* (London, George Allen & Unwin, 1930).

Williamson, Edwin, *The Penguin History of Latin America* (London, Penguin Press, 1992).

Wittmayer Baron, Salo, *A Social and Religious History of the Jews, Vol. XIII* (New York, Columbia University Press, 1969).

Zavala, Sílvio, 'En Busca del Tratado de Vasco de Quiroga, "De Debellandis Indis"' (in *Historia Mexicana*, vol. XVII, no. 4, 1968).

——: *Ensayo Bibliográfico en Torno de Vasco de Quiroga* (Mexico, Colegio Nacional, 1991).

——: *La 'Utopia' de Tomás Moro en la Nueva España* (Mexico, Antigua Librería Robredo, de José Porrúa e Hijos, 1937).

——: *Los Esclavos Indios en Nueva España* (Mexico, El Colegio Nacional Luis González Obregón, 1968).

——: *New Viewpoints on the Spanish Colonization of America* (Philadelphia, University of Pennsylvania Press, 1943).

——: *Recuerdo de Vasco de Quiroga* (Mexico, Editorial Porrúa, 1987).

——: *Servidumbre Natural y Libertad Cristiana – Según los Tratadistas Españoles de los Siglos XVI y XVII* (Buenos Aires, Peuser S.A., 1944).

——: *Sir Thomas More in New Spain: A Utopian Adventure of the Renaissance* (London, The Hispanic and Luso-Brazilian Councils, 1965).

——: *Vasco de Quiroga* (Morelia, Secretaria de Difusión Cultural, 1993).

THOMAS MORE AND HIS UTOPIAN INFLUENCE

Ackroyd, Peter, *The Life of Thomas More* (London, Chatto & Windus, 1998).

Augustijn, Cornelius, *Erasmus: His Life Works and Influence*, tr. J. C. Grayson (Toronto, University of Toronto Press, 1991).

Baker-Smith, Dominic, 'Utopia and the Franciscans' (in Cousins, A. D. and Grace, Damian (1995)).

Bracherer, Leicester and Lynch, Charles Arthur (eds.), *The Latin Epigrams of Thomas More* (Chicago, University of Chicago Press, 1953).

Chambers, R. W., *Thomas More* (London, Jonathan Cape, 1935).

Cousins, A. D. and Grace, Damian (eds.), *More's Utopia and the Utopian Inheritance* (Lanham Ma., University Press of America, 1995).

Donner, H. W., *Introduction to Utopia* (London, Sidgwick & Jackson, 1945).

Hexter, J. H., *More's Utopia: The Biography of an Idea* (New York, Harper & Row, 1965; first published 1952).

More, Thomas, *A Dialogue of Comfort Against Tribulation*, ed. Mgr P. E. Hallett (London, Burns, Oates & Washburne, 1937).

——: *Utopia*, tr. Paul Turner (Harmondsworth, Penguin, 1965; first published 1516).

Pavkovic, Aleksander, 'Prosperity, Equality and Intellectual Needs in More's Utopia' (in Cousins, A. D. and Grace, Damian (1995)).

Smith, Preserved, *Erasmus: A Study of His Life, Ideals and Place in History* (New York, Harper and Brothers, 1923).

Surtz, Edward L., *The Praise of Wisdom: A Commentary on the Religious and Moral Problems and Backgrounds of St. Thomas More's* Utopia (Chicago, Loyola University Press, 1957).

UTOPIAS AND LITERATURE ABOUT UTOPIAS

Bacon, Francis, *New Atlantis* in *Three Early Modern Utopias*, ed. Susan Bruce, (Oxford, Oxford University Press, 1999; first published 1627).

Bellamy, Edward, *Looking Backward: 2000–1887* (Mineola NY, Dover Publications, 1996; first published 1888).

Berlin, Isaiah, *Four Essays on Liberty* (Oxford, Oxford University Press, 1969).

Bruce, Susan, 'Introduction' (in *Three Early Modern Utopias*, ed. Susan Bruce, (Oxford, Oxford University Press, 1999).

Butler, Samuel, *Erewhon* (London, Heron Books, 1969; first published 1872).

Callenbach, Ernest, *Ecotopia: A Novel About Ecology, People and Politics* (London, Pluto Press, 1978; first published 1975).

Campanella, Thomas, *The City of the Sun* (London, Journeyman Press, 1981; first published 1623).

Davis, J. C., *Utopia and the Ideal Society: A Study of English Utopian Writing, 1516–1700* (Cambridge, Cambridge University Press, 1981).

Eliav-Feldon, Miriam, *Realistic Utopias: The Ideal Imaginary Societies of the Renaissance 1516–1630* (Oxford, Clarendon Press, 1982).

Huxley, Aldous, *Brave New World* (London, Chatto & Windus, 1984; first published 1932).

——: *Island* (London, Flamingo, 1994; first published 1962).

Koestler, Arthur, *Darkness at Noon* (London, Hutchinson, 1973; first published 1940).

Kumar, Krishnan, 'The End of Socialism? The End of Utopia? The End of History' (in Kumar and Bann (1993)).

Kumar, Krishnan and Bann, Stephen (eds.), *Utopias and the Millennium* (London, Reaktion Books, 1993).

Le Guin, Ursula, *The Dispossessed* (London, Victor Gollancz, 1999; first published 1974).

Maravall, José Antonio, *Utopía y Contrautopía en el 'Quijote'* (Santiago de Compostela, Editorial Pico Sacro, 1976).

Marin, Louis, 'The Frontiers of Utopia' (in Kumar and Bann (1993)).

Marx, Karl, 'The Communist Manifesto' (in McLellan (1972)).

——: 'The Future Results of British Rule in India' (in McLellan (1972)).

——: 'The German Ideology' (in McLellan (1972)).

McLellan, David (ed.), *Karl Marx: Selected Writings* (Oxford, Oxford University Press, 1972).

Morris, William, 'News From Nowhere' (pp. 41–230 of *News From Nowhere and Other Writings*, ed. Clive Wilmer (London, Penguin, 1993; first published 1890).

O'Neill, John, 'McTopia: Eating Time' (in Kumar and Bann (1993)).

Plato, *Republic*, tr. G.M.A. Grube (Indianapolis, Hackett Publishing Company, 1992).

Popper, Karl, *The Open Society and Its Enemies* (London, Routledge, 1945, 2 vols).

Rousseau, Jean Jacques, *The Social Contract and Discourses* (London, J. M. Dent, 1913).

Russell, Bertrand, *In Praise of Idleness* (London, Routledge, 1994; first published 1935).

Schumacher, E. F., *Small is Beautiful* (London, Abacus, 1974; first published 1963).

Zamyatin, Yevgeny, *We*, tr. Bernard Guilbert Gueney (London, Jonathan Cape, 1970; first published 1924).

INDEX